E.G. Rajan

Symbolic Computing

Signal and Image Processing

E.G. Rajan

Symbolic Computing

Signal and Image Processing

BSP **BS Publications**
A unit of **BSP Books Pvt., Ltd.**

4-4-309/316, Giriraj Lane, Sultan Bazar,
Hyderabad - 500 095
Phone : 040 - 23445605, 23445688

Published by :

BS Publications
A unit of **BSP Books Pvt., Ltd.**

4-4-309/316, Giriraj Lane, Sultan Bazar,
Hyderabad - 500 095
Phone : 040 - 23445605, 23445688
e-mail : info@bspbooks.net

ISBN : 978-93-52300-34-1 (HB)

Dedicated
to
my country
Bharath

Preface

ॐ

Om. Acharya poorva roopam; Anteyvas uttara roopam; Vidya sandhi; Pravachanam sandhanam

(Om. Teacher is like a first syllable; Student is like a second syllable; Education is like the join of the two syllables; Guidance is like the grammar that allows the join of two syllables in order to evolve a meaningful word)

Shikshavalli, Taitiriya Upanishad

The purpose of this book

This book gives the reader a first-time exposure to certain ideas and concepts related to ***non-numerical signal and image processing***. The material covered here has been the result of many years of fundamental research carried out with the purpose of evolving a logico-mathematical framework for ***symbolic computing***. This book provides certain latest technologies that may serve as a reportoire of tools that are of significant use in formulating ***DNA computing*** paradigms.

Much care has been taken while preparing the manuscript so that it is useful to a wide spectrum of readers. Consequently, this book has been organized to ensure that the reader understands every concept without the need of any cross-reference. At the same time the scientific rigor has been kept in tact. The content is self-explanatory, covering all the basic fundamentals. Some of the already published research work due to the author has also been inserted at appropriate places in order to give a research flair to the readers. The intention of the author is to present this as a reference book. In fact, this book is an outcome of a number of classroom experiments and relevant courses taught by the author in the department of Electrical Engineering of the Indian Institute of Technology, Kanpur, India and invited seminars and institute lectures offered at various elite universities in the United States of America. Though the book is meant for scientists working in R & D organizations and Academic Institutions, students from universities, people with different background like Employees, Researchers and of course a ***Common Man*** too can read this book. People working in medical and genetic science also will find this book very useful since the techniques discussed in the book have a direct bearing on certain applications related to medicine and biology like ***bioinformatics***. No prerequisite knowledge is required to go through this book.

Organization of the book

This book is divided into *five parts* (i) Symbolic Signal Processing, (ii) A Language Theoretic Approach To Signal Processing, (iii) Theory Of Constructive Signal Processing, (iv) Symbolic Image Processing and (v) Applications of Cellular Logic Array Processing. The first part deals with certain relevant details about the notion of a normal algorithm and its generalization and the basic techniques involved in implementing nonnumerical signal processing operations using normal algorithms. The purpose of the second part is to introduce a formal language and a special automaton for the study of constructive (normal algorithmic) signal processing systems. Part III provides a compressive introduction to symbolic processing of digital images using Cellular Logic Algorithms. A cellular logic algorithm is essentially a realization of a Cellular Automaton by a Generalised Markov Algorithm. With images treated as arrays of symbols, which we refer as *Array Configurations*, from an alphabet $\mathcal{A}$, our concern is to consider the realization of various pattern generating and image processing operations in terms of pattern matching and substitution operations using cellular automata rules. The fourth part of the book describes various application areas and certain important outcomes of our own research in symbolic processing of signals and images.

About the contributors

This book has been brought to this form due to the efforts of a team of my students. My undergraduate and graduate students have been the driving force behind this book-writing project. They were involved in collecting literature from almost all possible sources, in criticizing my lecture notes and in preparing the soft copy of the material. The list of the students who have actively participated in this book project has been given at the end of the preface.

About the supporting organizations

Pentagram Research Centre (P) Ltd. Hyderabad was the major supporter for this project in extending technical, materialistic and logistic support to us in a very big way. The International School for Information Technology of Dr. Swaminadhan Research Foundation, National Institute of Research and Social Action, Hyderabad was kind enough to support us in every possible way. Vasavi College of Engineering, Hyderabad extended their library support. Surya Academy, Chennai played a great role in extending various technical information related to Information Technology. M/s B S Publications, Hyderabad was solely responsible in extending materialistic and financial support in bringing out this book in this form.

About individuals

Thanks are due to my wife Mrs. G. Chitra, the Managing Director of Pentagram Research Centre Private Limited, Hyderabad for her untiring support in the form of infrastructure, funding, and constant encouragement.

Thanks are due to Mr. Anil Shah and Mr. Nikhil Shah, the Directors of the B S Publications, Hyderabad for their confidence in me and in my large team and for their timely support. Mr K.S. Raju, Mr Madan Mohan and Mr. Naresh of B.S. Publications helped our team in all possible ways. All these efforts would have become void but for my friend and colleague Mr. Jesudas of the B S Publications. His untiring and never-ending visits to my house and office, and his charming smile (not artificial) indeed kept me fit even at difficult times and made us succeed in this project ultimately. Many thanks Mr. Jesudas !

The whole manuscript was edited by a big team and the role played by Mr. K. Pramod Sankar is highly commendable.

Dr. E. G. Rajan

President, Pentagram Research Centre (P) Ltd, Hyderabad
Hon. Director, International School of Information Technology, NIRSA, Hyderabad
Professor, Vasavi College of Engineering, Hyderabad

My Student Contributors

- Prof. A. G. Ramakrishnan, Department of EE, Indian Institute of Science, Bangalore
- Prof. E. Nagabhooshanam, (Ph.D), Chaitanya Bharathi Institute of Technology, Hyderabad
- Prof. A.V. Narasimha Rao, (Ph.D), Chaitanya Bharathi Institute of Technology, Hyderabad
- Prof. K.Kishore, (Ph.D), Vasavi College of Engineering, Hyderabad
- Prof. Jyothi Patil, (Ph.D), PDA College of Engineering, Gulbarga
- Prof. K. Venu, School of Physics, University of Hyderabad
- Prof. Ramanamurthy, School of Mathematics, Osmania University
- Prof. P. Veera Narayana Reddy, (M.Tech), Alpha Engineering College, Kurnool
- Prof. B. Prabhakara Reddy, (M.Tech), Gates Institute of Technology, Ananthapur
- Prof. Asma, (M.Tech), KBN College of Engineering, Gulbarga
- Prof. Sameena, (M.Tech), KBN College of Engineering, Gulbarga
- Mr. K. Pramod Sankar, Final year student, Vidya Jyothi Instt. Of Tech., Hyderabad
- Mr. Sai Thejasvee. M., Final year, Department of CSE.,MJ college of Engineering.
- Mr. Mohd. Riyazuddin, Final year, Department of ECE.,MJ college of Engineering.
- Mr. Naveen Shankpal, Final year, Department of ECE, MJ College of Engineering
- Mr. Randhir Korlapati, Final year, Department of ECE, MJ College of Engineering

Contents

Part IV

Symbolic Image Processing

Part – V

Applications of Cellular Logic Array Processing

Part I

Abstract

This part consists of four sections. In section 2, we review certain relevant details about the notion of a normal algorithm and its generalization. In section 3, we provide a few string manipulating techniques, which would be useful in constructing normal algorithms for implementing any nonnumerical signal processing operation. In section 4, we actually demonstrate one method of implementing operations such as cyclic shifting and linear convolution of nonnegative integer sequences using a set of normal algorithms constructed over specific alphabets.

Symbolic Signal Processing

Section 1

Nonnumerical Representation And Processing Of Signals And Images

1.1 Introduction

In very broad set theoretic terms, to filter is to separate, to partition a given set of entities into disjoint subsets, based on whether they have or do not have a stipulated property. One could, in principle, conceive of a 'Boolean Genie', as it were, that could instantly appear on our rubbing the Alladin's Lamp, and as instantly carry out the partitioning, if at all possible, by examining the entities all at once for the stipulated property. In the absence of the Lamp, however, we must be content with a more earthly procedure for such a partitioning, one that is a function of time and space, and which depends for its realization on a physical device, be it a sieve, an electronic circuit, or a computer.

In the study and design of such filtering procedures for signals, one crucial underlying principle seems to be the following: ***System models of signal processing operations and those of sources from which signals originate should belong to the same class***. It is implied here that signals are to be thought of as outputs of sources, and that their description is not really complete unless we specify source models.

To go by the general pattern of relationships that this principle suggests, it is only appropriate that for signals that evolve with time and whose sources can be modeled as time-invariant systems governed by differential or difference equations, e.g., audio signals, we should look for processors that can likewise be modeled as time-invariant systems. For pictures and images on the other hand, there is good reason to believe that the traditional 2-D extensions of time-invariant systems governed by differential equations and partial differential equations do not serve as canonical models. It is not surprising therefore that the traditional filter theory does not measure up to the task in this case and one has to look for alternative formulations.

E. G. Rajan, *Symbolic Computing - Signal and Image Processing*
ISBN 81-7800-047-4

It is significant to note in this connection that for a large class of pictures and images of high complexity, an effective modeling tool for sources generating them has been found to be that of ***Cellular Automata*** [26]. Invoking the principle just set forth, it is then reasonable to surmise that filtering operations on pictures and images, such as those of thinning, edge detection, segmentation, erosion and dilation may be canonically modeled and realized using cellular automata.

There is yet another point that the principle prompts us to take into account. In the traditional theory of filtering, we are able to numericalize our problems by viewing signals as members of a vector space over which it is possible for us to characterize their properties or attributes of interest in terms of the notion of spectrum. But in the case of pictures and images, some of the pertinent attributes are such that a straightforward numericalization of this kind is not possible, and the notion of spectrum in its present form is not very useful. Interesting and promising new possibilities, however, emerge if instead of working with numerical representations of signals and systems, we study filtering operations as formal symbol manipulating algorithms. Markov's ***Normal Algorithms*** [20] seem to provide a rich repertoire of tools for this purpose [32].

The motivating factor for this kind of choice is that there would seem to open up through it, interesting possibilities of relating the area of signal processing to developments in other areas such as those of abstract measurement theory and computable real analysis.

Following ideas drawn from abstract measurement theory [35], and quantum logic [21], [30], it has been suggested [36] that the notion of a signal needs to be looked at in terms of a triple $< \bar{X}, X, \phi >$. In this triple, $\bar{X}$ is an algebraic or relational structure whose primitives and postulates are decided by empirical considerations about the physical phenomena the signals of interest characterize, and X is a numerical structure, called a representation of $\bar{X}$, which is a homomorphic image of $\bar{X}$ through the mapping ϕ. Formulation of $\bar{X}$ is generally carried out using tools of logic and formal languages. In the case of quantum logic, for instance, it is logic of propositions characterizing what are called 'yes-no experiments'. The representation X on the other hand is formulated using tools of Analysis, and may consist of just the real line treated as a vector space, or may even be a lattice of subspaces of an appropriate Hilbert space. If signals are to be studied in this light, then the nonnumeric interpretation adopted here is going to be of considerable significance. It acquires added significance if we take into account the fact that there has emerged in recent years the area of ***Computable Analysis*** [1], [8] as an alternative to real Analysis, in which the place of real numbers is taken over by computable real numbers, that is, those real numbers whose arbitrarily precise rational approximations can be obtained using computer programs or algorithms. For signal processing operations and algorithms set within the framework of computable analysis, symbolic interpretations would seem to be of central interest.

In general, given a string of symbols one can transform it into another desired string by systematically rearranging or rewriting the symbols contained in the given string according to a finite set of rules. A prescription, which gives a set of such rewriting rules along with the details of how they should be applied, is known as a *string manipulating algorithm.* The concept of a *normal algorithm* refers to one such string manipulating algorithm. Essentially, a normal algorithm is an ordered list of a finite number of what are called *substitution formulas.* A substitution formula is analogous to a semi-Thue production of Chomsky type-0 grammar.

1.2 Scope Of the Book

In the volume, five basic issues concerning the study of systems for symbolic processing of signals and images are considered. They are:

(i) Is it possible to represent signals as strings of symbols from finite alphabets and process them using symbol manipulating normal algorithms?

(ii) A set X of nonnumerical signal representations (i.e., a set of strings of symbols from an alphabet, say $\mathcal{A}$) could also be called a *language* because is a subset of the free monoid $\mathcal{A}^*$ (i.e., the monoid consisting of all possible words from the alphabet $\mathcal{A}$, together with the associative binary operation of concatenation of words). Considering that rewriting systems defined by a grammar, as also automata, are language recognizers, can they be used to describe signal processing normal algorithms?

(iii) What are the various properties of normal algorithmic signal processing systems?

(iv) Is it possible to represent images as arrays of symbols from finite alphabets and process them using pattern-directed normal algorithms?

(v) What are the potential applications of such a study?

This volume consists of a total number of twenty two sections, under five parts and each part deals with one of these basic issues.

The **first part** consists of four sections. In section 2, we review certain relevant details about the notion of a normal algorithm and its generalization. In section 3, we provide a few string manipulating techniques, which would be useful in constructing normal algorithms for implementing any nonnumerical signal processing operation. In section 4, we actually demonstrate one method of implementing operations such as cyclic shifting and linear convolution of nonnegative integer sequences using a set of normal algorithms constructed over specific alphabets.

The **second part** consists of sections 5 and 6. In this part, we take up the second basic issue of describing normal algorithmic signal processing systems as rewriting systems defined by a grammar and as automata. In the theory of formal languages, a set of words from an alphabet is defined as a language and any subset of it as a sublanguage. According to this definition, a nonnumerical representation of a signal over an alphabet could be treated as a language. Here we interpret the operational rule of a normal algorithm in a slightly different way and show that for any given normal algorithm one can obtain a functionally equivalent Turing machine. By this we are able to formulate a type-0 grammar of Chomsky type, which defines the class of all normal algorithms over an alphabet as serial rewriting systems. In section-6, we introduce the notion of a *Cyclic Normal Automaton* for normal algorithms and demonstrate with an example how a cyclic normal automaton over a nonnumerical alphabet recognizes a language corresponding to a signal space.

The sections 7,8,9 and 10 form the **third part** of this book. In this part, we consider a structure $C_{\mathfrak{R}} = \langle \mathcal{N}_{\mathcal{A}}, \circ, \simeq \rangle$ (where $\mathcal{N}_{\mathcal{A}}$ denotes a class of normal algorithms over $\mathcal{A}$, o denotes the operation of composition and $\simeq$ denotes the relation of functional equivalence) which finitely specifies nonnumerical signal processing operations and we develop a theory for it in a language of constructive logic. In addition, we provide constructive interpretations to (i) Lyndon-Keisler homomorphism theorem and

(ii) Thampuran's extended topological filters and show that the properties of a $C_{\mathfrak{R}}$ – type signal processing system could be studied with the help of either of these two. Section-7 provides a theory denoted by Th ($\mathfrak{R}$), for the structure $C_{\mathfrak{R}}$ and a short list of properties of $C_{\mathfrak{R}}$ – type systems. In section-8, we consider Lyndon-Keisler homomorphism theorem and its improved version by Fujiwara. We present a characterization theorem, which is analogous to Fujiwara's version of the homomorphism theorem for $C_{\mathfrak{R}}$ – type systems, in a language of constructive logic. In section-9, we reformulate the notion of an extended filter in constructive terms (the resulting filter is called a ***constructive extended filter***) and establish a connection between the notions of a normal algorithm and a constructive extended filter. In section 10, we study, on the lines of Erlandson, certain computational aspects of extended topological filters in terms of quantifiable measures such as (i) ***ambiguity*** of a filter, (ii) ***discrimination*** of a filter, (iii) ***resolution*** of a filter and (iv) ***distance*** between two filters. In so doing, we describe these measures in terms of normal algorithmic operators acting from a metric lattice of constructive extended filters into the metric space of constructive real numbers.

The **fourth part** of this book contains the sections 11, 12, 13, 14, 15, 16 and 17. In section 11, we describe the concept of ***Cellular Automata***, which forms the basis for our approach to image processing. In section 12, we discuss the normal algorithmic realizations of cellular automata and the notion of a ***Generalized Cellular Logic Scheme***. Section 13 provides various techniques for generating patterns using such realizations. In section 14, we describe fast algorithms for processing 2-D and 3-D images. Section 15 introduces the state-of-the-art technique of representing digital images on a hexagonal grid of pixels and their processing using cellular logic algorithms. In section 16, we introduce the notion of a ***Geometric Filter***, and its relevance in the processing of digital images. Section 17 subsequently describes the concept of ***Pextrum*** and ***Pextral Coding*** of digital images.

Lastly, the **fifth part** of the book consists of five sections and they describe various application areas and certain important outcomes of our own research in symbolic processing of signals and images. Section 18 provides the basic areas of research related to symbolic processing of signals and images. Section 19 explores the possibility of modeling solidification process as a thinning lattice gas automaton. The moving boundaries of isotherms in a solidification process correspond to the boundary removal of a digital image, which is also referred as thinning. In section 20, we explain the technique of modeling fluid flow using cellular automata, which are also known as lattice gas automata. Though this approach to study fluid dynamics is different from conventional techniques, it has been class-room tested and validated by comparing certain results with those due to traditional techniques. Section 21 describes one application of cellular logic array processing techniques to examine the laser scanned data of metal surfaces. Lastly section 22 describes an important application of modeling of collision processes using cellular logic array processing.

1.3 Preliminary Concepts Required For Further Study

1.3.1 Signals, Systems, Monoids And $\mathcal{J}$ - Class Relations

While the precise definitions of various terms to be used in this book will be introduced in the text as the need arises, it is appropriate to clarify here itself as to how we intend to interpret the two basic terms – **signals** and **systems**. By a *signal* we mean a word from a free monoid $\mathcal{A}^*$ of an alphabet $\mathcal{A}$ (i.e., the monoid consisting of all possible words from the alphabet $\mathcal{A}$ and the identity element Λ that is also known as the null string, together with the associative binary operation of concatenation of words).

By a ***Signal Space*** we mean the free monoid $\mathcal{A}^*$ itself or a subset of it. By a ***Signal Processing System*** we understand a binary on $\mathcal{A}^*$, with the first members of the ordered pairs constituting this relation called ***Inputs*** and the second members called ***Outputs***.

An alternative way of looking at systems is that in terms of four ***equivalence relations*** introduced by Green [26], which hold for semi groups as well as free monoids [26].

These are:

(i) ***Right*** or ***$\mathfrak{R}$ – class congruences***:
$a, b \in \mathcal{A}^*$, $a \,\mathfrak{R}\, b$ if $a\mathcal{A}^* = b\,\mathcal{A}^*$

(ii) ***Left*** or ***$\mathcal{L}$-class congruences***:
$a, b \in \mathcal{A}^*$, $a \,\mathcal{L}\, b$ if $\mathcal{A}^* a = \mathcal{A}^* b$

(iii) ***𝒥-Class congruences***:
a, b $\in \mathcal{A}^*$, a𝒥b if $\mathcal{A}^* a \mathcal{A}^* = \mathcal{A}^* b \mathcal{A}^*$

(iv) ***ℋ-Class congruences***:
a, b $\in \mathcal{A}^*$, a ℋ b if aℜb and aℒ b

Definition 1.3.1.1

An alphabet 𝒜, together with a finite set 𝒥 of 𝒥-class equivalence relations is called an *𝒥-class presentation* of the free monoid $\mathcal{A}^*$. Similarly one can obtain four more types of presentations based on the remaining four equivalence relations 𝒟, ℛ, ℒ and ℋ.. We may now say that a system is an *𝒥-class presentation.*

1.3.2 Study Of Systems In Terms Of Associative Calculi

With systems treated in this manner, we find the notion of an ***Associative Calculus*** of Markov [23] to be of immediate use because of the fact that this notion has a direct correspondence with the notion of an 𝒥-class presentation of a free monoid. The correspondence between these two notions is described below.

Let us consider an alphabet 𝒜, and a symbol ↔ which is not in 𝒜. Let 'a' and 'b' be two strings of symbols from the alphabet 𝒜. Now, the string a ↔ b from 𝒜 U { ↔ } is called a ***Defining Formula*** in the theory of associative calculus [23]. By virtue of this formula one can transform a given string into another in the following manner: If the given string is 'uav' it is transformed into 'ubv' where u and v are two more strings in the free monoid $\mathcal{A}^*$. On the other hand, if the given string is 'ubv' then it is transformed into 'uav'. A string (sequence of symbols) from an alphabet is also called a word. Now, one can clearly see from the above technique of transforming a word into another by virtue of a defining formula, that a defining formula is one kind of interpretation of an 𝒥-class equivalence relation. For example, the defining formula a ↔ b over an alphabet 𝒜 can be seen to have a direct correspondence with the equivalence relation a 𝒥 b in the free monoid $\mathcal{A}^*$. A finite set of such defining formulas (𝒥-class relations) over an alphabet 𝒜 is called a ***Defining System***. Let us denote a defining system by the symbol 𝒟.

Associative Calculus

Now, the couple $< \mathcal{A}, \mathcal{D} >$ is what is known in Markov's terms as an *Associative Calculus.* Let us denote an associative calculus over an alphabet $\mathcal{A}$ by the symbol $\mathcal{R}$ such that $\mathcal{R} = < \mathcal{A}, \mathcal{D} >$.

An associative calculus $\mathcal{R}$ over an alphabet $\mathcal{A}$ leads to operations on certain words in $\mathcal{A}^*$ not by means of prescription, that is, to act precisely in such and such way using the $\mathcal{J}$-class relations of the defining system $\mathcal{D}$ in such and such sequence; but by means of permission, that is, to apply the relations without imposing on them any limitations in their choice and their repetitive use. An associative calculus $\mathcal{R}$ is said to be applicable to a word P in the free monoid $\mathcal{A}^*$ only when the word P is transformed into another, say Q, after an exhaustive use of the defining system $\mathcal{D}$. In such a case, the word P is said to be equivalent to the word Q in $\mathcal{R}$ which is denoted by $\mathcal{R}: P \perp\!\!\perp Q$.

Thus an associate calculus $\mathcal{R}$ over alphabet $\mathcal{A}$ generates a system of words $S_{\mathcal{R}}$ which are equivalents with respect to its defining system $\mathcal{D}$. The system of words $S_{\mathcal{R}}$ along with the associative binary operation of concatenation o, forms a mathematical structure $K = <S_{\mathcal{R}}, o>$ where K is called an ***Associative System***.

Thus with the free monoid $\mathcal{A}^*$ being treated as the non-numerical formal structure of a signal space, an associative calculus over the alphabet $\mathcal{A}$ admits of being treated as a non-numerical signal processing system.

In other words, with a signal space over an alphabet $\mathcal{A}$, one can construct a suitable associative calculus over $\mathcal{A}$ in order to carry out a desired non-numerical signal processing operation by symbol manipulation.

Unsolvable Word Problems In the Use Of Associative Calculi

In spite of its neat formalism, the theory of associative calculi and systems suffers from various word problems. One of the problems is about the existence of an algorithm, which would ascertain the equivalence of a word Q to another word P in an associative calculus. Another problem is about the existence of an algorithm that would precisely recognize an invariant property of an associative system. The first problem has been negatively solved independently by Post and Markov [21]. Markov has demonstrated the unsolvability of the second problem [23]. All of these amount to saying that one cannot conveniently carry out various non-numerical signal processing operations in terms of associative calculi, and it is mainly because of the following two reasons.

(i) All the word problems of the theory of associative calculus were found to be tied up with the need for a precise definition of the notion of an *algorithm,* which is closely linked with the notion of ***Computability***.

(ii) Monoid property of an associative calculus is not a ***Hereditary Property***. The notion of a hereditary property is to be understood in the following manner: Let $\mathcal{R}_1$ and $\mathcal{R}_2$ be two (associative) calculi over the alphabets $\mathcal{A}_1$ and $\mathcal{A}_2$ respectively. By a homomorphism of $\mathcal{R}_1$ into $\mathcal{R}_2$ we mean an algorithm, say $\mathcal{N}$, (precisely known as a normal algorithm; Ref. Section 2 for details) over the union of $\mathcal{A}_1$ and $\mathcal{A}_2$ which transforms each and every word from $\mathcal{A}_1$ into some word from $\mathcal{A}_2$ and for any P, Q $\in S\mathcal{R}_1$ the condition $\mathcal{N}(PQ) = \mathcal{N}(P)\,\mathcal{N}(Q)$ holds. The homomorphism becomes an isomorphism if the following condition is satisfied: $\mathcal{R}_1$: P $\perp\perp$ Q $\Leftrightarrow$ $\mathcal{R}_2$: $\mathcal{N}(P) \perp\perp \mathcal{N}(Q)$. In other words, two calculi $\mathcal{R}_1$ and $\mathcal{R}_2$ over the alphabets $\mathcal{A}_1$ and $\mathcal{A}_2$ respectively, are called *isomorphic* to each other only if the derivability of Q from P in $\mathcal{R}_1$ implies the derivability of $\mathcal{N}(Q)$ from $\mathcal{N}(P)$ in $\mathcal{R}_2$ and vice versa. Now let us consider two calculi $\mathcal{R}_1$ and $\mathcal{R}_2$. If there exists an isomorphism of $\mathcal{R}_1$ into $\mathcal{R}_2$ then $\mathcal{R}_1$ is said to be **imbeddable** in $\mathcal{R}_2$. There can be some properties of $\mathcal{R}_2$ which are preserved in $\mathcal{R}_1$.

In general, those properties of an associative calculus which are preserved in every one of its imbeddable calculus are known as hereditary properties.

Since signal spaces are treated here as monoids, all the invariant properties of systems which are preserved in their homomorphic images cannot be conveniently studied using associative calculi.

So now, we turn our attention to A. A. Markov's notion of a ***Normal Algorithm*** for developing a theory for symbolic signal processing.

1.4 Prime Sources Of Support

The material content of this book is the result of a prolonged research carried out by the author with his team of students, scientists and colleagues from the Indian Institute of Technology, Kanpur, Vasavi College of Engineering, Hyderabad, Chaitanya Bharathi Institute of Technology, Hyderabad and mainly from the Pentagram Research Centre Private Limited, Hyderabad. Professor V. P. Sinha of Dhirubhai Ambani Institute of Information and Communication Technology, Gandhi Nagar, Professor Tony G. Constantinides of the Imperial College of Science, Technology and Medicine, London, Professor Claudio Moraga of the Universitat Dortmund, Germany, Professor S. C. Dutta Roy (now retired from the Indian Institute of Technology, Delhi), Professor Padma Sri B. Deekshatalu, Former Director of the National Remote Sensing Agency, Hyderabad (currently he is the Indian Space Research Organization Professor to University of Hyderabad) and Professor Bharata Ratna A.P.J. Abdul Kalam, Former Adviser to Defense Minister, Government of India (currently he is the First Citizen and the President of the Union of India) have been the prime source of motivation, support and criticism in the development of this paradigm.

The central philosophy behind such a development is a meta logical framework blended with the Ancient Indian pedagogy called ***Special Theory of Nondualism*** due to Srimad Ramanujacharya and the ***Constructive Mathematical Logic*** due to Andreii Andreevich Markov, Shanin, Kushner and others of the Steklov Institute of Advanced Studies, Moscow. So, the fundamental philosophy observed throughout this book is the abstraction of ***Potential Realizability of Infinity***, and **not** the idealization of abstraction of actual infinity.

Now, the author presents this book to the reader for a careful study and for constructive criticism.

Section 2

Normal Algorithms

2.1 Why Normal Algorithms?

In the precise formulation of the concept of an algorithm, notions of recursive functions, Turing machines, Post's working hypothesis and Markov's normal algorithms play equivalent roles.

While the first three of these notions occupy a well-established place in theoretical computer science and other related areas including that of signal processing, the notion of normal algorithms have received very little attention from the point of view of applications in these areas. Potentials for such applications would, however, seem to be enormous, considering the fact that normal algorithms play a key role in the works of Markov [20], Shanin [23], [24] and others on constructive real numbers and Analysis. Our choice of normal algorithms from amongst the equivalent notions just mentioned is based on these considerations.

2.2 What Is Meant By A Normal Algorithm?

In what follows, we review very briefly that part of the formalism from Markov's monograph, which is essential for describing the concept and the working principle of a normal algorithm in general [20].

By an *alphabet* we mean a finite, unordered list of primitive symbols known as letters. For example, $\mathcal{A} = \{ 0 \mid - \}$ denotes an alphabet $\mathcal{A}$ which contains the three letters 0, | and - . Binary operations between alphabets are interpreted in exactly the same way as the set-theoretic operations such as *union, intersection and difference* are understood. We shall use the same symbols $\cup$, $\cap$ and \ to denote respectively the union, intersection and the difference operations between alphabets. Similarly all the relation symbols such as $\subseteq$, $\subset$, $\supseteq$, $\supset$ and other symbols like $\in$ and $\notin$ are also used, which convey the same meaning as they do in set theory.

E. G. Rajan, *Symbolic Computing - Signal and Image Processing*
ISBN 81-7800-047-4

By a *generic variable,* we mean a variable whose values are the letters taken from an alphabet. We shall use the symbols ξ, η and μ and their subscripted versions to denote generic variables, irrespective of the alphabets over which they range. But, whenever a generic variable is used, we shall define the alphabet over which it will range.

A string of letters drawn from an alphabet $\mathcal{A}$ and written one after another is called a *word* from the given alphabet. The word consisting of no letters is called *empty word* or the *null word,* which is denoted by the symbol Λ. The concatenation of two words from an alphabet is also a word from the same alphabet.

Definition 2.2.1 [22]

A word U is called the *left factor* of a word P if the condition UV = P holds for P, where V is another word. In this case, V is called the *right factor* of P. In general, a word V is called a factor of another word P if the condition UVW = P holds for P where U and W are two other words.

In a word of the form UVW, the factors U and W are called the delimiters of the factor V.

Now let us consider an alphabet $\mathcal{A}$ and two other symbols $\rightarrow$ and $\cdot$ that are not in $\mathcal{A}$. Then words of the types: (i) $P \rightarrow Q$ and (ii) $P \rightarrow \cdot\, Q$ from the alphabet $\mathcal{A} \cup \{\, \cdot \rightarrow \}$ are called *substitution formulas;* the former is called a simple substitution formula and the latter a terminal substitution formula. P and Q are words in the free monoid $\mathcal{A}^*$ of the alphabet $\mathcal{A}$, and are known as the left and the right parts of the corresponding formula.

Substitution formulas of the type (i) $\rightarrow Q$ (ii) $P \rightarrow$ and (iii) $\rightarrow \cdot$ whose blank parts are empty words, are admissible formulas, and those of the first type, we call *injection formulas.*

By application of a substitution formula to a word, we mean the replacement of the left part of the formula that occurs in the given word, by the right part of the formula.

An ordered list of simple and terminal substitution formulas is called a *scheme.* Let us denote such a scheme by the symbol $\mathcal{S}$. Now, the ordered pair $< \mathcal{A}, \mathcal{S} >$ consisting of a specific alphabet $\mathcal{A}$ and a scheme $\mathcal{S}$ is known as a *normal algorithm,* denoted in general by the symbol $\mathcal{N}$. By the operation of $\mathcal{N}$ on a word, say P, we mean the application of the formulas of its scheme to the word P in accordance with the following rules:

(i) If none of the left parts of the substitution formulas of $\mathcal{N}$ is a factor of P, then $\mathcal{N}$ is not applicable to P; symbolically we say $\neg!\mathcal{N}(P)$.

(ii) If at least one of the left parts of the substitution formulas of $\mathcal{N}$ is a factor of P, then $\mathcal{N}$ is definitely applicable to P (i.e., P is an input to $\mathcal{N}$) and we say $!\mathcal{N}(P)$.

(iii) If $!\mathcal{N}(P)$, then from the ordered list of $\mathcal{N}$, the first substitution formula that is applicable to P is identified and the right part of the identified formula is substituted for the first occurrence in P this formula's left part. Let the result of this substitution be the word Q. If the applied formula is of the terminal type, the word resulting from the substitution is treated as the desired word transformed by N and we write N: $P \vdash \cdot\, Q$. If the applied formula is of the simple type, then the word produced by the substitution is again subjected to $\mathcal{N}$ as outlined in the earlier steps. In this case, we express the one-step transformation as $\mathcal{N}: P \vdash Q$. The process of applying $\mathcal{N}$ can stop at some step either naturally (i.e., when no formula could be applied further) or by means of a terminal formula.

In general, instead of the expression $\mathcal{N}: P_0 \vdash P_1$, $\mathcal{N}: P_1 \vdash P_2, \ldots,$ $\mathcal{N}: P_{n-1} \vdash P_n$ we shall use the briefer expressions $\mathcal{N}: P_0 \vdash P_1 \vdash P_2 \vdash \ldots \vdash P_n$ or $\mathcal{N}: P_0 \models_n P_n$ or $\mathcal{N}: P_0 \models P_n$. Similarly, instead of the expression $\mathcal{N}: P_0 \vdash P_1$, $\mathcal{N}: P_1 \vdash P_2 \ldots \mathcal{N} : P_{n-1} \vdash \cdot P_n$ we shall use the briefer expressions $\mathcal{N}: P_0 \vdash P_1 \vdash P_2 \vdash \ldots \vdash \cdot P_n$ or $\mathcal{N}: P_0 \models_n \cdot P_n$ or $\mathcal{N}: P_0 \models \cdot P_n$.

The rules are illustrated in the diagram shown in figure 2.2.1. Here the symbol δ stands for the empty word Λ if the corresponding formula is simple and for the symbol $\cdot$ if the formula is a terminal one.

Note that the process of application of a normal algorithm would come to an instant stop if the applied formula were a terminal formula.

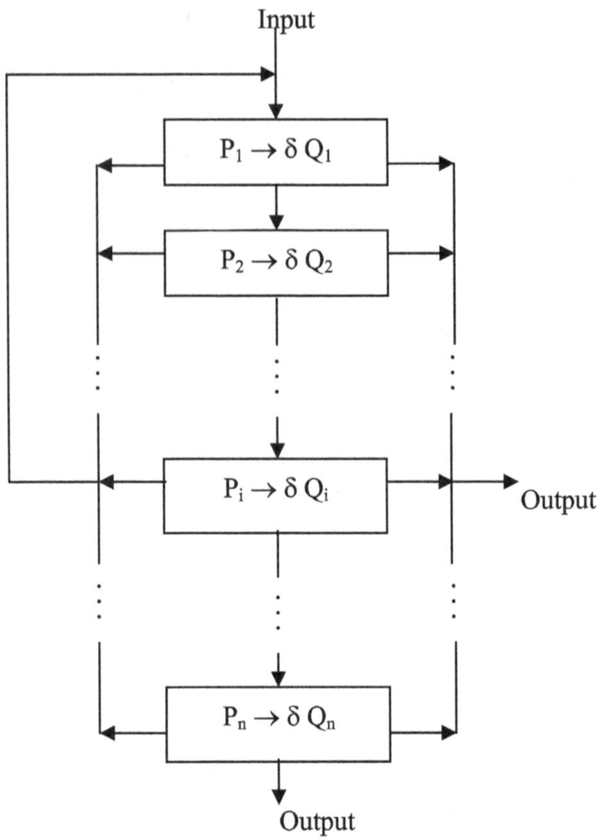

Fig. 2.2.1: Functional block diagram of a normal algorithm

2.3 How To Construct Normal Algorithms?

2.3.1. Relevant Notations And Definitions

In theoretical studies dealing with computations, it is customary to assume that there is no scarcity for storage space and there is no restriction on the repeated use of an algorithm. Markov refers to this assumption as the concept of potential realizability [20]. In keeping with this concept, we are allowed to construct alphabets by adding a new letter to every realized alphabet; to construct words by concatenating a letter to every realized word and to construct normal algorithms from ones already constructed.

Their realization is *potential* that is, the process of their construction is not limited by insufficient space and means. Let $\mathcal{A}$ be an alphabet. Then, the free monoid $\mathcal{A}^*$ is potentially realizable.

Definition 2.3.1.1 [22]

Let P be a word in $\mathcal{A}^*$ where $\mathcal{A}$ is an alphabet and μ be a letter in $\mathcal{A}$. Then the length of the word P , that is, the number of symbols required to form P is denoted by [P]. The number of occurrences of a letter μ in P is denoted by $[P]_\mu$.

Note that $\sum_{\mu \in \mathcal{A}} |P|_\mu = [P]$

Definition 2.3.1.2

A word P is called *multilinear* if for every letter μ in the alphabet $\mathcal{A}$ the condition $|P|_\mu < 2$ holds for P.

In the study of normal algorithms, there is a need to distinguish between the equivalence of normal algorithms, and that of the words representing them. As we shall see later, different words may represent the same normal algorithm. In order to take care of this distinction, three different types of equivalence are used.

Definition 2.3.1.3

Two words P and Q from an alphabet $\mathcal{A}$ are *graphically equivalent* only when they are composed of the same letters, arranged in the same order. Their equivalence is denoted as $P \doteq Q$, where the symbol $\doteq$ represents the relation of graphical equivalence.

Definition 2.3.1.4

Let $\mathcal{N}_1$ and $\mathcal{N}_2$be two normal algorithms in an alphabet $\mathcal{A}$. If $\mathcal{N}_1$ transforms a particular word P from $\mathcal{A}$ into a word Q from $\mathcal{A}$, and $\mathcal{N}_2$ also transforms the same word P into the same word Q, then $\mathcal{N}_1$ and $\mathcal{N}_2$ are said to be *conditionally equivalent* with respect to the word P. Now, if $\mathcal{N}_1$ and $\mathcal{N}_2$ have the same set of input-output pairs consisting of words from the free monoid $\mathcal{A}^*$, then the two normal algorithms are said to be *functionally equivalent* with respect to every admissible input P from A* and we express it as $\mathcal{N}_1(P) \simeq \mathcal{N}_2(P)$. At times we use a briefer expression $\mathcal{N}_1 \simeq \mathcal{N}_2$ instead of $\mathcal{N}_1(P) \simeq \mathcal{N}_2(P)$.

Definition 2.3.1.5

Let P be a word from an alphabet $\mathcal{A}$. The first symbol in the word P is known as its *initial* and the last symbol in P is known as its *ending*. Any factor of P starting with the initial of P is known as the *head* of P. Similarly, any factor of P ending with the ending of P is known as the *tail* of P. The null string Λ, is an empty word from the alphabet $\mathcal{A}$ and so it cannot be the head or tail of P.

Definition 2.3.1.6

Let P be a word from an alphabet $\mathcal{A}$. Then, the word that is obtained by writing the sequence of letters of P in the reverse order is called the *inverse* of the word P and is denoted by P^{-1}.

Definition 2.3.1.7

Two words P and Q from an alphabet $\mathcal{A}$ are said to be *relatively prime* to each other if P and Q do not have any common head or tail.

Definition 2.3.1.8

Let us consider an alphabet of two symbols, say, $\mathcal{A} = \{\ \alpha\ \beta\ \}$. Then, words of the form $\alpha\beta\alpha$, $\alpha\beta\beta\alpha$, $\alpha\beta\beta\beta\alpha$, and so on, are called (α, β) - links. Any word from this alphabet which can be factored into (α,β)– links is called an (α, β) – *chain.*

In general, a normal algorithm $\mathcal{N}$ is called a normal algorithm over an alphabet, say $\mathcal{A}$, if it is constructed in some extension of $\mathcal{A}$ (i.e., in the disjoint union of the alphabets $\mathcal{A}$ and δ, where δ is called the alphabet of *auxiliary symbols).*

Auxiliary symbols are used as markers that separate desired factors in a word from $\mathcal{A}$.

A normal algorithm meant for a specific operation, say * on certain words from the alphabet $\mathcal{A}$, is denoted by $\mathcal{N}^*$. The symbol * may be replaced by any conventional operation symbol or by a suitable acronym which denotes the required operation. At times, it may be required to indicate the domain D of the operation corresponding to $\mathcal{N}^*$. Then the normal algorithm is denoted by $\mathcal{N}^*_D$. The symbol D may be replaced by any symbol denoting a finite or a potentially infinite set of words from the given alphabet. If the domain of an operation of a normal algorithm $\mathcal{N}^*$ over an alphabet $\mathcal{A}$ is the free monoid $\mathcal{A}^*$ itself, then we shall not, in general, indicate the domain. But if it becomes necessary that we should indicate the domain, then instead of denoting the normal algorithm as $\mathcal{N}^*_{\mathcal{A}}$ we shall denote it as $\mathcal{N}^*_{\mathcal{A}}$ in order to reduce the notational complexity. For example, $\mathcal{N}^*_{\mathcal{A}1\cap\mathcal{A}2}$ denotes a normal algorithm that carries out the operation * on words in the free monoid $(\mathcal{A}_1 \cap \mathcal{A}_2)^*$ where $\mathcal{A}_1$ and $\mathcal{A}_2$ are alphabets; whereas, $\mathcal{N}^*_{X\cap Y}$ denotes a normal algorithm that carries out the operation * on words that are common to both the sets X and Y of words from the given alphabet.

2.3.2 Guidelines For Constructing Simple Normal Algorithms

In this subsection, we provide certain guidelines that are helpful in the construction of a normal algorithm meant for a desired operation on words. Before that, we present two simple examples of normal algorithms and see how they work.

Example 2.3.2.1.

Let us consider the alphabet $\mathcal{A} = \{ a\ b \}$, and the normal algorithm $\mathcal{N}^{ANN}$ whose scheme is as follows:

$\mathcal{N}^{ANN}$:	Substitution formulas	Formula number
	$a \rightarrow$	(0)
	$b \rightarrow$	(1)

The substitution formulas of this scheme convey the meaning that both the letters a and b are to be substituted by null strings Λ if they are found in any given word from $\mathcal{A}$. Since the alphabet $\mathcal{A}$ consists of only two letters a and b, it can be seen that $\mathcal{N}^{ANN}$ annihilates (erases) every word that is obtained from $\mathcal{A}$. So, the construction of an annihilating normal algorithm over an alphabet consisting of n letters requires n substitution formulas of the type shown above. However, one can simplify the scheme of $\mathcal{N}^{ANN}$ over any arbitrary alphabet $\mathcal{A}$, by making use of the *generic variable* μ as shown below:

$\mathcal{N}^{ANN}$:	Substitution formula		Formula number
	$\mu \rightarrow$	$(\mu \in \mathcal{A})$	(0)

Example 2.3.2.2

Let us take another example of a normal algorithm $\mathcal{N}^{RAN}$, that right-adjoins (concatenates) a particular word say Q, to any other word, say P, from a given alphabet $\mathcal{A}$. In this example we observe the significant use of an auxiliary symbol.

$\mathcal{N}^{RAN}$:	Substitution formula		Formula number
	$\alpha\,\mu \rightarrow \mu\alpha$	$(\mu \in \mathcal{A}, \alpha \notin \mathcal{A})$	(0)
	$\alpha \quad \rightarrow .\, Q$	$(Q \in \mathcal{A}^*)$	(1)
	$\rightarrow \alpha$		(2)

The working of $\mathcal{N}^{RAN}$ is demonstrated with the help of the following example. Let us consider the alphabets $\mathcal{A}_0 = \{ O \mid \}$ and $\delta = \{\alpha\}$ and the words P = O|O| and Q = O|O from A_0. $\mathcal{N}^{RAN}$ right adjoins Q to P in the following manner: first the auxiliary symbol α is left adjoined to the left of P (formula (2)) , so that the word O|O| is transformed into αO|O|. Then α moves to the right through the word (formula (0)) so that the word αO|O| is transformed into O|O|α after four steps. Now, α is replaced by the word O|O (formula (1)) so that the word O|O|α is transformed into the word O|O|O|O| and the process of applying $\mathcal{N}^{RAN}$ terminates.

$\mathcal{N}^{RAN}$ causes the following elementary transformations of P = O|O| :

Sr.No.	Elementary transformations	Formula used
0	O|O| (input string)	-
1	αO|O|	2
2	Oα|O|	0
3	O|αO|	0
4	O|Oα|	0
5	O|O|α	0
6	O|O|O|O	1 (process terminates)

In principle, any number of auxiliary symbols may be used in a scheme. However, as Markov has shown in [20], one needs atmost two auxiliary symbols in constructing any type of normal algorithm. This is achieved by means of an operation that Markov calls *translation.* As we shall use this notion of translation later, in section-6, we feel that a brief description of it, here, would be appropriate. With this idea in mind, we recall some details of it from [20].

Let us consider a two-lettered alphabet, say, $\mathcal{B} = \{ \alpha \beta \}$ and an alphabet of auxiliary symbols, say, $\mathcal{E} = \{ \Gamma_1 \Gamma_2 \ \ldots. \ \Gamma_n \}$ in addition to the basic alphabet $\mathcal{A}$. Let $\mathcal{C} = \mathcal{A} \cup \mathcal{B}$ and $\mathcal{G} = \mathcal{A} \cup \mathcal{E}$ and ζ be the generic variable that ranges in G. Then the translation of a letter ζ from the alphabet $\mathcal{G}$ is defined as (i) $[\zeta]^{\mathcal{T}} = \zeta$ if $\zeta \in \mathcal{A}$; (ii) $[\zeta]^{\mathcal{T}} = \alpha \beta^{i} \alpha$, $(1 \leq i \leq n)$ if $\zeta \in \mathcal{E}$. In other words all the n letters from the alphabet $\mathcal{E}$ are represented as (α, β) – links from the two-lettered alphabet $\mathcal{B}$. Now, the translation of a word $P = \zeta_1 \zeta_2 \ldots \zeta_i \ldots \zeta_K$ from the alphabet $\mathcal{G}$ is obtained by replacing each letter ζ_i ; $(1 \leq i \leq k)$ in P, by its corresponding translation. The translation of the word P is then denoted by $[P]^{\mathcal{T}}$. [NOTE: $[\Lambda]^{\mathcal{T}} = \Lambda$]. In the same manner, the translation of a normal algorithm N over the alphabet $\mathcal{G}$ is obtained by replacing the left as well as the right parts of all the substitution formulas of the scheme, by their corresponding translations.

Based on these details, we now give a result of Markov, *translation theorem*, which forms one of the central notions of constructive mathematics.

Theorem 2.3.2.1 [20]

Let a normal algorithm $\mathcal{N}$ be applicable to a word P from an alphabet, say, $\mathcal{A}$. Then,

$$[\mathcal{N}]^{\mathcal{T}}([P]^{\mathcal{T}}) \simeq [\mathcal{N}(P)]^{\mathcal{T}}.$$

Thus, generic variables and auxiliary symbols could be seen to play an important role in the construction of normal algorithms.

Now let us see the guidelines that are useful in constructing a normal algorithm for implementing a desired operation on words. These guidelines are just guidelines only and are not to be taken as a systematic procedure.

Guidelines

(i) Normal algorithms are applicable only to words from alphabets. So, by computation we mean the transformation of a given word into a desired word. Now, the computation for which a normal algorithm is sought has to be broken into certain basic symbolic operations similar to what is done to a problem prior to writing a computer program for it.

(ii) The order in which the basic symbolic operations of the computation process are to be carried out, is identified.

(iii) Substitution formulas have to be constructed corresponding to each basic operation of the computation process. For example, let us take the case of constructing a substitution formula corresponding to the basic operation of addition of any two positive integers. We proceed in the following manner.

Firstly, we take two positive integers say 3 and 5, and see how they are added symbolically. The integers 3 and 5 are coded as the words |||* ||||| with the auxiliary symbol * acting as a marker. Now if we erase the marker * the resulting string |||||||| corresponds to the integer 8. By this method, the operation of addition of any two positive integers can be carried out symbolically. The substitution formula that carries out this symbolic operation is: * → · .

(iv) Let us assume that the given computation can be carried out by means of a sequence of b basic symbolic operations. As outlined in the previous step, we can construct one or more substitution formulas corresponding to each of the b basic operations. We note that a basic operation on a word transforms it into another word and the transformation due to this basic operation depends on the word that has been transformed by the previous basic operation. Given an ordered sequence of b basic symbolic operations constituting a computation and an input word P, we exhaust the possibility of carrying out all the other basic operations starting from the bth operation before trying out the first operation and we repeat this procedure for every transformed word. By doing this, we are in a position to maintain the dependency relation in the sequence of basic operations. So, while writing the scheme, the block of substitution formulas corresponding to the bth basic operation has to be written first. Next, the block of substitution formulas corresponding to the $(b-1)^{th}$ basic operation has to be written. This procedure has to be continued till the block of substitution formulas corresponding to the first basic operation is written.

(v) The left parts of the substitution formulas contained in a block might be of different lengths. Now, each block has to be reconstructed with their substitution formulas written in the decreasing order of lengths of their left parts. This is done in order to maintain the dependency relation between the substitution formulas in a block. The ordered list of all the substitution formulas constructed in the above manner, gives rise to a scheme of the required normal algorithm.

2.3.3 Basic Theorems On the Combination Of Normal Algorithms

Markov presented in his monograph, a series of theorems that allow the construction of new normal algorithms using certain algorithms that have already been constructed.

In view of their importance in constructing normal algorithms, we list these theorems here. For the proofs, the reader is referred to [20].

Theorem 2.3.3.1

For any pair of normal algorithms $\mathcal{N}_1$ and $\mathcal{N}_2$, constructed over alphabets $\mathcal{A}$ and $\mathcal{B}$ respectively, one can construct a normal algorithm $\mathcal{N}_3$ over the alphabet C where $C = \mathcal{A} \cup \mathcal{B}$, such that $\mathcal{N}_3$ (P) = $\mathcal{N}_2$ ($\mathcal{N}_1$ (P)) where P is a word from C. This is known as the *composition theorem.*

Theorem 2.3.3.2

For any pair of normal algorithms $\mathcal{N}_1$ and $\mathcal{N}_2$ constructed over an alphabet $\mathcal{A}$, one can construct a normal algorithm $\mathcal{N}_3$ over $\mathcal{A}$ such that $\mathcal{N}_3$(P) = $\mathcal{N}_1$ (P) $\mathcal{N}_2$ (P), where P is a word form $\mathcal{A}$. This is known as the *union theorem.*

Theorem 2.3.3.3

For any normal algorithms $\mathcal{N}_1$, $\mathcal{N}_2$, and $\mathcal{N}_3$ over the alphabets $\mathcal{A}$, $\mathcal{B}$ and $\mathcal{C}$ respectively, one many construct a normal algorithm $\mathcal{N}_4$ over the alphabet $\mathcal{G}$, where $\mathcal{G} = \mathcal{A} \cup \mathcal{B} \cup \mathcal{C}$, such that

(i) $\mathcal{N}_4 (P) \simeq \mathcal{N}_2 (P)$ (P is a word from $\mathcal{G}$ and $\mathcal{N}_3 (P) = \Lambda$)

(ii) $\mathcal{N}_4 (P) \simeq \mathcal{N}_1 (P)$ (P is a word from $\mathcal{G}$ and $\mathcal{N}_3 (P) \neq \Lambda$)

This is known as the *branching theorem.*

In many cases, the need arises for the repeated application of a normal algorithm over and over again until the resulting word satisfies a specific condition. In such cases, the following theorem, known as *repetition theorem* is of use.

Theorem 2.3.3.4

For any two normal algorithms $\mathcal{N}_1$ and $\mathcal{N}_2$ over the alphabets $\mathcal{A}$ and $\mathcal{B}$ respectively, one may construct a normal algorithm $\mathcal{N}_3$ over the alphabet $\mathcal{C}$ where, $\mathcal{C} = \mathcal{A} \cup \mathcal{B}$ such that $\mathcal{N}_3$ transforms a word P from $\mathcal{C}$ into a word Q if and only if there exists a sequence of words P_0, P_1, P_2, …, P_n ; $(n \geq 0)$ satisfying the following conditions:

(i) $P_0 = P$

(ii) $P_i = \mathcal{N}_1 (P_{i-1}) ; (0 < i \leq n)$

(iii) $P_n = Q$

(iv) $\mathcal{N}_2 (P_i) \neq \Lambda ; (0 < i < n)$

(v) $\mathcal{N}_2 (P_n) = \Lambda$

2.3.4 The Notion Of A Generalized Markov Algorithm (GMA)

The purpose of this sub section is to introduce a generalization to the already established concept of Markov Algorithms. The need to go in for this generalization arises from the fact that images are not one-dimensional strings as such, and so, their processing using normal algorithms is not a straight-forward procedure. Since a normal algorithm over an alphabet $\mathcal{A}$, is a map of type $\mathcal{A}^* \rightarrow \mathcal{A}^*$, it is difficult to realize computable mappings of the type $(\mathcal{A}^*)^n \rightarrow \mathcal{A}^*$. For example, it is inconvenient to process array of more than one-dimension consisting of symbols from an alphabet $\mathcal{A}$, using a simple normal algorithm over $\mathcal{A}$. However, efforts were made to solve this problem by actually providing an extension to the concept of Markov Algorithms. The concept of a *Generalized Markov Algorithm* (GMA) is one such extension, which was formulated by Caracciolo Di Fornio for the purpose of defining string processing languages [7].

As described by Caracciolo in [7], the concept of Generalized Markov Algorithm (GMAs) is obtained by admitting certain higher order type substitution formulas, without altering the original sequencing scheme and functional rules.

There are two kinds of higher orders substitution formulas, one representing algebraic expressions of the types $D(f_1 + f_2) \rightarrow D(f_1) + D(f_2)$ and $D(f_1 \cdot f_2) \rightarrow D(f_1) \cdot D(f_2) + (f_1) \cdot D(f_2)$, and the other representing expressions of the type $XY \rightarrow X\,\phi\,[X, Y]$ where ϕ denotes a mapping from the set $A_X \cdot A_Y$ of all pairs of strings respectively belonging to X and Y into $\mathcal{A}^*$. Normal algorithms of the first kind are called *Simple-Generalized Markov Algorithms* (S-GMAs) and those of the second kind *Conditional Functional-Generalized Markov Algorithms* (CF-GMAs). In addition, a CF-GMA admits conditional clauses of the type *provided $\beta(P)$*, where $\beta(P)$ is a Boolean function depending on P which has to be satisfied in order to make the formula $P \rightarrow Q$ admissible.

It is to be noted here that both the concepts of S-GMAs and CF-GMAs were developed with an idea of providing a basic tool for defining the string processing languages PANON-1 and PANON-2 [7]. Though a PANON program is itself a string, which is operated on by structural production rules, the rules from the argument string allow traditional numerical computations. So, it does not provide the capabilities of the required pattern-directed rewriting system in the true sense.

In order to overcome this difficulty, we consider here a particular type of generalization for Markov Algorithms. As per this generalization, different factors located at various places in a string are together viewed as a pattern, that is, a subset of $(\mathcal{A} \cup \mathcal{E})^*$ and substituted by their values. For example, let us consider the string $P_1P_2 \ldots P_i \ldots P_n \Box Q_1\, Q_2 \ldots Q_i \ldots Q_n$ from an alphabet $\mathcal{A} \cup \mathcal{E}$, where P_i, Q_i ; $1 \leq i \leq n$ are words from $\mathcal{A}$ and $\Box$ is a symbol from $\mathcal{E}$. Now, a formula of the type $\lfloor P_1 \rfloor \lfloor Q_1 \rfloor \rightarrow R$, where the symbols $\rfloor$ and $\lfloor$ denote respectively the right and the left parenthesis, is an admissible substitution formula as per this generalization. We refer to this substitution formula as Conjoint Substitution Formula, the details of which are given in section 12. The result of applying this formula to the string $P_1 P_2 \ldots P_i \ldots P_n \square Q_1 Q_2 \ldots Q_i \ldots Q_n$ would be $RP_2 \ldots P_i \ldots P_n \square Q_2 \ldots Q_i \ldots Q_n$ or $P_2 \ldots P_i \ldots P_n \square RQ_2 \ldots Q_i \ldots Q_n$, and this depends on the type of rewriting chosen as to whether R has to replace P_1 or Q_1 .

So all computable mappings of the type $(\mathcal{A}^*)^n \rightarrow \mathcal{A}^*$ can be realized in terms of mappings of the type $(\mathcal{A} \cup \mathcal{E})^* \rightarrow \mathcal{A}^*$ using this concept of a Generalized Markov Algorithm, of course, with the help of simple pattern-directed *search and replace* procedures.

To summarize, we have thus arrived at a level of understanding as to (i) why we prefer normal algorithms for our study (ii) what normal algorithms are and (iii) how we can go about developing a few, in order to meet out any desired computational requirement.

In the next section, we shall see some important techniques using which we can actually construct normal algorithms for implementing desired signal processing operations.

Section 3

Normal Algorithms For Implementing Nonnumerical Signal Processing Operations

In this section, we describe certain string manipulating techniques, which could be used in constructing normal algorithms for signal processing purposes.

3.1. Preliminaries

The term *string manipulation* is interpreted in a restricted sense, as a rearrangement of letters in a given string consisting of symbols drawn from an alphabet. In general, by string manipulation we mean the transformation of a given string into another desired string by either (i) rearranging the letters contained in the given string in a desired fashion, or (ii) erasing arbitrary symbol(s) in the given string, independent of their position or (iii) introducing arbitrary symbol(s) anywhere in the given string.

In the course of constructing normal algorithms for implementing various traditional signal processing operations, we found that any desired normal algorithmic signal processing system could be constructed with the help of a minimal set of certain basic and advanced string manipulation techniques. The following definitions are required for explaining those techniques.

Definition 3.1.1 [23]

Let us consider an alphabet $\mathcal{A}$, and an extra symbol $*$ which is not in $\mathcal{A}$. Then, a word of the form P $*$ Q from $\mathcal{A} \cup \{*\}$, P, Q $\in \mathcal{A}^*$, is defined as A *$*$-pair of words from $\mathcal{A}$* , P its *left $*$-term* and Q its *right $*$-term.* Likewise, with P, Q and R as words from $\mathcal{A}$, P $*$ Q $*$ R is a *$*$- triple of words from $\mathcal{A}$,* Q its *kernel,* P$*$ its *left delimiter* and $*$ R its *right delimiter.* P, Q and R are called *$*$-terms.*

E. G. Rajan, *Symbolic Computing - Signal and Image Processing*
ISBN 81-7800-047-4

Definition 3.1.2

(□ *)-*term* is a word of the form □ P ∗ where P is from an alphabet $\mathcal{A}$ and the symbol □ and ∗ are extra symbols which are not in $\mathcal{A}$. We prefer to call the symbols □ and ∗ *delimiters.*

Definition 3.1.3

(∗ ∗)-*term* or a ∗-*delimited term* is a word of the form ∗ P ∗ where P is from an alphabet $\mathcal{A}$.

Definition 3.1.4 [22]

Let P and Q be two words from an alphabet $\mathcal{A}$, where P can be factored as $P_1 P_2 P_3 \ldots\ldots P_n$ and Q as $Q_1 Q_2 Q_3 \ldots Q_n$. Then, the *shuffle* of P and Q is the subset of the free monoid $\mathcal{A}^*$, defined by :

$$P‡Q = \{R \mid R = P_1 Q_1 P_2 Q_2 \ldots P_i Q_i \ldots P_n Q_n; 1 \leq i \leq n;\ n \geq 0;\ P_i, Q_i \in \mathcal{A}^*\}$$

Definition 3.1.5

Let us consider the shuffle P ‡ Q where $|P| \neq |Q|$. In such a case, P ‡ Q is known as an *improper shuffle.*

Definition 3.1.6

Let P and Q be two words from an alphabet $\mathcal{A}$, where P can be factored as $P_1P_2P_3 \ldots P_n$. Then, Q-dilution of P is the subset of the free monoid $\mathcal{A}^*$, defined by:

$$P†Q = \{R \mid R = P_1QP_2QP_3 \ldots QP_i \ldots QP_n;\ 1 \leq i \leq n;\ n>1;\ P_i, Q \in \mathcal{A}^*\}$$

With these definitions, we are now ready to examine the following string manipulating techniques.

3.2 Basic String Manipulating Techniques

3.2.1. Transposition Technique-Type 1

Interchanging the positions of two adjacent symbols in a string is known as *transposition.* As per this technique, we can transpose two *specific* symbols in a string. For example, let us consider the alphabet of Arabic numerals and a substitution formula 23 → 32. This formula is applicable to the word 105723649 and the transformed word is 105732649.

3.2.2 Transposition Technique-Type 2

In this technique, we use generic variables along with specific symbols. The purpose of using this technique is to shift a specified symbol in a string towards the left or the right. For example, let us consider the alphabet of Arabic numerals and two substitution formulas: (1) F1: 3μ → μ3 and (2) F2: μ4 → 4μ. μ is a generic variable that ranges over the given alphabet. Let P = 1234567 be a word to which both the formulas F1 and F2 are applicable. If F1 is applied to P just once, the word 1234567 is transformed into the word 1243567. On the other hand if F1 is repeatedly applied, the word 1234567 is ultimately transformed into the word 1245673 and the process of applying F1 is naturally terminated. In the same way, by applying F2 just once, P can be transformed into 1243567 or by applying F2 repeatedly, the word P can be transformed into 4123567.

3.2.3 Transposition Technique-Type 3

In this technique, we make use of auxiliary symbols along with generic variables. Let us consider an alphabet $\mathcal{A}$ and an auxiliary symbol α which is not in $\mathcal{A}$. Then, substitution formulas of the types: (1) αμ → μα and (2) ξα → αξ where μ and ξ are individual generic variables which range in $\mathcal{A}$, constitute this technique. For example, let us refer to subsection 2.3.2 where the scheme of the normal algorithm N^{RAN} is provided. As per the 2nd formula of the scheme, the auxiliary symbol is introduced in a given string. It is shifted to the right end of the string by means of the repeated application of the 0th formula of the scheme, that is, αμ → μα which falls under this category. One would find a frequent use of this transposition technique while constructing various normal algorithms. [Note: Formulas of the type αβ → βα , where α and β are auxiliary variables, also belong to this category.]

3.2.4 Transposition Technique-Type 4

Techniques of types 1 to 3 are of use in situations where at least one of the pair of symbols to be transposed is a specific one. There are, however, situations in which we are interested in carrying out certain manipulations such as (1) right adjoining the initial of an arbitrary word to its ending, or (2) left adjoining the ending of a word to its initial. Since the initial and the ending of an arbitrary word are unknown, we cannot specify the corresponding symbols which have to be right (left) shifted. Therefore, we introduce here transposition technique - type 4, which makes use of substitution formulas of the types (1) $\delta\mu\xi \rightarrow \xi\delta\mu$, a right shift formula and (2) $\mu\xi\Gamma \rightarrow \xi\Gamma\mu$, a left shift formula. Here, δ and Γ are auxiliary symbols and μ and ξ are generic variables. A repeated application of the first formula causes a complete right shift of an arbitrary symbol represent by μ which is to the *right of the shift operator,* that is, the auxiliary symbol δ. Likewise, a repeated application of the second formula causes a complete left shift of an arbitrary symbol represented by ξ which is to the *left of the shift operator*, that is, the auxiliary symbol Γ.

For example, consider the alphabet $\mathcal{A}$ = {a b c d}, and the auxiliary alphabet $\mathcal{E} = \{\alpha\ \delta\ \Gamma\}$. Let μ and ξ be the generic variables that range over $\mathcal{A}$, and let P = abcd be a word from $\mathcal{A}$.

Example 3.2.4.1

Normal algorithm for right shift operations

$\mathcal{N}^{RS}$:

Substitution formulas	Formula number
$\delta\mu\xi \rightarrow \xi\delta\mu$	0
$\delta \rightarrow \cdot$	1
$\rightarrow \delta$	2

Now, N^{RS} : abcd $\vdash$ δabcd $\vdash$ bδacd $\vdash$ bcδad $\vdash$ bcdδa $\vdash$ $\cdot$ bcda

Example 3.2.4.2

Normal algorithm for left shift operations

$\mathcal{N}^{LS}$:

Substitution formulas	Formula number
$\mu\xi\Gamma \rightarrow \xi\Gamma\mu$	0
$\alpha\mu \rightarrow \mu\alpha$	1
$\alpha \rightarrow \Gamma$	2
$\Gamma \rightarrow \cdot$	3
$\rightarrow \alpha$	4

Now, $\mathcal{N}^{LS}$: abcd $\vdash$ αabcd $\vdash$ aαbcd $\vdash$ abαcd $\vdash$ abcαd $\vdash$ abcdα $\vdash$ abcdΓ $\vdash$ abdΓc $\vdash$ adΓbc $\vdash$ dΓabc $\vdash$ $\cdot$ dabc

Besides carrying out transformations of symbols in a given string, at times we also need to have some of the symbols removed or erased from them. For this purpose, we introduce the following annihilating techniques.

3.2.5 Annihilation Technique – Type 1

By annihilation of a symbol in a word, we mean substitution of that symbol by null string Λ. By annihilating formula type 1, we mean a substitution formula whose left part is the symbol to be erased and the right part is the null string. For example, let $\mathcal{A}$ = { a b c d } be an alphabet and μ be a generic variable in $\mathcal{A}$. Then, depending on the need one can incorporate in a scheme, any of the following basic annihilating formulas: F1: $\mu \rightarrow$; F2: a $\rightarrow$; F3: b $\rightarrow$; F4: c $\rightarrow$ and F5: d $\rightarrow$.

Let P be any word from $\mathcal{A}$. Then the following statements are valid:

(1) If F1 is applied to P just once, the initial of P will be erased.
(2) If F1 is applied repeatedly, the entire word P will be erased.
(3) If F2 is applied to P just once, the first occurring letter a in P will be erased.
(4) If F2 is applied repeatedly, then $|P|_a - 0$
(5) Statements (3) and (4) are true for other formulas F3, F4 and F5 also.

3.2.6 Annihilation Technique - Type 2

Annihilating formulas of type 1 cannot, in general, be used for erasing a left factor or a right factor of a given string. To be more precise, let us say that we have to erase the right factor V in a word P=UV. Assume that at least one common symbol occurs both in U and V. Then, in the process of erasing all symbols in V with the help of type 1 annihilating formulas, the common symbol present in U will also get erased.

In order to overcome this difficulty, we provide here annihilating formulas of the following types: F1: □ μ → □ and F2: ξτ → τ , where the auxiliary symbols □ and τ we call *right annihilator* and *left annihilator* respectively. μ and ξ are the generic variables over an alphabet $\mathcal{A}$. Annihilation of the right factor V of a given word P from $\mathcal{A}$, where P = UV, is carried out first by rewriting P as U□V and then by applying the formula F1 repeatedly till V is erased. Now by applying the type 1 annihilating formula: $\square \rightarrow$ to the word U$\square$ we obtain the word U. Likewise, we can use formula F2 for annihilating the left factor of a word.

The following example illustrates the use of these two annihilators in erasing the initial and the ending of any realizable word from a given alphabet.

Example 3.2.6.1

Let us consider the alphabets $\mathcal{A} = \{\ a\ b\ \}$; $\mathcal{E} = \{\ \alpha\ \tau\ \square\ \}$; and a word P = abba from $\mathcal{A}$.

$\mathcal{N}^{EXC}$:	Substitution formulas		Formula number
	$\tau\mu \rightarrow \mu\tau$	$(\mu \in \mathcal{A})$	0
	$\square\mu \rightarrow$		1
	$\xi\tau \rightarrow \cdot$	$(\xi \in \mathcal{A})$	2
	$\rightarrow \square\tau$		3

Now, N^{EXC} : abba $\vdash$ $\square\tau$abba $\vdash$ $\square$aτbba $\vdash$ $\square$abτba $\vdash$ $\square$abbτa $\vdash$

$\square$abbaτ $\vdash$ bbaτ $\vdash$ $\cdot$ bb

3.2.7 Annihilation Technique - Type 3

Finally we introduce a technique for carrying out string manipulations such as: (1) annihilation of alternate symbols in a string, (2) extraction of a word P from its Q-diluted form, that is, from P † Q , (3) truncation of P or Q from the $*$-pair P $*$ Q. In such cases, substitution formulas of the following types could be used:

$$F1: \square * \mu \rightarrow \square * \qquad \text{and} \qquad F2: \xi * \tau \rightarrow * \tau$$

We illustrate the use of these formulas by means of the following examples:

Let us consider the alphabets $\mathcal{A} = \{a\ b\}$, $\mathcal{B} = \{*\}$, $\mathcal{C} = \{\tau\ \theta\ \square\}$ and the words P = abba and Q = bab from $\mathcal{A}$, such that abba $*$ bab is from $\mathcal{A} \cup \mathcal{B}$.

Example 3.2.7.1

Normal algorithm for truncating the right *-term in a *-pair

$\mathcal{N}^{REX}$:

Substitution formulas		Formula number
$\square\mu \rightarrow \mu\square$	$(\mu \in \mathcal{A})$	0
$\square{*}\mu \rightarrow \square{*}$		1
$\square{*} \rightarrow \cdot$		2
$\rightarrow \square$		3

Now, N^{REX} :

abba*bab ⊢ □abba*bab ⊢ a□bba*bab ⊢ ab□ba*bab ⊢ abb□a*bab ⊢ abba□*bab ⊢ abba□*ab ⊢ abba□*b ⊢ abba□* ⊢ · abba

Example 3.2.7.2

Normal algorithm for truncating the left *-term in a *-pair

$\mathcal{N}^{LEX}$:

Substitution formulas		Formula number
$\tau\mu \rightarrow \mu\tau$	$(\mu \in \mathcal{A})$	0
$\xi{*}\tau \rightarrow {*}\tau$	$(\xi \in \mathcal{A})$	1
$\tau{*} \rightarrow {*}\tau\theta$		2
${*}\tau\theta \rightarrow \cdot$		3
$\rightarrow \tau$		4

Now, N^{LEX}

abba*bab ⊢ τabba*bab ⊢ aτbba*bab ⊢ abτba*bab ⊢ abbτa*bab ⊢ abbaτ*bab ⊢ abba*τθbab ⊢ abb*τθbab ⊢ ab*τθbab ⊢ a*τθbab ⊢ *τθbab ⊢ · bab

Exclusively with the techniques of transposition, annihilation and injection [subsection 2.2], we can construct a scheme for any desired normal algorithm. In what follows, we provide some more techniques, which will be of use in constructing normal algorithms for signal processing purposes.

3.3 Advanced String Manipulating Techniques

3.3.1 Cyclic Permutations In Any Desired Factor Of a Word

In general, a rearrangement of a word $P = \xi_1\xi_2\ldots\xi_m$, where $\xi_1, \ldots,$ ξ_m are generic variables in an alphabet, is a word $P' = \xi_{i1}\ \xi_{i2\ldots}\xi_{im}$ where

$i1i2_{...}im$ is a permutation of 1234…m. The class of all possible permutations of a word is known as the *rearrangement class* of P, of which *cyclic permutations* of P form a subset [19]. A cyclic permutation in a word can be achieved by means of modified versions of shifting algorithms $\mathcal{N}^{RS}$ or $\mathcal{N}^{LS}$ [Subsection 3.2].

The technique proposed here is concerned with the problem of constructing a normal algorithm that causes cyclic permutations in any desired factor of a given string. We bring out details of this technique with the help of an example.

Let $\mathcal{A}$ be an alphabet and $P = \xi_1\ \xi_{2...}\xi_i\ \xi_{i+1}\ \xi_{i+2}\ \xi_{i+3...}\xi_m$ be a word from $\mathcal{A}$, where ξ_i ; $1 \le i \le m$ are generic variables in $\mathcal{A}$. Let us say that we are interested in having a cyclic permutation in the factor $\xi_i\,\xi_{i+1}\,\xi_{i+2}\,\xi_{i+3}$ of the word P. To do this, we proceed in two steps: (1) we inject two auxiliary symbols □ and * in P, in such a way that the desired factor becomes a (□*)-term [Definition 3.1.3] and (2) we introduce certain transposition-type3 formulas in the scheme of the shifting algorithm so that the algorithm is made available only to the (□*)-term. Note that the auxiliary symbols □ and * act here as delimiters to the desired factor.

For example, the following scheme $\mathcal{N}^{MLS}$, is a modified version of $\mathcal{N}^{LS}$, and it is applicable only to a (□*)-term:

Normal algorithm for Modified Left Shift Operation

$\mathcal{N}^{MLS}$:

Substitution formulas		Formula number
$\mu\xi\Gamma \rightarrow \xi\,\Gamma\mu$	$(\mu,\xi \in \mathcal{A})$	0
$\alpha\Box \rightarrow \Box\,\alpha$		1
$\alpha\,\mu \rightarrow \mu\,\alpha$		2
$\alpha \rightarrow \Gamma$		3
$\Gamma \rightarrow \cdot$		4
$\rightarrow \alpha$		5

Let $\mathcal{A}$ = { a b } P = abab and P' = a □ba*b

Now, $\mathcal{N}^{MLS}$:

a□ba*b ⊢ αa□ba*b ⊢ aα□ba*b ⊢ a□αba*b ⊢ a□bαa*b
⊢ a□baα*b ⊢ a□baΓ*b ⊢ a□aΓb*b ⊢ · a□ab*b

Although we have evolved the algorithm $\mathcal{N}^{MLS}$ with reference to a specific factor of a given word, it may be seen that it is of a perfectly general nature. To be more precise, given any word and a factor of it to be cyclically permuted, the formulas of $\mathcal{N}^{MLS}$ can be used.

Sometimes, we come across a situation in which a particular factor of a multi-factored string has to be cyclically permuted. For example, let us consider a word P from an alphabet $\mathcal{A}$, consisting of m factors: $P = P_1 P_2 ... P_i ... P_m$. We may be interested in getting the ith factor of the string P, to be cyclically permuted. In order to do this, we take the following steps: (1) Firstly, we inject m distinct delimiters $d_1, d_2, d_3, \dots, d_i, \dots, d_m$ in such a way that the given string P is expressed as the shuffle $P \ddagger d = P_1d_1P_2d_2...d_{i-1}P_id_i...P_md_m$. (2) Next, we introduce i-1 substitution formulas of transposition-type3, in the scheme of the modified shifting algorithm $\mathcal{N}^{MLS}$ so that the remodified algorithm is made available only to the (d_{i-1}, d_i)-term of $P\ddagger d$.

Now the following scheme $\mathcal{N}^{CPF}$, causes cyclic permutation in the (d_{i-1}, d_i)-term of a shuffle $P \ddagger d = P_1d_1P_2d_2...d_{i-1}P_id_i...P_md_m$.

Normal algorithm for Cyclic Permutation Operation

$\mathcal{N}^{CPF}$:	Substitution formulas	Formula number
	$\mu\xi\Gamma \rightarrow \xi\Gamma\mu$	0
	$\alpha d_1 \rightarrow d_1\alpha$	1
	⋮	⋮
	$\alpha d_i \rightarrow d_i\alpha$	i
	$\alpha\mu \rightarrow \mu\alpha$	i + 1
	$\alpha \rightarrow \Gamma$	i + 2
	$\Gamma \rightarrow \cdot$	i + 3
	$\rightarrow \alpha$	i + 4

Now, $\mathcal{N}^{CPF}(P\ddagger d) = P_1d_1...d_{i-1}P'_id_i...P_md_m$, where P'_i is the cyclic permutation of the factor P_i ,

We now move on to a further generalization of the shifting algorithm, using which, factors of a given word are separately and simultaneously cyclic permuted.

3.3.2 Cyclic Permutations In All the Factors Of a Word

Given a factored string P from an alphabet $\mathcal{A}$, P = $P_1P_{2...}P_m$; our problem is to carry out cyclic permutations of all the m factors separately. In order to do this, we first of all rewrite the word P as ∗-diluted string [Definition 3.1.7]. This gives us the string P†∗= P_1∗P_2∗… ∗P_m. We know that cyclic permutation in a string is carried out by a shift operator Γ right adjoined to the string. So, in order to carry out cyclic permutations in all the factors of the given word P, that is, in every ∗-term of the string P†∗ our next step is to inject the shift operator Γ in P†∗ as follows: P_1Γ∗P_2Γ∗…Γ∗P_mΓ. Now the following scheme carries out cyclic permutations in all ∗-terms of P†∗, one by one from the left, sequentially.

$\mathcal{N}^{FCP}$:	Substitution formulas		Formula number
	ξ α μ Γ → μ Γ ξ α	(ξ, μ ∈ $\mathcal{A}$)	00
	α μ Γ → μ Γ α		01
	β μ → α μ β		02
	α α → β		03
	β β → Γ		04
	Γα → Γ		05
	Γ μ → μΓ		06
	β α → β		07
	Γ ∗ α → ∗ β		08
	β ∗ μ → β ∗ β μ		09
	Γ → ·		10
	→ α		11

Now, let us consider an alphabet $\mathcal{A}$ = {a b}, a word P = abba and P†∗ = ab ∗ ba .

Then, $\mathcal{N}^{FCP}$:

ab∗ba ⊢ αab∗ba ⊢ ααab∗ba ⊢ βab∗ba ⊢ αaβb∗ba ⊢ αaαbβ∗ba ⊢ αaαbβ∗βba ⊢ αaαbβ∗αbβa ⊢ αaαbβ∗αbαaβ ⊢ ααaαbβ∗αbαaβ ⊢ βaαbβ∗αbαaβ ⊢ αaβαbβ∗αbαaβ ⊢ αaβbβ∗αbαaβ ⊢ αaαbββ∗αbαaβ ⊢ αaαbΓ∗αbαaβ ⊢ αbΓaα∗αbαaβ ⊢ bΓαaα∗αbαaβ ⊢ bΓaα∗αbαaβ ⊢ baΓα∗αbαaβ ⊢ baΓ∗αbαaβ ⊢ ba∗βbαaβ ⊢ ba∗αbβαaβ ⊢ ba∗αbβaβ ⊢ ba∗αbαaββ ⊢ ba∗αbαaΓ ⊢ ba∗αaΓbα ⊢ ba∗aΓαbα ⊢ ba∗aΓbα ⊢ ba∗abΓα ⊢ ba∗abΓ ⊢ · ba∗ab

The techniques discussed so far (i.e., transposition, annihilation, injection and cyclic permutation), enable us to construct substitution formulas required for different symbol manipulations in words from the union of a basic alphabet $\mathcal{A}$, an alphabet $\mathcal{E}$ of auxiliary symbols and an alphabet $\mathcal{D}$ of delimiters. Now, with a formal characterization of substitution formulas, our study of string manipulating techniques would be complete.

3.3.3 Pattern Matching Technique

In general, the operation of examining strings of symbols from an alphabet, for the occurrence of specific strings known as *patterns* is defined as *pattern matching* [15]. As per this definition, a substitution formula is a prescription for pattern matching and substitution. In other words, the left part of a substitution formula, which is a specific pattern, is examined for its occurrence in a given string of symbols and replaced by the right part of the formula, *the value of the pattern.* So, a normal algorithm over an alphabet $\mathcal{A}$, is a prescription for systematically examining a set of strings from the free monoid $\mathcal{A}^*$ for the occurrence of a finite number of patterns and substituting them with their values.

Let us consider a basic alphabet $\mathcal{A}$, an alphabet $\mathcal{D}$ consisting of delimiters and an alphabet $\mathcal{E}$ consisting of auxiliary symbols. Now, patterns are those strings from $(\mathcal{A} \cup \mathcal{D} \cup \mathcal{E})^*$ which are used as left parts of various substitution formulas constructed over the union of these disjoint alphabets.

We are interested in two kinds of patterns that we call (1) Simple patterns and (2) Complex patterns. A simple pattern is a string either from $\mathcal{A}^*$ or $(\mathcal{A} \cup \mathcal{D})^*$that is used as left part of a substitution formula. A complex pattern is a string from $(\mathcal{A} \cup \mathcal{D} \cup \mathcal{E})^*$ containing at least one symbol from $\mathcal{E}$, and which is used as left part of a substitution formula. Simple and Complex patterns are further divided into *regular simple patterns, irregular simple patterns, regular complex patterns and irregular complex patterns.* Regular patterns are those, whose constructions are governed at least by any one of the rules of the string manipulating techniques discussed so far. Irregular patterns are special patterns of both simple and complex types, whose constructions are not governed by any rule, but are used as left parts of certain substitution formulas.

We now proceed to verify, in the next section, the usefulness of these string manipulating techniques, by actually constructing normal algorithms for carrying out the traditional signal processing operations of cyclic shifting and linear convolution of nonnegative integer sequences.

Section 4

Realization Of Certain Normal Algorithmic Signal Processing Operations

In this section, we demonstrate the use of the string manipulating techniques of secion-3, in nonnumerical signal processing. First, we construct a normal algorithm for carrying out *cyclic shifting* in a string of arbitrary length. Next, we outline a general method for constructing normal algorithmic systems for signal processing operations on symbolic sequences in general. As an illustration, we then construct a normal algorithmic system for carrying out linear convolution of nonnegative integer sequences.

4.1. Cyclic Shifting By a Normal Algorithm $\mathcal{N}^{cs}$

When the normal algorithm $\mathcal{N}^{LS}$ [Example 3.2.4.2] is applied to a word, say P from an alphabet $\mathcal{A}$, the ending of P is shifted to its left by the shift operator Γ which gets annihilated after the shifting is over. As we shall see later, there are situations in which we make use of Γ not only as a left shift operator, but also as a part of certain patterns to be substituted by their values. In order to do this, there has to be a provision in the scheme of $\mathcal{N}^{LS}$ for bringing Γ back to the right of the word whose ending is left shifted. With this idea in mind, the following scheme of $\mathcal{N}^{CS}$ has been constructed over $\mathcal{A} \cup \{\ \alpha\ \beta\ \Gamma\ \}$. $\mathcal{N}^{CS}$ causes one cyclic shift (left shift) in any string of arbitrary length, in the free monoid $\mathcal{A}^*$.

$\mathcal{N}^{CS}$:

Substitution formulas		Formula number
$\xi\,\alpha\,\mu\,\Gamma \rightarrow \mu\,\Gamma\,\xi\,\alpha$	$(\xi, \mu \in \mathcal{A})$	0
$\alpha\,\mu\,\Gamma \rightarrow \mu\,\Gamma\,\alpha$		1
$\beta\,\mu \rightarrow \alpha\,\mu\,\beta$		2
$\alpha\,\alpha \rightarrow \beta$		3
$\beta\,\beta \rightarrow \Gamma$		4
$\Gamma\alpha \rightarrow \Gamma$		5

E. G. Rajan, *Symbolic Computing - Signal and Image Processing*
ISBN 81-7800-047-4

$\Gamma\mu \rightarrow \mu\Gamma$ 6

$\beta\alpha \rightarrow \beta$ 7

$\Gamma \rightarrow .$ 8

$\rightarrow \alpha$ 9

Let us consider the alphabets $\mathcal{A}$ = {O |} and $\mathcal{E}$ = {α β Γ} and apply $\mathcal{N}^{CS}$ to a word |O|O from $\mathcal{A}$.

Now, $\mathcal{N}^{CS}$:

Formula number	Elementary transformations
-	|O|O ← (Input string)
9	α|O|O
9	αα|O|O
3	β|O|O
2	α|βO|O
2	α|αOβ|O
2	α|αOα|βO
2	α|αOα|αOβ
9	αα|αOα|αOβ
3	β|αOα|αOβ
2	α|βαOα|αOβ
7	α|βOα|αOβ
2	α|αOβα|αOβ
7	α|αOβ|αOβ
2	α|αOα|βαOβ
7	α|αOα|βOβ
2	α|αOα|αOββ
4	α|αOα|αOΓ
0	α|αOαOΓ|α
0	α|αOΓOα|α
0	αOΓ|αOα|α
1	OΓα|αOα|α
5	OΓ|αOα|α
6	O|ΓαOα|α
5	O|ΓOα|α
6	O|OΓα|α
5	O|OΓ|α
6	O|O|Γα
5	O|O|Γ
8	O|O| ← (Output string)

$\mathcal{N}^{CS}$ causes one cyclic shift in the word |O|O after 29 elementary transformations such that |O|O becomes O|O|. In fact, the number of transformations that a word P of length n undergoes when $\mathcal{N}^{CS}$ is applied to it for one cyclic shift, can be computed with the help of the simple rule a+(n-1)d where a=11 and d=6. It can be observed that the process of applying $\mathcal{N}^{CS}$ to a word P comes to an end after a single cyclic shift, on the application of the 8th substitution formula of the scheme. So, if we require consecutive cyclic shifts in a word P, $\mathcal{N}^{CS}$ has to be applied consecutively (n-1) number of times to the intermediate strings. But, this can be done in a different manner. Let us replace the terminal formula $\Gamma \to \cdot$ of the scheme of $\mathcal{N}^{CS}$ by the simple formula $\Gamma \to$ and make use of Theorem 2.3.3.4 in achieving a control over the number of cyclic shifts. Now, the scheme of $\mathcal{N}^{CS}$ with the above modification is labeled as $\mathcal{N}^{CCS}$ where the acronym ccs stands for *Consecutive Cyclic Shifts*. The generality of the scheme of $\mathcal{N}^{CCS}$ has been verified by implementing it on a personal computer.

For example, one can develop a program for the scheme of $\mathcal{N}^{CCS}$ for carrying out two cyclic shifts in a word P $\doteq$ O|OO|||O|| from the alphabet $\mathcal{A}$ = {O |}. Then the output would be the following:

Give the number of characters in the input string: 10
Give the input string: O|OO|||O||
Specify number of cyclic shifts: 2

Formula Number	Elementary Transformations	
-	O|OO|||O||	← (Input string)
9	αO|OO|||O||	
9	ααO|OO|||O||	
3	βO|OO|||O||	
2	αOβ|OO|||O||	
2	αOα|βOO|||O||	
2	αOα|αOβO|||O||	
2	αOα|αOαOβ|||O||	
2	αOα|αOαOα|β||O||	
2	αOα|αOαOα|α|β|O||	
2	αOα|αOαOα|α|α|βO||	
2	αOα|αOαOα|α|α|αOβ||	
2	αOα|αOαOα|α|α|αOα|β|	
2	αOα|αOαOα|α|α|αOα|α|β	
9	ααOα|αOαOα|α|α|αOα|α|β	
3	βOα|αOαOα|α|α|αOα|α|β	

2 αOβα|αOαOα|α|α|αOα|α|β
7 αOβ|αOαOα|α|α|αOα|α|β
2 αOα|βαOαOα|α|α|αOα|α|β
7 αOα|βOαOα|α|α|αOα|α|β
2 αOα|αOβαOα|α|α|αOα|α|β
7 αOα|αOβOα|α|α|αOα|α|β
2 αOα|αOαOβα|α|α|αOα|α|β
7 αOα|αOαOβ|α|α|αOα|α|β
2 αOα|αOαOα|βα|α|αOα|α|β
7 αOα|αOαOα|β|α|αOα|α|β
2 αOα|αOαOα|α|βα|αOα|α|β
7 αOα|αOαOα|α|β|αOα|α|β
2 αOα|αOαOα|α|α|βαOα|α|β
7 αOα|αOαOα|α|α|βOα|α|β
2 αOα|αOαOα|α|α|αOβα|α|β
7 αOα|αOαOα|α|α|αOβ|α|β
2 αOα|αOαOα|α|α|αOα|βα|β
7 αOα|αOαOα|α|α|αOα|β|β
2 αOα|αOαOα|α|α|αOα|α|ββ
4 αOα|αOαOα|α|α|αOα|α|Γ
0 αOα|αOαOα|α|α|αOα|Γ|α
0 αOα|αOαOα|α|α|α|ΓOα|α
0 αOα|αOαOα|α|α|Γ|αOα|α
0 αOα|αOαOα|α|Γ|α|αOα|α
0 αOα|αOαOα|Γ|α|α|αOα|α
0 αOα|αOα|ΓOα|α|α|αOα|α
0 αOα|α|ΓOαOα|α|α|αOα|α
0 αOα|Γ|αOαOα|α|α|αOα|α
0 α|ΓOα|αOαOα|α|α|αOα|α
1 |ΓαOα|αOαOα|α|α|αOα|α
5 |ΓOα|αOαOα|α|α|αOα|α
6 |OΓα|αOαOα|α|α|αOα|α
5 |OΓ|αOαOα|α|α|αOα|α
6 |O|ΓαOαOα|α|α|αOα|α
5 |O|ΓOαOα|α|α|αOα|α
6 |O|OΓαOα|α|α|αOα|α
5 |O|OΓOα|α|α|αOα|α
6 |O|OOΓα|α|α|αOα|α
5 |O|OOΓ|α|α|αOα|α

```
6    |O|OO|Γα|α|αOα|α
5    |O|OO|Γ|α|αOα|α
6    |O|OO||Γα|αOα|α
5    |O|OO||Γ|αOα|α
6    |O|OO|||ΓαOα|α
5    |O|OO|||ΓOα|α
6    |O|OO|||OΓα|α
5    |O|OO|||OΓ|α
6    |O|OO|||O|Γα
5    |O|OO|||O|Γ
8    |O|OO|||O|   ← [ First cyclic shift is over after
9    α|O|OO|||O|     65 elementary transformations ]
9    αα|O|OO|||O|
3    β|O|OO|||O|
2    α|βO|OO|||O|
2    α|αOβ|OO|||O|
2    α|αOαβOO|||O|
2    α|αOα|αOβO|||O|
2    α|αOα|αOαOβ|||O|
2    α|αOα|αOαOα|β||O|
2    α|αOα|αOαOα|α|β|O|
2    α|αOα|αOαOα|α|α|βO|
2    α|αOα|αOαOα|α|α|αOβ|
2    α|αOα|αOαOα|α|α|αOα|β
9    αα|αOα|αOαOα|α|α|αOα|β
3    β|αOα|αOαOα|α|α|αOα|β
2    α|βαOα|αOαOα|α|α|αOα|β
7    α|βOα|αOαOα|α|α|αOα|β
2    α|αOβα|αOαOα|α|α|αOα|β
7    α|αOβ|αOαOα|α|α|αOα|β
2    α|αOα|βαOαOα|α|α|αOα|β
7    α|αOα|βOαOα|α|α|αOα|β
2    α|αOα|αOβαOα|α|α|αOα|β
7    α|αOα|αOβOα|α|α|αOα|β
2    α|αOα|αOαOβα|α|α|αOα|β
7    α|αOα|αOαOβ|α|α|αOα|β
2    α|αOα|αOαOα|βα|α|αOα|β
7    α|αOα|αOαOα|β|α|αOα|β
2    α|αOα|αOαOα|α|βα|αOα|β
```

7 α|αOα|αOαOα|α|β|αOα|β
2 α|αOα|αOαOα|α|α|βαOα|β
7 α|αOα|αOαOα|α|α|βOα|β
2 α|αOα|αOαOα|α|α|αOβα|β
7 α|αOα|αOαOα|α|α|αOβ|β
2 α|αOα|αOαOα|α|α|αOα|ββ
4 α|αOα|αOαOα|α|α|αOα|Γ
0 α|αOα|αOαOα|α|α|α|ΓOα
0 α|αOα|αOαOα|α|α|Γ|αOα
0 α|αOα|αOαOα|α|Γ|α|αOα
0 α|αOα|αOαOα|Γ|α|α|αOα
0 α|αOα|αOα|ΓOα|α|α|αOα
0 α|αOα|α|ΓOαOα|α|α|αOα
0 α|αOα|Γ|αOαOα|α|α|αOα
0 α|α|ΓOα|αOαOα|α|α|αOα
0 α|Γ|αOα|αOαOα|α|α|αOα
1 |Γα|αOα|αOαOα|α|α|αOα
5 |Γ|αOα|αOαOα|α|α|αOα
6 ||ΓαOα|αOαOα|α|α|αOα
5 ||ΓOα|αOαOα|α|α|αOα
6 ||OΓα|αOαOα|α|α|αOα
5 ||OΓ|αOαOα|α|α|αOα
6 ||O|ΓαOαOα|α|α|αOα
5 ||O|ΓOαOα|α|α|αOα
6 ||O|OΓαOα|α|α|αOα
5 ||O|OΓOα|α|α|αOα
6 ||O|OOΓα|α|α|αOα
5 ||O|OOΓ|α|α|αOα
6 ||O|OO|Γα|α|αOα
5 ||O|OO|Γ|α|αOα
6 ||O|OO||Γα|αOα
5 ||O|OO||Γ|αOα
6 ||O|OO|||ΓαOα
5 ||O|OO|||ΓOα
6 ||O|OO|||OΓα
5 ||O|OO|||OΓ
8 ||O|OO|||O ← [Second cyclic shift is over after 130 elementary transformations]

4.2 How To Realize a Constructive Signal Processing Operation?

Here, the term *Constructive Signal Processing* refers to the symbolic processing of signals by normal algorithms, irrespective of the fact whether sample values of signals are expressed as numbers or words.

Definition 4.2.1

By a *Constructive Signal Processing system,* we mean an ordered pair $< \mathfrak{R}, X >$, Where, $\mathfrak{R}$ represents a normal algorithm and X is a subset of $(\mathcal{A} \cup \mathcal{D})^*$ that is recognized by $\mathfrak{R}$. $\mathcal{A}$ is a basic alphabet in which signals are represented and $\mathcal{D}$ is an alphabet of delimiters.

Now, we outline a general method for constructing normal algorithms for implementing binary operations between numerical data sequences.

Let us consider two numerical data sequences p(n) and q(n) of M and N data samples respectively. Let r(n) be the result of an arithmetic operation, say $\cdot$ between p(n) and q(n), that is $r(n) = p(n)\cdot q(n)$ Our interest is to carry out this operation symbolically, by means of a normal algorithm. We proceed as follows.

Firstly, we code the data samples of p(n) and q(n) as words from a suitable alphabet $\mathcal{A}$ so that the data sequences p(n) and q(n) are expressed respectively as

$$P\dagger d_p = P_1 d_p P_2 d_p \ldots P_i d_p \ldots d_p P_M, \qquad 1 \le i \le M$$

and

$$Q\dagger d_q = Q_1 d_q Q_2 d_q \ldots Q_j d_q \ldots d_q Q_N, \qquad 1 \le i \le M$$

where d_p and d_q are two different delimiters from the alphabet $\mathcal{D}$. Next, we express these coded strings as a $*$-pair $(P\dagger d_p) * (Q\dagger d_q)$, where the symbol * is a delimiter from the alphabet $\mathcal{D}$.

Now, the $*$-pair is to be manipulated in such a way that the resulting string say $R\dagger d_r$ corresponds to the output r(n). A normal algorithm meant for this purpose would cause the following sequence of string manipulations.

Let $d_k(P\dagger d_P)*(Q\dagger d_q) \doteq d_kP_1d_p\ldots d_pP_M*Q_1d_q\ldots d_qQ_N$ where d_k is another delimiter. d_k is used to identify P_1 at any stage of the manipulation. First, the $*$-pair pattern consisting of the right most factor P_M of $P\dagger d_p$ and the left most factor Q_1 of $Q\dagger d_q$ is substituted by its value $P_M*Q_1R_{M1}$. R_{M1} is the result of a suitable manipulation P_M and Q_1 , and it corresponds to the value of the intended operation between the last sample of the first data sequence p(n) and the first sample of the second data sequence q(n). Now P_M is shifted to the left end such that the resulting string would be of the form:

$$P_M\, d_k\, P_1\, d_p\ldots P_{M-1}d_p*Q_1\, R_{M1}\, d_q\, \ldots\, d_q\, Q_N$$

By assigning a value $d_p*Q_1\, d_c$ to the pattern d_p*Q_1 a delimiter d_c is injected in the first d_q-term, which is used here in order to identify R_{M1} at any stage of the manipulation. Now, d_p is shifted to the left end such that the resulting string would be of the form:

$$d_pP_Md_kP_1d_p\ldots P_{M-1}*Q_1\, d_c\, R_{M1}\, d_q\ldots d_qQ_N$$

The above procedure is repeated for the $*$-pair pattern $P_{M-1}*Q_1$ such that the resulting string would be of the form:

$$d_pP_{M-1}\, d_pP_Md_kP_1d_p\ldots P_{M-2}*Q_1d_cR_{(M-1)1}\, d_cR_{M1}d_q\ldots d_qQ_N$$

We shall repeat this procedure till we arrive at a string, which would be of the form:

$$P_1\, d_p\ldots d_p\, P_Md_k*Q_1R_{11}d_cR_{21}d_c\ldots d_cR_{M1}\, d_qQ_2\, d_q\ldots d_qQ_N\, .$$

Now, we shall make use of the delimiter d_k in two ways: (i) d_k is used as a type-3 annihilator such that Q_1 is erased by assigning the value d_k* to the pattern d_k*Q_1 and (ii) d_k is allowed to inject a right shift operator δ into the right $*$-term when either a value $d_k*\delta\, d_c$ is assigned to the pattern d_k*d_c , or a value $d_k*\delta R_{ij}$, $1 \le i \le M$, $1 \le j \le N$ is assigned to the pattern d_k*R_{ij} or a value $d_k*\delta d_r$ is assigned to the pattern d_k*d_q . The moment δ is introduced, R_{11} , d_c and d_r will be shifted to the right. This is repeated till all the M generated values are shifted to the right end. Now, the delimiter d_k is shifted to the left such that the resulting string would be of the form $d_kP_1\, d_p\ldots d_pP_M*Q_2\, d_q\ldots d_qQ_N\, d_r\delta R_{M1}\delta d_c\delta R_{(M-1)1}\ldots\delta d_c\delta R_{11}$

This procedure is repeated for all the remaining (N-1) d_q-terms of $Q\dagger d_q$ after which $P\dagger d_p$ together with the delimiters d_k, $*$ and the right operator δ are erased by means of a type-3 and a type-2 annihilation formulas. The resulting string $R\dagger d_r$ corresponds to the result of the operation between the two coded strings of p(n) and q(n) and it would be of the form $R_{MN}\, d_c\, R_{(M-1)N}\, d_c\ldots d_cR_{1N}\, d_rR_{M(N-1)}d_cR_{(M-1)(N-1)}d_c\ldots d_r\ldots R_{M1}d_c\, R_{(M-1)1}\, d_c\ldots d_cR_{11}$.

Now, the values of R_{ij} ; $1 \leq i \leq M$; $1 \leq j \leq N$ are decoded such that the output r(n) due to the operation $*$ between p(n) and q(n), is obtained.

Note that the operation $\cdot$ between p(n) and q(n) is carried out by manipulating the corresponding coded $*$-pair with the help of left shifting, right shifting, transposition, annihilation and pattern matching substitution formulas.

4.3 Linear Convolution Of Nonnegative Integer Sequences By a Constructive System $\mathfrak{R}^{con}$

In 4.2, a general method as to how one can construct a normal algorithmic signal processing system was outlined. In what follows, we provide a specific example of one way of constructing a normal algorithmic system $\mathfrak{R}^{CON}$ that carries out the operation of linear convolution of nonnegative integer sequences of arbitrary lengths. We shall make use of the string manipulating techniques of section 3 in obtaining our constructive system $\mathfrak{R}^{CON}$.

Let us consider two discrete time signals x(n) and y(n) of samples M and N respectively, which are to be convolved with the help of normal algorithms. Let the convolved output be z(n) of M+N-1 samples. Now, the required system $\mathfrak{R}^{CON}$ is constructed as per the following steps:

STEP # 1

We need the following alphabets for the construction of $\mathfrak{R}^{CON}$
$\mathcal{A}_0 = \{ 0 \mid \}$; $\mathcal{D}_1 = \{ , \}$; $\mathcal{D}_2 = \{ \square \}$; $\mathcal{D}_3 = \{ * \}$;
$\mathcal{E} = \{ a\ b\ \alpha\ \beta\ \Gamma\ \delta\ \theta\ \sigma\ \omega\ \nu \}$; $\mathcal{D} = \mathcal{D}_1 \cup \mathcal{D}_2 \cup \mathcal{D}_3$; $\mathcal{A}_{11} = \mathcal{A}_0 \cup \mathcal{D}_1$;
$\mathcal{A}_{12} = \mathcal{A}_0 \cup \mathcal{D}_2$; $\mathcal{A}_{13} = \mathcal{A}_{11} \cup \mathcal{A}_{12}$; $\mathcal{A}_0 = \{ 0\ 1\ 2\ 3\ 4\ 5\ 6\ 7\ 8\ 9 \}$;
$\mathcal{A}_{14} = \mathcal{A}_{13} \cup \mathcal{D}_3$

Further, we consider the sets N = {x|x is a natural number in the traditional sense} and S = {x|x is a nonnegative integer sequence} .

We also need the following subsets of certain free monoids for the construction of $\mathfrak{R}^{CON}$ [Ref: Table 4.3.1]:

Table 4.3.1: Subsets recognized by $\Re^{CON}$

Sl.No.	Free Monoids	Subsets	Sample elements of the subsets
1	A^*_0	N ={x|x is a word (natural number) from A_0}	4
2	$(A_0 \cup \mathcal{D}_1)^*$	S ={x|x is a nonnegative integer sequence}	2,4,6,8,12
3	A^*_0	X_0 ={x|x=O or $\|^i$; i ≥ 1 }	||||
4	A^*_{11}	X_{11} ={x|x=P or P†, ; P∈X_0 }	|,||,|||
5	A^*_{12}	X_{12} ={x|x=P or P†□; P∈X_0 }	||□|||□||||
6	A^*_{13}	X'_{13}={x|x∈X_{11}or X_{12} }	|,||,||| or ||□|||□||||
7	A^*_{13}	X''_{13}={x|x=P†□ ; P∈X_{11}}	|,||,|||□||,|||□||,|
8	A^*_{14}	X_{14} ={x|x=□P*Q ; P∈X_{11} ; Q ∈ X_{12} or X''_{13} }	□|,||,|||*||□|||□|||| or □|,||,*||,|||□|,||,|||

STEP # 2

Firstly, we code the data samples of x(n) and y(n) from N over the alphabet $\mathcal{A}_0$ in the following manner: The number 0 is represented as the string O and the number 1 is represented as the string | from the alphabet $\mathcal{A}_0$. The number 2 is represented as the string || and the number 3 is coded as the string |||. In this fashion, any non-negative integer can be coded in the alphabet $\mathcal{A}_0$. Since convolution is a binary operation, we express the coded strings of x(n) and y(n) as a ∗-pair over the union of the alphabets $\mathcal{A}_0$, $\mathcal{D}_1$, $\mathcal{D}_2$ and $\mathcal{D}_3$ so that the *-pair is of the form:

$$\Box X\dagger,*Y\dagger\Box \doteq \Box X_1 , X_2 ,..., X_i ,..., X_M *Y_1\Box Y_2 \Box_{...}\Box Y_j\Box_{...}\Box Y_N$$

where X_i , $(1 \le i \le M)$ and Y_j , $(1 \le j \le N)$ are coded strings from $\mathcal{A}_0$ corresponding to the data samples of x(n) and y(n) respectively. We acquire three normal algorithms in order to obtain the above *-pair: (i) $\mathcal{N}^\dagger$, that transforms x(n) into X† , (ii) $\mathcal{N}^\dagger$□ that transforms y(n) into Y†□ and (iii) $\mathcal{N}$* that forms the *-pair □X†, Y†□ . For brevity, we shall call the string □X†,Y†□ as *Preconvolution String.*

STEP # 3

Convolution is basically a multiplication operation. Firstly, let us consider the following normal algorithm $\mathcal{N}^{MUL}$ which allows one way of carrying out the multiplication operation between two coded strings of nonnegative integers that are expressed as a *-pair. $\mathcal{N}^{MUL}$ has been constructed over $\mathcal{A}_0 \cup \mathcal{D}_3 \cup \mathcal{E}$.

$\mathcal{N}^{MUL}$:

Substitution formula			Formula number
a|	→	| ba	0
b|	→	| b	1
O*|	→	O*	2
|*O	→	*O	3
|*|	→	*a|	4
*|	→	*	5
a	→		6
*b	→	|*	7
*	→	·	8

For example, let us consider a ∗-pair |||∗|| of strings from $\mathcal{A}_0$ and apply $\mathcal{N}^{MUL}$ to it.

$\mathcal{N}^{MUL}$:

Formula Number	Elementary Transformations
-	|||∗|| ⟵ Input String
4	||∗a||
0	||∗|ba|
0	||∗|b|ba|
1	||∗||bba
4	|∗a||bba
0	|∗|ba|bba
0	|∗|b|babba
1	|∗||bbabba
4	∗a||bbabba
0	∗|ba|bbabba
0	∗|b|babbabba
1	∗||bbabbabba
5	∗|bbabbabba
5	∗bbabbabba
6	∗bbbbabba
6	∗bbbbbba
6	∗bbbbbb
7	|∗bbbbb
7	||∗bbbb
7	|||∗bbb
7	||||∗bb
7	|||||∗b
7	||||||∗
8	|||||| ← (Output string)

The string |||||| corresponds to the number 6 which is the product of the numbers 3 and 2. Now, the multiplication operation can be carried out in the $*$-pair:

$$\Box X\dagger,*Y\dagger\Box \doteq \Box X_1, X_2, \ldots, X_i, \ldots, X_M * Y_1 \Box Y_2 \Box \ldots \Box Y_j \Box \ldots \Box Y_N$$

by means of a normal algorithm which makes use of the technique of $\mathcal{N}^{MUL}$.

$\mathcal{N}^{PP}$ is one such normal algorithm constructed over $\mathcal{A}_0 \cup \mathcal{D} \cup \mathcal{E}$. It contains certain pattern substitutions and certain already known algorithms. The scheme of $\mathcal{N}^{PP}$ is given below. [Note: (i) μ, $\xi \in A_0$. (ii) The acronyms TPT stands for *Transposition Type,* AT for *Annihilation Type,* PTS for *Pattern* Substitution and SPL for *Special* type. A special type formula is constructed by making use of known techniques as per the need. (iii) One can develop a computer program LINCON for implementing $\mathfrak{R}^{CON}$.

Sl. No.	**Substitution Formulas**	**Type of the Formula**	**Remarks**
00	$\mu\alpha\xi\Gamma \rightarrow \xi\Gamma\mu\alpha$	TPT-4	The formulas 00 to 12, 59 and 60 form a modified scheme of $\mathcal{N}^{CCS}$
01	$\Box\alpha\xi\Gamma \rightarrow \xi\Gamma\Box\alpha$	TPT-4	
02	$\mu\alpha\Box\Gamma \rightarrow \Box\Gamma\mu\alpha$	TPT-4	
03	$\alpha\Box\Gamma \rightarrow \Box\Gamma\alpha$	TPT-4	
04	$\alpha\xi\Gamma \rightarrow \xi\Gamma\alpha$	TPT-4	
05	$\beta\mu \rightarrow \alpha\mu\beta$	SPL	
06	$\alpha\alpha \rightarrow \beta$	SPL	
07	$\beta\beta \rightarrow \Gamma$	SPL	
08	$\Gamma\alpha \rightarrow \Gamma$	AT-2	
09	$\Gamma\mu \rightarrow \mu\Gamma$	TPT-3	
10	$\Gamma\Box \rightarrow \Box\Gamma$	TPT-3	
11	$\beta\alpha \rightarrow \beta$	AT-2	
12	$\beta\Box \rightarrow \alpha\Box\beta$	SPL	
13	$\mu*\nu \rightarrow *\nu$	AT-3	Formulas 13,14 and 15 form the scheme of $\mathcal{N}^{LEX}$
14	$\Box*\nu \rightarrow *\nu$	AT-3	
15	$*\nu \rightarrow \nu$	AT-2	
16	$\nu\delta \rightarrow \nu$	AT-2	
17	$\nu\sigma \rightarrow \nu$	AT-2	
18	$\nu\vert \rightarrow \vert\nu$	Composition of TPT-3 and letter substitution	
19	$\nu\Box \rightarrow \Box\nu$	TPT-3	

<table>
<tr><td>20</td><td>νμ</td><td>→</td><td>μν</td><td>TPT-3</td><td></td></tr>
<tr><td>21</td><td>δσ</td><td>→</td><td>δ</td><td>AT-2</td><td></td></tr>
<tr><td>22</td><td>Γβ</td><td>→</td><td>Γ</td><td>AT-2</td><td></td></tr>
<tr><td>23</td><td>O*|</td><td>→</td><td>Oβ*O|</td><td>PTS</td><td></td></tr>
<tr><td>24</td><td>O*O</td><td>→</td><td>O*aO</td><td>PTS</td><td></td></tr>
<tr><td>25</td><td>,*</td><td>→</td><td>,β*,</td><td>PTS</td><td></td></tr>
<tr><td>26</td><td>|*O</td><td>→</td><td>|*aO</td><td>PTS</td><td></td></tr>
<tr><td>27</td><td>a|</td><td>→</td><td>|ba</td><td>SPL</td><td></td></tr>
<tr><td>28</td><td>δbμ</td><td>→</td><td>μδb</td><td>TPT-4</td><td></td></tr>
<tr><td>29</td><td>aOa</td><td>→</td><td>aaO</td><td>TPT-3</td><td></td></tr>
<tr><td>30</td><td>aOO</td><td>→</td><td>aO</td><td>AT-1</td><td></td></tr>
<tr><td>31</td><td>aa</td><td>→</td><td>a</td><td>AT-1</td><td></td></tr>
<tr><td>32</td><td>b|</td><td>→</td><td>|b</td><td>TPT-3</td><td></td></tr>
<tr><td>33</td><td>δb□</td><td>→</td><td>□δb</td><td>TPT-4</td><td rowspan="4">Formulae 28 33 to 37, 39 to 44 form the scheme of $\mathcal{N}^{RS}$</td></tr>
<tr><td>34</td><td>δba</td><td>→</td><td>aδb</td><td>TPT-4</td></tr>
<tr><td>35</td><td>δbb</td><td>→</td><td>bδb</td><td>TPT-4</td></tr>
<tr><td>36</td><td>δbσ</td><td>→</td><td>σδb</td><td>TPT-4</td></tr>
<tr><td>37</td><td>δμξ</td><td>→</td><td>ξδμ</td><td>TPT-4</td><td></td></tr>
<tr><td>38</td><td>□*δ□</td><td>→</td><td>□*□</td><td>AT-3</td><td></td></tr>
<tr><td>39</td><td>δμ□</td><td>→</td><td>□δμ</td><td>TPT-4</td><td></td></tr>
<tr><td>40</td><td>δμσ</td><td>→</td><td>σδμ</td><td>TPT-4</td><td></td></tr>
<tr><td>41</td><td>δμa</td><td>→</td><td>aδμ</td><td>TPT-4</td><td></td></tr>
<tr><td>42</td><td>δμb</td><td>→</td><td>bδμ</td><td>TPT-4</td><td></td></tr>
<tr><td>43</td><td>δ□μ</td><td>→</td><td>μδ□</td><td>TPT-4</td><td></td></tr>
<tr><td>44</td><td>δ□□</td><td>→</td><td>□δ□</td><td>TPT-4</td><td></td></tr>
<tr><td>45</td><td>σμξ</td><td>→</td><td>ξσμ</td><td>TPT-4</td><td></td></tr>
<tr><td>46</td><td>□*|</td><td>→</td><td>□*</td><td>AT-3</td><td rowspan="4">Formulas 46, 47, 49, 50 and 51 form the scheme of $\mathcal{N}^{REX}$.</td></tr>
<tr><td>47</td><td>□*O</td><td>→</td><td>□*</td><td>AT-3</td></tr>
<tr><td>48</td><td>□*ba</td><td>→</td><td>□*δb</td><td>PTS</td></tr>
<tr><td>49</td><td>□*b</td><td>→</td><td>□*δ|</td><td>composition of AT-3 and letter substitution</td></tr>
<tr><td>50</td><td>□*a</td><td>→</td><td>□*δ</td><td>Composition of AT-3 and PTS</td><td></td></tr>
<tr><td>51</td><td>□*σ</td><td>→</td><td>□*σ</td><td>Composition of AT-3 and PTS</td><td></td></tr>
<tr><td>52</td><td>Γ*□</td><td>→</td><td>*δ□</td><td>Composition of AT-3 and PTS</td><td></td></tr>
</table>

53	Γ*,	→	*σ,	PTS
54	Γ*b	→	*σb	PTS
55	Γ*|	→	*a|	PTS
56	Γ*O	→	*σO	PTS
57	Γ*aO	→	*OaO	PTS
58	Γ*δ	→	*νδ	Composition of AT-3 and PTS
59	ν	→	·	AT-1
60		→	α	SPL

$\mathcal{N}^{PP}$ transforms the pre-convolution string □X†,*Y†□ into another string of the form (P†□)$^{-1}$ which is the inverse of P†□ [Definition 2.3.4]. The string P†□≐ P_{11},P_{21},…,P_{M1}□P_{12},P_{22},…,P_{M2}□ … □P_{1N} ,P_{2N} ,…,P_{MN} is called the *Partial Product string,* and every □-term of P†□ corresponds to the *partial product component* of the multiplication of y(n) by x(n).

For example, let us consider two data sequences x(n) = 1, 0 and y(n) = 2, 1 and apply $\mathcal{N}^{PP}$ to the pre-convolution string □|,O*||□| . After 269 elementary transformations we would obtain the string O, |□O,|| which is the inverse of the partial product string P†□. [NOTE: We have made use of a program LINCON in obtaining the required string].

Formula Number	Elementary Transformations	Remarks
	The pre-convolution String is □|,O*||□|	Data sequences to be convolved: x(n) = 1,0 and y(n) = 2,1
23	□|,Oβ*O||□| →	Product of 0 and 2 is obtained in the coded form as O
60	α□|,Oβ*O||□|	
60	αα□|,Oβ*O||□|	
7	β□|,Oβ*O||□|	
12	α□β|,Oβ*O||□|	
5	α□α|β,Oβ*O||□|	
5	α□α|α,βOβ*O||□|	
5	α□α|α,αOββ*O||□|	

7 α□α|α,αOΓ*O||□|
0 α□α|αOΓ,α*O||□|
0 α□αOΓ|α,α*O||□|
0 αOΓ□α|α,α*O||□|
4 OΓα□α|α,α*O||□|
8 OΓ□α|α,α*O||□|
10 O□Γα|α,α*O||□|
8 O□Γ|α,α*O||□|
9 O□|Γα,α*O||□|
8 O□|Γ,α*O||□|
9 O□|,Γα*O||□|
8 O□|,Γ*O||□| ⟶ The coded string of 0 left shifted
56 O□|,*σO||□|
25 O□|,β*,σO||□|
45 O□|,β*,|σO|□|
45 O□|,β*,||σO□|
60 αO□|,β*,||σO□|
60 ααO□|,β*,||σO□|
7 βO□|,β*,||σO□|
5 αOβ□|,β*,||σO□|
12 αOα□β|,β*,||σO□|
5 αOα□α|β,β*,||σO□|
5 αOα□α|α,ββ*,||σO□|
7 αOα□α|α,Γ*,||σO□|
0 αOα□α,Γ|α*,||σO□|
0 αOα,Γ□α|α*,||σO□|
0 α,ΓOα□α|α*,||σO□|
4 ,ΓαOα□α|α*,||σO□|
8 ,ΓOα□α|α*,||σO□|
9 ,OΓα□α|α*,||σO□|
8 ,OΓ□α|α*,||σO□|
10 ,O□Γα|α*,||σO□|
8 ,O□Γ|α*,||σO□|
9 ,O□|Γα*,||σO□|

8 ,O□|Γ*,||σO□|

53 ,O□|*σ,||σO□|

45 ,O□|*|σ,|σO□|

45 ,O□|*||σ,σO□|

60 α,O□|*||σ,σO□|

60 αα,O□|*||σ,σO□|

7 β,O□|*||σ,σO□|

5 α,βO□|*||σ,σO□|

5 α,αOβ□|*||σ,σO□|

12 α,αOα□β|*||σ,σO□|

5 α,αOα□α|β*||σ,σO□|

60 αα,αOα□α|β*||σ,σO□|

7 β,αOα□α|β*||σ,σO□|

5 α,βαOα□α|β*||σ,σO□|

11 α,βOα□α|β*||σ,σO□|

5 α,αOβα□α|β*||σ,σO□|

11 α,αOβ□α|β*||σ,σO□|

12 α,αOα□βα|β*||σ,σO□|

11 α,αOα□β|β*||σ,σO□|

5 α,αOα□α|ββ*||σ,σO□|

7 α,αOα□α|Γ*||σ,σO□|

0 α,αOα|Γ□α*||σ,σO□|

0 α,α|ΓOα□α*||σ,σO□|

0 α|Γ,αOα□α*||σ,σO□|

4 |Γα,αOα□α*||σ,σO□|

8 |Γ,αOα□α*||σ,σO□|

9 |,ΓαOα□α*||σ,σO□|

8 |,ΓOα□α*||σ,σO□|

9 |,OΓα□α*||σ,σO□|

8 |,OΓ□α*||σ,σO□|

10 |,O□Γα*||σ,σO□|

8 |,O□Γ*||σ,σO□|

55 |,O□*a||σ,σO□|

27 |,O□*|ba|σ,σO□|

27	|,O□*|b|baσ,σO□|	
32	|,O□*||bbaσ,σO□|	
46	|,O□*|bbaσ,σO□|	
46	|,O□*bbaσ,σO□|	→ Product of 1 and 2 is obtained in the coded form as bb.
49	|,O□*δbbaσ,σO□|	
35	|,O□*bδbaσ,σO□|	
34	|,O□*baδbσ,σO□|	
36	|,O□*baσδb,σO□|	
28	|,O□*baσ,δbσO□|	
36	|,O□*baσ,σδbO□|	
28	|,O□*baσ,σOδb□|	
33	|,O□*baσ,σO□δb|	
28	|,O□*baσ,σO□|δb	
48	|,O□*δbσ,σO□|δb	
36	|,O□*σδb,σO□|δb	
28	|,O□*σ,δbσO□|δb	
36	|,O□*σ,σδbO□|δb	
28	|,O□*σ,σOδb□|δb	
33	|,O□*σ,σO□δb|δb	
28	|,O□*σ,σO□|δbδb	
51	|,O□*δ,σO□|δbδb	
40	|,O□*σδ,O□|δbδb	
37	|,O□*σOδ,□|δbδb	
39	|,O□*σO□δ,|δbδb	
37	|,O□*σO□|δ,δbδb	
51	|,O□*δO□|δ,δbδb	
39	|,O□*□δO|δ,δbδb	
37	|,O□*□|δOδ,δbδb	→ Coded string corresponding to the first partial product component right shifted.
60	α|,O□*□|δOδ,δbδb	
60	αα|,O□*□|δOδ,δbδb	
7	β|,O□*□|δOδ,δbδb	
5	α|β,O□*□|δOδ,δbδb	
5	α|α,βO□*□|δOδ,δbδb	
5	α|α,αOβ□*□|δOδ,δbδb	

12 α|α,αOα□β*□|δOδ,δbδb
60 αα|α,αOα□β*□|δOδ,δbδb
7 β|α,αOα□β*□|δOδ,δbδb
5 α|βα,αOα□β*□|δOδ,δbδb
11 α|β,αOα□β*□|δOδ,δbδb
5 α|α,βαOα□β*□|δOδ,δbδb
11 α|α,βOα□β*□|δOδ,δbδb
5 α|α,αOβα□β*□|δOδ,δbδb
11 α|α,αOβ□β*□|δOδ,δbδb
12 α|α,αOα□ββ*□|δOδ,δbδb
7 α|α,αOα□Γ*□|δOδ,δbδb
0 α|α,α□ΓOα*□|δOδ,δbδb
0 α|α□Γ,αOα*□|δOδ,δbδb
0 α□Γ|α,αOα*□|δOδ,δbδb
3 □Γα|α,αOα*□|δOδ,δbδb
8 □Γ|α,αOα*□|δOδ,δbδb
9 □|Γα,αOα*□|δOδ,δbδb
8 □|Γ,αOα*□|δOδ,δbδb
9 □|,ΓαOα*□|δOδ,δbδb
8 □|,ΓOα*□|δOδ,δbδb
9 □|,OΓα*□|δOδ,δbδb
8 □|,OΓ*□|δOδ,δbδb
52 □|,O*δ□|δOδ,δbδb
43 □|,O*|δ□δOδ,δbδb
23 □|,Oβ*O|δ□δOδ,δbδb → Product of 0 and 1 is obtained in the coded form as O.
60 α□|,Oβ*O|δ□δOδ,δbδb
60 αα□|,Oβ*O|δ□δOδ,δbδb
7 β□|,Oβ*O|δ□δOδ,δbδb
12 α□β|,Oβ*O|δ□δOδ,δbδb
5 α□α|β,Oβ*O|δ□δOδ,δbδb
5 α□α|α,βOβ*O|δ□δOδ,δbδb
5 α□α|α,αOββ*O|δ□δOδ,δbδb
7 α□α|α,αOΓ*O|δ□δOδ,δbδb
0 α□α|αOΓ,α*O|δ□δOδ,δbδb

0	α□αOΓ|α,α*O|δ□δOδ,δbδb
0	αOΓ□α|α,α*O|δ□δOδ,δbδb
4	OΓα□α|α,α*O|δ□δOδ,δbδb
8	OΓ□α|α,α*O|δ□δOδ,δbδb
10	O□Γα|α,α*O|δ□δOδ,δbδb
8	O□Γ|α,α*O|δ□δOδ,δbδb
9	O□|Γα,α*O|δ□δOδ,δbδb
8	O□|Γ,α*O|δ□δOδ,δbδb
9	O□|,Γα*O|δ□δOδ,δbδb
8	O□|,Γ*O|δ□δOδ,δbδb
56	O□|,*σO|δ□δOδ,δbδb
25	O□|,β*,σO|δ□δOδ,δbδb
45	O□|,β*,|σOδ□δOδ,δbδb
60	αO□|,β*,|σOδ□δOδ,δbδb
60	ααO□|,β*,|σOδ□δOδ,δbδb
7	βO□|,β*,|σOδ□δOδ,δbδb
5	αOβ□|,β*,|σOδ□δOδ,δbδb
12	αOα□β|,β*,|σOδ□δOδ,δbδb
5	αOα□α|β,β*,|σOδ□δOδ,δbδb
5	αOα□α|α,ββ*,|σOδ□δOδ,δbδb
7	αOα□α|α,Γ*,|σOδ□δOδ,δbδb
0	αOα□α,Γ|α*,|σOδ□δOδ,δbδb
0	αOα,Γ□α|α*,|σOδ□δOδ,δbδb
0	α,ΓOα□α|α*,|σOδ□δOδ,δbδb
4	,ΓαOα□α|α*,|σOδ□δOδ,δbδb
8	,ΓOα□α|α*,|σOδ□δOδ,δbδb
9	,OΓα□α|α*,|σOδ□δOδ,δbδb
8	,OΓ□α|α*,|σOδ□δOδ,δbδb
10	,O□Γα|α*,|σOδ□δOδ,δbδb
8	,O□Γ|α*,|σOδ□δOδ,δbδb
9	,O□|Γα*,|σOδ□δOδ,δbδb
8	,O□|Γ*,|σOδ□δOδ,δbδb
53	,O□|*σ,|σOδ□δOδ,δbδb
45	,O□|*|σ,σOδ□δOδ,δbδb

60	α,O□|*|σ,σOδ□δOδ,δbδb
60	αα,O□|*|σ,σOδ□δOδ,δbδb
7	β,O□|*|σ,σOδ□δOδ,δbδb
5	α,βO□|*|σ,σOδ□δOδ,δbδb
5	α,αOβ□|*|σ,σOδ□δOδ,δbδb
12	α,αOα□β|*|σ,σOδ□δOδ,δbδb
5	α,αOα□α|β*|σ,σOδ□δOδ,δbδb
60	αα,αOα□α|β*|σ,σOδ□δOδ,δbδb
7	β,αOα□α|β*|σ,σOδ□δOδ,δbδb
5	α,βαOα□α|β*|σ,σOδ□δOδ,δbδb
11	α,βOα□α|β*|σ,σOδ□δOδ,δbδb
5	α,αOβα□α|β*|σ,σOδ□δOδ,δbδb
11	α,αOβ□α|β*|σ,σOδ□δOδ,δbδb
12	α,αOα□βα|β*|σ,σOδ□δOδ,δbδb
11	α,αOα□β|β*|σ,σOδ□δOδ,δbδb
5	α,αOα□α|ββ*|σ,σOδ□δOδ,δbδb
7	α,αOα□α|Γ*|σ,σOδ□δOδ,δbδb
0	α,αOα|Γ□α*|σ,σOδ□δOδ,δbδb
0	α,α|ΓOα□α*|σ,σOδ□δOδ,δbδb
0	α|Γ,αOα□α*|σ,σOδ□δOδ,δbδb
4	|Γα,αOα□α*|σ,σOδ□δOδ,δbδb
8	|Γ,αOα□α*|σ,σOδ□δOδ,δbδb
9	|,ΓαOα□α*|σ,σOδ□δOδ,δbδb
8	|,ΓOα□α*|σ,σOδ□δOδ,δbδb
9	|,OΓα□α*|σ,σOδ□δOδ,δbδb
8	|,OΓ□α*|σ,σOδ□δOδ,δbδb
10	|,O□Γα*|σ,σOδ□δOδ,δbδb
8	|,O□Γ*|σ,σOδ□δOδ,δbδb
55	|,O□*a|σ,σOδ□δOδ,δbδb
27	|,O□*|baσ,σOδ□δOδ,δbδb
46	|,O□*baσ,σOδ□δOδ,δbδb → Product of 1 and 1 is obtained in the coded form as b
48	|,O□*δbσ,σOδ□δOδ,δbδb
36	|,O□*σδb,σOδ□δOδ,δbδb
28	|,O□*σ,δbσOδ□δOδ,δbδb

36 |,O □*σ,σδbOδ □δOδ,δbδb

28 |,O □*σ,σOδbδ □δOδ,δbδb

51 |,O □*δ,σOδbδ □δOδ,δbδb

40 |,O □*σδ,Oδbδ □δOδ,δbδb

37 |,O □*σOδ,δbδ □δOδ,δbδb

51 |,O □*δOδ,δbδ □δOδ,δbδb

60 α|,O □*δOδ,δbδ □δOδ,δbδb

60 αα|,O □*δOδ,δbδ □δOδ,δbδb

7 β|,O □*δOδ,δbδ □δOδ,δbδb

5 α|β,O □*δOδ,δbδ □δOδ,δbδb

5 α|α,βO □*δOδ,δbδ □δOδ,δbδb

5 α|α,αOβ □*δOδ,δbδ □δOδ,δbδb

12 α|α,αOα □β*δOδ,δbδ □δOδ,δbδb

60 αα|α,αOα □β*δOδ,δbδ □δOδ,δbδb

7 β|α,αOα □β*δOδ,δbδ □δOδ,δbδb

5 α|βα,αOα □β*δOδ,δbδ □δOδ,δbδb

11 α|β,αOα □β*δOδ,δbδ □δOδ,δbδb

5 α|α,βαOα □β*δOδ,δbδ □δOδ,δbδb

11 α|α,βOα □β*δOδ,δbδ □δOδ,δbδb

5 α|α,αOβα □β*δOδ,δbδ □δOδ,δbδb

11 α|α,αOβ □β*δOδ,δbδ □δOδ,δbδb

12 α|α,αOα □ββ*δOδ,δbδ □δOδ,δbδb

7 α|α,αOα □Γ*δOδ,δbδ □δOδ,δbδb

0 α|α,α □ΓOα*δOδ,δbδ □δOδ,δbδb

0 α|α □Γ,αOα*δOδ,δbδ □δOδ,δbδb

0 α □Γ|α,αOα*δOδ,δbδ □δOδ,δbδb

3 □Γα|α,αOα*δOδ,δbδ □δOδ,δbδb

8 □Γ|α,αOα*δOδ,δbδ □δOδ,δbδb

9 □|Γα,αOα*δOδ,δbδ □δOδ,δbδb

8 □|Γ,αOα*δOδ,δbδ □δOδ,δbδb

9 □|,ΓαOα*δOδ,δbδ □δOδ,δbδb

8 □|,ΓOα*δOδ,δbδ □δOδ,δbδb

9 □|,OΓα*δOδ,δbδ □δOδ,δbδb

8 □|,OΓ*δOδ,δbδ □δOδ,δbδb

58 □|,O*vδOδ,δbδ□δOδ,δbδb
13 □|,*vδOδ,δbδ□δOδ,δbδb
13 □|*vδOδ,δbδ□δOδ,δbδb
13 □*vδOδ,δbδ□δOδ,δbδb
14 *vδOδ,δbδ□δOδ,δbδb
15 vδOδ,δbδ□δOδ,δbδb ⟶ Left excision of the *-pair has been carried out
16 vOδ,δbδ□δOδ,δbδb
20 Ovδ,δbδ□δOδ,δbδb
16 Ov,δbδ□δOδ,δbδb
20 O,vδbδ□δOδ,δbδb
16 O,vbδ□δOδ,δbδb
18 O,|vδ □δOδ,δbδb
16 O,|v □δOδ,δbδb
19 O,| □vδOδ,δbδb
16 O,| □vOδ,δbδb
20 O,| □Ovδ,δbδb
16 O,| □Ov,δbδb
20 O,| □O,vδbδb
16 O,| □O,vbδb
18 O,| □O,|vδb
16 O,| □O,|vb
18 O,| □O,||v
The inverse of the partial product string is:
59 O,| □O,||

The number of elementary transformation is: 269

The complexity of symbol manipulation in terms of elementary transformations for the multiplication of any two nonnegative integers say i and j by $\mathcal{N}^{PP}$, is determined by the following rules :

[NOTE : $\mathcal{N}^{PP}$ has to be applied only to the *–pair I*J where I and J are the coded strings from $\mathcal{A}_0$ corresponding to the numbers i and j. Let t_{ij} be the number of elementary transformations of I*J after which the string corresponding to the product of i and j is obtained.]

RULE 1 : $t_{00} = 43$
RULE 2 : $t_{01} = 39$
RULE 3 : $t_{10} = 43$ [NOTE : $t_{01} \neq t_{10}$]
RULE 4 : For all $i > 1$, $t_{i0} = t_{(i-1)o} + (12i + 16)$
RULE 5 : For all $j > 1$, $t_{0j} = t_{0(j-1)} + 2$
RULE 6 : For all $i > 0$, $t_{i1} = t_{io} + i(i-1)$
RULE 7 : For all $i \geq 1$ and $j > 1$, $t_{ij} = t_{i(j-1)} + ij(i+1) + (3i+1)$

The following table 4.3.2 contains certain values of t_{ij} , $(i, j \leq 8)$

Table 4.3.2: Complexity of symbol manipulation due to $\mathcal{N}^{PP}$ in multiplying two nonnegative integers

i \ j	0	1	2	3	4	5	6	7	8	→
0	43	39	41	43	45	47	49	51	53	→
1	43	43	51	61	73	87	103	121	141	→
2	83	85	104	129	160	197	240	289	344	→
3	135	141	175	221	279	349	431	525	631	→
4	199	211	264	337	430	543	676	829	1002	→
5	275	295	371	477	613	779	975	1201	1457	→
6	363	393	496	641	828	1057	1328	1641	1996	→
7	463	505	639	829	1075	1377	1735	2149	2619	→
8	575	631	800	1041	1354	1739	2196	2725	3326	→
↓	↓	↓	↓	↓	↓	↓	↓	↓	↓	→

STEP # 4

As mentioned in STEP 3, the string:

$P\dagger\square \doteq P_{11}, P_{21}, \ldots, P_{M1} \square P_{12}, P_{22}, \ldots, P_{M2} \square \ldots \square P_{1N}, P_{2N}, \ldots, P_{MN}$

is called the partial product string, and every □-term of $P\dagger\square$ corresponds to the partial product component to the multiplication of y(n) by x(n) . In the traditional signal processing, the linear or aperiodic convolution of x(n) of M samples and y(n) of N samples is computed by

$$z(n) = \sum_{K=0}^{M+N-1} y(n)x(n-k)$$

such that the convolved output z(n) consists of M+N-1 samples. Let us take for example, x(n) = 1,2,3 and y(n) = 2,3,4 and compute their convolution directly.

		y(n) 2	3	4
x(n)	1	2	3	4
	2	4	6	8
	3	6	9	12

Partial product components: < 2, 4, 6 >, < 3, 6, 9 >, < 4,8,12 >

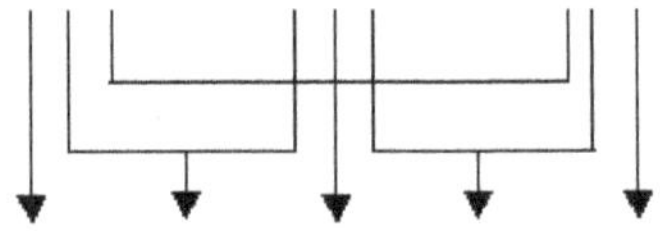

The convolved output z(n) = 2, 7, 16, 17, 12.

From the above computation, we observe that the first one element of the first component is taken as the first as the first convolved output sample; two elements, 4 from the first component and 3 from the second component are added to get the second sample; three elements, 6 from the first component, 6 from the second component and 4 from the third component are added to get the third sample; two elements, 9 from the second component and 8 from the third component are added to get the fourth sample; and the remaining one element from the third component is taken as the firth sample of the sequence z(n). Now, the ordered sequence of numbers that are marked above with underline, can be seen to be of a palindrome type. Let us denote it by L. Then, L in this case is 1,2,3,2,1.

In general, three types of such palindrome sequences can be formed in the case of linear convolution of data sequences of M and N samples.

(i) 1,2,3,...,(n-1),n,(n-1),...,3,2,1 for M = N = n

(ii) $1,2,3,\ldots,(M-1),\underbrace{M,M,M,\ldots,M}_{\text{N-M+1 times}},(M-1),\ldots,3,2,1$ for M < N

(ii) $1,2,3,\ldots,(N-1),\underbrace{N,N,N,\ldots,N}_{\text{M-N+1times}},(N-1),\ldots,3,2,1$ for N < M

On the basis of this simple observation, we develop in what follows, a normal algorithm $\mathcal{N}^{CA}$ which chooses appropriate elements from (P† □)$^{-1}$ and add them so that a string Z†, = $Z_1, Z_2, \ldots, Z_k, \ldots, Z_{M+N-1}$ is obtained. Each ,-term of Z†, corresponds to a sample of the convolved output z(n) of x(n) and y(n).

Two nonnegative integers, that is, words from $\mathcal{A}_0$ which are separated by a delimiter could be added just by removing the delimiter itself. For example, the representations of two integers 3 and 4 over the alphabet $\mathcal{A}_0$ can be added using the following scheme $\mathcal{N}^+_N$ constructed over $\mathcal{A}_0 \cup \mathcal{D}_3$.

$\mathcal{N}^+_N$:	Substitution formula	Formula number
	O* →	0
	*O →	1
	* →	2
	→·	3

$\mathcal{N}^+_N$: ||| * |||| ⊢ ||||||| ⊢ · |||||||

However, this algorithm fails in adding selected number representations in a string such as in the case of adding P_{11}, P_{12} and P_{13} in the string P_{11}, P_{21}, P_{31} □ P_{12}, P_{22}, P_{32} □ P_{13}, P_{23}, P_{33}. In such cases, the following prescription would be of use in carrying out specific number of Choose and Add operations in arbitrarily long sequences similar to the one given above:

Prescription for Choose and Add operations

(i) Let us consider a string P† □. Each □-term is a ,-system of words P_{ij} from $\mathcal{A}_0$. Let us assume that there are ℓ number of □-terms in P† □ and that our purpose is to choose the first ,-term of every □-term and add them.

(ii) Let L be the word from $\mathcal{A}_0$ corresponding to the number ℓ. Now we shall form the *-pair L*P† □ and apply the following scheme $\mathcal{N}^{CA}$ constructed over $\mathcal{A}_0 \cup \mathcal{D} \cup \mathcal{E}$:

$\mathcal{N}^{CA}$:	Substitution formula				Formula number
	$\delta\mu\square$	$\rightarrow$	$\square\delta\mu$	$(\mu \in \mathcal{A}_0)$	00
	$\delta\mu\xi$	$\rightarrow$	$\xi\delta\mu$	$(\xi \in \mathcal{A}_0)$	01
	$\delta\mu,$	$\rightarrow$	$,\delta\mu$		02
	$\vert{*}\mu\xi$	$\rightarrow$	$\vert{*}\delta\mu\xi$		03
	$\vert{*}\mu$	$\rightarrow$	${*}\delta\mu$		04
	$\vert{*},$	$\rightarrow$	${*},\nu$		05
	${*},$	$\rightarrow$	${*}$		06
	$\nu\nu\square$	$\rightarrow$	$\nu\square\nu$		07
	$\nu\mu$	$\rightarrow$	$\mu\nu$		08
	$\nu,$	$\rightarrow$	$,\nu$		09
	$\nu\square,$	$\rightarrow$	$\square$		10
	$\nu\square\mu$	$\rightarrow$	$\nu\square\delta\mu$		11
	δ	$\rightarrow$			12
		$\rightarrow$	$\cdot$		13

Now, let ℓ be the number of $\square$-terms in the string:

$$P\dagger\square \doteq P_{11},P_{21},\ldots,P_{M1}\square P_{12},P_{22},\ldots,P_{M2}\square\ldots.\square P_{1N},P_{2N},\ldots,P_{MN}$$

where, $\ell = M+N-1$ and let us apply $\mathcal{N}^{CA}$ to the *-pair :

$$\underbrace{||||||\ldots\ldots\ldots\ldots}_{\ell \text{ times}}|{*}P_{11},P_{21},\ldots,P_{M1}\square P_{12},\ldots.,P_{M2}\square\ldots\square P_{1N},\ldots.,P_{MN}\ .$$

Due to the formula (03) and (04) $\mathcal{N}^{CA}$ the first ,-term P_{11} is shifted to the right, letter by letter, so that the resulting string would be of the form :

$$\underbrace{||||||\ldots\ldots\ldots}_{\ell-1 \text{ times}}|{*},P_{21},\ldots.,P_{M1}\square P_{12},\ldots,P_{M2}\square\ldots\square P_{1N},\ldots,P_{MN}\ \delta P_{11}\ .$$

Now, the repetitive application of the formula (05) to the above string injects $\ell - 1$ number of choose operators ν in the right $*$-term which in turn get distributed to the remaining $(\ell - 1)$ $\square$-terms with the help of formulas (07), (08) and (09) of the scheme, as shown below:

$${*}P_{21},\ldots,P_{M1}\nu\square P_{12},\ldots.,P_{M2}\nu\square P_{13},\ldots\nu\square_{\ldots}\nu\square P_{1N},\ldots,P_{MN}\delta P_{11}\ .$$

Now, with the help of formula (11), that is, $\nu\square\mu \rightarrow \mu\square\delta\mu$ the first ,-term of each of the remaining $(\ell - 1)$ $\square$-terms is chosen one by one and shifted to right. After completing shifting of all the chosen ,-terms, the shift operator δ is erased with the help of formula (12), and the required string of the following form:

$$P_{21},\ldots,P_{M1}\square P_{22},\ldots,P_{M2}\square P_{23},\ldots\ \square\ldots\square P_{2N},\ldots,P_{MN}P_{1N}P_{1(N-1)}\ldots P_{12}\,P_{11}$$

is obtained. Now, the factor $P_{1N}\ P_{1(N-1)}\ldots P_{12}\ P_{11}$ is the string corresponding to the addition of the first ,-term of all the □-terms of the string P†□ .

A modified version of $\mathcal{N}^{CA}$ is the following scheme $\mathcal{N}^{CA}$ which carries out the required type of Choose and Add operations in an inverse partial product string. Note that the serial numbers given in this scheme are in continuation with those given in the partial product scheme.

Sl. No.	Substitution Formulas			Type of the Formula	Remarks
61	μαξΓ	→	ξΓμα	TPT-4	
62	□αξΓ	→	ξΓ□α	TPT-4	
63	μα□Γ	→	□Γμα	TPT-4	
64	α□Γ	→	□Γα	TPT-4	
65	αξΓ	→	ξΓα	TPT-4	
66	βμ	→	αμβ	SPL	
67	αα	→	β	SPL	
68	ββ	→	Γ	SPL	
69	Γα	→	Γ	AT-2	
70	Γμ	→	μΓ	TPT-3	
71	Γ□	→	□Γ	TPT-3	
72	βα	→	β	AT-2	
73	β□	→	α□β	SPL	
74	μ*θ	→	*θ	AT-3	
75	□*θ	→	*θ	AT-3	
76	*θ	→	θ	AT-2	
77	θδ	→	θ	AT-2	
78	θμ	→	μθ	TPT-3	
79	δμ□	→	□δμ	TPT-4	
80	δμξ	→	ξδμ	TPT-4	
81	|*,	→	|*ω	PTS	
82	,*,ω	→	,*ω	PTS	
83	,*ω	→	,*ν	PTS	
84	νω	→	ων	TPT-3	
85	νν□	→	ν□ν	TPT-3	
86	,*μ	→	,β*,μ	PTS	

87	„	→	,	SPL	
88	OO	→	O	AT-1	
89	|O	→	|	AT-1	
90	O|	→	|	AT-1	
91	νμ	→	μν	TPT-3	
92	ν□,	→	□	Composition of two formulas of AT-1	Known as 'Excising formula"
93	ν□μ	→	ν□δμ	SPL	
94	Γ*ω	→	*,ω	PTS	
95	Γ*□	→	*	Composition of two formulas of AT-1	
96	Γ*,	→	*δ,	PTS	
97	Γ*μ,	→	*δμ,	PTS	
98	Γ*δ	→	*θ	PTS	
99	Γ*μ	→	Γ*δμ	PTS	
100	θ	→	·	AT-1	
101		→	α	SPL	

It was shown in STEP 3, that $\mathcal{N}^{PP}$ transforms the ∗-pair □|,O*|| □| into the inverse partial product string $(P\dagger\square)^{-1} \doteq$ O,| □O,|| . By means of a normal algorithm $\mathcal{N}^{PL}$ (whose scheme is given below) we shall obtain the ∗-pair whose left ∗-term is the corresponding palindrome string |,||,| left delimited by □ and the right *-term is the inverse partial product string O,| □O,|| .

$\mathcal{N}^{PL}$: Substitution formula Formula number

→	*		0
→	L	(L = |,||,|)	1
→	·□		2

$\mathcal{N}^{PL}$: O,| □O,|| ⊢ *O,| □O,|| ⊢ |,||,|*O,| □O,|| ⊢· □|,||,|*O,| □O,||

Now N^{CA} transforms □|,||,|∗O,| □O,|| into the string Z†, ≐ ||,|,O where Z†, corresponds to the convolved output sequence z(n) = 2,1,0 . [NOTE: We have made use of a program LINCON in obtaining all the 306 elementary transformations, which are given below.]

Note: [$\mathcal{N}^{PL}$: O,|□O,|| ⊨ □|,||,|*O,| □O,||]
$\mathcal{N}^{CA}$ (LINCON):
Adjoin palindrome string to the partial product string, choose and add:
Input string: □|,||,|*O,| □O,|| ⊨

101 α□|,||,|*O,| □O,||
101 αα□|,||,|*O,| □O,||
67 β□|,||,|*O,| □O,||
73 α□β|,||,|*O,| □O,||
66 α□α|β,||,|*O,| □O,||
66 α□α|α,β||,|*O,| □O,||
66 α□α|α,α|β|,|*O,| □O,||
66 α□α|α,α|α|β,|*O,| □O,||
66 α□α|α,α|α|α,β|*O,| □O,||
66 α□α|α,α|α|α,α|β*O,| □O,||
101 αα□α|α,α|α|α,α|β*O,| □O,||
67 β□α|α,α|α|α,α|β*O,| □O,||
73 α□βα|α,α|α|α,α|β*O,| □O,||
72 α□β|α,α|α|α,α|β*O,| □O,||
66 α□α|βα,α|α|α,α|β*O,| □O,||
72 α□α|β,α|α|α,α|β*O,| □O,||
66 α□α|α,βα|α|α,α|β*O,| □O,||
72 α□α|α,β|α|α,α|β*O,| □O,||
66 α□α|α,α|βα|α,α|β*O,| □O,||
72 α□α|α,α|β|α,α|β*O,| □O,||
66 α□α|α,α|α|βα,α|β*O,| □O,||
72 α□α|α,α|α|β,α|β*O,| □O,||
66 α□α|α,α|α|α,βα|β*O,| □O,||
72 α□α|α,α|α|α,β|β*O,| □O,||
66 α□α|α,α|α|α,α|ββ*O,| □O,||
68 α□α|α,α|α|α,α|Γ*O,| □O,||
61 α□α|α,α|α|α|Γ,α*O,| □O,||
61 α□α|α,α|α|Γ|α,α*O,| □O,||
61 α□α|α,α|Γ|α|α,α*O,| □O,||
61 α□α|α|Γ,α|α|α,α*O,| □O,||

61 α□α|Γ|α,α|α|α,α*O,| □O,||

61 α|Γ□α|α,α|α|α,α*O,| □O,||

65 |Γα□α|α,α|α|α,α*O,| □O,||

69 |Γ□α|α,α|α|α,α*O,| □O,||

71 |□Γα|α,α|α|α,α*O,| □O,||

69 |□Γ|α,α|α|α,α*O,| □O,||

70 |□|Γα,α|α|α,α*O,| □O,||

69 |□|Γ,α|α|α,α*O,| □O,||

70 |□|,Γα|α|α,α*O,| □O,||

69 |□|,Γ|α|α,α*O,| □O,||

70 |□|,|Γα|α,α*O,| □O,||

69 |□|,|Γ|α,α*O,| □O,||

70 |□|,||Γα,α*O,| □O,||

69 |□|,||Γ,α*O,| □O,||

70 |□|,||,Γα*O,| □O,||

69 |□|,||,Γ*O,| □O,||

97 |□|,||,*δO,| □O,||

80 |□|,||,*,δO|□O,||

80 |□|,||,*,|δO□O,||

79 |□|,||,*,|□δOO,||

80 |□|,||,*,|□OδO,||

80 |□|,||,*,|□O,δO||

80 |□|,||,*,|□O,|δO|

80 |□|,||,*,|□O,||δO

86 |□|,||,β*,,|□O,||δO

87 |□|,||,β*,|□O,||δO

101 α|□|,||,β*,|□O,||δO

101 αα|□|,||,β*,|□O,||δO

67 β|□|,||,β*,|□O,||δO

66 α|β□|,||,β*,|□O,||δO

73 α|α□β|,||,β*,|□O,||δO

66 α|α□α|β,||,β*,|□O,||δO

66 α|α□α|α,β||,β*,|□O,||δO

66 α|α□α|α,α|β|,β*,|□O,||δO

66 α|α□α|α,α|α|β,β*,|□O,||δO

66 α|α□α|α,α|α|α,ββ*,|□O,||δO

68 α|α□α|α,α|α|α,Γ*,|□O,||δO

61 α|α□α|α,α|α,Γ|α*,|□O,||δO

61 α|α□α|α,α,Γ|α|α*,|□O,||δO

61 α|α□α|α,Γ,α|α|α*,|□O,||δO

61 α|α□α,Γ|α,α|α|α*,|□O,||δO

61 α|α,Γ□α|α,α|α|α*,|□O,||δO

61 α,Γ|α□α|α,α|α|α*,|□O,||δO

65 ,Γα|α □α|α,α|α|α*,|□O,||δO

69 ,Γ|α □α|α,α|α|α*,| □O,||δO

70 ,|Γα □α|α,α|α|α*,|□O,||δO

69 ,|Γ □α|α,α|α|α*,| □O,||δO

71 ,| □Γα|α,α|α|α*,|□O,||δO

69 ,| □Γ|α,α|α|α*,|□O,||δO

70 ,| □|Γα,α|α|α*,| □O,||δO

69 ,| □|Γ,α|α|α*,|□O,||δO

70 ,| □|,Γα|α|α*,| □O,||δO

69 ,| □|,Γ|α|α*,| □O,||δO

70 ,|□|,|Γα|α*,|□O,||δO

69 ,|□|,|Γ|α*,| □O,||δO

70 ,| □|,||Γα*,| □O,||δO

69 ,| □|,||Γ*,|□O,||δO

96 ,| □|,||*δ,| □O,||δO

80 ,| □|,||*|δ,□O,||δO

79 ,| □|,||*| □δ,O,||δO

80 ,| □|,||*|□Oδ,,||δO

80 ,| □|,||*| □O,δ,||δO

80 ,| □|,||*|□O,|δ,|δO

80 ,| □|,||*|□O,||δ,δO

101 α,|□|,||*|□O,||δ,δO

101 αα,|□|,||*|□O,||δ,δO

67 β,|□|,||*|□O,||δ,δO

66 α,β|□|,||*|□O,||δ,δO

66 α,α|β□|,||*|□O,||δ,δO
73 α,α|α□β|,||*|□O,||δ,δO
66 α,α|α□α|β,||*|□O,||δ,δO
66 α,α|α□α|α,β||*|□O,||δ,δO
66 α,α|α□α|α,α|β|*|□O,||δ,δO
66 α,α|α□α|α,α|α|β*|□O,||δ,δO
101 αα,α|α□α|α,α|α|β*|□O,||δ,δO
67 β,α|α□α|α,α|α|β*|□O,||δ,δO
66 α,βα|α□α|α,α|α|β*|□O,||δ,δO
72 α,β|α□α|α,α|α|β*|□O,||δ,δO
66 α,α|βα□α|α,α|α|β*|□O,||δ,δO
72 α,α|β□α|α,α|α|β*|□O,||δ,δO
73 α,α|α□βα|α,α|α|β*|□O,||δ,δO
72 α,α|α□β|α,α|α|β*|□O,||δ,δO
66 α,α|α□α|βα,α|α|β*|□O,||δ,δO
72 α,α|α□α|β,α|α|β*|□O,||δ,δO
66 α,α|α□α|α,βα|α|β*|□O,||δ,δO
72 α,α|α□α|α,β|α|β*|□O,||δ,δO
66 α,α|α□α|α,α|βα|β*|□O,||δ,δO
72 α,α|α□α|α,α|β|β*|□O,||δ,δO
66 α,α|α□α|α,α|α|ββ*|□O,||δ,δO
68 α,α|α□α|α,α|α|Γ*|□O,||δ,δO
61 α,α|α□α|α,α|Γ|α*|□O,||δ,δO
61 α,α|α□α|α|Γ,α|α*|□O,||δ,δO
61 α,α|α□α|Γ|α,α|α*|□O,||δ,δO
61 α,α|α|Γ□α|α,α|α*|□O,||δ,δO
61 α,α|Γ|α□α|α,α|α*|□O,||δ,δO
61 α|Γ,α|α□α|α,α|α*|□O,||δ,δO
65 |Γα,α|α□α|α,α|α*|□O,||δ,δO
69 |Γ,α|α□α|α,α|α*|□O,||δ,δO
70 |,Γα|α□α|α,α|α*|□O,||δ,δO
69 |,Γα□α|α,α|α*|□O,||δ,δO
70 |,|Γα□α|α,α|α*|□O,||δ,δO
69 |,|Γ□α|α,α|α*|□O,||δ,δO

71 |,|□Γα|α,α|α*|□O,||δ,δO
69 |,|□Γ|α,α|α*|□O,||δ,δO
70 |,|□|Γα,α|α*|□O,||δ,δO
69 |,|□|Γ,α|α*|□O,||δ,δO
70 |,|□|,Γα|α*|□O,||δ,δO
69 |,|□|,Γ|α*|□O,||δ,δO
70 |,|□|,|Γα*|□O,||δ,δO
69 |,|□|,|Γ*|□O,||δ,δO
99 |,|□|,|Γ*δ|□O,||δ,δO
79 |,|□|,|Γ*□δ|O,||δ,δO
80 |,|□|,|Γ*□Oδ|,||δ,δO
80 |,|□|,|Γ*□O,δ|||δ,δO
80 |,|□|,|Γ*□O,|δ||δ,δO
80 |,|□|,|Γ*□O,||δ|δ,δO
95 |,|□|,|*O,||δ|δ,δO
101 α|,|□|,|*O,||δ|δ,δO
101 αα|,|□|,|*O,||δ|δ,δO
67 β|,|□|,|*O,||δ|δ,δO
66 α|β,|□|,|*O,||δ|δ,δO
66 α|α,β|□|,|*O,||δ|δ,δO
66 α|α,α|β□|,|*O,||δ|δ,δO
73 α|α,α|α□β|,|*O,||δ|δ,δO
66 α|α,α|α□α|β,|*O,||δ|δ,δO
66 α|α,α|α□α|α,β|*O,||δ|δ,δO
66 α|α,α|α□α|α,α|β*O,||δ|δ,δO
101 αα|α,α|α□α|α,α|β*O,||δ|δ,δO
67 β|α,α|α□α|α,α|β*O,||δ|δ,δO
66 α|βα,α|α□α|α,α|β*O,||δ|δ,δO
72 α|β,α|α□α|α,α|β*O,||δ|δ,δO
66 α|α,βα|α□α|α,α|β*O,||δ|δ,δO
72 α|α,β|α□α|α,α|β*O,||δ|δ,δO
66 α|α,α|βα□α|α,α|β*O,||δ|δ,δO
72 α|α,α|β□α|α,α|β*O,||δ|δ,δO
73 α|α,α|α□βα|α,α|β*O,||δ|δ,δO

72 α|α,α|α □β|α,α|β*O,||δ|δ,δO
66 α|α,α|α □α|βα,α|β*O,||δ|δ,δO
72 α|α,α|α □α|β,α|β*O,||δ|δ,δO
66 α|α,α|α □α|α,βα|β*O,||δ|δ,δO
72 α|α,α|α □α|α,β|β*O,||δ|δ,δO
66 α|α,α|α □α|α,α|ββ*O,||δ|δ,δO
68 α|α,α|α □α|α,α|Γ*O,||δ|δ,δO
61 α|α,α|α □α|α|Γ,α*O,||δ|δ,δO
61 α|α,α|α □α|Γ|α,α*O,||δ|δ,δO
61 α|α,α|α|Γ □α|α,α*O,||δ|δ,δO
61 α|α,α|Γ|α □α|α,α*O,||δ|δ,δO
61 α|α|Γ,α|α □α|α,α*O,||δ|δ,δO
61 α|Γ|α,α|α □α|α,α*O,||δ|δ,δO
65 |Γα|α,α|α □α|α,α*O,||δ|δ,δO
69 |Γ|α,α|α □α|α,α*O,||δ|δ,δO
70 ||Γα,α|α □α|α,α*O,||δ|δ,δO
69 ||Γ,α|α □α|α,α*O,||δ|δ,δO
70 ||,Γα|α □α|α,α*O,||δ|δ,δO
69 ||,Γ|α □α|α,α*O,||δ|δ,δO
70 ||,|Γα □α|α,α*O,||δ|δ,δO
69 ||,|Γ*pα|α,α*O,||δ|δ,δO
71 ||,| □Γα|α,α*O,||δ|δ,δO
69 ||,| □Γ|α,α*O,||δ|δ,δO
70 ||,| □|Γα,α*O,||δ|δ,δO
69 ||,| □|Γ,α*O,||δ|δ,δO
70 ||,| □|,Γα*O,||δ|δ,δO
69 ||,| □|,Γ*O,||δ|δ,δO
97 ||,| □|,*δO,||δ|δ,δO
80 ||,| □|,*,δO||δ|δ,δO
80 ||,|*p|,*,|δO|δ|δ,δO
80 ||,| □|,*,||δOδ|δ,δO
86 ||,| □|,β*,,||δOδ|δ,δO
87 ||,| □|,β*,||δOδ|δ,δO
101 α||,| □|,β*,||δOδ|δ,δO
101 αα||,| □|,β*,||δOδ|δ,δO

67 β||,|□|,β*,||δOδ|δ,δO

66 α|β|,|□|,β*,||δOδ|δ,δO

66 α|α|β,|□|,β*,||δOδ|δ,δO

66 α|α|α,β|□|,β*,||δOδ|δ,δO

66 α|α|α,α|β□|,β*,||δOδ|δ,δO

73 α|α|α,α|α□β|,β*,||δOδ|δ,δO

66 α|α|α,α|α□α|β,β*,||δOδ|δ,δO

66 α|α|α,α|α□α|α,ββ*,||δOδ|δ,δO

68 α|α|α,α|α□α|α,Γ*,||δOδ|δ,δO

61 α|α|α,α|α□α,Γ|α*,||δOδ|δ,δO

61 α|α|α,α|α,Γ□α|α*,||δOδ|δ,δO

61 α|α|α,α,Γ|α□α|α*,||δOδ|δ,δO

61 α|α|α,Γ,α|α□α|α*,||δOδ|δ,δO

61 α|α,Γ|α,α|α□α|α*,||δOδ|δ,δO

61 α,Γ|α|α,α|α□α|α*,||δOδ|δ,δO

65 ,Γα|α|α,α|α □α|α*,||δOδ|δ,δO

69 ,Γ|α|α,α|α □α|α*,||δOδ|δ,δO

70 ,|Γα|α,α|α □α|α*,||δOδ|δ,δO

69 ,|Γ|α,α|α □α|α*,||δOδ|δ,δO

70 ,||Γα,α|α □α|α*,||δOδ|δ,δO

69 ,||Γ,α|α □α|α*,||δOδ|δ,δO

70 ,||,Γα|α □α|α*,||δOδ|δ,δO

69 ,||,Γ|α □α|α*,||δOδ|δ,δO

70 ,||,|Γα □α|α*,||δOδ|δ,δO

69 ,||,|Γ □α|α*,||δOδ|δ,δO

71 ,||,| □Γα|α*,||δOδ|δ,δO

69 ,||,| □Γ|α*,||δOδ|δ,δO

70 ,||,| □|Γα*,||δOδ|δ,δO

69 ,||,| □|Γ*,||δOδ|δ,δO

96 ,||,| □|*δ,||δOδ|δ,δO

80 ,||,| □|*|δ,|δOδ|δ,δO

80 ,||,| □|*||δ,δOδ|δ,δO

101 α,||,|□|*||δ,δOδ|δ,δO

101 αα,||,|□|*||δ,δOδ|δ,δO

67 β,||,|□|*||δ,δOδ|δ,δO

66 α,β||,|□|*||δ,δOδ|δ,δO

66 α,α|β|,|□|*||δ,δOδ|δ,δO

66 α,α|α|β,|□|*||δ,δOδ|δ,δO

66 α,α|α|α,β|□|*||δ,δOδ|δ,δO

66 α,α|α|α,α|β□|*||δ,δOδ|δ,δO

73 α,α|α|α,α|α□β|*||δ,δOδ|δ,δO

66 α,α|α|α,α|α□α|β*||δ,δOδ|δ,δO

101 αα,α|α|α,α|α□α|β*||δ,δOδ|δ,δO

67 β,α|α|α,α|α□α|β*||δ,δOδ|δ,δO

66 α,βα|α|α,α|α□α|β*||δ,δOδ|δ,δO

72 α,β|α|α,α|α□α|β*||δ,δOδ|δ,δO

66 α,α|βα|α,α|α□α|β*||δ,δOδ|δ,δO

72 α,α|β|α,α|α□α|β*||δ,δOδ|δ,δO

66 α,α|α|βα,α|α□α|β*||δ,δOδ|δ,δO

72 α,α|α|β,α|α□α|β*||δ,δOδ|δ,δO

66 α,α|α|α,βα|α□α|β*||δ,δOδ|δ,δO

72 α,α|α|α,β|α□α|β*||δ,δOδ|δ,δO

66 α,α|α|α,α|βα□α|β*||δ,δOδ|δ,δO

72 α,α|α|α,α|β□α|β*||δ,δOδ|δ,δO

73 α,α|α|α,α|α□βα|β*||δ,δOδ|δ,δO

72 α,α|α|α,α|α□β|β*||δ,δOδ|δ,δO

66 α,α|α|α,α|α□α|ββ*||δ,δOδ|δ,δO

68 α,α|α|α,α|α□α|Γ*||δ,δOδ|δ,δO

61 α,α|α|α,α|α|Γ□α*||δ,δOδ|δ,δO

61 α,α|α|α,α|Γ|α□α*||δ,δOδ|δ,δO

61 α,α|α|α|Γ,α|α□α*||δ,δOδ|δ,δO

61 α,α|α|Γ|α,α|α□α*||δ,δOδ|δ,δO

61 α,α|Γ|α|α,α|α□α*||δ,δOδ|δ,δO

61 α|Γ,α|α|α,α|α□α*||δ,δOδ|δ,δO

65 |Γα,α|α|α,α|α□α*||δ,δOδ|δ,δO

69 |Γ,α|α|α,α|α□α*||δ,δOδ|δ,δO

70 |,Γα|α|α,α|α□α*||δ,δOδ|δ,δO

69 |,Γ|α|α,α|α□α*||δ,δOδ|δ,δO

70 |,|Γα|α,α|α □α*||δ,δOδ|δ,δO
69 |,|Γ|α,α|α □α*||δ,δOδ|δ,δO
70 |,||Γα,α|α □α*||δ,δOδ|δ,δO
69 |,||Γ,α|α □α*||δ,δOδ|δ,δO
70 |,||,Γα|α □α*||δ,δOδ|δ,δO
69 |,||,Γ|α □α*||δ,δOδ|δ,δO
70 |,||,|Γα □α*||δ,δOδ|δ,δO
69 |,||,|Γ □α*||δ,δOδ|δ,δO
71 |,||,| □Γα*||δ,δOδ|δ,δO
69 |,||,| □Γ*||δ,δOδ|δ,δO
99 |,||,| □Γ*δ||δ,δOδ|δ,δO
80 |,||,| □Γ*|δ|δ,δOδ|δ,δO
99 |,||,| □Γ*δ|δ|δ,δOδ|δ,δO
98 |,||,| □*θ|δ|δ,δOδ|δ,δO
75 |,||,|*θ|δ|δ,δOδ|δ,δO
74 |,||,*θ|δ|δ,δOδ|δ,δO
74 |,||*θ|δ|δ,δOδ|δ,δO
74 |,|*θ|δ|δ,δOδ|δ,δO
74 |,*θ|δ|δ,δOδ|δ,δO
74 |*θ|δ|δ,δOδ|δ,δO
74 *θ|δ|δ,δOδ|δ,δO
76 θ|δ|δ,δOδ|δ,δO
78 |θδ|δ,δOδ|δ,δO
77 |θ|δ,δOδ|δ,δO
78 ||θδ,δOδ|δ,δO
77 ||θ,δOδ|δ,δO
78 ||,θδOδ|δ,δO
77 ||,θOδ|δ,δO
78 ||,Oθδ|δ,δO
77 ||,Oθ|δ,δO
78 ||,O|θδ,δO
77 ||,O|θ,δO
78 ||,O|,θδO
77 ||,O|,θO
78 ||,O|,Oθ
90 ||,|,Oθ
100 ||,|,O

The string Z† = ||,|,O is obtained after 306 elementary transformations. One can construct another normal algorithm $\mathcal{N}^{DC}$ which would convert the string ||,|,O as 2,1,0.

Table 4.3.3: Types of maps corresponding to the Normal Algorithms that constitute $\mathfrak{R}^{CON}$

Sl. No.	Normal Algorithm	Alphabet over which constructed	Type of the map	Function
1	$\mathcal{N}^{\dagger,}$	$\mathcal{A}_0 \cup \mathcal{A}_{11}$	$S \rightarrow X_{11}$	Forms ,-diluted strings from $\mathcal{A}_0$ representing natural number sequences
2	$\mathcal{N}^{\dagger}$□	$\mathcal{A}_0 \cup \mathcal{A}_{12}$	$S \rightarrow X_{12}$	Forms □-diluted strings from A_0 representing natural number sequences
3	$\mathcal{N}^{ID}$	Any alphabet $\mathcal{A}$	$\mathcal{A}^* \rightarrow \mathcal{A}^*$	Transforms any string to the same string
4	$\mathcal{N}^*$	$\mathcal{A}_{14}$	$X'_{13} \rightarrow X_{14}$	Forms the pre-convolution string
5	$\mathcal{N}^{PP}$	$\mathcal{A}_{14}$	$X_{14} \rightarrow X''_{13}$	Transforms the pre-convolution string into inverse partial product string.
6	$\mathcal{N}^{PL}$	$\mathcal{A}_{14}$	$X''_{13} \rightarrow X_{14}$	Forms the *-pair whose left *-term is the suitable palindrome string with □ as the left delimiter and whose right *-term is the inverse partial product string.

7	$\mathcal{N}^{CA}$	$\mathcal{A}_{14}$	$X_{14} \rightarrow X_{11}$	Transforms the *-pair formed by N^{PL} into a string corresponding to the convolved output sequence.
8	$\mathcal{N}^{DC}$	$\mathcal{A}_0 \cup \mathcal{A}_{11}$	$X_{11} \rightarrow S$	Decodes the string due to $\mathcal{N}^{CA}$ into the corresponding nonnegative integer sequence.

STEP # 5

One can construct another normal algorithm $\mathcal{N}^{DC}$ over the alphabet $\mathcal{A}_0 \cup \mathcal{D}_1 \cup N$ that decodes $Z^{\dagger}$, as convolved output z(n).

That is, $\mathcal{N}^{DC}$ (||,|,O) = 2,1,0 .

So far, we outlined the construction details of certain normal algorithms which form the system $\mathfrak{R}^{CON}$. In what follows, we indicate the type of maps corresponding to those normal algorithms ad show how they are combined to form the system $\mathfrak{R}^{CON}$ [Table 4.3.3 and Fig. 4.3.1]. For convenience, we recall from **STEP # 1**, the alphabets over the union of which $\mathfrak{N}^{CON}$ has been constructed:

$\mathcal{A}_0 = \{ O \mid \}$; $\mathcal{D}_1 = \{ , \}$; $\mathcal{D}_2 = \{ \square \}$; $\mathcal{D}_3 = \{ * \}$;
$\mathcal{E} = \{ a\, b\, \alpha\, \beta\, \Gamma\, \delta\, \theta\, \sigma\, \omega\, \nu \}$; $\mathcal{D} = \mathcal{D}_1 \cup \mathcal{D}_2 \cup \mathcal{D}_3$;
$\mathcal{A}_{11} = \mathcal{A}_0 \cup \mathcal{D}_1$; $\mathcal{A}_{12} = \mathcal{A}_0 \cup \mathcal{D}_2$; $\mathcal{A}_{13} = \mathcal{A}_{11} \cup \mathcal{A}_{12}$;
$\mathcal{A}_0 = \{0\ 1\ 2\ 3\ 4\ 5\ 6\ 7\ 8\ 9\}$;
$\mathcal{A}_{14} = \mathcal{A}_{13} \cup \mathcal{D}_3$

Let us also consider N = { x | x is natural number in the traditional sense } and $\mathcal{S}$ = { x | x is a non-negative integer sequence }. The block diagram of the operational scheme of the constructive system $\mathfrak{R}^{CON}$ is shown in figure 4.3.1 .

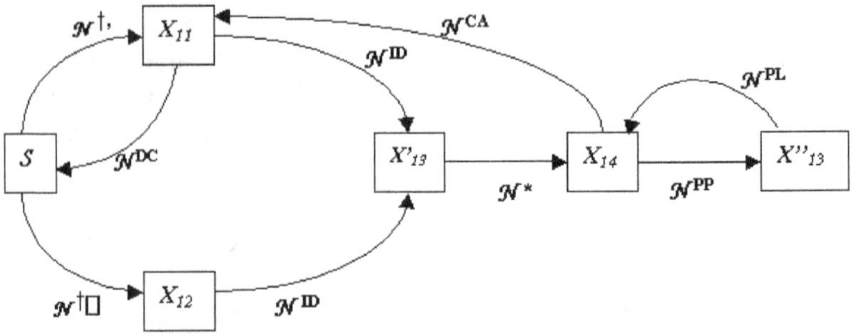

Figure 4.3.1: Operational scheme of $\mathfrak{R}^{CON}$

The first part of this book is over with this section. In section 1.2, we raised a question whether it is possible to represent signals as strings of symbols from finite alphabets and process them using string manipulating normal algorithms. The highlight of what we learnt in this part is not only an affirmative answer to this question but also the state-of-the-art approach to carry out non-numerical signal processing operations.

Part II

Abstract

The purpose of this part is to introduce a formal language and a special automaton for the study of constructive (normal algorithmic) signal processing systems. The motivation for such a study is provided by the fact that a constructive signal processing system $\mathfrak{R}$ over an alphabet $\mathcal{A}$, is in essence a mapping that recognizes a subset X (that is a language) of the free monoid $\mathcal{A}^*$ and maps it onto another subset Y of words in $\mathcal{A}^*$. With X and Y as the input and output signal spaces, $\mathfrak{R}$ admits of being treated as a system described by a grammar and also as an automaton.

A Language Theoretic Approach To Signal Processing

Section 5

Study Of Normal Algorithmic Signal Processing Systems In Terms Of Formal Languages Generated By a Grammar

5.1 Formal Representation Of Signals And Systems Over Alphabets

The starting point of our study is the *formal representability* of words and algorithms over alphabets by Elementary Formal Systems (EFS) of Smullyan [14]. An elementary formal system over an alphabet $\mathcal{A}$ is defined as a set of alphabets, $\mathcal{A}$, $\mathcal{V}$, $\mathcal{P}$ and $\mathcal{J}$, together with a set of axioms. $\mathcal{A}$ is a given alphabet whose words are the basic elements of interest in the EFS. $\mathcal{V}$ is an alphabet of two types of variables, the first type consisting of proper variables that range over the free semigroup $\mathcal{A}^+$ and the other type consisting of improper variables that range over the free monoid $\mathcal{A}^*$. $\mathcal{P}$ is an alphabet of predicates, each of which assigned with a unique positive integer called its degree. $\mathcal{J}$ is an alphabet containing two symbols called the implication sign and punctuation sign. The set of axioms of the system are strings from the above distinct alphabets and are known as well formed formulas (wff).

Any string of symbols from the alphabet $\mathcal{A} \cup \mathcal{V}$ is known as a term generally denoted by t, of the system. By an atomic formula F, we mean a string from the alphabet $\mathcal{A} \cup \mathcal{V} \cup \mathcal{P}$ of the form $pt_1t_2 \ldots t_m$ where p is a predicate of degree m and $t_1, t_2, \ldots, t_m$ are terms. A well formed formula is defined as word $F\dagger \rightarrow$ in $\mathcal{A} \cup \mathcal{V} \cup \mathcal{P} \cup \mathcal{J}$ where $F\dagger \rightarrow \; = F_1 \rightarrow F_1 \rightarrow \ldots \rightarrow F_i \rightarrow \ldots \rightarrow F_n$ and $F_i : (1 \leq i \leq n)$ is an atomic formula. $F_1, F_2, \ldots, F_i, \ldots, F_{n-1}$ are called as premises and F_n as the conclusion. Any atomic formula is also a wff, which means that it is by itself a premise and the conclusion. If all the variables of a wff are substituted by strings from $\mathcal{A}$, then the resulting string is known as an instance of the wff. A variable-free wff is known as a sentence. A theorem of an EFS is either an axiom

E. G. Rajan, *Symbolic Computing - Signal and Image Processing*
ISBN 81-7800-047-4

or a string which is derivable from the set of axioms of the EFS with the help of the following rules of inference:

(i) Instantiation : Substitution of strings from $\mathcal{A}$ for variables

(ii) Modus Ponens : The rule by which a formula can be inferred from another atomic formula.

Let p be a predicate of degree n from $\mathcal{P}$, and let W be a set of n-tuples of words from $\mathcal{A}^*$. Then, we say that p represents W if $px_1x_2...x_n$ is provable in the EFS over $\mathcal{A}$ for every n-tuple $x_1x_2...x_n$ in W.

As an illustration of an EFS, let us consider the basic alphabet $\mathcal{A}_0$={O |} in which the natural number system can be formally represented as shown below. The relevant alphabets for the EFS in this case are:

(i) $\mathcal{A}_0$ = {O |}
(ii) $\mathcal{V}$ = {x}
(iii) $\mathcal{P}$ = {N}, where N is of degree 1.
(iv) $\mathcal{I}$ = {$\rightarrow$}

and the axioms are :

(i) NO (i.e., in set-theoretic terms, $O \in N$)

(ii) $Nx \rightarrow Nx|$ (if the word represented by the variable x is in N then the word x | is also in N.)

Using these axioms, the system of natural numbers is formally represented over $\mathcal{A}_0$ as N={O, O|, O||, O|||, O||||,……}. N is called the system of Constructive Natural Numbers [13], [24].

Remark: We note that in the above example we have used the same symbol N for denoting the predicate and the set of natural numbers.

Now, we show with the help of the following two propositions, that signal spaces and constructive signal processing systems are formally representable over finite alphabets. Here, we refer to subsets of a free monoid as signal spaces and algorithms such as associative calculi and normal algorithms as constructive systems.

Proposition 5.1.1

Let $S_{\mathcal{R}}$ be a subset of a free monoid $\mathcal{A}^*$ and let $\mathcal{R}$ be an associative calculus that recognizes $S_{\mathcal{R}}$. Then $S_{\mathcal{R}}$ is representable in an elementary formal system $E_{\mathcal{R}}$ over $\mathcal{A}$.

Proof:

Recall from section 1 that elements of the set $S_{\mathcal{R}}$ are equivalents with reference to the defining system $\mathcal{D}$ of $\mathcal{R}$, where $\mathcal{D}$ is an unordered list of $\mathcal{J}$-class equivalence relations. We construct an EFS $E_{\mathcal{R}}$ for representing the $S_{\mathcal{R}}$.

Alphabets:

(i)	$\mathcal{A}$	(A given alphabet)
(ii)	$\mathcal{V} = \{ \alpha\ \beta\ x\ y\ v\ w \}$	(α and β are improper variables and x, y, v and w are proper variables.)
(iii)	$\mathcal{P} = \{ f\ r\ \mathcal{D}\ S_{\mathcal{R}} \}$	($S_{\mathcal{R}}$ is a predicate of degree 1 and f, r and $\mathcal{D}$ are predicates of degree 2.)
(iv)	$\mathcal{J} = \{ \rightarrow , \}$	(Punctuation symbols)

Axioms:

(i)	$S_{\mathcal{R}}x$:	(x is an element of $S_{\mathcal{R}}$)
(ii)	$fx, \alpha x\beta \rightarrow ryx \rightarrow \mathcal{D}vw$	(If x is the factor of a word $\alpha x\beta$ then y is the replacement of x which in turn implies that a word $v \doteq \alpha x\beta$ is a $\mathcal{D}$-equivalent of $w \doteq \alpha y\beta$.)
(iii)	$fy, \alpha y\beta \rightarrow rxy \rightarrow \mathcal{D}vw$	(If y is the factor of a word $\alpha y\beta$ then x is the replacement of y which in turn implies that a word $v \doteq \alpha y\beta$ is a $\mathcal{D}$–equivalent of $w \doteq \alpha x\beta$)
(iv)	$\mathcal{D}vw$	(v is a $\mathcal{D}$–equivalent of w)

Let $< x_i , y_i >$, $1 \leq i \leq n$ be the n ordered $\mathcal{J}$-class relations of the defining system $\mathcal{D}$ of an associative calculus $\mathcal{R}$. For any pair of equivalent words v and w in $S_{\mathcal{R}}$, $\mathcal{D}$vw is provable in $E_{\mathcal{R}}$ by the inductive instantiation of axioms (ii), (iii) and (iv), using the $\mathcal{J}$–class relation of $\mathcal{D}$. Now, given any two arbitrary words v and w in $\mathcal{A}+$, if $\mathcal{D}$vw is provable in $E_{\mathcal{R}}$, then v, w $\in S_{\mathcal{R}}$. Hence, $S_{\mathcal{R}}$ is representable in an elementary formal system $E_{\mathcal{R}}$ over $\mathcal{A}$.

Proposition 5.1.2

Let $W_{\mathcal{N}}$ be a subset of a free monoid $\mathcal{A}^*$ and let $\mathcal{N}$ be a normal algorithm that recognizes $W_{\mathcal{N}}$. Then, $W_{\mathcal{N}}$ is representable in an EFS, $E_{\mathcal{N}}$ over $\mathcal{A}$.

Proof:

As we recall from subsection 2.2, a normal algorithm $\mathcal{N}$ over an alphabet $\mathcal{A}$ is interpreted as an $\mathcal{J}$-class presentation of the free monoid $\mathcal{A}^*$ defined by an ordered list of n $\mathcal{J}$-class partial order relations corresponding to the n substitution formulas of $\mathcal{N}$. We now, construct an EFS, $\mathcal{E}_{\mathcal{N}}$ for representing the set $W_{\mathcal{N}}$.

Alphabets:

(i)	$\mathcal{A}$	(The given alphabet)
(ii)	$\mathcal{V}$={ α β x y v w }	(α and β are improper variables and x,y,v and w are proper variables)
(iii)	$\mathcal{P}$ = { a f r $W_{\mathcal{N}}$ }	(a and $W_{\mathcal{N}}$ are predicates of degree 1 and r and f are predicates of degree 2)
(iv)	$\mathcal{J}$= { →, }	(Punctuation symbols)

Axioms:

(i)	$W_{\mathcal{N}}$x	(i.e., set theoretically x∈$W_{\mathcal{N}}$)
(ii)	fx, αxβ → ryx→av	(If x is a factor of a word v $\doteq$ αxβ they y is a replacement of x in v which implies that v is amenable to $\mathcal{N}$)
(iii)	av	(v is amenable to $\mathcal{N}$)

Let < x_i , y_i > , $1 \le i \le n$ be the n ordered $\mathcal{J}$-class partial order relations of the scheme $\mathcal{S}$ of a normal algorithm $\mathcal{N}$. For a word v in $W_{\mathcal{N}}$, the axiom av is provable in $E_{\mathcal{N}}$ by the inductive instantiation of the axioms (ii) and (iii) using the relations of $\mathcal{S}$. Now, given a word v in $\mathcal{A}^*$, if av is provable in $E_{\mathcal{N}}$ then $v \in W_{\mathcal{N}}$. Hence, $W_{\mathcal{N}}$ is formally representable in $E_{\mathcal{N}}$. This completes the proof.

Since $S_{\mathcal{R}}$ and $W_{\mathcal{N}}$ are formally representable in the elementary formal system $E_{\mathcal{R}}$ and $E_{\mathcal{N}}$ respectively, the classes of associative calculi and normal algorithms are formally representable over an alphabet $\mathcal{A}$.

5.2 Formulation Of a String Manipulation Language For Constructive Signal Processing

Since subsets of a free monoid and algorithms such as associative calculi and normal algorithms are formally representable in EFS' over alphabets, the possibility exists of studying signal spaces and constructive systems in an EFS type language. We find that Fitting's notion of EFS type string manipulation languages [05], is useful for this purpose. Before attempting to formulate one such language for constructive signal processing, we review some of the basic details regarding the EFS language of Fitting.

5.2.1 Fitting's Basic String Manipulation Language EFS(str(L))

EFS(str(L)) is a representative example of an EFS language for a data structure of character strings over an alphabet, say L.

Definition 5.2.1.1 [05]

EFS(str(L)) over an alphabet L is defined to be a collection of the following:

(i) An alphabet L of distinct symbols

(ii) A data structure $< L^* , CON_L >$ where L^* is the free monoid of L and CON_L is a 3-place relation $< u, v, w >$ such that for any three u, v, $w \in L^*$, w is the word obtained by right concatenating v to u.

(iii) A set of identifiers which are words consisting of capital letters from the English alphabet.

(iv) An alphabet consisting of variables x, y, z....
(v) An alphabet consisting of punctuation symbols {→ ( ) ,}

The notions *term*, *atomic statement* and *wff* of EFS(str(L)) have to be understood as they have been defined already. A work space W of an EFS, in general, consists of the following:

(i) A specification of a domain.
(ii) A list of reserved identifiers. (The term *identifiers* refers to predicate labels. A reserved identifier will not occur in the position of the conclusion of a statement (wff)).
(iii) A specification of what relations the reserved identifiers represent. Such relations are the given relations of W.

Every elementary formal system is associated with its basic work space. For instance, the basic work space of EFS(str(L)) consists of the following:

(i) The domain L*.
(ii) The only reserved identifier CON.
(iii) The label CON represents the concatenation relation CON_L on L.

A procedure P in a work space W is a list of acceptable statements written one below the other like a PASCAL program. The first statement is known as the header and the block of remaining statements as the body of the procedure. The header designates an unreserved identifier together with degree n of the predicate for which the identifier is the label. The identifier in the header represents the name of the procedure and its output as well.

Example 5.2.1.1

EFS language	:	EFS(str(L))
Data structure	:	$< L^* , CON_L >$
Work space (W)	:	(i) Elements of L*
		(ii) CON (the reserved identifier with degree 3)
		(iii) CON represents concatenation of an element v to the right of another u such that uv = w ; u,v,w ∈ L*
Name of the procedure	:	FAC(2)

FAC (2):

FAC(x,x);
FAC(x, Λ);
CON(x, y, z)→CON(v, z, y)→FAC(y, x)

The language recognized by the procedure FAC is L* x L* . The computation of a procedure P in a work space W gives rise to sequences of statements of the following kinds:

(i) A substitution instance of a procedure statement
(ii) An instance of a given relation of W
(iii) An assignment statement T where its previous line is $X_1 \rightarrow X_2 \rightarrow \ldots \rightarrow T$ and $X_1, X_2, \ldots, T$ are atomic statements.

A sequence of statements resulting from a computation of a procedure P is known as a trace, which is analogous to what is called a *derivation* in mathematical logic. A *restricted trace* is the sequence of statements governed by the first two conditions for a trace and by a third condition known as the *restricted assignment rule*. This rule allows statements of the form X → F where X is atomic and the assignment F need not be.

The basic work space of an EFS can be expanded by adding to it more and more reserved identifiers as needed. For example, the basic work space W of EFS(str(L)) could be expanded as W' by adding FAC as a reserved identifier. Now we shall construct a procedure GREQ in W' which would compute the graphical equivalence between two words, in the following manner:

Let the basic alphabet be L = { O | }

GREQ(2):

GREQ(x, x);
FAC(y, x)→FAC(x, y)→GREQ(x, y)

A trace of GREQ would be of the form:

GREQ(2) :

GREQ(|O| , |O|) ;
FAC(|O|, |O|)→FAC(|O|, |O|)→GREQ(|O|, |O|)

EFS(str(L)) has an enormous language (subset) recognizing power. This can be inferred from the following argument:

Let, P be the class of all possible procedures which could be constructed in W of EFS(str(L)). Then, P is said to consist of basic or first level procedures. The procedures which are constructible only in W' and not in W are called second level procedures. As already mentioned, W' is an expanded work space of W with an additional reserved identifier which has been used previously as an unreserved identifier in W. Every such unreserved identifier, let us call it "i", when individually added to W as a reserved identifier, forms an expanded work space W'_i in which a class P'_i of second level procedures can be constructed. Likewise, the basic work space W along with two distinct reserved identifiers "i" and "j" , forms the work space W'_{ij} , in which P'_{ij} , a class of third level procedures can be constructed. The generalization of the basic work space expansion in the above manner exhibits the language recognizing power of EFS(str(L)) .

5.2.2 The String Manipulation Language EFS(spl($\mathcal{A}$)) For Constructive Signal Processing

With the material covered in subsection 1 as the required background, we shall now formulate a string manipulation language EFS(spl($\mathcal{A}$)) for constructive signal processing.

Definition 5.2.2.1

EFS(spl($\mathcal{A}$)) over an alphabet $\mathcal{A}$ is defined to be the collection of the following :

(i) An alphabet $\mathcal{A}$ of n distinct symbols

(ii) A data structure $<\mathcal{A}^*, CON_{\mathcal{A}}, SBT_{\mathcal{A}}>$ where $\mathcal{A}^*$ is the free monoid of $\mathcal{A}$; $CON_{\mathcal{A}}$ is a 3-place relation $<u, v, w>$ such that w is the concatenated string uv: $(u,v \in \mathcal{A}^*)$; and $SBT_{\mathcal{A}}$ is a 2-place relation $<u, v>$ such that v is substitute of u where $u, v \in \mathcal{A}^*$.

(iii) A set of identifiers denoting predicate labels. [A break symbol "_" could be used in writing identifier labels. For example, FAC_OF is a valid identifier whereas "FAC_" or "_OF" are not]

(iv) An alphabet consisting of variables of two types:
(1) u, v, w, x, y, z which range over $\mathcal{A}^*$ and
(2) ξ, μ, η which range over $\mathcal{A}$. [The variables could be subscripted or superscripted as per requirement.]

(v) An alphabet consisting of punctuation symbols: {→( ) ,}

The basic work space W of EFS(spl($\mathcal{A}$)) consists of the following:

(i) The domain $\mathcal{A}^*$
(ii) CON and SBT are the only reserved identifiers
(iii) CON represents the concatenation relation $CON_{\mathcal{A}}$ on $\mathcal{A}$. SBT represents the substitution relation $SBT_{\mathcal{A}}$ on $\mathcal{A}$.

In general, the output of an EFS procedure is called a *generated relation*. Let R be a reserved identifier denoting the predicate R of degree n. Then, a procedure of the type S(n): $R(x_1, x_2,\ldots, x_n) \rightarrow S(x_1, x_2,\ldots, x_n)$ we express as:

$S(x_1, x_2,\ldots, x_n) \Leftrightarrow R(x_1, x_2,\ldots.. x_n)$ or more briefly as $S(n) \Leftrightarrow R(n)$.

The following types of expressions are admissible:

(i) $S(n) \Leftrightarrow R(n)$
(ii) $S(n+1) \Leftrightarrow R(n)$
(iii) $T(n) \Leftrightarrow R(n) \vee S(n)$ [$\vee$ denotes logical connective AND. Note: This symbol $\vee$ is not the same as the null word symbol Λ]
(iv) $T(n) \Leftrightarrow R(n) \vee S(n)$ [$\vee$ denotes logical connective OR. Note: This symbol $\vee$ is not the same as the English symbol V]

At times, one might come across a situation where a relation R denoted by reserved identifier R is of degree greater than that of its generated relation S by one. In such a case, $S(n) \Leftrightarrow R(n+1)$ is not an admissible expression. On the other hand, the projection S of R is expressed as $S(x_1, x_2,\ldots x_n) \Leftrightarrow (\exists\, y)R(x_1, x_2,\ldots x_n, y)$ which means that there is a y for which $R(x_1, x_2,\ldots x_n, y) \rightarrow S(x_1, x_2,\ldots x_n)$ is valid.

With these details, we now show that given an alphabet $\mathcal{A}$ and a normal algorithm over it, one can always construct a functionally equivalent EFS procedure in the language EFS(spl($\mathcal{A}$)).

Let us consider the following EFS (spl($\mathcal{A}$)) procedure RRW(2), whose work space W' is the basic work space W of EFS(spl($\mathcal{A}$)) along with the reserved identifier FAC denoting the relation (factor of) FAC of rank 2. Let RRW(2) be a generated relation that represents the binary relation *rewritten string of.* Now, we construct a procedure which will do the same job, that a substitution formula in a normal algorithm would do.

RRW(2):
SBT(Λ, x) → RRW(Λ, x) ;
SBT(x, Λ) → RRW(x, Λ) ;
FAC(Q, x) → SBT(x, y) → FAC(Q_1, y) → RRW (Q, Q_1)

A trace of RRW(2) for $\mathcal{A}$ = { O | } would be of the following form:

RRW(2):
SBT(Λ, |O|) → RRW(Λ, |O|) ;
SBT(|O|, Λ) → RRW(|O|, Λ) ;
FAC(||O||O, |O|) → SBT(|O|, OO|) →
FAC(|OO||O, OO|) → RRW(||O||O, |OO||)

So, given an alphabet $\mathcal{A}$, one can realize any substitution formula over $\mathcal{A}$ with the help of the procedure RRW(2). In other words, for any normal algorithm $\mathcal{N}$ over $\mathcal{A}$, there is a functionally equivalent EFS(spl($\mathcal{A}$)) procedure.

Example 5.2.2.1

Let us construct a procedure for the cyclic permutation of a string of symbols from an alphabet $\mathcal{A}$:

Language used	:	EFS(spl($\mathcal{A}$))
Data structure	:	< $\mathcal{A}$* , $CON_{\mathcal{A}}$, $SBT_{\mathcal{A}}$ >
Work space W"	:	Basic work space W, together with the reserved Identifiers (i) FAC and (ii) RRW.
Name of the procedure	:	CPS(2) [CPS represents the binary relation *Cyclically Permuted String of*]

CPS(2):

CPS(Λ, Λ);
CPS(ξ, ξ);
CON(u, ξ, x)→CON(ξ, u, x_1)→SBT(x, x_1)→RRW(x, x_1)→CPS(x, x_1).

The fact that for a normal algorithm over an alphabet $\mathcal{A}$ there is a functionally equivalent EFS(spl($\mathcal{A}$)) procedure, admits the possibility of obtaining EFS(spl($\mathcal{A}$)) procedures for constructive signal processing systems. We shall verify this in the following.

Firstly, we introduce here the notion of a reserved alphabet as an EFS analogue to the alphabet of auxiliary symbols. By a reserved alphabet, we mean an alphabet that is included in the work space whose symbols do not appear in the output of a procedure.

Next, we show one method of implementing a binary operation between two discrete data sequences p(n) and q(n) by means of an EFS(spl($\mathcal{A}$)) procedure.

As outlined is subsection 4.2, the data samples are coded as words from a suitable alphabet $\mathcal{A}$ so that the data sequences p(n) of M samples and q(n) of N samples could be expressed as the coded strings $P\dagger d_p$ and $Q\dagger d_q$ respectively, where $P\dagger d_p = P_1 d_p\ P_2 d_p \ldots P_i\ d_p \ldots d_p P_M$, $1 \leq i \leq M$ and $Q\dagger d_q = Q_1 d_q\ Q_2 d_q \ldots Q_j d_q \ldots d_q Q_N$, $1 \leq j \leq N$, d_p and d_q are two different delimiters from the delimiter alphabet $\mathcal{D}$. Now, these coded strings are expressed as $*$-pair: $(P\dagger d_p)*(Q\dagger d_q)$, where the auxiliary symbol $*$ is a delimiter from the alphabet $\mathcal{D}$. Then, the $*$-pair is manipulated by means of a suitable normal algorithmic system $\mathfrak{R}$ in such a way that the resulting string $R\dagger d_r$ corresponds to the output r(n) due to the intended operation between the given data sequences p(n) and q(n).

A $*$-system of words from an alphabet $\mathcal{A}$ is an admissible term in an EFS procedure. Let the symbol $*$ denote a binary operation. Then, the $*$-terms like (u*v) and ((u*v)*(w*x)) are admissible atomic terms in an EFS procedure. A sequence of atomic terms is called a *formation sequence.* If the last term of a formation sequence happens to be a $*$-term then the $*$-term is called a type-1 term. Such type-1 terms are allowed in the procedure statements of EFS(spl($\mathcal{A}$)) also. This means $*$-pair inputs to normal algorithms also act as inputs to EFS(spl($\mathcal{A}$)) procedures.

As described in [05], an input accepting procedure would consist of the header statement of the form shown below.

OUT_NAME (n) INPUT IN_NAME (k):

(Procedure Body of OUT_NAME).

OUT_NAME represents the name of a procedure and the identifier corresponding to the output, which is an n-place relation. IN_NAME represents the input to the procedure and it is a k-place relation. IN_NAME is neither a reserved identifier nor a generated relation. If the IN_NAME and OUT_NAME are simultaneously n-place relations, then the corresponding input accepting procedure is said to give rise to a monotone operator ϕ which is nothing but a mapping from a set of n-place relations to another set of n-place relations satisfying the condition:

$$X \subseteq Y \Rightarrow \phi(X) \subseteq \phi(Y);\ X, Y \in D, \text{ the domain of the EFS.}$$

By a *constructive signal processing system*, we mean a normal algorithm or a set of normal algorithms combined in a manner that is allowed by any of the combination theorems of Markov. In the same way, procedures that are written in various work spaces of EFS(spl($\mathcal{A}$)), can be combined on the basis of the following theorems:

Theorem 5.2.2.1

For any three relations $R(n_1)$, $S(n_2)$ and $T(n_3)$, if $S(n_2)$ is the generated relation of $R(n_1)$ being applied to a procedure P_i in W'_i and $T(n_3)$ is the generated relation of $S(n_2)$ being applied to a procedure P_j in W'_j, then one can construct a procedure P_k in W'_k which is the union of W_i and W_j such that $T(n_3)$ is a generated relation of $R(n_1)$ being applied to P_k .

Proof:

Let us assume that $n_1 = n_2 = n_3 = n$. Then .ϕ_i, ϕj, and ϕ_k , can be treated as the monotone compact operators defined by the input accepting procedures P_i , P_j and P_k . Now, as Fitting shows in [05], if the input to an operator defined by a procedure is a generated relation, then so is the output.

In the light of this proposition, we observe that if R is an input relation to ϕ_i such that its output generated relation S when applied to ϕ_j yields the generated relation T. Then, there exists a monotone operator ϕ_k which is the composition of ϕ_i and ϕ_j such that $\phi_j\ (\phi_i\ (R)) = T = \phi_k(R)$. The generalizations $\phi_i\, \phi_j = \phi_k$ to relations with $n_1 \neq n_2 \neq n_3$ yields $P_iP_j = P_k$ which is known as the composition of procedures.

Theorem 5.2.2.2

For any three relations $R(n_1)$, $S(n_2)$ and $T(n_3)$, if $S(n_2)$ is the generated relation of $R(n_1)$ being applied to a procedure P_i in W'_i and $T(n_3)$ is the generated relation of $R(n_1)$ being applied to a procedure P_j in W'_j then one can construct a procedure P_k in W'_k so that the generated relation of $R(n_1)$ being applied to P_k in W'_k is the union of the relations $S(n_2)$ and $T(n_3)$.

Proof :

The theorem is applicable to only those inputs which are applicable to both P_i and P_j. Let us assume that $n_1 = n_2 = n_3 = n$. Then one can construct monotone operators corresponding to P_i , P_j and P_k which satisfy the union property such as $[\phi_i \cup \phi_j](R) = \phi_i(R) \cup \phi_j(R) = \phi_k(R)$. This theorem can also be generalized for input accepting procedures which generate relations of unequal arities.

We now give three additional theorems concerning the combination of procedures. Note that these theorems can be proved on the same lines as theorem 5.2.2.2. Theorem 5.2.2.4 is a reformulation of a result of Fitting [05].

Theorem 5.2.2.3

For any three relations $R(n_1)$, $S(n_2)$ and $T(n_3)$, if $S(n_2)$ is the generated relation of $R(n_1)$ being applied to a procedure P_i in W'_i and $T(n_3)$ is the generated relation of $R(n_1)$ being applied to a procedure P_j in W'_j, then one could construct a procedure P_k in W'_k so that the generated relation of $R(n_1)$ being applied to P_k in W'_k is the intersection of the relations $S(n_2)$ and $T(n_3)$.

Theorem 5.2.2.4

For any three procedures P_i , P_j and P_k in W'_i , W'_j and W'_k respectively, one can construct another procedure P_ℓ and W'_ℓ so that, (i) if P_k does not accept R then neither P_ℓ too; (ii) if P_k accepts R then $P_\ell(R)$ is equivalent to $P_i(R)$ when $P_k(R)$ satisfies a condition C and $P_\ell(R)$ is equivalent to $P_j(R)$ when $P_k(R)$ does not satisfy the condition C.

Theorem 5.2.2.5

For an input accepting procedure P_i in W'_i one can construct another procedure P_j in W'_j such that S is the generated relation of R applied to P_i and (i) S is the least fixed point for P_j so that $P_j(S) = S$ and S is the output or (ii) S is again fed to P_i and the corresponding generated relation is tested for the least fixed point. P_i is repeatedly applied till its output becomes the least fixed point of P_j.

Remarks:

(i) The notion of a type-1 term allows us to feed a *-system of strings from the basic alphabet as the input to an input accepting EFS(spl($\mathcal{A}$)) procedure.

(ii) The notion of a reserved alphabet allows auxiliary symbols in the statements of an EFS(spl($\mathcal{A}$)) procedure.

(iii) Complex EFS(spl($\mathcal{A}$)) procedures can be constructed by making use of the above combination theorems.

Finally we remark here, that the string manipulation language EFS(spl($\mathcal{A}$)) is a useful computational aid in realizing constructive signal processing operations.

5.3 Languages Generated By M–Grammar Based On Semi-Thue Productions of Post Words

So far we explored the possibilities of studying constructive signal processing systems in terms of formal languages. Using the concept of *Elementary Formal System* of Smullyan, we proposed a string manipulation language EFS(spl($\mathcal{A}$)) as an extension to that of Fitting's EFS(str(L)). Finally we gave a method of implementing signal processing operations by means of certain EFS(spl($\mathcal{A}$)) procedures.

In this subsection, we consider the problem of finitely specifying the potentially infinite languages of a free monoid recognized by constructive signal processing systems, by means of a set of rules called *M-Grammar.*

5.3.1 The Problem of Generating Markov Class Rewriting Systems By a Type-0 Phrase Structure Grammar

We start with the following definition.

Definition 5.3.1.1

A Markov class rewriting system (process) is defined as an ordered pair $<\Sigma, S>$ where the alphabet Σ is the union of the terminal (basic) alphabet $\mathcal{A}$ and the alphabet $\mathcal{E}$ consisting of non terminals (auxiliary variables); and S is a totally ordered list of semi-Thue productions, which are pattern substitution formulas of the type:

$$\text{any string of } \Sigma^* \rightarrow \text{any string of } \Sigma^* .$$

With this definition in mind, we shall view a normal algorithm as a Markov class rewriting process, or more generally, as a Markov class rewriting system. Now, the following two theorems of the established literature highlight the fact that Markov class rewriting systems can be defined only by a type-0 grammar of Chomsky hierarchy.

Theorem 5.3.1.1 (Detlovs) [06]

The class of normally computable partial word functions is equivalent to the class of partial recursive word functions.

Theorem 5.3.1.2 (Davis and Chomsky) [20]

A language $L \subseteq \mathcal{A}^*$ is generated by a formal grammar $<\Sigma, P, \mathcal{A}>$ if and only if it is recursively enumerable.

The languages recognized by the class of normal algorithms over an alphabet $\mathcal{A}$ are recursively enumerable and so can be finitely specified only by a type-0 grammar.

Definition 5.3.1.2 [20]

A (Type-0) phrase structure grammar G_T, also called a semi-Thue process, is an ordered quadruple $< \Sigma, P, S, \mathcal{A} >$, where,

(i) Σ is a total alphabet,

(ii) $\mathcal{A}$ is the terminal alphabet,

(iii) $\Sigma \setminus \mathcal{A}$ is the alphabet of non terminals,

(iv) P is a set of semi-Thue rewriting rules of the type: String 1 $\rightarrow$ String 2, where String 1 can be any string of terminals and non terminals that contains at least one non terminal and String 2 is any string of terminals and non terminals whatsoever, and,

(v) S is known as a Start symbol which is in $\Sigma \setminus \mathcal{A}$.

G_T defines a semi-Thue rewriting system $< \Sigma , P >$.

From the above definition it is clear that a type-0 grammar does not allow semi-Thue productions of the form $\Lambda \rightarrow$ String 2, where String2 is from Σ. But the notion of a normal algorithm does allow substitution formulas of the form $\Lambda \rightarrow$ String 2. Therefore, it is not possible to define Markov class rewriting systems directly by a type-0 grammar of Chomsky hierarchy. We overcome this difficulty by introducing a grammar, which we call M-grammar, for describing Markov class rewriting systems. To do this, we restructure substitution formulas as semi-Thue productions corresponding to certain representations of a Turing machine, called quadruples that operate on special words known as *Post words*. Post words are words of the type hkq_wlh where h is an auxiliary letter, k and l are words from an alphabet S and q_w is a letter from a state alphabet of a Turing machine.

5.3.2 Formulation of M-Grammar

Babikov [16] proposed a method for realizing normal algorithms in terms of Turing machines by representing normal algorithms in an index alphabet of a semi-Thue system. Using this method, every substitution of a normal algorithm is replaced by a certain system of substitutions of a semi-Thue system, which operates on Post words, and thus the appropriate Turing Machine is determined. Babikov refers to Post words as words of the type hkq_wlh where h is an auxiliary letter, k and l are words from all alphabet $S\cup\{\Lambda\}$ over which the normal algorithm is constructed, q is a letter from Q and w is a word from $S\cup\{1, 2, 3,\ldots, m\}$; m = f(n) is a finite integer function of n. Our M-grammar is primarily based on this idea. We proceed as follows. Recall that a Turing machine is described by a set of quadruples of the following types:

(i) $q_i\, s_j\, s_k\, q_l$: (being in the state q_i the machine scans the symbol s_j , prints s_k in the place of s_j and goes into state q_l)

(ii) $q_i\, s_j\, R\, q_l$: (being in the state q_i the machine scans the symbol s_j , moves to the right adjacent square and goes into state q_l)

(ii) $q_i\, s_j\, L\, q_l$: (being in the state q_i the machine scans s_j , moves to the left adjacent square and goes into state q_l)

For deterministic Turing machines, no two quadruples can have the same pair q_is_j.

Now, let us consider a deterministic Turing machine $\mathcal{M}$ with the alphabet $S = \{s_1, s_2, \ldots, s_k\}$ and the state alphabet $Q = \{q_1, q_2, \ldots, q_n\}$. The semi-Thue productions corresponding to the quadruples of this Turing machine are as follows:

(i) $q_i\, s_j\, s_k\, q_l$ corresponds to the semi Thue production $q_i\, s_j \rightarrow q_l\, s_k$

(ii) $q_i\, s_j\, Rq_i$ corresponds to: 1. $q_is_js_k \rightarrow s_j\, q_i\, s_k$; (k=0, 1, 2,... K)
2. $q_is_jh \rightarrow s_j\, q_i\Lambda h$

(iii) $q_i\, s_j\, Lq_i$ corresponds to: 1. $s_kq_is_j \rightarrow q_i\, s_ks_j$; (k=0, 1, 2,…,K)
2. $hq_is_j \rightarrow hq_i\Lambda s_j$

Let us assume the configuration of $\mathcal{M}$ at a particular stage of computation to be

$$\begin{array}{c} s_2s_1s_0s_3 \\ \uparrow \\ q_4 \end{array}$$

This corresponds to the Post word $hs_2q_4s_1s_0s_3h$. Let us assume that $\mathcal{M}$ contains the quadruple $q_4s_1s_3s_5$ so that the corresponding semi Thue production is of the form $q_4s_1 \rightarrow q_5s_3$. According to this production rule, the Post word $hs_2q_4s_1s_0s_3h$ is written as $hs_2q_5s_3s_0s_3h$. In a similar manner, the rewriting of Post words by virtue of the production rules corresponding to the remaining two types of quadruples of $\mathcal{M}$ can be verified. A system of semi Thue productions corresponding to certain quadruples of a Turing machine $\mathcal{M}$ and which operate on Post words, is called a semi-Thue system denoted by $\Sigma(\mathcal{M})$.

All the three types of semi Thue production rules allow only letter to letter substitution. But a word to word substitution formula of a normal algorithm, as we know, is a restriction-free mapping of the type $\Sigma^* \rightarrow \Sigma^*$. So the question that arises here is whether it is possible to restructure the substitution formulas of a normal algorithm as semi-Thue production rules, which operate on Post words.

In this context, we propose the following technique by which a word to word substitution is realized by a block of letter to letter substitutions. Firstly we shall agree to the following assumption:

Assumption: *Any configuration of a Post word can be represented in infinite number of ways by including any number of blanks corresponding to null strings, in between any two symbols in the configuration.*

On the basis of this assumption, we can make the lengths of the pair of words that form a substitution formula, equal, by padding the shorter word with the required number of Λ's. For example, we can restructure the substitution formulas: (i) $\beta\xi \rightarrow \alpha\xi\beta$ and (ii) $\Box{*}\xi \rightarrow \Box{*}$ as (i) $\beta\xi\Lambda \rightarrow \alpha\xi\beta$ and (ii) $\Box{*}\xi \rightarrow \Box{*}\Lambda$ respectively. For convenience, we shall call this technique *End Justification*. End justification is done in two ways, that is, the pair of a substitution formula is either left justified by suffixing the shorter word with Λ's or right justified by prefixing the shorter word with Λ's. After the end justification of the pair of words, the word to word substitution due to the corresponding substitution formula which is a map of the type $\Sigma^* \rightarrow \Sigma^*$ could be replaced by a block of letter to letter substitutions of the type $\Sigma \cup \{\Lambda\} \rightarrow \Sigma \cup \{\Lambda\}$. Now, the block of semi-Thue production rules corresponding to the block of letter to letter substitutions is obtained in the manner described above. We illustrate this technique of restructuring a substitution formula in the following example.

Example 5.3.2.1

Let us consider a substitution formula $s_1s_2s_1s_3 \rightarrow s_2s_2s_1$. Then, the end justified version of this formula would be of the form $s_1s_2s_1s_3 \rightarrow s_2s_2s_1\Lambda$ and the corresponding block of semi-Thue productions are as given in table 5.3.2.1.

Table 5.3.2.1: Semi-Thue productions corresponding to the end justified substitution formula $s_1s_2s_1s_3 \rightarrow s_2s_2s_1\Lambda$

Sl.No.	Post words	Semi-Thue productions	Remarks
1	$q_{i0}s_1s_2q_{i1}$	$q_{i0}s_1 \rightarrow q_{i1}s_2$	letter substitution
2	$q_{i1}s_2Rq_{i1}$	$q_{i1}s_2s_2 \rightarrow s_2q_{i1}s_2$	right move
3	$q_{i1}s_2s_2q_{i2}$	$q_{i1}s_2 \rightarrow q_{i2}s_2$	letter substitution
4	$q_{i2}s_2Rq_{i2}$	$q_{i2}s_2s_1 \rightarrow s_2\, q_{i2}s_1$	right move
5	$q_{i2}s_1s_1q_{i3}$	$q_{i2}s_1 \rightarrow q_{i3}s_1$	letter substitution
6	$q_{i3}s_1Rq_{i3}$	$q_{i3}s_1s_3 \rightarrow s_1q_{i3}s_3$	right move
7	$q_{i3}s_3\Lambda q_{i4}$	$q_{i3}s_3 \rightarrow q_{i4}\Lambda$	letter substitution

Now, the semi-Thue system $\Sigma(\mathcal{M})$ consisting of the above production rules operates on the corresponding Post words, thus simulating the effect of the formula: $s_1s_2s_1s_3 \underset{\Sigma(\mathcal{M})}{\rightarrow} s_2\, s_2\, s_1$.

Let us consider a normal algorithm $\mathcal{N}$ over an alphabet $\mathcal{A}$ whose scheme consists of n substitution formulas. Then, each of the n formulas can be replaced by the appropriate blocks of semi-Thue rewriting rules. The totally ordered list of all such blocks gives rise to what we call as End-justified Post Turing (EPT) rewriting system whose definition is given below:

Definition 5.3.2.1

An EPT rewriting system is an RE-analogue (Recursively Enumerable) of a Markov class rewriting system and is defined as the 4-tuple $<\Sigma, Q, h, P>$ where Σ is the total alphabet; Q is the state alphabet consisting of $\{q_{ij}$: $0 \leq i \leq m$; $0 \leq j \leq n$ such that q_{ij} represents states corresponding to the ith block of end justified words of length n$\}$; h is an auxiliary symbol known as *end marker* and which is used in the construction of Post words and P is the subset of the Cartesian product $(h\Sigma^*q_{ij}\Sigma^*h)X(h\Sigma^*q_{kl}\Sigma^*h)$, known as the finite list of semi-Thue productions which operate on Post words.

We shall demonstrate the working principle of an EPT rewriting system by means of the following example:

Example 5.3.2.2

Let us consider the scheme of the cyclic shifting normal algorithm, $\mathcal{N}^{CS}$ [Ref. Subsection 4.1.1 of [23]]. The semi-Thue system corresponding to $\mathcal{N}^{CS}$ is the totally ordered list of ten blocks of semi-Thue rewriting rules as given in the following tables 5.3.2.2.

Table 5.3.2.2: Semi-Thue system corresponding to $\mathcal{N}^{CS}$

Sl.No.	Semi-Thue productions	Remarks
0	$q_{INI}\ \Sigma \rightarrow q_{00}\ \Sigma$	Input
1	$q_{00} \backslash \xi \rightarrow q_{10}\ \Sigma\backslash\xi$	Block 0 Corresponding to the formula $\xi\alpha\mu\Gamma \rightarrow \mu\Gamma\xi\alpha$
2	$q_{00}\ \xi \rightarrow q_{01}\ \mu$	
3	$q_{01}\ \mu\Sigma \rightarrow \mu\ q_{02}\ \Sigma$	
4	$q_{02}\ \Sigma\backslash\alpha \rightarrow q_{10}\ \Sigma\backslash\alpha$	
5	$q_{02}\ \alpha \rightarrow q_{03}\ \Gamma$	
6	$q_{03}\ \Gamma\Sigma \rightarrow \Gamma q_{04}\ \Sigma$	
7	$q_{04}\ \Sigma\backslash\mu \rightarrow q_{10}\ \Sigma\backslash\mu$	
8	$q_{04}\ \mu \rightarrow q_{05}\ \xi$	
9	$q_{05}\ \xi\Sigma \rightarrow \xi q_{06}\ \Sigma$	
10	$q_{06}\ \Sigma\backslash\Gamma \rightarrow q_{10}\ \Sigma\backslash\Gamma$	
11	$q_{06}\ \Gamma \rightarrow q_{07}\ \alpha$	
12	$q_{07}\ \alpha \rightarrow \alpha q_{08}\ \Lambda$	
13	$q_{08}\ \Lambda \rightarrow q_{00}\ \Lambda$	
14	$q_{10}\ \Sigma\backslash\alpha \rightarrow q_{20}\ \Sigma\backslash\alpha$	Block 1 corresponding to the formula $\alpha\mu\Gamma\rightarrow\mu\Gamma\alpha$
15	$q_{10}\ \alpha \rightarrow q_{11}\ \mu$	
16	$q_{11}\ \mu\Sigma \rightarrow \mu q_{12}\ \Sigma$	
17	$q_{12}\ \Sigma\backslash\mu \rightarrow q_{20}\ \Sigma\backslash\mu$	
18	$q_{12}\ \mu \rightarrow q_{13}\ \Gamma$	
19	$q_{13}\ \Gamma\Sigma \rightarrow \Gamma\ q_{14}\ \Sigma$	
20	$q_{14}\ \Sigma\backslash\Gamma \rightarrow q_{20}\ \Sigma\backslash\Gamma$	
21	$q_{14}\ \Gamma \rightarrow q_{15}\ \alpha$	
22	$q_{15}\ \alpha \rightarrow \alpha q_{16}\ \Lambda$	
23	$q_{16}\ \Lambda \rightarrow q_{00}\ \Lambda$	
24	$q_{20}\ \Sigma\backslash\beta \rightarrow q_{30}\ \Sigma\backslash\beta$	
25	$q_{20}\ \beta \rightarrow q_{21}\ \alpha$	
26	$q_{21}\ \alpha\Sigma \rightarrow \alpha q_{22}\ \Sigma$	
27	$q_{22}\ \Sigma\backslash\mu \rightarrow q_{30}\ \Sigma\backslash\mu$	

28	$q_{22}\mu \to q_{23}\mu$	Block 2 corresponding to the formula $\beta\mu \to \alpha\mu\beta$
29	$q_{23}\mu\Lambda \to \mu q_{24}\Lambda$	
30	$q_{24}\Lambda \to q_{25}\beta$	
31	$q_{25}\beta \to \beta q_{26}\Lambda$	
32	$q_{26}\Lambda \to q_{00}\Lambda$	
33	$q_{30}\,\Sigma\backslash\alpha \to q_{40}\,\Sigma\backslash\alpha$	Block 3 corresponding to the formula $\alpha\alpha \to \beta$
34	$q_{30}\,\alpha \to q_{31}\,\beta$	
35	$q_{31}\,\beta\Sigma \to \beta q_{32}\,\Sigma$	
36	$q_{32}\,\Sigma\backslash\alpha \to q_{40}\,\Sigma\backslash\alpha$	
37	$q_{32}\,\alpha \to q_{33}\,\Lambda$	
38	$q_{33}\,\Lambda \to q_{00}\,\Lambda$	
39	$q_{40}\,\Sigma\backslash\beta \to q_{50}\,\Sigma\backslash\beta$	Block 4 corresponding to the formula $\beta\beta \to \Gamma$
40	$q_{40}\,\beta \to q_{41}\,\Gamma$	
41	$q_{41}\,\Gamma\Sigma \to \Gamma q_{42}\,\Sigma$	
42	$q_{42}\,\Sigma\backslash\beta \to q_{50}\,\Sigma\backslash\beta$	
43	$q_{42}\,\beta \to q_{43}\,\Lambda$	
44	$q_{43}\,\Lambda \to q_{00}\,\Lambda$	
45	$q_{50}\,\Sigma\backslash\Gamma \to q_{60}\,\Sigma\backslash\Gamma$	Block 5 corresponding to the formula $\Gamma\,\alpha \to \Gamma$
46	$q_{50}\,\Gamma \to q_{51}\,\Gamma$	
47	$q_{51}\,\Gamma\Sigma \to \Gamma q_{52}\,\Sigma$	
48	$q_{52}\,\Sigma\backslash\alpha \to q_{60}\,\Sigma\backslash\alpha$	
49	$q_{52}\,\alpha \to q_{53}\,\Lambda$	
50	$q_{53}\,\Lambda \to q_{00}\,\Lambda$	
51	$q_{60}\,\Sigma\backslash\Gamma \to q_{70}\,\Sigma\backslash\Gamma$	Block 6 corresponding to the formula $\Gamma\,\mu \to \mu\,\Gamma$
52	$q_{60}\,\Gamma \to q_{61}\,\mu$	
53	$q_{61}\,\mu\Sigma \to \mu q_{62}\,\Sigma$	
54	$q_{62}\,\Sigma\backslash\mu \to q_{70}\,\Sigma\backslash\mu$	
55	$q_{62}\,\mu \to q_{63}\,\Gamma$	
56	$q_{63}\,\Gamma \to q_{64}\,\Lambda$	
57	$q_{64}\,\Lambda \to q_{00}\,\Lambda$	
58	$q_{70}\,\Sigma\backslash\beta \to q_{80}\,\Sigma\backslash\beta$	Block 7 corresponding to the formula $\beta\,\alpha \to \beta$
59	$q_{70}\,\beta \to q_{71}\,\beta$	
60	$q_{71}\,\beta\Sigma \to \beta q_{72}\,\Sigma$	
61	$q_{72}\,\Sigma\backslash\alpha \to q_{80}\,\Sigma\backslash\alpha$	
62	$q_{72}\,\alpha \to q_{73}\,\Lambda$	
63	$q_{73}\,\Lambda \to q_{00}\,\Lambda$	

64	$q_{80}\ \Sigma\backslash\Gamma \rightarrow q_{90}\ \Sigma\backslash\Gamma$	Block 8 corresponding to the formula $\Gamma \rightarrow \cdot$
65	$q_{80}\ \Gamma \rightarrow q_{FIN}\ \Lambda$	
66	$q_{90}\ \Lambda \rightarrow q_{91}\ \alpha$	Block 9 corresponding to the formula $\rightarrow \alpha$
67	$q_{91}\ \alpha \rightarrow \alpha q_{92}\ \Lambda$	
68	$q_{92}\ \Lambda \rightarrow q_{00}\ \Lambda$	

Definition 5.3.2.2

M-grammar is defined as a 7-tuple $G_M = \langle\Sigma,Q,INI,FIN,h,\psi,P\rangle$, where $\Sigma = S\cup\{\Lambda\}$ is the total alphabet consisting of the terminal and the non terminal alphabets and the null string Λ; Q is the state alphabet, the number of elements of which depends on the scheme of a normal algorithm; INI $\notin$ Q is the initial state and FIN $\notin$ Q is the final state such that $Q' = Q\cup\{INI\}\cup\{FIN\}$; h is the end marker of a Post word from $\Sigma\cup Q'\cup\{h\}$; ψ is the start axiom from $\Sigma\cup Q'\cup\{h\}$ and P is the totally ordered list of semi-Thue productions operating on Post words.

M-grammar defines EPT rewriting systems. The direct derivation relation of an EPT system is denoted by $\Rightarrow$ and defined as follows. For some Post words u and v from $\Sigma \cup Q' \cup \{h\}$, $u \underset{G_M}{\Rightarrow} v$ means that there are certain $x_1,x_2,x_3\in\Sigma^*$ and $q_{ij},q_{kl}\in Q'$ such that $\langle u,v\rangle\in P$, that is , $\langle(hx_1q_{ij}x_2h), (hx_1q_{kl}x_3h)\rangle \in P$ and $(q_{ij}x_2x_3q_{kl})$ is a quadruple of a Turing machine. The language generated by G_M is defined as $L(G_M)$ where, $L(G_M)=\{w\in h\mathcal{A}^*Q'\mathcal{A}^*h: \psi\in h\Sigma^*Q'\Sigma^*h \overset{*}{\underset{G_M}{\Rightarrow}} w\}$

G_M generates potentially infinite languages of an alphabet and such a family of languages is denoted by L(M). Now the following theorem ascertains the *Recursive Enumerability* (RE) of the languages generated by G_M:

Theorem 5.3.2.1: L (M) = L (RE)
(RE stands for Recursively Enumerable)

The proof of this theorem is the direct consequence of the theorem 5.3.1.2. Finally we remark here, that a language recognized by a constructive signal processing system is a subset of L(M).

Section 6

Special Automata For Normal Algorithms And Their Transcriptions

It was shown in the previous section 5, that symbolic signal processing operations could be carried out by means of Markov class EPT rewriting systems that are described by M-grammar. It was also mentioned in the beginning of section 5, that a language is a subset of a free monoid and is recognized by a finite state machine (automaton). A language L is recognized by an automaton in such a manner that if we start with its initial state and feed a string from the free monoid, the final state will belong to a designated set if and only if the string belongs to L. The notions of automata and codes are closely associated with each other, in the sense that, a subset of a free monoid is not only known as a language but also as a code and the finite state machine that recognizes it, is called an automaton. Any signal representation is a code by itself and any finite state machine that simulates a signal processing system is an automaton.

In this section, we shall interpret signals as variable length codes over alphabet and normal algorithms as special automata, and briefly demonstrate a syntactic method of implementing signal processing operations by means of a system of such automata of appropriate normal algorithms.

There are occasions when it becomes necessary to encode the schemes of certain normal algorithms such that their coded forms become amenable to some other normal algorithms. Hence, we shall treat a constructive signal processing system either as a code or as an automaton depending on the requirement. Before going into the details, we shall review some of the preliminaries required for our study from [03], [06], [07] and [10]. As tutorial aids, examples relevant to our study are added to clarify the main ideas.

E. G. Rajan, *Symbolic Computing - Signal and Image Processing*
ISBN 81-7800-047-4

6.1 Codes And Automata

Let A be an alphabet and $\mathcal{A}^*$ be its free monoid. Then, a word $w \in \mathcal{A}^*$ is called primitive if is not a power of any other word. For example, the word P = |O|O| from the alphabet $\mathcal{A}_0$ = {O |} is a primitive word whereas the word Q = |O|O is not, because Q is the second power of the word |O. Two words x and y are said to be conjugate if there exist two other words u and v such that x = uv and y = vu. Conjugacy relation is an equivalence relation. Equivalence classes for this relation are called conjugacy classes. It is at times convenient to say of conjugate words x and y that x is a conjugate of y or equivalently y is a conjugate of x. [Note: The string Λ is a conjugate of itself.]

Given a pair of conjugate words, one can obtain a word of the pair from the other with the help of the cyclic shifting normal algorithm N^{CS} [subsection 4.1.1]. For example, x = O|O|O| and y = |O|O|O are two conjugate words from the alphabet $\mathcal{A}_0$ = {O |} such that $x = N^{CS}(y)$ and $y=N^{CS}(x)$. Likewise, in the case of an arbitrary pair of conjugate words, x and y, we can get x from y by n applications of N^{CS}, $x = (N^{CS})^n(y)$, for some n, $0 \leq n \leq |y|$.

[Note: |y| denotes the length of the word y and $(N^{CS})^n(y)$ denotes the n number of successive applications of the normal algorithm N^{CS} to the word y.]

Proposition 6.1.1

Let C be a conjugacy class of words of length ℓ with exponent n. Let x be a word in C of the form $x = r^n$ where the primitive word r is a root. Then, for any other word y in C there is a root q such that $y = q^n$. Further, the cardinality of C is ℓ / n.

Proof:

Let x be a word in C such that $x = r^n$ and let | r | be p. Then $|x| = pn = \ell$. Now, the normal algorithm N^{CS} could be applied successively to the word x up to a maximum of p-1 times without affecting the condition that all words of C have the same exponent n. In that case the conjugacy class C would consist of the following p words: x, $N^{CS}(x)$, $(N^{CS})^2(x)$, $(N^{CS})^3(x)$, …. , $(N^{CS})^{p-1}(x)$ where $p = \ell / n$.

Example 6.1.1

Let us consider the alphabet $\mathcal{A}$ = {a b c}, a conjugacy class C={x|x is a word of length 12 and exponent 4} and a word x = abcabcabcabc in C where r = abc and n = 4 . Now, $N^{CS}(x)$ = cabcabcabcab where r = cab and n = 4 and $(N^{CS})^2(x)$ = bcabcabcabca where r = bca and n = 4. So, the cardinality of C is 3.

Definition 6.1.1

A subset of X of $\mathcal{A}^*$ is called a *code over the alphabet* $\mathcal{A}$ if for all n, m ≥ 1 and $x_1 x_2 x_3 \ldots x_n$, $x'_1 x'_2 x'_3 \ldots x'_m \in X$, the condition $x_1x_2x_3\ldots x_n = x'_1x'_2x'_3\ldots x'_m$ implies n = m and $x_i = x'_i$ for i = 1,2,3,…n.

Any subset of a code is also a code. If $X \subset \mathcal{A}^*$ is a code, then X^n is also a code for all n > 0. In general, coding is defined as an injective morphism β , β : $\mathcal{B}^* \to \mathcal{A}^*$ for alphabets $\mathcal{A}$ and $\mathcal{B}$, such that the following conditions hold :

(i) For every $\xi \in \mathcal{B}$ there is one and only one $\beta(\xi)$ in $\mathcal{A}^*$.

(ii) There is a proper subset X of $\mathcal{A}^*$ such that β induces a bijection of $\mathcal{B}$ onto X .

The family of all possible codings from $\mathcal{B}$ onto X is denoted by COD($\mathcal{B}$, X) . Let β: $\mathcal{B}^* \to \mathcal{A}^*$ be an injective morphism. Then, $\beta(\mathcal{B}) = X$, where X is a proper subset of the free monoid $\mathcal{A}^*$ is known as the coding morphism for X.

Definition 6.1.2

The subset $X \subset \mathcal{A}^*$ is a prefix (suffix) code if no element of X is a proper left (right) factor of another element in X, that is, $X\mathcal{A}^+ \cap X = \phi$ for prefix code ($\mathcal{A}^+X \cap X = \phi$ for suffix code). The code $X \subset \mathcal{A}^*$ is known as biprefix if X is both prefix and suffix.

Every submonoid M of a free monoid $\mathcal{A}^*$ has a unique minimal set of generators $X = (M-\Lambda)-(M-\Lambda)^2$ where Λ is the null string and X is a code.

Definition 6.1.3

Let $\mathcal{A}$ be an alphabet. Then, an *automaton* over $\mathcal{A}$ is defined as a triple A = <Q, I, T> where Q is a set of states, I and T are subsets of Q and are respectively known as the initial and final states.

Edge is an element from the 3-tuple $Q x \mathcal{A} x Q$ and the set of all edges of an automaton is denoted by $\mathcal{F} \subseteq Q x \mathcal{A} x Q$. A path of length n in an automaton is a sequence $c = \{f_1, f_2, \ldots, f_n\}$ of consecutive edges, where $f_1 = (q_i, a_i, q_{i+1})$, $1 \le i \le n$. The label of a path c of length n is the word $w = a_1a_2a_3\ldots a_n$ where $c = \{f_1, f_2, \ldots.., f_n\}$ and $f_1 = (q_1, a_1, q_2)$, $f_2 = (q_2, a_2, q_3)$, $f_3 = (q_3, a_3, q_4), \ldots, f_n = (q_n, a_n, q_{n+1})$. In short, a path c of length n with the label w is denoted by

$$c: q_1 \xrightarrow{w} q_{n+1}$$

A path $c: q_i \rightarrow q_t$ is called successful if and only if $q_i \in I$ and $q_t \in T$. The set of all successful paths of an automaton A is denoted by L(A). A state $q \in Q$ is accessible or co-accessible if there exists accordingly a path c which is either $c: i \rightarrow q$ and $i \in I$ or $c: q \rightarrow t$ and $t \in T$. An automaton whose every state is both accessible and co-accessible, is known as a *trim automaton* A° = <P, I∩P, T∩P> where P is a set of states which are accessible and co-accessible. Then, it can be verified that L(A) = L(A°).

An automaton A = <Q, I, T> is deterministic if the cardinality of I is 1 and if for any $p \in Q$ the edges (p, a, q) and (p, a, r) belong to the set F implies q = r. For every $p \in Q$ and $a \in A$, the transition function for an automaton A is defined as

$$\begin{aligned} p.a &= q \quad \text{if } (p, a, q) \in \mathcal{F} \\ &= \phi \quad \text{otherwise} \end{aligned}$$

This is a partial function of the type $Q \times \mathcal{A} \rightarrow Q$. An automaton is complete if for every $p \in Q$ and every $a \in A$ there exists at least one $q \in Q$ so that $(p,a,q) \in F$.

Theorem 6.1.1

Let us consider an alphabet $\mathcal{A}$ and a subset X of the free monoid $\mathcal{A}^*$. Then X is said to be recognizable if X is recognized by a finite automaton.

Proof:

Let ϕ: $\mathcal{A}^* \rightarrow$ M be a morphism onto a finite monoid M and let us assume that ϕ recognizes X. Then, a finite automaton can be defined as A= <M, Λ, ϕ (X)> with the transition function m.a = mϕ(a). Let w be a word in X. Then, Λ.w $\in \phi$(X) if any only if $\phi(w) \in \phi(X)$. Then L(A) = X. Hence, X is recognizable.

Definition 6.1.4

An *asynchronous automaton* is a generalized notion of an automaton. It has edges labeled either by a letter or by the null string such that $F \subset Q \times (\mathcal{A} \cup \Lambda) \times Q$.

Theorem 6.1.2

If $X \subset \mathcal{A}^*$ is recognizable by an automaton A, then X* is also recognizable. If $X,Y \subset \mathcal{A}^*$ are recognizable, then XY is also recognizable.

Proof

Now $X \subset \mathcal{A}^*$. Since $X^*=(X-\Lambda)^*$, $\Lambda \notin X$ is a valid assumption. Let A = <Q, I, T> be a finite automaton recognizing X and let $\mathcal{F}$ be the set of its edges. Since $\Lambda \notin X$, edges of the types $q_i \xrightarrow{\Lambda} q_i$ or $q_i \xrightarrow{\Lambda} q_j$; $q_i, q_j \in Q$ are not in $\mathcal{F}$. This means $I \cap T = \phi$. Now let us construct another asynchronous automaton B = <Q, I, T> whose set of edges is $\mathcal{F}'$ where $\mathcal{F}' = \mathcal{F} \cup (T \times \{\Lambda\} \times I)$.

In the light of the definition of a successful path, we observe that the number of successful paths in B amounts to the free semigroup X^+. This means $L(B) = X^+$. Any successful path in B may contain an edge of the form c: $i_k \xrightarrow{w_k} t_k$; $t_k \in T$, $i_k \in I$ and an edge of the form c: $t_k \xrightarrow{\Lambda} i_k$. In other words, any word w in X^+ can be recognized as a successful path in B such as:

$$c: i_1 \xrightarrow{w_1} t_1 \xrightarrow{\Lambda} i_2 \xrightarrow{w_2} t_2 \xrightarrow{\Lambda} i_3 \xrightarrow{w_3} \ldots \xrightarrow{\Lambda} i_n \xrightarrow{w_n} t_n$$

and $i_1 = i$ and $t_n = j$; $i \in I$; $j \in T$.

Since X^+ is recognizable X* is also recognizable if we assume that $I \cap T \neq \phi$, that is, $\Lambda \in X$.

Now let us consider two finite automata A_1 = <P, I, S> and A_2 = <Q, J, T> with sets of edges $\mathcal{F}_1$ and $\mathcal{F}_2$ respectively. We shall construct an asynchronous automaton A_3 with the set of edges $\mathcal{F}_3$ where $\mathcal{F}_3 = \mathcal{F}_1 \cup \mathcal{F}_2 \cup (S \times \{\Lambda\} \times J)$. Now, A_3 recognizes XY.

Definition 6.1.5

To each automaton A = <Q, I, T> with the set of edges $\mathcal{F}$ over an alphabet $\mathcal{A}$, a function $\phi: A \rightarrow N^{Q \times Q}$ is associated which is defined as:

$$(p, \phi(a), q) = 1 \text{ if } (p, a, q) \in F$$
$$= 0 \text{ otherwise.}$$

N is the semiring of natural numbers. N^{QXQ} is called the monoid of N relations over Q, that is, to each pair $(q_i, q_j) \in Q \times Q$ is related a number from N by virtue of the function ϕ. ϕ is the morphism of the type: $\mathcal{A}^* \rightarrow N^{QXQ}$ if the following conditions hold:

(i) $\phi(\Lambda) = I_Q$; (I_Q is the identity relation $(q_i, q_i) \in N^{QXQ}$).

(ii) For any u, v $\in \mathcal{A}^*$, $(q_i, \phi(uv), q_j) = \sum_{q_k \in Q} (q_i, \phi(u), q_k)(q_k, \phi(v), q_j)$

Then the morphism ϕ is known as the representation of the automaton A over N.

Definition 6.1.6

The formal power series, otherwise known as the behavior of an automaton A = <Q, I, T> over an alphabet $\mathcal{A}$ is defined by:

$$(|A|, w) = \sum_{i \in I,\, t \in T} (i, \phi(w), t)$$

and designated by |A|. The support of |A| could be seen to be the set recognized by A, i.e., the set L(A).

Definition 6.1.7

To every automaton A = <Q, I, T> over $\mathcal{A}$, there corresponds another automaton called A*, whose construction is as explained below:

Let us consider a new state q_* which is not in Q and construct an automaton B = $<Q \cup q_*, q_*, q_*>$ with the set of edges $\mathcal{G} = \mathcal{F}_1 \cup \mathcal{F}_2 \cup \mathcal{F}_3 \cup \mathcal{F}_4$ where

$\mathcal{F}_1$ = set of edges of A

$\mathcal{F}_2$ = $\{(q_*, a, q) : \exists i \in I((i, a, q) \in \mathcal{F}_1)\}$

$\mathcal{F}_3$ = $\{(q, a, q_*) : \exists t \in T((q, a, t) \in \mathcal{F}_1)\}$

$\mathcal{F}_4$ = $\{(q_*, a, q_*) : \exists i \in I, \exists t \in T((i, a, t) \in \mathcal{F}_1)\}$

The restriction of B to the set of its states, which are both accessible and co-accessible yields the trim part of B, which is the desired automaton A*.

Example 6.1.2

Let us consider the alphabet $\mathcal{A}_O$ = {O |} and the subset X = {O|O, O||O, O|||O}. The automaton A which recognizes X and its corresponding automaton A* are shown in figures 6.1.1 and 6.1.2 respectively.

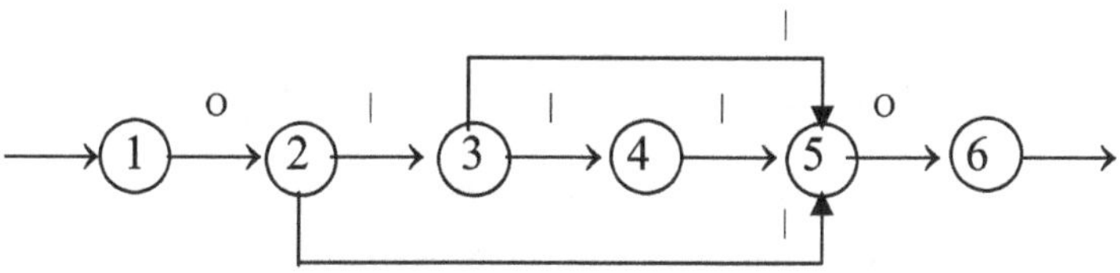

Figure 6.1.1: The automaton that recognizes the subset X = {O|O, O||O, O|||O}

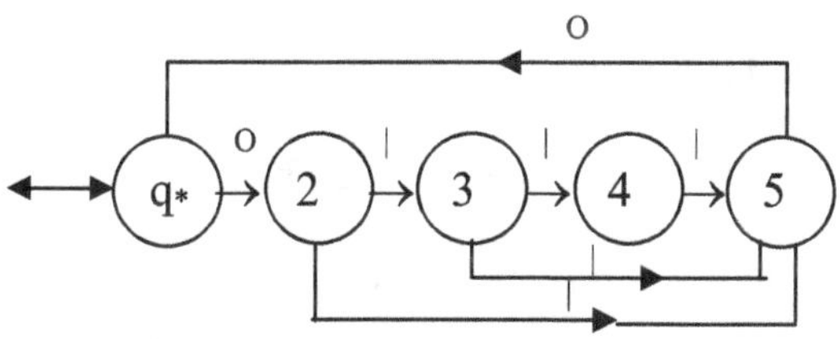

Figure 6.1.2: The trim automaton that recognizes X = {O|O, O||O, O|||O}

Example 6.1.3

Let us consider the alphabet $\mathcal{A}_O$ = {O |} and the subset X=O||*O. The automaton A which recognizes X and its corresponding automaton A* are shown in figures 6.1.3 and 6.1.4 respectively.

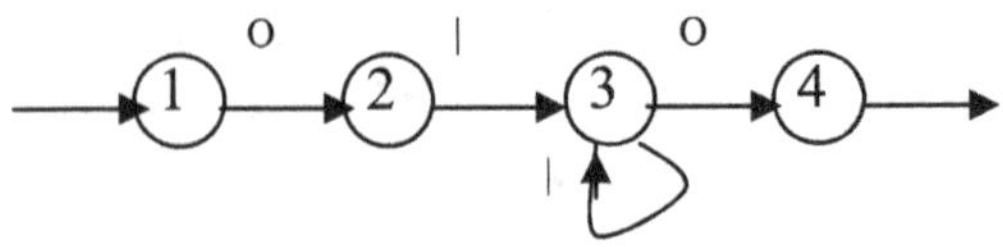

Figure 6.1.3: The automaton that recognizes the subset X = O||*O

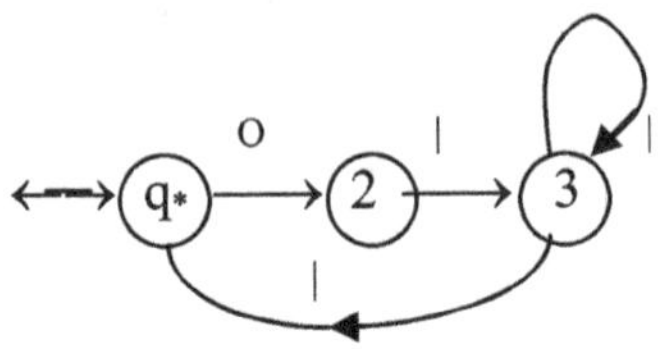

Figure 6.1.4: The trim automaton that recognizes the subset X = O||*O

6.2 An Alphabetic Encoding Of Normal Algorithms

As mentioned earlier, it becomes necessary at times to encode the scheme of certain normal algorithms such that their coded forms become amenable to some other normal algorithms. Markov devised a method known as transcribing a normal algorithm, by which the scheme of a normal algorithm $\mathcal{N}$ could be coded as a string from a two-lettered alphabet [08].

6.2.1 Transcriptions Of Normal Algorithms

In general, the scheme of a normal algorithm $\mathcal{N}$ operating in a certain way on words from a basic alphabet, say, $\mathcal{A}$ is constructed over a larger alphabet $\mathcal{B} = \mathcal{A} \cup \mathcal{E}$ and $\mathcal{E}$ is the alphabet of auxiliary symbols. Let $\mathcal{C}$ be another alphabet where $\mathcal{C} = \mathcal{B} \cup \{x\ y\ z\}$ and the symbols x, y and z are not contained either in $\mathcal{A}$ or in $\mathcal{E}$. Now the normal algorithm $\mathcal{N}$ is represented in the alphabet $\mathcal{C}$ in the following manner:

The substitution formulas of $\mathcal{N}$ are written down in the order of succession of its scheme, placing the symbol z at the end of each substitution formula and replacing all arrows (→) and dots (·) by the symbols x and y respectively. For example, the following scheme:

$$\mathcal{N}: \quad \alpha\,\mu \rightarrow \cdot\, \mu\alpha \qquad\qquad (\mu \in \mathcal{A},\ \alpha \in \mathcal{E})$$
$$\rightarrow \alpha$$

could be represented in the alphabet $\mathcal{C}$ as a string of the form:

$$\alpha\mu xy\mu\alpha zx\alpha z$$

Now let us introduce a convenient ordering of symbols in the alphabet $\mathcal{C}$. Let us also denote by r_i; $(1\leq i \leq n)$ any one of the n symbols of $\mathcal{C}$ and translate [Refer theorem 2.3.2.1] every symbol of $\mathcal{C}$ by using the coding rule II: $r_i \rightarrow O|^iO$ in the alphabet $A_O = \{O\ |\}$. II is an injective morphism of the type $\mathcal{C}^* \rightarrow \mathcal{A}^*_O$ such that $II(\mathcal{C}) = X$ is the coding morphism for $X=\{O|^iO\ ;\ 1\leq i \leq n\}$. It is not hard to see that the subset X consisting of (O, |)-links [Definition 2.3.1.8] is a biprefix code [Definition 6.1.2] over the alphabet $\mathcal{A}_O$.

If all the symbols of the string from $\mathcal{C}$ which represents a normal algorithm $\mathcal{N}$ are replaced by their translations by applying the coding rule II, then the resulting string in $\mathcal{A}_O$ is called the transcription of $\mathcal{N}$ and is denoted by $\{\mathcal{N}\}$.

For example, let us consider the following scheme:

$$\mathcal{N}:\quad \alpha\,\mu \rightarrow \cdot\mu\alpha \qquad\qquad (\mu\in\mathcal{A},\ \alpha\in\mathcal{E})$$
$$\rightarrow \alpha$$

This is represented in the alphabet $\mathcal{C}$ as a string of the form:

$$\alpha\mu xy\mu\alpha zx\alpha z$$

Let us now define II as follows:

II:

$$x \rightarrow O|O$$
$$z \rightarrow O||O$$
$$\mu \rightarrow O|||O$$
$$\alpha \rightarrow O||||O$$
$$y \rightarrow O|||||O$$

Then $\{\mathcal{N}\} \doteq O||||OO|||OO|OO|||||OO|||OO||||OO||OO|OO||||OO||O$

In general, transcription of any normal algorithm over an arbitrary alphabet is a word from the set X = O||*O. The set X is a subset of the free monoid $\mathcal{A}^*_O$ and so is a code.

In what follows, we study some of the important properties of this code.

6.2.2 Structural Properties Of the Biprefix Code X = O||*O

Proposition 6.2.2.1

X is a biprefix code

Proof

$X \subset A^*_O$. $X\mathcal{A}^+_O \cap X = \phi$. $\mathcal{A}^+_O X \cap X = \phi$. So, X is a biprefix code.

Propostion 6.2.2.2

The submonoid X * of $\mathcal{A}^*_O$ generated by X = O||*O is free.

Proof

$X \subset \mathcal{A}^*_O$. Let II: $\mathcal{C}^* \to \mathcal{A}^*_O$ be a coding morphism for X. Then II is injective and a bijection from $\mathcal{C}$ into X. II is a bijection from $\mathcal{C}^*$ onto II ($\mathcal{C}^*$). Hence, X* is free and its minimal set of generators X is given by

$$(X^*-\Lambda)-(X^*-\Lambda)^2$$

Definition 6.2.2.1 [03]

Let M be a monoid and N be a submonoid of M. Then, N is called right unitary in M if $\forall u, v \in M$ $(u, uv \in N \Rightarrow v \in N)$, that is, $(N^+)^{-1}N = N$. For convenience, we shall write N^{-1} instead of $(N^+)^{-1}$.

N is left unitary in M if $\forall u, v \in M$ $(u, vu \in N \Rightarrow v \in N)$, that is, $N(N^+)^{-1} = N$. The submonoid N is called biunitary if it is both left and right unitary. N is said to be stable in M if $\forall u, v, w \in M$ $(u, v, uw, wv \in N \Rightarrow w \in N)$.

Proposition 6.2.2.3

The free submonoid X* of $\mathcal{A}^*_O$ generated by the set X is biunitary and stable in $\mathcal{A}^*_O$.

Proof

Let us assume $u = O|^iO$, $v = O|^jO$ and $w = O|^kO$ such that u, v, w $\in \mathcal{A}^*_O$. Now u, v, uw, wv $\in$ X* because $O|^iO$, $O|^jO$, $O|^iOO|^kO$, $O|^kOO|^jO$ $\in$ X* and so w $\in$ X*. Hence, X* is stable in $\mathcal{A}^*_O$. Using similar arguments, we can see that X* is biunitary in $\mathcal{A}^*_O$.

The relationships between the unitariness and stability properties of X is shown in figure 6.2.2.1.

In $X \subset \mathcal{A}^*$ is a code then every subset of X is itself a code. This brings out the notion of maximal codes. A code is maximal over an alphabet $\mathcal{A}$ if X is not contained in any other code over $\mathcal{A}$. That is, for $X \subset X'$, if X' is a code then $X = X'$. Maximality is not algorithmically verifiable, but it is decidable for recognizable codes. Propositions like: "*Any code X over $\mathcal{A}$ is contained in some maximal code*" are provable only by means of nonconstructive methods, which admit the existence of a least upper bound in the set of codes over A. However, as outlined in [03], the extremal properties of codes could be studied in terms of what is known as *completeness* by replacing an extremal property by a combinatorial one.

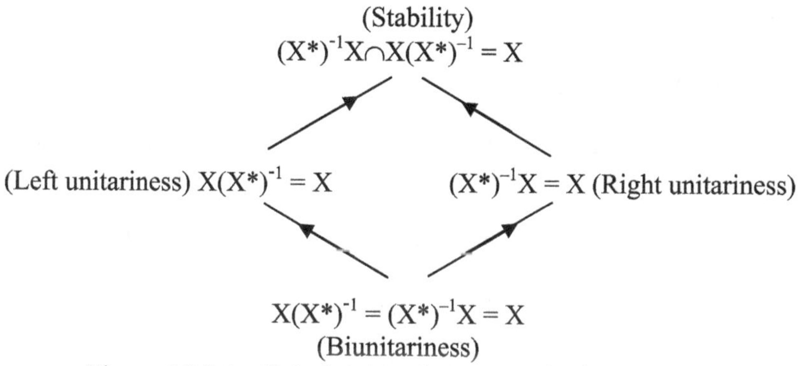

Figure 6.2.2.1: Relationships between unitariness and stability properties of the code X = U||*U

Definition 6.2.2.2 [03]

Let P be a subset of the semigroup $\mathcal{A}^+$ where $\mathcal{A}$ is an alphabet. An element m in $\mathcal{A}^+$ is completable in P, if there exist u and v in $\mathcal{A}^+$ such that $umv \in P$. P is said to be *dense* in $\mathcal{A}^+$ of every element of $\mathcal{A}^+$ is completable in P. P is said to be complete if P* is dense. Every dense set is also complete. A subset of a monoid, which is not dense is called *thin set*. All maximal codes are complete. All thin complete codes are maximal.

Proposition 6.2.2.4

The biprefix code X is thin and not maximal.

Proof

X would be thin if there is at least one element in $\mathcal{A}^*_O$ which is incompletable in X. One such element which is incompletable in X is |O|. So X is thin. Moreover, the element |O| is incompletable in X* also. This means X* is not dense. Hence, X is incomplete and not maximal.

Proposition 6.2.2.5

Let X_i and X_j be two thin biprefix codes, which are finite subsets of X. Then $X_i X_j$ is thin.

Proof

Let us consider two words u and v in $\mathcal{A}^*_O$ which are incompletable in X_i and X_j respectively. Then the word uv is incompletable in $X_i X_j$. So $X_i X_j$ is thin.

Definition 6.2.2.3 [03]

Given a subset N of a monoid M, the set of those elements of M which are factors of elements in N is defined as F(N), where $F(N) = M^{-1}NM^{-1} = \{m \in M | \exists u,v \in M: umv \in N\}$ and $\bar{F}(N) = M - F(N)$. N is a proper subset of F(N). A code $X \subset \mathcal{A}^+$ is called *very thin* if there exists a word in X* which is not a factor of any word in X. In other words, X is very thin if and only if $X^* \cap \bar{F}(X) \neq \phi$. For example, let us consider the code $X = \{O^n|O^n : n \geq 0\}$ over the alphabet $\mathcal{A}_O = \{O\ |\}$. This code is very thin because the element $|^2$ which is not a factor of any element of X, is present in $X^* \cap \bar{F}(X)$.

Proposition 6.2.2.6

Let X be a subset of the code X = O||*O. Then X is very thin.

Proof

Since no other element in X* excepting the set X, is a factor of any element of X, F(X) = X. Then $\bar{F}(X) = X^* - X$ and $X^* \cap \bar{F}(X) = \bar{F}(X)$.

There is no element in $\bar{F}$ (X), which is a factor of any of the elements of X. Hence, X is a very thin code and every subset of it is also very thin.

Definition 6.2.2.4

A code X is *purely thin* if and only if $X^* \cap \bar{F}(X) = \bar{F}(X)$.

Proposition 6.2.2.7

The code X is purely thin.

Proof

The code X satisfies the condition $X^* \cap \bar{F}(X) = \bar{F}(X)$. So it is purely thin.

6.2.2 Literal Representation of X = O||*O

Literal representation of codes over an alphabet is a convenient method of representing them graphically in the form of a tree whose selected nodes (nodes which are shaded) correspond to words in the code set. Given a finite alphabet $\mathcal{A}$, the literal representation of the corresponding free monoid is constructed in the following manner.

The alphabet is totally ordered and words of equal length are lexicographically ordered. The set of words of a specific length form a level in the tree. All the nodes of a level are lexicographically labeled from top to bottom. The zeroth level consists of a single node known as the root corresponding to the null string. The first right level consists of n nodes where n is the number of symbols in the alphabet. Labeling of these n nodes is done from top to bottom in accordance with the lexicographic order introduced in the alphabet. The second right level consists of n^2 nodes, each being labeled lexicographically from top to bottom with the corresponding n^2 words of length 2. By repeating this procedure the literal representation of the free monoid could be potentially realized. For example, the literal representation of the free monoid $\mathcal{A}^*_O$ of the alphabet $\mathcal{A}_O$ = {O |} is shown in figure 6.2.3.1. Since X is a subset of $\mathcal{A}^*_O$ its literal representation is a sub tree of the tree of $\mathcal{A}^*_O$. The sub tree corresponding to the code X is shown in figure 6.2.3.2. [Note: The dark nodes correspond to the words in X].

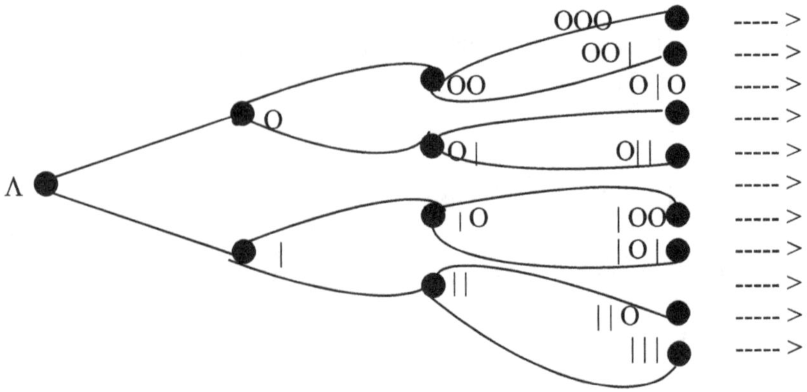

Figure 6.2.3.1: Literal representation of the free monoid $\mathcal{A}^*_O$

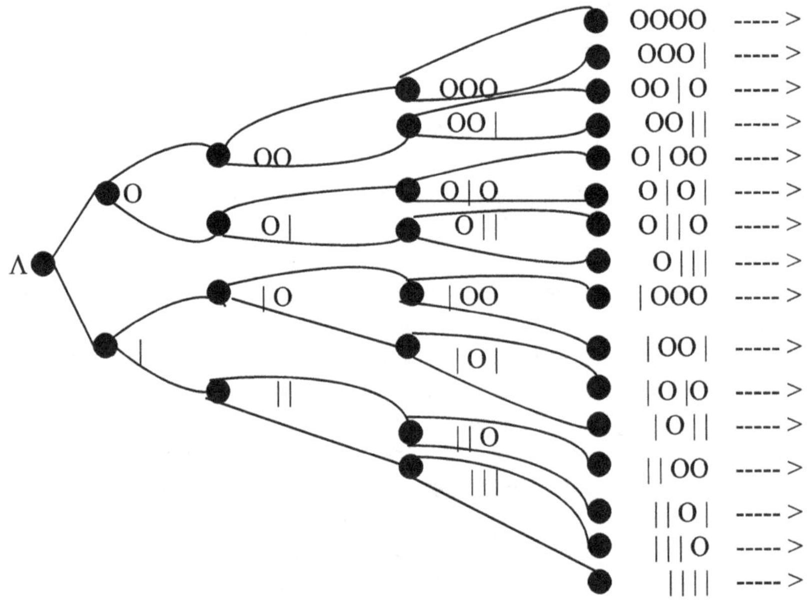

Figure 6.2.3.2: Literal representation of the code X = O||*O

The advantage of the literal representation of codes lies in the easy readability of words and compact diagrammatic representation of reasonably big codes. Given a finite alphabet $\mathcal{C}$, [Subsection 6.2.1] the corresponding code set X is also finite. Now the literal representation of X yields a method for verifying whether the transcription of a normal algorithm (which is nothing but a (O,|)-chain from the code set X) is actually in X* or not. In other words, the verification of a valid factor of the transcription of a normal algorithm is done by tracing the path from the root, letter by letter, so that a leaf (dark node) is reached. This procedure is repeated for all the factors of the entire coded string. The successful completion of all such verifications corresponding to a given (O,|)-chain determines the syntactic correctness of the transcription of a normal algorithm.

6.3 The Notion Of a Cyclic Normal Automaton

The notion of an unambiguous automaton plays an important role in the study of variable length codes, in the sense that, computations in the monoids of functions are replaced by computations in the monoids of unambiguous relations. In this sub section, we present a technique of interpreting normal algorithms in terms of unambiguous automata.

While the precise definitions of various terms to be used in this book are introduced in the text as the need arise, it is appropriate to clarify here itself as to how we intend to interpret the two basic terms – *signals and systems*. By a signal we mean a word from a free monoid $\mathcal{A}^*$ of an alphabet $\mathcal{A}$. By a *signal space* we mean the free monoid $\mathcal{A}^*$ itself or a subset of it, i.e., a *language*. By a signal *processing system* we understand a binary relation on $\mathcal{A}^*$, with the first members of the ordered pairs constituting this relation called inputs and the second members called outputs.

Refer to section 1.3. An alternative way of looking at systems is that in terms of four equivalence relations introduced by Green [06], which hold for semigroups as well as free monoids [10]. These are:

(i) Right or $\mathcal{R}$-class congruences: a, b $\in \mathcal{A}^*$, a $\mathcal{R}$b if a$\mathcal{A}^*$ = b$\mathcal{A}^*$

(ii) Left or $\mathcal{L}$- congruences: a, b $\in \mathcal{A}^*$, a $\mathcal{L}$ b if $\mathcal{A}^*$a = $\mathcal{A}^*$b

(iii) $\mathcal{J}$-class congruences: a, b $\in \mathcal{A}^*$, a $\mathcal{J}$ b if $\mathcal{A}^*$a$\mathcal{A}^*$ = $\mathcal{A}^*$b$\mathcal{A}^*$

(ii) $\mathcal{H}$-class congruences: a, b $\in \mathcal{A}^*$, a $\mathcal{H}$b if a $\mathcal{R}$b and a $\mathcal{L}$ b

An alphabet $\mathcal{A}$, together with a finite set $\mathcal{T}$ of $\mathcal{J}$- class equivalence relations is called an $\mathcal{J}$-class presentation of the free monoid $\mathcal{A}^*$.

Similarly one can obtain four more types of presentations based on the remaining four equivalence relations $\mathcal{D}$, $\mathcal{R}$, $\mathcal{L}$ and $\mathcal{H}$.

A normal algorithm say $\mathcal{N}$, in an alphabet $\mathcal{A}$ has a direct correspondence with a $\mathcal{J}$-class presentation of the free monoid $\mathcal{A}^*$, which is defined by certain $\mathcal{J}$-class partial order relations. Let a substitution formula $P \rightarrow Q$ be contained in the scheme of $\mathcal{N}$. This formula is applicable only to those words of $\mathcal{A}^*$ for which P is a factor. In other words, this substitution formula is a partial map of the type $\mathcal{A}^*P\mathcal{A}^* \rightarrow \mathcal{A}^*Q\mathcal{A}^*$ which in turn is interpreted as the partial order relation $P\mathcal{J}Q$. So, a normal algorithm $\mathcal{N}$ with the scheme $\mathcal{S}$ consisting of n substitution formulas, is a $\mathcal{J}$-class presentation of the free monoid $\mathcal{A}^*$ defined by an ordered list of n $\mathcal{J}$-class partial order relations corresponding to the n substitution formulas. So, we may now say that a system is a $\mathcal{J}$-class presentation.

Definition 6.3.1 [03]

Unambiguous Relations

Let us consider an N-relation [Refer definition 6.1.5] between two sets P and Q which is a mapping m: $P \times Q \rightarrow N$ where N is the complete semiring of natural numbers which admits least upper bound. The N-relation of m is said to be unambiguous if $m \in \{0, 1\}^{PXQ}$ where $0,1 \in N$. Assume P = Q. Then a monoid M of unambiguous relations over Q is defined as a submonoid of $\{0, 1\}^{QXQ}$ with the identity element I_Q. The following property holds for M.

$\forall m,n \in M \;\; p,q \in Q \; \exists r \in Q \; ((p, mn, q) = 1 \Rightarrow \; (p, m, r) = (r, n, q) = 1 \,)$

M is transitive if it satisfies the following property:

$$\forall p,q \in Q \; \exists m \in M \; ((p, m, q) = 0 \vee 1)$$

Now, a monoid M of unambiguous partial order relations over a set Q is defined as a submonoid of $\{O, O|\}^{QXQ}$ with the identity I_Q where O and O| are the constructive natural numbers [Refer subsection 1.1] corresponding to 0 and 1 from N. The system of constructive natural numbers is denoted by the symbol $\wp$. A $\wp$-relation m is unambiguous only when $m \in \{O, O|\}^{QXQ}$. Let us consider a normal algorithm $\mathcal{N}$ over an alphabet $\mathcal{A}$, whose scheme $\mathcal{S}$ consists of n substitution formulas. Since $\mathcal{N}$ is a $\mathcal{J}$-class semi-Thue presentation of the free monoid $\mathcal{A}^*$ defined by a totally ordered list of n $\mathcal{J}$-class partial order relations corresponding to the n substitution formulas, one could construct n unambiguous $\wp$-relations corresponding to the n $\mathcal{J}$-class partial order relations of the scheme $\mathcal{S}$.

This indicates the possibility of interpreting normal algorithms in terms of unambiguous automata. Now, let us go into the details.

Definition 6.3.2 [03]

Unambiguous Automata

Let A be an automaton over an alphabet $\mathcal{A}$. Then, A is unambiguous if and only if its representation $\phi_A(\mathcal{A}^*)$ is unambiguous [Refer definition 6.1.5].

Theorem 6.3.1

If A=<Q, Λ, Λ>, then A is trim if and only if $\phi_A(\mathcal{A}^*)$ is transitive.

Definition 6.3.3

Normal Automaton

This is defined as a quintuple $\langle X, Y, Q, \lambda, \delta \rangle$, where X is the set of admissible inputs, Y is the set of outputs, Q is the set of states corresponding to the number of substitution formulas, λ is the next state function of the type λ: Q x X → Q, and δ is the output function of the type δ: Q x X → Y and whose construction is governed by the following rules:

For any state $q_i \in Q$ let the input string be w_i and the left part of the corresponding i[th] substitution formula be u_i.

Then, (i) $\lambda(q_i, w_i) = q_0$ if u_i is a factor of w_i, that is, $u_i \le w_i$. (q_0 is the initial state)
$= q_{i+1}$ otherwise

(ii) $\delta(q_i, w_i) = w_0$ if $u_i \le w_i$. (w_0 is the input string at the initial state)
$= w_{i+1}$ otherwise

Definition 6.3.3 has been coined with the purpose of interpreting the scheme $\mathcal{S}$ of a normal algorithm $\mathcal{N}$ over an alphabet $\mathcal{A}$. But, this definition does not fully characterize the class of normal algorithms over an alphabet $\mathcal{A}$, based on their common operational semantics. However, the following modified definition gives rise to a syntactic construction, which describes the operational scheme of normal algorithms over an alphabet $\mathcal{A}$.

Definition 6.3.4

Cyclic Normal Automaton

This is defined as a 7-tuple $<X, Y, Q, q_{ini}, q_{fin}, \lambda, \delta>$ where X is the set of admissible inputs; Y is the set of outputs; Q is the set of n states corresponding to the n substitution formulas of the scheme $\mathcal{S}$ of a normal algorithm $\mathcal{N}$ over an alphabet $\mathcal{A}$; $q_{ini} \notin Q$ is the input state; $q_{fin} \notin Q$ is the output state; λ is the next state function of the type λ: Q x X $\rightarrow$ Q and δ is the output function of the type δ: Q x X $\rightarrow$ Y and whose construction is governed by the following rules:

For any state q_i, let the input string during the mth iteration of the scheme be w_{mi} and the left part of the corresponding i[th] substitution formula be u_i. Let us assume that the ith substitution formula is of simple type.

Then,

(i) $\lambda(q_i, w_{mi}) = q_o$ if $(u_i \leq w_{mi})$ or $\neg(u_n \leq w_{mn})$ (q_0 is the first state)
$= q_{i+1}$ otherwise

(ii) $\delta(q_i, w_{mi}) = w_{(m+1)o}$ if $(u_i \leq w_{mi})$ or $\neg(u_n \leq w_{mn})$
$= w_{m(i+1)}$ otherwise

Let us assume that the ith substitution formula is of terminal type. Then,

(i) $\lambda(q_i, w_{mi}) = q_{fin}$ if $(u_i \leq w_{mi})$
$= q_{i+1}$ otherwise

(ii) $\delta(q_i, w_{mi}) = y{:}y \in Y$ if $(u_i \leq w_{mi})$
$= w_{m(i+1)}$ otherwise .

As an illustration, a 6-state cyclic normal automaton corresponding to a scheme consisting of six simple substitution formulas is shown in figure 6.3.1. We shall represent a cyclic normal automaton by the symbol C. Then the representation associated with C is a morphism $\phi_C: \mathcal{A}^* \rightarrow \{O, O|\}^{QXQ}$; $O, O| \in \wp$ such that:

(i) $\phi(\Lambda) = I_Q$ (identity element)

(ii) $(q_i, \phi(w_{mj}), q_j) = O|$ if there is an edge connecting q_i and q_j
$= O$ Otherwise .

Any cyclic normal automaton C over an alphabet A is unambiguous because, for every $q_i, q_j \in Q$ and $w_{mj} \in A^*$, $(q_i, \phi_C(w_{mj}), q_j) \in \{O, O|\}$.

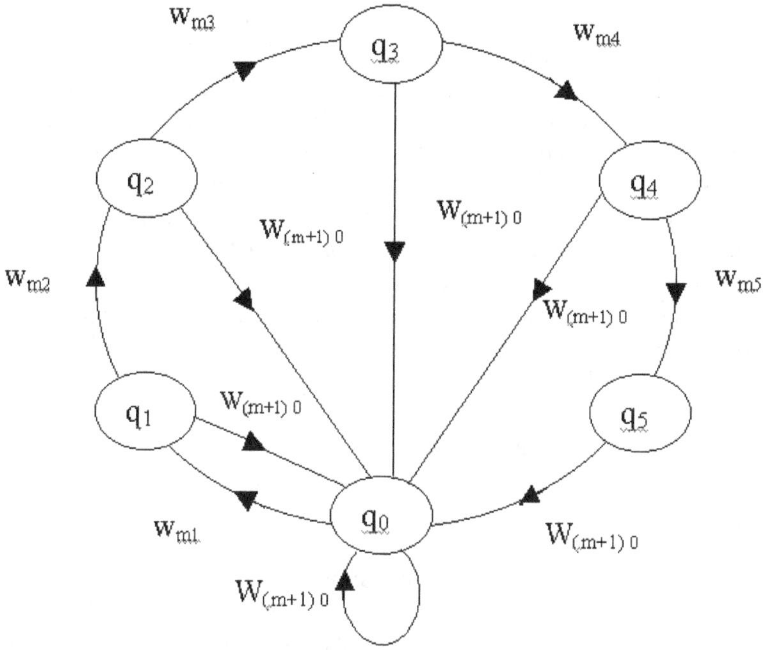

Figure 6.3.1 A 6-state cyclic normal automaton

6.3 Implementation Of Signal Processing Operations In Terms Of Rewriting Cyclic Normal Automata

In subsection 5.3, it was shown that signal processing operations could be carried out by means of EPT rewriting systems. Here, we show that such EPT rewriting systems can be modeled as finite state machines, which we shall call as *Rewriting Cyclic Normal Automata* (RCNA). An RCNA is basically a cyclic normal automaton with certain additional factors.

Definition 6.4.1

Rewriting Cyclic Normal Automata

Let us consider a normal algorithm N consisting of n totally ordered substitution formulas $\{u_i \rightarrow v_i: 1 \leq i \leq n\}$ and its EPT version. We shall define a rewriting cyclic normal automaton for the EPT system in the following manner:

Let Q be the set of states corresponding to the semi-Thue productions contained in the scheme of the EPT rewriting system where $Q = \{q_{ij} \mid 0 \leq i \leq n-1; 0 \leq j \leq k$: i represents the ith substitution formula, j represents the jth semi-Thue production of the ith substitution formula and k represents the number of states, that is, the number of semi-Thue productions corresponding to the ith substitution formula$\}$. For convenience, the state corresponding to the ith substitution formula is termed as a *major state* and the states corresponding to the k semi-Thue productions of the ith substitution formula as *minor states*. Let $u_i \rightarrow v_i$ be the ith substitution formula. Then, the number of minor states corresponding to the ith major state is given by the following rules.

(i) if $|u_i| = |v_i| = \ell_m$, then $k = 2\ell_m$

[NOTE: $|u_i|$ is the length of u_i]

(ii) if $|u_i| < |v_i|$ then $k = 2\ell_m$

(ii) if $|u_i| > |v_i|$ then $k = 2\ell_m\text{-}1$

Now, the rewriting cyclic normal automaton is defined as the triple <Q , INI, FIN> where INI $\not\subset$ Q is the initial state and FIN $\not\subset$ Q is the final state and whose set of edges $\mathcal{F}$ contains edges of the following types:

(i) $q_{ij} \xrightarrow{\Sigma \setminus \mu / \Leftarrow} q_{(i+1)0}$ (being in the state q_{ij} if the symbol μ is not found in the corresponding input string, go to the next state $q_{(i+1)0}$ and read the same string)

(ii) $q_{ij} \xrightarrow{\mu / \xi} q_{i(j+1)}$ (being in the state q_{ij} if the symbol μ is found in the corresponding input string, recognize it as ξ and go to state $q_{i(j+1)}$)

(iii) $q_{ij} \xrightarrow{\mu / \rightarrow} q_{i(j+1)}$ (being in the state q_{ij} if the symbol μ is found in the corresponding input string, go to state $q_{i(j+1)}$ and read the symbol next to μ)

(iii) $q_{ij} \xrightarrow{\Lambda / \vdash} q_{00}$ (being in the state q_{ij} rewrite the input string with the recognized symbols duely substituted and go to state q_{oo})

We shall demonstrate the working of an RCNA by means of the following example:

Example 6.4.1

Let us consider the EPT rewriting system corresponding to the cyclic shifting normal algorithm N^{CS} [Refer to example 5.3.2.2].

The RCNA for the above EPT system is defined by $C^{CS} = \langle Q, INI, FIN \rangle$ where

$Q = \{q_{00}, q_{01}, q_{02}, q_{03}, q_{04}, q_{05}, q_{06}, q_{08}, q_{09}, q_{10}, q_{11}, q_{12}, q_{13}, q_{14}, q_{15}, q_{16}, q_{20}, q_{21}, q_{22}, q_{23}, q_{24}, q_{25}, q_{26}, q_{30}, q_{31}, q_{32}, q_{33}, q_{40}, q_{41}, q_{42}, q_{43}, q_{50}, q_{51}, q_{52}, q_{53}, q_{60}, q_{61}, q_{62}, q_{63}, q_{64}, q_{70}, q_{71}, q_{72}, q_{73}, q_{80}, q_{90}, q_{91}, q_{92}\}$

with the set of edges $\mathcal{F}$ where,

$\mathcal{F} = \{(q_{INI}, \Sigma^*, q_{00}),$ $(q_{00}, \Sigma\backslash\xi/\Leftarrow, q_{10}),$ $(q_{00}, \xi/\mu, q_{01}),$
$(q_{01}, \mu/\rightarrow, q_{02}),$ $(q_{02}, \Sigma\backslash\alpha/\Leftarrow, q_{10}),$ $(q_{02}, \alpha/\Gamma, q_{03}),$
$(q_{03}, \Gamma,\rightarrow, q_{04}),$ $(q_{04}, \Sigma\backslash\mu/\Leftarrow, q_{10}),$ $(q_{04}, \mu/\xi, q_{05}),$
$(q_{05}, \mu/\rightarrow, q_{06}),$ $(q_{06}, \Sigma\backslash\Gamma/\Leftarrow, q_{10}),$ $(q_{06}, \Gamma/\alpha, q_{07}),$
$(q_{07}, \alpha/\rightarrow, q_{08}),$ $(q_{08}, \Lambda/\vdash, q_{00}),$ $(q_{10}, \Sigma\backslash\alpha/\Leftarrow, q_{20}),$
$(q_{10}, \alpha/\mu, q_{11}),$ $(q_{11}, \mu/\rightarrow, q_{12}),$ $(q_{12}, \Sigma\backslash\mu/\Leftarrow, q_{20}),$
$(q_{12}, \mu/\Gamma, q_{13}),$ $(q_{13}, \Gamma/\rightarrow, q_{14}),$ $(q_{14}, \Sigma\backslash\Gamma/\Leftarrow, q_{20}),$
$(q_{14}, \Gamma/\alpha, q_{15}),$ $(q_{15}, \alpha/\rightarrow, q_{16}),$ $(q_{16}, \Lambda/\vdash, q_{00}),$
$(q_{20}, \Sigma\backslash\beta/\Leftarrow, q_{30}),$ $(q_{20}, \beta/\alpha, q_{21}),$ $(q_{21}, \alpha/\rightarrow, q_{22}),$
$(q_{22}, \Sigma\backslash\mu/\Leftarrow, q_{30}),$ $(q_{22}, \mu/\mu, q_{23}),$ $(q_{23}, \mu/\rightarrow, q_{24}),$
$(q_{24}, \Lambda/\beta, q_{25}),$ $(q_{25}, \beta/\rightarrow, q_{26}),$ $(q_{26}, \Lambda/|, q_{00}),$
$(q_{30}, \Sigma\backslash\alpha/\Leftarrow, q_{40}),$ $(q_{30}, \alpha/\beta, q_{31}),$ $(q_{31}, \beta/\rightarrow, q_{32}),$
$(q_{32}, \Sigma\backslash\alpha/\Leftarrow, q_{40}),$ $(q_{32}, \alpha/\Lambda, q_{33}),$ $(q_{33}, \Lambda/\vdash, q_{00}),$
$(q_{40}, \Sigma\backslash\beta/\Leftarrow, q_{50}),$ $(q_{40}, \beta/\Gamma, q_{41}),$ $(q_{41}, \Gamma/\rightarrow, q_{42}),$
$(q_{42}, \Sigma\backslash\beta/\Leftarrow, q_{50}),$ $(q_{42}, \beta/\Lambda, q_{43}),$ $(q_{43}, \Lambda/\vdash, q_{00}),$
$(q_{50}, \Sigma\backslash\Gamma/\Leftarrow, q_{60}),$ $(q_{50}, \Gamma/\Gamma, q_{51}),$ $(q_{51}, \Gamma/\rightarrow, q_{52}),$
$(q_{52}, \Sigma\backslash\Gamma/\Leftarrow, q_{60}),$ $(q_{52}, \alpha/\Lambda, q_{53}),$ $(q_{53}, \Lambda/\vdash, q_{00}),$
$(q_{60}, \Sigma\backslash\Gamma/\Leftarrow, q_{70}),$ $(q_{60}, \Gamma/\mu, q_{61}),$ $(q_{61}, \mu/\rightarrow, q_{62}),$
$(q_{62}, \Sigma\backslash\mu/\Leftarrow, q_{70}),$ $(q_{62}, \mu/\Gamma, q_{63}),$ $(q_{63}, \Gamma/\Lambda, q_{64}),$
$(q_{64}, \Lambda/\vdash, q_{00}),$ $(q_{70}, \Sigma\backslash\beta/\Leftarrow, q_{80}),$ $(q_{70}, \beta/\beta, q_{71}),$
$(q_{71}, \beta/\rightarrow, q_{72}),$ $(q_{72}, \Sigma\backslash\alpha/\Leftarrow, q_{80}),$ $(q_{72}, \alpha/\Lambda, q_{73}),$
$(q_{73}, \Lambda/\vdash, q_{00}),$ $(q_{80}, \Sigma\backslash\Gamma/\Leftarrow, q_{90}),$ $(q_{80}, \Gamma/\Lambda, q_{FIN}),$
$(q_{90}, \Lambda/\alpha, q_{91}),$ $(q_{91}, \alpha/\rightarrow, q_{92}),$ $(q_{92}, \Lambda/\vdash, q_{00})\}$

The graphical representation of C^{CS} is shown in figure 6.4.1

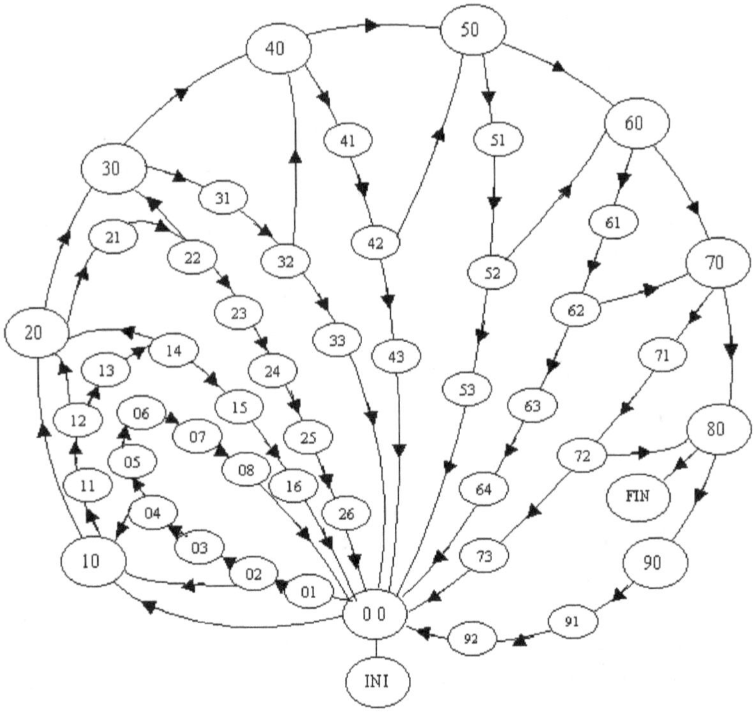

Figure 6.4.1: Graphical representation of the rewriting cyclic normal auotmaton

Proposition 6.4.1

The family of languages recognized by Turing machines is also recognized by Rewriting Cyclic Normal Automata.

Proof

This is a direct consequence of theorem 5.3.2.1.

6.4.1 Principle Of Normalization Of Automata

With a view to answering the question, in what measure does the precise notion of a normal algorithm relate to the less precise but more general notion of an algorithm in some algorithm in some alphabet, Markov proposed the principle of normalization which states:

Every algorithm in an alphabet $\mathcal{A}$ is fully equivalent relative to some normal algorithm over $\mathcal{A}$ [08].

This principle asserts that given a well defined algorithm in an alphabet $\mathcal{A}$ with a specific set of input output pairs, one can construct correspondingly an equivalent normal algorithm relative to that alphabet with the same set of input output pairs.

In what follows, we interpret this principle in terms of normal automata [Refer to definitions 6.3.3 and 6.3.4] and a more general notion of a family of automata over an alphabet.

In [25], Schutzenberger defines the notion of a family of automata over an alphabet in the following manner:

Definition 6.4.1.1

A family of automata Ξ over an alphabet $\mathcal{A}$ consists of machines characterized by the following restrictions:

(i) Their output consists in the acceptance (or rejection) of input words belonging to the set F of all words in the letters of a finite alphabet A.

(ii) The automaton operates sequentially on the successive letters of the input word without the possibility of coming back on the previously read letters and, thus, all the information to be used in the further computations has to be stored in the internal memory.

(iii) The unbounded part of the memory, V_N, is the finite dimensional vector space of the vectors with N integral coordinates; this part of the memory plays only a passive role and all the control of the automaton is performed by the finite part.

(iv) Only elementary arithmetic operations are used and the amount of computation allowed for each input letter is bounded in terms of the total number of additions and subtractions.

(v) The rule by which it is decided to accept or reject a given input word is submitted to the same type of requirements and it involves only the storage of a finite amount of information.

It is in this context, we propose the following principle of normalization of automata, which relates the notion of normal automata with that of a family of automata.

Every automaton A belonging to the family of automata Ξ over a finite alphabet $\mathcal{A}$ is fully equivalent relative to A to some normal automaton over $\mathcal{A}$.

This principle highlights the following conjecture:

Every family of automata over a potentially realizable alphabet is normalisable and therefore it is impossible to construct a nonnormalisable automaton.

6.4.2 Construction Of Flower Automata For Transcriptions Of Normal Algorithms

Berstel and Perrin have described in [03], the construction of a universal automaton known as *Flower Automaton*, which recognizes a submonoid of $\mathcal{A}^*$ where $\mathcal{A}$ is an alphabet. The importance of this type of automaton lies in the fact that it allows a new state $q_* = (\Lambda, \Lambda)$ in its construction by virtue of which one could describe and type of finite state machine as a flower automaton. The null string Λ is the identity element of the submonoid, which is recognized by it.

In this subsection, we show that transcripted versions of normal algorithms could be represented by such flower automata.

As shown in subsection 6.2, the transcription of a normal algorithm $\mathcal{N}$ is a word over the biprefix code set X = O||*O. The characteristic series of X denoted by $\underline{X}$ is given by

$$(\underline{X}, x) = \begin{cases} 1 & \text{if } x \in X \\ 0 & \text{else.} \end{cases}$$

A trim automaton A° [Refer to definition 6.1.3] with a unique initial and a unique final states is unambiguous if and only if its behavior |A°| [Refer to definition 6.1.5] is a characteristic series. Now let us construct an automaton $A_D(X)$ = <Q, I, T> over the alphabet $\mathcal{A}_0 = \{O \mid\}$ where $Q = \{(u, v) \in \mathcal{A}^*_0 \times \mathcal{A}^*_0 \mid uv \in X\}$, $I = \Lambda \times X$, $T = X \times \Lambda$ with edges of the type $(u, v) \xrightarrow{a} (u', v')$ such that ua = u' and v = av' and uav ∈ X. The behavior of this automaton $|A_D(X)|$ is equal to the characteristics series $\underline{X}$. $A_D(X)$ is unambiguous and it recognizes X. Now we define the flower automaton for the transcription of a normal algorithm in the following manner:

Definition 6.4.2.1

The flower automaton for X is defined as the trim part of the automaton $B_D(X)$ derived from $A_D(X)$ using the canonical construction given in definition 21.7. The introduction of a new state $q_* = (\Lambda, \Lambda)$ in the construction of B_D (X) allows only four types of edges in the flower automaton:

(i) $(u, av) \xrightarrow{a} (ua, v)$ for $uav \in X$ and $(u, v) \neq (\Lambda, \Lambda)$

(ii) $(\Lambda, \Lambda) \xrightarrow{a} (a, v)$ for $av \in X$ and $v \neq \Lambda$

(iii) $(u, a) \xrightarrow{a} (\Lambda, \Lambda)$ for $ua \in X$ and $u \neq \Lambda$

(iv) $(\Lambda, \Lambda) \xrightarrow{a} (\Lambda, \Lambda)$ for $a \in X$

Example 6.4.2.1

The flower automaton corresponding to the transcription O|OO||OO|||OO||||O is shown in figure 6.4.2.1.

Proposition 6.4.2.1

To each cyclic normal automaton, we can associate a flower automaton.

Proof

It is a direct consequence of their respective constructions and the transcribability of normal algorithms.

Every normal algorithm is transcribable by a coding morphism. One can transcribe a normal algorithm using different coding morphisms. Different coding morphisms yield different transcriptions of different lengths for the same normal algorithm. But the coding morphism that yields the shortest length transcription is the most efficient one, and this length is taken as an estimate of *complexity* of the normal algorithm.

The flower automaton pertaining to the complexity of a normal algorithm is called a *minimal flower automaton.*

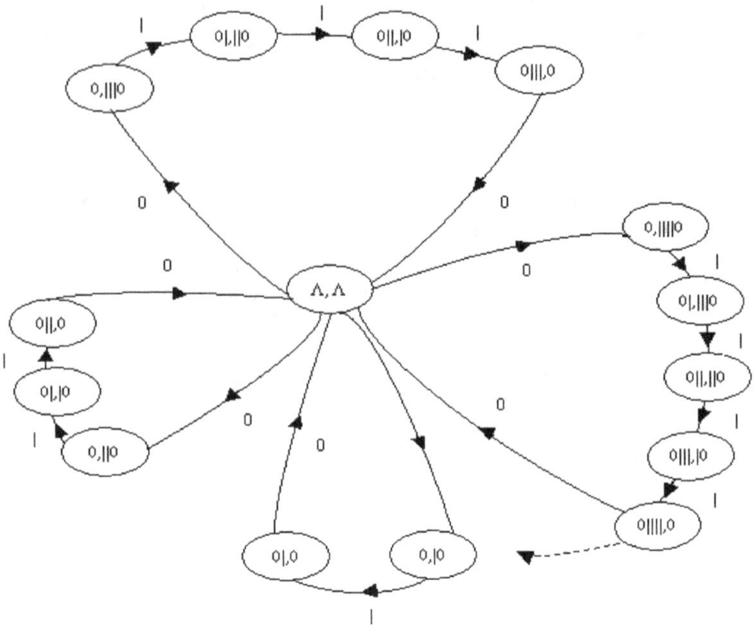

Figure 6.4.2.1: The flower automaton corresponding to the transcription O|OO||OO|||OO||||O

Part III

Abstract

This part consists of the sections 7,8,9 and 10. In this part, we consider a structure $C_{\mathfrak{R}} = < \mathcal{N}_{\mathcal{A}}, \text{o}, \simeq >$ (where $\mathcal{N}_{\mathcal{A}}$ denotes a class of normal algorithms over $\mathcal{A}$, o denotes the operation of composition and $\simeq$ denotes the relation of functional equivalence) which finitely specifies nonnumerical signal processing operations and we develop a theory for it in a language of constructive logic. In addition, we provide constructive interpretations to Lyndon-Keisler homomorphism theorem and Thampuran's extended topological filters and show that the properties of a $C_{\mathfrak{R}}$–type signal processing system could be studied with the help of either of these two.

Theory Of Constructive Signal Processing

Section 7

The Logic Of Constructive Signal Processing

The purpose of this section is to study constructive signal processing systems in the framework of a *constructive logic* introduced by Markov [40], [41], [42], [43], [44], [45], [46]. This constructive logic is built on a *hierarchical system of languages* denoted by $Я_\alpha$: $\alpha = 0, 1, 2, 3, 4, 5, \ldots, \omega, \omega|$, whose main constituents are *alphabets, words* and *normal algorithms.*

We first present a summary of the basic notions of this logic that are relevant for us and then introduce a theory Th($\mathfrak{R}$) for constructive signal processing. In later sections, we make use of this theory in the study of constructive systems in terms of homorphisms and extended topological filters.

7.1 The Languages $\{Я_\alpha\}$

7.1.1 Language $Я_0$

The starting point of Markov's logic is the language $Я_0$. A *Literoid* is a nonempty word form a one-letter alphabet. *Variables* are nonempty words from a one-letter alphabet. Literoids and variables are also known as *atoms. Verboids* are formed by concatenating literoids to verboids. The null string Λ is a verboid. By a *term* we mean either a verboid or an atom. Let us assume that there occurs a variable X in a term U. Substitution of the variable X by another term T is a permissible operation. By an *operation,* we mean the action of a normal algorithm $\mathcal{N}$ on a term. The result of the operation of substitution of X by T in U by means of a normal algorithm $\mathcal{N}$ is also a term and is denoted by $\Im\lfloor XU \square T \rfloor$ where $\square$ is an auxiliary symbol and the symbols $\lfloor$ and $\rfloor$ play the role of the left and the right parentheses respectively. For example, for any term T, $\Im\lfloor X\Lambda \square T \rfloor \cong \Lambda$ where the symbol $\cong$ stands for *equal by*

E. G. Rajan, *Symbolic Computing - Signal and Image Processing*
ISBN 81-7800-047-4

definition. The notion of *result of the operation of substitution* could be extended to all the remaining languages.

An *elementary formula* is a string of the form T σ U where T and U are terms and σ is a *comparer.* By a *comparer,* we refer to any one of the symbols $=$ or $\neq$ or $\doteq$ or $\not\doteq$ where the symbols $=$ and $\neq$ compare two terms and the symbols $\doteq$ and $\not\doteq$ compare two words or verboids.

The only logical connectives that are permitted in $Я_0$ are (i) & (conjunction) and (ii) V (disjunction). The quantifier symbols $\forall$ and $\exists$ are allowed in a restricted manner. Quantifiers and connectives are called *logical symbols.* Formulas of $Я_0$ are constructed using the following rules

(i) If A is an elementary formula then it is a formula $Я_0$. We shall designate a formula of $Я_0$ as Fm0.

(ii) If A and B are Fm0's and λ is a connective, then λAB is an Fm0.

(iii) If A is an Fm0, Q is a quantifier, X is a variable, U is a term and β is a limiter (either the symbol $<$ or the symbol $>$), then the string QUβXA is an Fm0.

The variable X is allowed to be substituted only by certain words or verboids. For example, the formula $\forall U<XA$ where U is a *constant term,* expresses that every formula of the type $\Im_0\llcorner XAQ\lrcorner$ is true where Q is the verboidal prefix of the *meaning of* U. Three items are to be explained now: (i) Constant Term: It is either the null string Λ or of the form PQ where P is a constant term and Q is a literoid. (ii) The meaning of a constant term is always a verboid determined by a normal algorithm (iii) $\Im_0\llcorner XAQ\lrcorner$ is the result of substituting the variable X by a term Q in the formula A which is also a formula. To be more specific, the quantification in an Fm0 is to be understood as that which allows the bounded variable to range in a predetermined, bounded set of words or verboids only.

The notion of a *parameter* is important in constructive logic. By parameters we mean the variables that occur either in an elementary formula or in the formulas A and B contained in the formula λAB or in U and A of the formula QUβXA excluding X. The term parameter conveys the same meaning as the term *free variable* conveys in classical logic.

As a result, we have the notion of a *closed formula* in constructive logic similar to that of a *sentence* in the classical logic.

In general, a closed formula of a language Я_α is a formula without parameters as defined in Я_α. Closed formulas of a language Я_α are designated as CFα's. The set of all formulas of a language Я_α is denoted by {Fmα} and the set of closed formulas by {CFα}. {CFα} is a subset of {Fmα}. So, {CF0} is the set of all closed formulas in the languages Я_0 and it is a subset of {Fm0}.

The language Я_0 does not allow the direct use of a negation symbol in an Fm0. However, it is possible to obtain an Fm0 which is semantically a negative equivalent of another by means of a normal algorithm $\mathcal{N}^{\neg}{}_{\text{Я}0}$ whose scheme is given below:

$\mathcal{N}^{\neg}{}_{\text{Я}0}$:

Substitution Formula		Formula Number
$\alpha\xi \rightarrow \xi\alpha$	(ξ denotes every symbol of Я_0 other than $=$, $\neq$, $\doteq$ and $\not\doteq$)	(00)
$\alpha= \rightarrow =\alpha$		(01)
$\alpha\neq \rightarrow \neq\alpha$		(02)
$\alpha\doteq \rightarrow \doteq\alpha$		(03)
$\alpha\not\doteq \rightarrow \not\doteq\alpha$		(04)
$\alpha\& \rightarrow \&\alpha$		(05)
$\alpha\vee \rightarrow \vee\alpha$		(06)
$\alpha\forall \rightarrow \forall\alpha$		(07)
$\alpha\exists \rightarrow \exists\alpha$		(08)
$\alpha \rightarrow \cdot$		(09)
$\rightarrow \alpha$		(10)

7.1.2 Language Я_1

The languages Я_1 allows the construction of the formula Fm1's by means of the following rules:

(i) If A is an Fm0, then it is also an Fm1.

(ii) It λ is a connective (& or $\vee$), A and B are Fm1's then the string λAB is an Fm1 provided either A or B is certainly not an Fm0.

(iii) If X is a variable and A is an Fm1 then $\exists$XA is an Fm1.

Parameters and closed formulas are defined in the same manner as they are defined in $\mathfrak{A}_0$.

$\mathfrak{A}_1$ describes the operation of normal algorithms in some alphabet $\mathcal{A}$ in the following manner:

Let x, y and z be variables. Let us denote the translation of a normal algorithm $\mathcal{N}$ by $[\mathcal{N}]^{\mathcal{T}}$ and its transcription by $\{\mathcal{N}\}$. In the same manner, the translation of a word P is denoted by $[P]^{\mathcal{T}}$. Now, the following types of constructions are permitted:

(i) $(x\neg)_{\mathcal{N}}$ is an Fm0 without parameters different from x such that $\mathfrak{I}_0 \lfloor x(x\neg)_{\mathcal{N}}[P]^{\mathcal{T}}\rfloor$ is a valid CF0 provided the word P is not accepted by $\mathcal{N}$.

(ii) $(x \vdash y)_{\mathcal{N}}$ is an Fm0 without parameters different from x and y such that $\mathfrak{I}_0 \lfloor y \mathfrak{I}_0 \lfloor x\ (x \vdash y)_{\mathcal{N}}\ [P]^{\mathcal{T}}\ [Q]^{\mathcal{T}}\rfloor$ is a valid CF0 provided the word P is simple rewritten as Q by $\mathcal{N}$.

(iii) $(x \vdash \cdot y)_{\mathcal{N}}$ is an Fm0 without parameters different from x and y such that $\mathfrak{I}_0 \lfloor y \mathfrak{I}_0 \lfloor x(x \vdash \cdot\ y)_{\mathcal{N}}\ [P]^{\mathcal{T}}\ [Q]^{\mathcal{T}}\rfloor$ is a valid CF0 provided the word P is concludingly rewritten as Q by $\mathcal{N}$.

(iv) $(x!)_{\mathcal{N}}$ is an Fm1 without parameters different from x such that $\mathfrak{I}_1 \lfloor x(x!)_{\mathcal{N}}[P]^{\mathcal{T}}\rfloor$ is a valid CF1 provided the word P from A is accepted by $\mathcal{N}$.

(v) $(x \Rightarrow y)_{\mathcal{N}}$ is an Fm1 without parameters different from x and y such that $\mathfrak{I}_1 \lfloor y \mathfrak{I}_1 \lfloor x(x \Rightarrow y)_{\mathcal{N}}\ [P]^{\mathcal{T}}\ [Q]^{\mathcal{T}}\rfloor$ is a valid CF1 provided P is simply transformed to Q by $\mathcal{N}$.

(vi) $(x \Rightarrow \cdot y)_{\mathcal{N}}$ is an Fm1 without parameters different from x and y such that $\mathfrak{I}_1 \lfloor y \mathfrak{I}_1 \lfloor x(x \Rightarrow \cdot y)_{\mathcal{N}}\ [P]^{\mathcal{T}}\ [Q]^{\mathcal{T}}\rfloor$ is a valid CF1 provided P is concludingly transformed to Q by $\mathcal{N}$.

(vii) $(x\!: y \Rightarrow z)_{\mathcal{N}}$ is a valid Fm1 without parameters different from x, y and z so that $\mathfrak{I}_1 \lfloor z \mathfrak{I}_1 \lfloor y \mathfrak{I}_1 \lfloor x(x\!: y \Rightarrow z)\{\mathcal{N}\}\rfloor\ [Q]^{\mathcal{T}}\ [R]^{\mathcal{T}}\rfloor$ is a valid CF1 provided the verboid $[Q]^{\mathcal{T}}$ which is the translated version of the word Q from $\mathcal{A}_0 = \{O\ |\}$, is transformed to the verboid $[R]^{\mathcal{T}}$ when the transcription of $\mathcal{N}$ is applied to it.

An important notion that $\mathfrak{A}_1$ introduces is the calculus $\mathcal{C}$, which is based on the notion of *deducibility* of a CF1 from another. Let S be a finite series of CF1's (that is, a finite number of CF1's are written one after the other in the form of a string). Now we shall call a CF1: C as an immediate consequence of S only in the following cases: (i) if there is a valid CF0, (ii) if A and B are in S such that $C \doteq \& AB$, (iii) if either A or B is in S such that $C \doteq \vee AB$ and (iv) if $\Im_1\lfloor XDQ \rfloor$ is in S such that $C \doteq \exists XD$. Now the notion of deducibility is to be understood in the following manner. If S is a deduction and a series of CF1's and C is an immediate consequence from S then SC is a deduction. Obviously the null string Λ is a deduction. In general, the notion of deducibility is extended to all the remaining languages, in the sense that, for every language Я_α there is a system of rules of deduction S_α using with a CFα could be deduced from another [41].

7.1.3 Language Я_2

The language Я_2 is richer than Я_1, in the sense that, it provides rules for the use of *implication* and *negation* of 0th order and *universal quantifier* in constructing Fm2's. Implication is denoted by the symbol $\supset$. An Fm2 is constructed using the following rules:

(i) If A is an Fm1 then it is also an Fm2.
(ii) If A and B are Fm1's then $\supset AB$ is an Fm2.
(iii) If A and B are Fm2's and one of them is certainly not an Fm1 then & AB is an Fm2.
(iv) If X is a variable and A is an Fm2 then $\forall XA$ is an Fm2.

It is important to note that CF2's cannot be combined using the logical connective of disjunction. Also existential quantifiers cannot be used in the construction of Fm2's. Fm2's of the form $\supset AB$ where A and B are Fm1's are called implications of the 0th order. The implication of the 0th order is to be understood in the following manner. Let S be a series of Fm1's. Let A and B be two Fm1's. Then the Fm2: $\supset AB$ is interpreted as *for an arbitrary S,* ((S is a deduction of A) or B).

The negation of the 0th order is defined as $\neg A \simeq A\ (\neq)$ where A is an Fm1. The following are the basic deductive rules of the language Я_2:

(i) $\dfrac{A \supset AB}{B}$ (ii) $\dfrac{\supset AB \supset BC}{\supset AC}$ (iii) $\dfrac{B}{\supset AB}$

(iv) $\dfrac{\supset AB \supset AC}{\supset A\&BC}$ (v) $\dfrac{\supset AC \supset BC}{\supset \vee ABC}$ (vi) $\dfrac{DE}{\&DE}$

(vii) $\dfrac{\&DE}{D}$ (viii) $\dfrac{\&DE}{E}$

(ix) $\dfrac{\mathfrak{I}_2\lfloor XHQ\rfloor \text{ for every verboid } Q}{\forall XH}$ (x) $\dfrac{\forall XH}{\mathfrak{I}_2\lfloor XHQ\rfloor}$

(xi) $\dfrac{\forall X\supset GA}{\supset\exists XHA}$

In addition to these rules, Я_2 provides a *semiformal system* S_2 consisting of thirteen rules of deduction, which decide the deducibility of a CF2 from another.

Let K be a CF2. Let Y be a condition, which could be meaningfully imposed on a CF2. Then Y is called *K-inductive* if the following thirteen conditions hold:

(i) K satisfies Y.
(ii) Every valid CF2 satisfies Y.
(iii) Whenever the CF2's A and $\supset AB$ satisfy Y, B satisfies Y.
(iv) Whenever the CF2's $\supset AB$ and $\supset BC$ satisfy Y, then $\supset AC$ satisfies Y.
(v) Whenever the CF2 B satisfies Y, then $\supset AB$ satisfies Y.
(vi) Whenever the CF2's $\supset AB$ and $\supset AC$ satisfy Y, then $\supset A\&BC$ satisfies Y.
(vii) Whenever the CF2's $\supset AC$ and $\supset BC$ satisfy Y, then $\supset\vee ABC$ satisfies Y.
(viii) Whenever D and E satisfy Y, then the CF2 & DE satisfies Y.
(ix) Whenever the CF2 & DE satisfies Y, then the CF2 D satisfies Y.
(x) Whenever the CF2 & DE satisfies Y, then the CF2 E satisfies Y.
(xi) Whenever we have a general method enabling us to establish for fixed X and H and for any verboid Q that the CF2: $\mathfrak{I}_2\lfloor XHQ\rfloor$ satisfies Y, then CF2 $\forall XH$ satisfies Y.
(xii) Whenever the CF2 $\forall XH$ satisfies Y, then CF2 $\mathfrak{I}_2\lfloor XHQ\rfloor$ satisfies Y.
(xiii) Whenever the CF2 $\forall X\supset GA$ satisfies Y, then the CF2 $\supset\exists XGA$ satisfies Y.

Theorem 7.1.3.1 [42]

If a condition Y is K-inductive, then every CF2 which is deducible from K satisfies the condition Y.

7.1.4 Language $Я_3$

This language is just an extension of $Я_2$ in the sense that it provides rules for the use of implication and negation of the first order. They are denoted by the symbols ⊃| and ¬| respectively. An Fm3 is constructed using the following rules:

(i) If A is an Fm2 then it is also an Fm3.
(ii) If A and B are Fm2's then ⊃|AB is an Fm3.
(iii) If C and D are Fm3's such that one of them is certainly not an Fm2, then & AB is an Fm3.
(iv) If X is a variable and E is an Fm3 but not an Fm2 then ∀XE is an Fm3.

The negation of the first order is defined as ¬|B ≅ ⊃|B(≠) where B is an Fm2.

Theorem 7.1.4.1 [43]

$$\frac{\neg|\neg A}{A} \quad \text{where A is arbitrary Fm1.}$$

¬A is a quasi elementary formula since ¬A is nothing but ⊃A(≠). The above theorem is known as *Markov's Principle of Constructive Choice.*

Let K be a CF3 and Y be a condition, which could be meaningfully imposed on K. Then Y is called 3K-inductive if thirteen conditions similar to the ones given in $Я_2$ hold. Now, if Y is 3K-inductive, then every CF3 which is 3-deducible [Refer to deducibility of CF2's] from K satisfies the condition Y. The notion of K-induction could be extended to all the remaining languages in a similar manner.

7.1.5 Languages $Я_4$, $Я_5$, ...

The languages $Я_4$, $Я_5$ and so on, are the generalizations of the successively extended languages $Я_0$, $Я_1$, $Я_2$ and $Я_3$. Any language $Я_3$ is identified by $Я_N$: N = 4, 5, 6, ... with the corresponding system of deductive rules S_N : N = 4, 5, 6, ... For every transition from a language $Я_N$ to its successor $Я_{N\,|}$, a new kind of implication emerges, an implication of order N-1. Thus a language $Я_N$ accumulates implications of orders 0 to N-2. However such an abundance of implications does no harm since they agree among themselves. An FmN| is constructed in the strength of the following rules:

(i) If A is an FmN then it is also an FmN|.
(ii) If A and B are FmN's then ⊃(N-1)AB is an FmN|.
(iii) If C and D are FmN|'s such that one of them is certainly not an FmN, then &CD is an FmN|.
(iv) If X is a variable and E is an FmN| but not an FmN then ∀XE is an FmN|.

N|-deducibility and N|K-induction are defined in exactly the same manner as they are defined in the previous languages.

In general, the negation of order N in the language $Я_{N||}$ is defined as ¬NA ≅ ⊃NA (≠) where A is an FmN|.

Theorem 7.1.5.1 [44]

$$\frac{\neg M \neg NA}{A}$$ (Proof is omitted here)

7.1.6 Language $Я_\omega$

The notion of *abstraction of potential realizability* [45] allows one to unite all the languages so far seen, to form what is known as $Я_\omega$. An Fmω is constructed as per the following rules:

(i) If A is an Fm1 then it is also an Fmω.
(ii) If C and D are Fmω's and one of them is certainly not an Fm1 then & CD is an Fmω
(iii) If E and F are Fmω's then ⊃EF is an Fmω.
(iv) If X is a variable and E is an Fmω then ∀XE is an Fmω.

Fmω's are known as *normal formulas.* Two Fmw's cannot be combined disjunctively nor they be existentially quantified. However, $Я_\omega$ allows the use of quasi disjunction and quasi existential quantifier in the construction of Fmω's. We shall denote quasi disjunction by the symbol $\underline{\vee}$ and the quasi existential quantifier by the symbol $\underline{\exists}$ and agree to their definitions as given in [21], so that the following hold:

(i) $\underline{\vee}$AB ≅ ¬&¬A¬B where A and B are Fmω's
(ii) $\underline{\exists}$XA ≅ ¬∀X¬A where X is a variable and A is an Fmω.

7.1.7 Language $Я_{\omega|}$

This language is an extension of $Я_{\omega}$ and is closed under all traditional logical connectives. Fmω|'s are constructed by virtue of the following rules:

(i) If A is an Fmω then it is also an Fmω|.

(ii) If A and B are Fmω's but one of them is certainly not an Fmω and λ is a logical connective either ⊃ or & then λAB is an Fmω|.

(iii) If A is an Fmω| but not an Fmω and X is a variable then ∀XA is an Fmω|.

(iv) If A is an Fmω| but not an Fm1 and X is a variable then the string ∃XA is an Fmω|.

The language $Я_1$ is a sublanguage of $Я_{\omega|}$. For any two Fmω|'s A and B in which one is certainly not an Fm1 the disjunctive formula ∨AB is defined as ∨AB $\cong$ ∃z&⊃(z=)A⊃(z≠)B where z is a variable other than the parameters of A and B.

The negation is defined as ¬A $\cong$ ⊃A(≠) where A is an Fmω|.

The rule Modus Ponens holds here: *Whenever the CFω|'s* A and B are such that both A and ⊃AB are true in $Я_{\omega|}$ *then* B *is also true in* $Я_{\omega|}$.

The principle of constructive choice is stated in $Я_{\omega|}$ as

⊃∀X∨D¬D⊃¬¬∃XD∃XD

The above principle plays the fundamental role in the formulation of a constructive theory for signals and systems as we shall see in the next subsection.

7.2 Normal Algorithmic Signal Processing Systems Represented By a Model $C_{\mathfrak{R}}$ Of the Constructive Theory Th($\mathfrak{R}$)

Let {CFα} be the set of closed formulas of the language $Я_{\alpha}$. Following standard terminology [20], any subset of {CFα} is known as a *constructive theory,* Φ_{α}, of that language, and a structure M is a model of that constructive theory Φ_{α} if every closed formula of the theory holds in M also. Consider now a constructive theory, Th($\mathfrak{R}$), defined by the following five closed formulas that are $Я_{\omega|}$-provable.

Th($\Re$):

(i)	Fmω|.1	$\supset\neg\neg\, !\mathcal{N}\lfloor P\rfloor\, !\mathcal{N}\lfloor P\rfloor$
(ii)	Fmω|.2	$\supset\mathcal{N}\lfloor P\rfloor \doteq Q!\mathcal{N}\lfloor P\rfloor$
(iii)	Fmω|.3	$\supset\forall xyz\Im_1\lfloor z\Im_1\lfloor y\Im_1\lfloor x(x\!: y\Rightarrow z)\{\mathcal{N}_i\}\rfloor\, [P]^{T}\rfloor\, [Q]^{T}\rfloor$ $\doteq\Im_1\lfloor z\Im_1\lfloor y\Im_1\lfloor x(x\!: y\Rightarrow z)\{\mathcal{N}_j\}\rfloor\, [P]^{T}\rfloor\, [Q]^{T}\rfloor$ $\{\mathcal{N}_i\}\simeq\{\mathcal{N}_j\}$
(iv)	Fmω|.4	$\supset\forall XYZ\ \&\&\ \mathcal{N}_i\lfloor X\rfloor \doteq Y\mathcal{N}_j\lfloor Y\rfloor \doteq Z\ \mathcal{N}_k\lfloor X\rfloor$ $\doteq Z\mathcal{N}_j\lfloor\mathcal{N}_i\lfloor X\rfloor\,\rfloor \doteq\mathcal{N}_k\lfloor X\rfloor$
(v)	Fmω|.5	$\supset\forall XYZ\ \&\&\ \mathcal{N}_i\lfloor X\rfloor \doteq Y\ \mathcal{N}_j\lfloor X\rfloor \doteq Z\mathcal{N}_k\lfloor X\rfloor$ $\doteq YZ\mathcal{N}_i\lfloor X\rfloor\,\mathcal{N}_j\lfloor X\rfloor \doteq\mathcal{N}_k\lfloor X\rfloor$

Now, we denote as $C_{\Re}$, the class of signal processing normal algorithms and show that $C_{\Re}$ in a model of Th($\Re$). Fmω|.1 is a different version of Markov's principle of constructive choice. According to this principle, if the assertion of the inapplicability of a normal algorithm $\mathcal{N}$ to some specific word P is refuted then $\mathcal{N}$ is applicable to P. By *applicability definiteness* of a normal algorithm $\mathcal{N}$ to string P, we mean the effective use of at least one of the substitution formulas of the scheme of $\mathcal{N}$ in rewriting P. The *applicability definiteness* (a-definiteness) of $\mathcal{N}$ to P is generally expressed as $!\mathcal{N}$(P). The basic supporting argument underlying Fmω|.1 is the notion of abstraction of potential realizability. By virtue of this notion, if the antecedent $\neg\neg!\mathcal{N}\lfloor P\rfloor$ is accepted then the process of applying $\mathcal{N}$ to P cannot continue forever and so it is possible to obtain the result of applying $\mathcal{N}$ to P by actually carrying out the operation of this algorithm step by step waiting for the conclusion of this operation. Since computation time and storage space are not considered to be the limiting factors in carrying out normal algorithmic signal processing operations, formula Fmω|.1 holds for $C_{\Re}$. Fmω|.2 is interpreted in the following manner: A normal algorithm $\mathcal{N}$ is said to be a-definite for a word P only when $\mathcal{N}$ is applicable to P and the process of applying it to P terminates either naturally or by a terminal substitution formula and the output Q is a word other than P. An important question that arises here is of immediate concern to us. Does Q indicate the *desired output* in $\mathcal{N}\lfloor P\rfloor \doteq Q$ of the formula Fmω.2? The answer is negative, because the a-definiteness of a normal algorithm for a word does not guarantee the transformed word to be the desired output due to the intended operation for which the very scheme has been constructed. For example, let us consider a normal algorithm $\mathcal{N}$ over an alphabet $\mathcal{A}$, whose scheme is constructed with the purpose of carrying out a specific operation on words from $\mathcal{A}$. Let us assume that this scheme contains the simple substitution formula $\rightarrow \alpha$. Then $\mathcal{N}$ is a-definite for every word in the free monoid $\mathcal{A}^*$ But a-definiteness of $\mathcal{N}$ to the free monoid does not imply that every word of the free monoid is transformed to the relevant output due to the intended operation. In order to overcome this difficulty, we shall introduce here the notion of *successive applicability* of a normal algorithm. A normal algorithm $\mathcal{N}$ is said to be *successful applicability definite* (sa-definite) for a word P only when the result of applying $\mathcal{N}$ to P is the *desired output* that satisfies the purpose for which the scheme of $\mathcal{N}$ has been constructed. sa-definiteness of a normal algorithm implies its a-definiteness. But the converse in not true always. We shall explain this by means of an example. Let us consider the alphabet $\mathcal{A}_2$ = {O | - /}. A word Q from this alphabet is said to represent a valid rational number q if Q is of the form R/S, where R and S are words that represent integers. An integer is a word O or any word made up of the only letter | with or without the symbol – left adjoined to it. For example, the word -||| represents the integer –3. The normal algorithm $\mathcal{N}_Q^{INV}$ whose scheme is given below, is sa-definite for every valid rational number q of the R/S in the sense that, the result of its application to Q$\doteq$R/S is the desired output S/R.

<table>
<tr><td>$\mathcal{N}_Q^{INV}$:</td><td colspan="3">Substitution formula</td><td>Formula number</td></tr>
<tr><td></td><td>O/</td><td>→</td><td>O</td><td>(00)</td></tr>
<tr><td></td><td>O|</td><td>→</td><td>O</td><td>(01)</td></tr>
<tr><td></td><td>/-</td><td>→</td><td>-/</td><td>(02)</td></tr>
<tr><td></td><td>|-</td><td>→</td><td>-|</td><td>(03)</td></tr>
<tr><td></td><td>α-</td><td>→</td><td>-α</td><td>(04)</td></tr>
<tr><td></td><td>αα</td><td>→</td><td>β</td><td>(05)</td></tr>
<tr><td></td><td>βα</td><td>→</td><td>β</td><td>(06)</td></tr>
<tr><td></td><td>β/</td><td>→</td><td>/β</td><td>(07)</td></tr>
<tr><td></td><td>βO</td><td>→</td><td>Oβ</td><td>(08)</td></tr>
<tr><td></td><td>β|</td><td>→</td><td>|β</td><td>(09)</td></tr>
<tr><td></td><td>α||</td><td>→</td><td>|α|</td><td>(10)</td></tr>
<tr><td></td><td>α|/</td><td>→</td><td>/α|</td><td>(11)</td></tr>
<tr><td></td><td>α/|</td><td>→</td><td>|α/</td><td>(12)</td></tr>
<tr><td></td><td>β</td><td>→</td><td>·</td><td>(13)</td></tr>
<tr><td></td><td></td><td>→</td><td>α</td><td>(14)</td></tr>
</table>

Let us consider two strings Q = -|||/|||| and Q' = -|||/ and apply $\mathcal{N}_Q^{INV}$ to Q and Q' independently. Now, $\mathcal{N}_Q^{INV}(-|||/||||) \doteq -||||/|||$. So, $\mathcal{N}_Q^{INV}$ is sa-definite for Q. On the other hand, $\mathcal{N}_Q^{INV}(-|||/) \doteq -/|||$. This proves that $\mathcal{N}_Q^{INV}$ is certainly a-definite but not sa-definite for Q'. Since all constructive signal processing operations of our interest consist of normal algorithms which are sa-definite for input strings corresponding to admissible signals, proposition 7.2.1 is true for $C_{\mathfrak{R}}$. This means Fmω|.2 is valid for $C_{\mathfrak{R}}$. Fmω|.3 describes the operational equivalence between two normal algorithms $\mathcal{N}_i$ and $\mathcal{N}_j$ over an alphabet $\mathcal{A}$, when the result of the operation of $\mathcal{N}_i$ on a word P is the same as the result of the operation of $\mathcal{N}_j$ on the same word P. More precisely Fmω|.3 is read as: if the result of the operation of the transcription of a normal algorithm $\mathcal{N}_i$ in $\mathcal{A}^*_O$ on a word P from an alphabet $\mathcal{A}$, transforming the translated verboid of P in $\mathcal{A}^*_O$ into the translated verboid of Q in $\mathcal{A}^*_O$ is graphically equivalent to the result of the operation of the transcription of a normal algorithm $\mathcal{N}_j$ and $\mathcal{A}^*_O$ on the same word P transforming its translated verboid into the same translated verboid of Q in $\mathcal{A}^*_O$, then the transcripted verboid of $\mathcal{N}_i$ is operationally equivalent to the transcripted verboid of $\mathcal{N}_j$. Using Fmω|.2 we obtain two formulas from Fmω|.3: (i) $\supset \mathcal{N}_i \lfloor P \rfloor \doteq Q!\mathcal{N}_i \lfloor P \rfloor$ and (ii) $\supset \mathcal{N}_j \lfloor P \rfloor \doteq Q!\mathcal{N}_j \lfloor P \rfloor$. Now, one can construct another normal algorithm $\mathcal{N}_k$ over $\mathcal{A} \cup \{*\}$ such that the formula $\mathcal{N}_k \lfloor \mathcal{N}_i \lfloor P \rfloor * \mathcal{N}_j \lfloor P \rfloor \rfloor \doteq \Lambda$ is valid only when $\mathcal{N}_i$ and $\mathcal{N}_j$ are functionally equivalent. Fmω|.3 asserts that a particular signal processing operation could be realized by any one of the functionally equivalent constructive systems. This allows us to name a constructive signal processing system pertaining to a particular operation by an abstract label. For example, let us agree that the abstract label $\mathfrak{R}^{CON}$ refers to a constructive system which implements linear convolution of nonnegative integer sequences. This does not mean that $\mathfrak{R}^{CON}$ refers only to the scheme given in subsection 4.2 [49]. Thus we see that Fmω|.3 is valid for $C_{\mathfrak{R}}$. Fmω|.4 and Fmω|.5 describe the operations of *composition* and *union* of normal algorithms respectively. Already in subsection 2.3.3 and in section 4, we have seen how various signal processing operations could be realized by means of constructive systems consisting of normal algorithms combined in an admissible manner by virtue of composition and union theorems. So, Fmω|.4 and Fmω|.5 are valid for $C_{\mathfrak{R}}$.

Thus with $C_{\mathfrak{R}}$ as model of Th($\mathfrak{R}$), we now have a formal basis for the study of the structural properties of $C_{\mathfrak{R}}$-type constructive signal processing systems.

Section 8

Homomorphisms In the Theory Of Constructive Signal Processing

Abstract

Homomorphisms play an important role in the study of systems. One of the important functions of homomorphisms is that they allow us to connect the results of one class of systems to those of an apparently different class of systems. A typical example of such connection to be found in classical systems theory is that provided in Steiglitz [53], where it is shown that the theory of continuous-time and discrete-time systems are connected to each other through a homomorphism induced by the bilinear transformation between the Hilbert spaces $L^2(-\infty,\infty)$ and $\ell_2(-\infty,\infty)$ What such a homomorphism essentially shows is that certain operations, relations and statements relating to these operations and relations are preserved under a particular mapping from $L^2(-\infty, \infty)$ to $\ell_2(-\infty,\infty)$.

One important question that arises about homomorphisms in general is: Are there any general conditions that operations and relations and statements involving them must satisfy so that they are preserved under homomorphisms? One way to deal with this question is that of Lyndon [39] who handles it in the framework of logic and algebra.

Since we are dealing with the notion of signals & systems in logical terms, Lyndon's results are directly relevant to us. In this section, we reformulate Lyndon's homomorphism theorem in terms of constructive mathematical logic and investigate its applications for normal algorithms and constructive signal processing systems.

We begin by listing out in the following subsection 8.1, a few relevant properties of various $C_{\Re}$-type constructive signal processing systems. Later we refer to this list.

E. G. Rajan, *Symbolic Computing - Signal and Image Processing*
ISBN 81-7800-047-4

8.1 A Short List Of Constructive Logical Formulas Pertaining To the Model $C_{\mathfrak{R}}$

Table 8.1.1 Constructive logical formulas

Sl. No.	Properties of $C_{\mathfrak{R}}$ relative to an alphabet	Constructive logical formula
01	Associated of words / verboids under concatenation operation. [Let $\mathcal{N}^c$ be the normal algorithm which would concatenate a word to another]	$\forall XYZ\mathcal{N}^c\lfloor \mathcal{N}^c\lfloor XY\rfloor Z\rfloor \doteq \mathcal{N}^c\lfloor X\mathcal{N}^c\lfloor YZ\rfloor\rfloor$
02	Concatenation of the identity element (Λ) to a word .	$\forall X\ \mathcal{N}^c\lfloor X\Lambda\rfloor \doteq \mathcal{N}^c\lfloor \Lambda X\rfloor \doteq X$
03	Definition of the relation V is a factor of X [Relation symbol: $\preccurlyeq$]	$\supset\forall X\exists UVW(X\doteq UVW)V \preccurlyeq X$
04	Reflexivity of the relation $\preccurlyeq$	$\forall X(X\preccurlyeq X)$
05	Antisymmetry of the relation $\preccurlyeq$	$\supset\forall XY\&(X\preccurlyeq Y)(Y\preccurlyeq X)(X\doteq Y)$
06	Transitivity of the relation $\preccurlyeq$	$\supset\forall XYZ\ \&\ (X\preccurlyeq Y)\ (Y\preccurlyeq Z)\ (X\preccurlyeq Z)$
07	Definition of the relation V is a proper left factor of X. [Relation symbol: <] [In general, the relation left factor of is denoted by the symbol : ≤]	$\supset\forall X\exists VW\ \&\ (X\doteq VW)\ (W\not\doteq\Lambda)\ (V<X)$
08	Transitivity of the relation <	$\supset\forall XYZ\ \&\ (X<Y)\ (Y<Z)\ (X<Z)$
09	Definition of the relation W is a proper right factor of X [Relation symbol: >]	$\supset\forall X\exists VW\ \&\ (X\doteq VW)\ (V\not\doteq\Lambda)\ (W>X)$
10	Transitivity of the relation >	$\supset\forall XYZ\ \&\ (X>Y)\ (Y>Z)\ (X>Z)$
11	Definition of the relation of comparability of left factors. [Relation symbol: $\underline{><}$]	$\supset\supset\forall X\exists VW\ \&\ (V\le X)\ (W\le X)\ V(V\le W)\ (W\le V)\ (V\ \underline{><}\ W)$
12	Symmetry of the relation $\underline{><}$	$\supset\forall UV\ (U\ \underline{><}\ V)\ (V\ \underline{><}\ W)$
13	Transitivity of the relation $\underline{><}$	$\supset\forall UVW\ \&\ (U\ \underline{><}\ V)\ (V\ \underline{><}\ W)(U\ \underline{><}\ W)$
14	Definition of the relation of graphical equivalence [Relation symbol: $\doteq$]	$\supset\forall XY\&\supset\forall Z\ (Z\le X)\ (Z\le Y)\ \supset\forall Z'(Z'\ge X)\ (Z'\ge Y)\ (X\doteq Y)$
15	Reflexivity of the relation $\doteq$	$\forall X\ (X\doteq X)$

16	Symmetry of the relation $\doteq$	$\supset\forall XY(X \doteq Y)(Y \doteq X)$
17	Transitivity of the relation $\doteq$	$\supset\forall XYZ\&(X \doteq Y)(Y \doteq Z)(X \doteq Z)$
18	Definition of the equi-divisibility of a free monoid	$\supset\forall VV'\exists WW'\&(V \geq\leq V')(VW \doteq V'W')\vee\exists S(V \doteq V'S)\exists T(V' \doteq VT)$
19	Invariance of words / verboids by the operation of double inversion. [Let $\mathcal{N}^{\sim}$ be the normal algorithm which would invert a word].	$\forall W\, \mathcal{N}^{\sim}\lfloor \mathcal{N}^{\sim}\lfloor W\rfloor\rfloor \doteq W$
20	Inversion of concatenation of two words / verboids is the reverse concatenation of their inversions	$\forall VW\, \mathcal{N}^{\sim}\lfloor \mathcal{N}^{C}\lfloor VW\rfloor\rfloor \doteq \mathcal{N}^{C}\lfloor \mathcal{N}^{\sim}\lfloor W\rfloor \mathcal{N}^{\sim}\lfloor V\rfloor\rfloor$
21	Inversion of a proper left factor of a word / verboid corresponds to the proper right factor of the inverted word.	$\supset\forall VW(V < W)(\mathcal{N}^{\sim}\lfloor V\rfloor > \mathcal{N}^{\sim}\lfloor W\rfloor)$
22	Definition of the conjugacy relation between two words [Relation symbol $\lhd$]	$\supset\forall XY\&\exists VW(X \doteq VW)(Y \doteq WV)(X \lhd Y)$
23	Reflexivity of the relation $\lhd$	$\supset\forall X(X \lhd X)$
24	Symmetry of the relation $\lhd$	$\supset\forall XY(X \lhd Y)(Y \lhd X)$
25	Transitivity of the relation $\lhd$	$\supset\forall XYZ\&(X \lhd Y)(Y \lhd Z)(X \lhd Z)$
26	Definition of the relation elementary transformation of between two words / verboids by a normal algorithm $\mathcal{N}$ [Relation symbol: $\vdash_{\mathcal{N}}$]	$\supset\exists VW\forall XY(\mathcal{N}\lfloor XVY\rfloor \doteq XWY)(V \vdash_{\mathcal{N}} W)$
27	Reflexivity of the relation $\vdash_{\mathcal{N}}$	$\forall X(X \vdash_{\mathcal{N}} X)$
28	Antisymmetry of the relation $\vdash_{\mathcal{N}}$	$\supset\forall XY\&(X \vdash_{\mathcal{N}} Y)(Y \vdash_{\mathcal{N}} X)(X \doteq Y)$
29	Transitivity of the relation $\vdash_{\mathcal{N}}$	$\supset\forall XYZ\&(X \vdash_{\mathcal{N}} Y)(Y \vdash_{\mathcal{N}} Z)(X \vdash_{\mathcal{N}} Z)$
30	Definition of the relation transformation of between words / verboids by virtue of a normal algorithm $\mathcal{N}$. [relation symbol: $\models_{\mathcal{N}}$]	$\supset\forall XY\mathcal{N}\lfloor X\rfloor \doteq Y(X \models_{\mathcal{N}} Y)$
31	Reflexivity of the relation $\models_{\mathcal{N}}$	$\forall X(X \models_{\mathcal{N}} X)$
32	Antisymmetry of the relation $\models_{\mathcal{N}}$	$\supset\forall XY\&(X \models_{\mathcal{N}} Y)(Y \models_{\mathcal{N}} X)(X \doteq Y)$

33	Transitivity of the relation $\models_{\mathcal{N}}$	$\supset\forall XYZ\&(X\models_{\mathcal{N}}Y)$ $(Y\models_{\mathcal{N}}Z)\,(X\models_{\mathcal{N}}Z)$
34	Definition of the relation contiguity of between words / verboids by virtue of an associative calculus $\mathfrak{R}$. [Relation symbol: $\perp_{\mathfrak{R}}$]	$\supset\exists VW\forall XY\vee(\mathfrak{R}\lfloor XVY\rfloor\doteq XWY)$ $\mathfrak{R}\lfloor XWY\rfloor\doteq XVY)\,(V\perp_{\mathfrak{R}}W)$
35	Reflexivity of the relation $\perp_{\mathfrak{R}}$	$\forall X(X\perp_{\mathfrak{R}}X)$
36	Symmetry of the relation $\perp_{\mathfrak{R}}$	$\supset\forall XY(X\perp_{\mathfrak{R}}Y)\,(Y\perp_{\mathfrak{R}}X)$
37	Transitivity of the relation $\perp_{\mathfrak{R}}$	$\supset\forall XYZ\&(X\perp_{\mathfrak{R}}Y)$ $(Y\perp_{\mathfrak{R}}Z)\,(X\perp_{\mathfrak{R}}Z)$
38	Definition of the relation $\mathfrak{R}$-defined equivalence of between words / verboids by virtue of an associative calculus $\mathfrak{R}$. [Relation symbol: $\perp\!\!\!\perp_{\mathfrak{R}}$]	$\supset\forall X\mathfrak{R}\lfloor X\rfloor\doteq Y(X\perp\!\!\!\perp_{\mathfrak{R}}Y)$
39	Reflexivity of the relation $\perp\!\!\!\perp_{\mathfrak{R}}$	$\forall X(X\perp\!\!\!\perp_{\mathfrak{R}}X)$
40	Symmetry of the relation $\perp\!\!\!\perp_{\mathfrak{R}}$	$\supset\forall XY(X\perp\!\!\!\perp_{\mathfrak{R}}Y)\,(Y\perp\!\!\!\perp_{\mathfrak{R}}X)$
41	Tramsitivity of the relation $\perp\!\!\!\perp_{\mathfrak{R}}$	$\supset\forall XYZ\&(X\perp\!\!\!\perp_{\mathfrak{R}}Y)\,(Y\perp\!\!\!\perp_{\mathfrak{R}}Z)$ $(X\perp\!\!\!\perp_{\mathfrak{R}}Z)$
42	Universal applicability of the identity normal algorithm $\mathcal{N}^{ID}$	$\forall X\mathcal{N}^{ID}\lfloor X\rfloor\doteq X$
43	Universal inapplicability of the empty normal algorithm $\mathcal{N}^{NL}$	$\neg!\forall X\mathcal{N}^{NL}\lfloor X\rfloor\doteq X$
44	Universal applicability of the cyclic shifting normal algorithm $\mathcal{N}^{CS}$	$!\forall X\mathcal{N}^{CS}\lfloor X\rfloor$

The formulas given in table 8.1.1 are from different languages of $\{\text{Я}_{\alpha}\}$, and they are $\text{Я}_{\omega 1}$- provable.

8.1 A Constructive Reformulation Of Lyndon's Homomorphism Theorem And Its Impact On the Model Theoretic Study Of $C_{\mathfrak{R}}$-systems

Lyndon's homomorphism theorem asserts that if $\mathcal{U}$ is a classical algebraic system, P is a first order property true in $\mathcal{U}$ and ϕ_P is the defining logical sentence of P in the classical first order predicate calculus, then P is true in all the homomorphic images of u if and only if ϕ_P is a positive sentence [30], [39].

Now, the problem of our immediate concern is how to use Lyndon's homomorphism theorem in studying various properties of the model $C_{\mathfrak{R}}$. We shall try to solve this problem by giving a constructive interpretation of Lyndon's homomorphism theorem, and for its application to various constructive models.

To arrive at such an interpretation, we invoke Markov's important result [47] that every Я$_2$-valid closed formula is Я$_\omega$-valid, and that a closed predicate formula (constructive sentence) is deducible in the classical predicate calculus if it is valid either in Я$_2$ or in Я$_\omega$. The converse form of this result is that for every sentence that is constructed in the classical predicate calculus without using the axiom of choice and the law of excluded middle, there is a closed predicate formula which is Я$_2$-valid or Я$_\omega$-valid. Thus, if we are able to show that for the sentences that constitute Lyndon's there are corresponding Я$_2$ or Я$_\omega$-valid closed formulas, then we get an interpretation of Lyndon's homorphism theorem that we are working for.

Now examining the standard statement of Lyndon's theorem, the only term that calls for special attention is the term 'first order property'. For languages of Я$_\alpha$ we interpret this term as follows. We first, call a closed formula that express a property of a constructive system as a *Defining Constructive Sentence* (DCS). A DCS is called positive if all of its predicate symbols and normal algorithmic operations occur positively. By a first order DCS, we mean a constructive sentence (closed formula) in which quantification is done only on words and verboids.

With these clarifications, we are now in a position to proceed towards interpreting Lyndon's homomorphism theorem in the following manner.

8.1.1 Fujiwara's Version Of Lyndon's Homomorphism Theorem

Lyndon formulated the homomorphism theorem with the help of his Interpolation Theorem, which is a generalization of Craig's modified version of Gentzen's Extended Hauptsatz of Herbrand's theorem [25], [38], [39].

A simpler proof for the homomorphism theorem was given by Keisler in his paper entitled Theory of models with generalized atomic formulas [37]. The notion of generalized atomic (GA) formulas was introduced by him in order to further generalize model theoretic concepts of subsystems and homomorphisms which are natural generalizations of various notions of modern algebra. As a result, more generalized notions such as F-subsystems and F-homomorphisms appeared when a set of atomic formulas were replaced by a GA-set of formulas.

The following definitions are useful in order to understand Keisler's version of Lyndon's homomorphism theorem.

Definition 8.2.1.1 [37]

A set F of formulas of a first order language L with identity, is generalized atomic (GA) if the following conditions hold:

(i) If $f(x_1, x_2, x_3, \ldots, x_n) \in F$ and $x_1, x_2, x_3, \ldots, x_n$ are mutually distinct, then
  (1) for any variable y_1 of L, $f(y_1, x_2, x_3 \ldots\ldots, x_n) \in F$
  (2) for any constant k of L, $f(k,, x_2, x_3 \ldots\ldots, x_n) \in F$
  (1 and 2 closed under substitution)

(ii) $f \in F$ and $\vdash f \equiv g$ implies $g \in F$ (closure with respect to logical equivalence)

(iii) $x_1 = x_2 \in F$ (where x_1 and x_2 are distinct variables.)

(iv) The identically false formula $O \in F$

Definition 8.2.1.2 [37]

Let F be a GA set. Then, $\mathcal{U}$ is said to be an F-subsystem of $\mathcal{V}$ if (i) the carrier of $\mathcal{U}$ is the subset of the carrier of $\mathcal{V}$, that is, $A \subseteq B$ and (ii) for any $f \in F$, an n-tuple $<a_1, a_2, a_3, \ldots, a_n> \in A_n$ satisfies f in $\mathcal{U}$ if and only if it satisfies f in $\mathcal{V}$.

Definition 8.2.1.3 [37]

A map h from B onto A is said to be an F-homomorphism from $\mathcal{V}$ to $\mathcal{U}$ if whenever $f \in F$ and an n-tuple $<b_1, b_2, b_3, b_4, \ldots, b_n> \in B_n$ satisfies f in $\mathcal{V}$, $<hb_1, hb_2, hb_3, hb_4, \ldots, hb_n>$ satisfies f in $\mathcal{U}$. Then $\mathcal{U}$ is called an F-homomorphic image of $\mathcal{V}$.

Definition 8.2.1.4 [11]

The triple $\langle R, F, \mu \rangle$ is said to be a signature of an algebraic system if the following conditions hold: (i) $R \cap F = \phi$ and (ii) $\mu: R \cup F \rightarrow N$ (set of natural numbers), where R is the set of relations or predicate symbols, F is the set of operation or function symbols, μ is the place or arity mapping.

Definition 8.2.1.5 [11]

An algebraic system $\mathcal{U}$ of a signature $\langle R, F, \mu \rangle$ is an ordered pair $\langle A, i^{\mu} \rangle$ where A is the carrier and i^{μ} is known as the interpretation of the signature in A, which is understood in the following manner: i^{μ} is a mapping of the set $R \cup F$ into relations and operations on the set A. Similarly, if $f \in F$ then, $i^{\mu}(f)$ is a μ(r)-place relation on A. Usually, $i^{\mu}(r)$ and $i^{\mu}(f)$ are written as r^{μ} and f^{μ} .

Definition 8.2.1.6 [37]

Let us consider two algebraic systems $\mathcal{U}$ and $\mathcal{V}$ with their respective carriers A and B. Let μ be any interpretation in $\mathcal{U}$ and λ be a unique interpretation in $\mathcal{V}$ such that μ and λ agree on all variables of the language L. Then, $\mathcal{V}$ is defined as an elementary extension of $\mathcal{U}$ if for all μ and λ and a formula ϕ of L, if ϕ holds in μ then it holds in λ also. Let F be a GA set. Then, given two systems $\mathcal{U}$ and $\mathcal{V}$ we shall say that $\mathcal{V}$ is an F extension of $\mathcal{U}$ only when $\mathcal{U}$ is an F-subsystem of $\mathcal{V}$.

Keisler's generalized form of Lyndon's homomorphism theorem is as follows:

Theorem 8.2.1.3 [37]

Given an L-system $\mathcal{V}$ and a GA set F. An L-system $\mathcal{U}$ has an elementary extension which is F-homomorphic to an elementary extension of $\mathcal{V}$ if and only if every sentence positive in F which holds in $\mathcal{V}$ also holds in $\mathcal{U}$. [NOTE: L refers to the first order language of the classical logic]

Tsuyoshi Fujiwara has modified theorem 8.2.1.3 in the following manner:

Theorem 8.2.1.4 [31]

Let L be a first order language with equality. Let F be a GA set of L. Then, $\mathcal{L}$F refers to the set of all formulas constructed by using the only connectives $\wedge$ and $\vee$ and the quantifiers $\forall$ and $\exists$. Let $\mathcal{U}$ and $\mathcal{V}$ be two structures of L. Then, the following two conditions are equivalent: (i) Every sentence in $\mathcal{L}$F that holds in $\mathcal{U}$ also holds in $\mathcal{V}$. (ii) There exist an elementary extension of $\mathcal{U}^*$ of $\mathcal{U}$ and an elementary extension of $\mathcal{V}^*$ of $\mathcal{V}$ such that $\mathcal{V}^*$ is an F-morphic image of $\mathcal{U}^*$.

8.2.2 Interpretation Of Lyndon's Homorphism Theorem In Constructive Algebraic Logic

In this subsection, we propose a preservation theorem of Lyndon type, based of Fujiwara's version of Lyndon's homomorphism theorem. This preservation theorem is applicable to various $C_{\Re}$ -systems.

Firstly we require the following clarifications: Let Φ be the class of closed predicate formulas that are either $Я_2$ or $Я_\omega$-provable. Then, Φ contains the following:

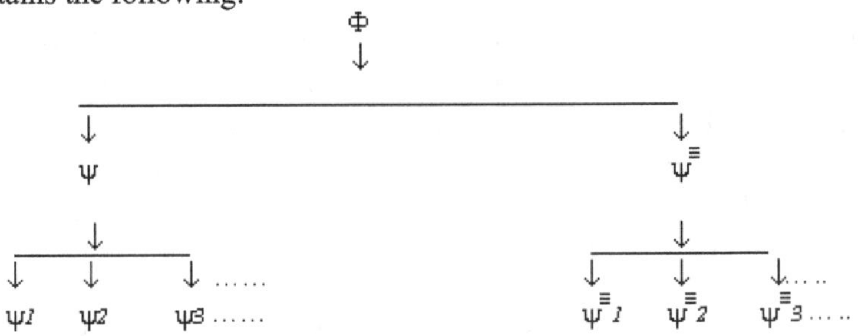

where,

ψ is the list of constructive sentences without identity $\equiv$

$\psi^{\equiv}$ is the list of constructive sentences with identity $\equiv$

ψ_1 is the list of first order constructive sentences without identity in which quantification is done only on elements of sets.

$\psi^{\equiv}_1$ is the list of first order constructive sentences with identity in which quantification is done only on elements of sets.

$\psi^{\equiv}_2$ is and ψ_2 are lists of second order constructive sentences according as whether the identity is considered or not.

For convenience let us consider an jth order constructive sentence without identity as CS_j and that with identity as CS_{ji} . For example, CS_{2i} refers to a sentence from the list $\psi^{\equiv}_2$. Let $\Phi_c = \psi_1 \cup \psi_1^{\equiv}$. Let us consider two sets of sentences from Φ_c and denote them by Δ_1 and Δ_2 . Let $\Re_1$ and $\Re_2$ with $|\Re_1|$ and $|\Re_2|$ as their carriers, be two systems defined by Δ_1 and Δ_2 respectively. Let F be the GE set of CS_1's and CS_{1i}'s of $\Delta_1 \cap \Delta_2$. Let M be a subset of $|\Re_1|$ x $|\Re_2|$. Then M is an F-morphism of $|\Re_1|$ onto $|\Re_2|$ if M satisfies the following conditions: (i) For any element a in $|\Re_1|$ there is an element b in $|\Re_2|$ such that $<a, b> \in M$. (ii) For any element b in $|\Re_2|$ there is an element a in $|\Re_1|$ such that $<a, b> \in M$ (iii) For any ϕ_i in F and any element $<a_1, b_1>, <a_2, b_2>, <a_3, b_3>, \ldots, <a_n, b_n>$ in M, $\Re_1 \models \phi_i(a_1, a_2, a_3, \ldots, a_n)$ implies $\Re_2 \models \phi_i(b_1, b_2, b_3, \ldots, b_n)$. An F-morphism is called an F-homomorphism if $<a, b>, <a, c> \in M$ implies b = c. If we consider the constructive sentences without negation from $\Delta_1 \cap \Delta_2$ which form a GE set denoted by $\mathcal{L}F$, then, M is an F-morphism of $|\Re_1|$ onto $|\Re_2|$ implies M is a $\mathcal{L}F$-morphism of $|\Re_1|$ onto $|\Re_2|$.

Using arguments analogous to those of Keisler [37], and invoking Markov's result stated earlier [47], we may now conclude with the following theorem.

Theorem 8.2.2.1

Let us consider two signal processing systems $\Re_1$ and $\Re_2$ belonging to the model $C_{\Re}$, and let $\Delta_1 \cap \Delta_2$ denote the two sets of closed predicate formulas corresponding to first order properties of the two systems respectively. Further, let $\mathcal{L}F$ denote the set of closed predicate formulas of $\Delta_1 \cap \Delta_2$ that do not contain negation. Then, every sentence in $\mathcal{L}F$ that holds for $\Re_1$ also holds for $\Re_2$.

8.2.3 The Problems Faced During the Homomorphic Study Of $C_{\Re}$.

We faced the following problems while testing theorem 8.2.2.1 by actually applying it to various $C_{\Re}$-systems.

(i) Let P be a property of a system $\Re_1$ and ϕ_P be its defining constructive sentence (DCS). If the DCS: ϕ_P happens to be negative, then by virtue of the theorem 8.2.2.1, it is not preserved in any homomorphic image. We note that implication is a defined concept, which makes use of negation and disjunction. Does it mean then all the implied statements given in the table 8.1.1 are not preserved under homomorphisms? Moreover, given a closed predicate formula, is it possible to obtain a logically equivalent GE formula from $\mathcal{L}$F?

(ii) The contrapositive form of Lyndon's theorem is difficult to be proved [30]. The converse is interpreted as that a first order property is reflected back from a homomorphic image to the real system if and only if its defining constructive sentence is necessary a negative sentence. Does it mean then, all those properties of the real system, which are preserved in a homomorphic image should be definable by a negative constructive sentence in the latter? If it is so, how can we represent, for example, associativity property of a system, which is preserved in a homomorphic image by a negative sentence?

(iii) Higher order properties of a constructive system cannot be tested for their validity in a homomorphic image by using theorem 8.2.2.1. For instance, the notions of sets and numbers are treated as normal algorithms and any quantification done over them in a closed formula will lead to a higher order constructive sentence from a $\psi_i \cup \psi^{\equiv}_i$. It is well known in classical algebraic logic that certain logical tools such as ultra filters and ultra products could be used in obtaining first order equivalents of certain higher order sentences. Is it possible to formulate and use similar constructive logical notions in obtaining first order equivalents of higher order closed formulas?

In the next section, we shall see that we can as such get rid of these problems by actually resorting to techniques established in Hammer's extended topology in the study of both first order and higher order system properties.

Section 9

A Constructive Reformulation Of Extended Topological Filters

Abstract

At the end of section 8, it was mentioned that notions like ultra filters and ultra products could be used in describing a higher order system property as a first order logical sentence. In the classical sense, ultra filters constitute a special class of topological filters over infinite spaces. These concepts of general topology are not of appropriate use in the case of $C_{\mathfrak{R}}$, because of the fact that they are primarily meant for infinite spaces, whereas the basic spaces of our concern in the study of the model $C_{\mathfrak{R}}$ are finite. In view of this fact, it is more appropriate in our case to use concepts from Hammer's extended topology, because the theory of his extended topology is applicable both to infinite and finite spaces [33], [34].

In this section, we reformulate the theory of extended topological filters in constructive logic and show that a normal algorithm over an alphabet $\mathcal{A}$ is an ordered sequence of constructive extended filter bases over the same alphabet $\mathcal{A}$.

9.1 The Notion Of A Constructive Set

Topological notions are based on the classical concept of a set, which is commonly understood as a finite or infinite collection of uniquely and simultaneously existing mathematical objects. But the concept of a set is not unique in constructive mathematics, for, it depends on the language Я$_{\alpha}$, $0 \leq \alpha \leq \omega|$, chosen to interpret the concept and hence it varies from case to case. We now present the interpretation that is to be used here.

E. G. Rajan, *Symbolic Computing - Signal and Image Processing*
ISBN 81-7800-047-4

In loose terms, a constructive set consists only of constructive objects. A mathematical object of analysis is known as a constructive object when it is represented as a word from some alphabet. The terms set and property are considered here to be synonymous. A constructive object is said to be a member of a set if it possess the corresponding property.

Definition 9.1.1 [15]

Let X_0 denote a collection of some words from an alphabet $\mathcal{A}$. Let $\mathcal{P}_0$ be some property satisfied by the elements of X_0. Then the property $\mathcal{P}_0$ is said to be potentially enumerable on X_0 if one could specify another property $\mathcal{P}_1$ which holds for those and only those elements of X_0.

Given an alphabet $\mathcal{A}$, if a variable s ranges over the entire free monoid $\mathcal{A}^*$ then s is known as a base variable. On the other hand, restricted variables are defined as those variables whose admissible values (words) are from a finite collection of words from $\mathcal{A}$. Now let us consider a one-parameter formula ϕ_α whose parameter [Refer subsection 7.1] is an individual base variable. Hereafter we shall not symbolically indicate the language in which the formulas are written. So, ϕ_α is simply written as ϕ. ϕ is called an algorithmically verifiable condition (recursive condition), if one can construct some normal algorithm which would verify the fulfillment of the condition imposed by ϕ. Let ϕ be a formula of the language $Я_{\omega|}$ of the type $\forall x\mathcal{B}(x)$ where $\mathcal{B}(x)$ is a normal formula and x is a restricted variable whose admissible values are from some finite collection, say, X of words from a specific alphabet $\mathcal{A}$. Then one can construct a normal algorithm $\mathcal{N}^{\in}$ which transforms every word chosen by x from X into O if $\mathcal{B}(x)$ holds or into O| if $\mathcal{B}(x)$ does not hold. Then X is said to be decided by the algorithm $\mathcal{N}^{\in}$. In other words, given an alphabet $\mathcal{A}$ and a property $\mathcal{P}$, one can construct a normal algorithm $\mathcal{N}^{\in}$ over $\mathcal{A}$ which would decide the set X of those constructive objects from $\mathcal{A}$ satisfying the property $\mathcal{P}$. Let us denote for convenience, this normal algorithm by $\mathcal{N}_X^{\in}$.

Borrowing the terminology from Bishop [05], we shall call this normal algorithm $\mathcal{N}_X^{\in}$ as the *preset deciding process*.

The following example illustrates how one could actually construct the preset deciding process over a specific alphabet for a given set property.

Example 9.1.1

Alphabet:	$\mathcal{A}_0 = \{ O \mid \}$
Preset to be decided:	$N = \{ O, O\mid, O\mid\mid, O\mid\mid\mid, O\mid\mid\mid\mid, \ldots \}$
Preset property:	$\mathcal{P} = \forall x \& (O \leq x) \neg (\mid O \leq x)$
	$\mathcal{P}$ is a property by which for any word x from $\mathcal{A}_0$ the symbol O is a left factor and the string $\mid O$ is not a factor.
Preset deciding process:	$\mathcal{N}_N^{\in} : \begin{cases} O\mid \to O \\ O \to \cdot \end{cases}$

[Note: This scheme transforms a word from $\mathcal{A}_0$ into a null string Λ if it satisfies $\mathcal{P}$].

A preset might contain more than one identical constructive objects, which satisfy the stipulated property whereas such a repetition is not allowed in the notion of a set. In order to overcome this difficulty, one can construct a normal algorithm $\mathcal{N}_X^{\doteq}$ which would regulate a preset X to contain only unique and nonrepetitive constructive objects, by operating on every pair of elements of X, say, y and z represented as y*z in the following manner:

(i) If $y \doteq z$, then $\mathcal{N}_X^{\doteq}(y*z) = y$ and
(ii) If $y \not\doteq z$, then $\mathcal{N}_X^{\doteq}$ is not sa-definite [Refer subsection 7.2] for y*z and the pair <y, z> remains unaltered.

Definition 9.1.2

A normal algorithm $\mathcal{N}_X^{\doteq}$ is defined as a *regulator of uniqueness in itself of a preset deciding process* $\mathcal{N}_X^{\in}$ if for every y and z from X the following holds:

$$\forall yz \& \supset (y \doteq z)\ \mathcal{N}_X^{\doteq} \lfloor y * z \rfloor \doteq y \supset (y \not\doteq z) \neg !\ \mathcal{N}_X^{\doteq} \lfloor y * z \rfloor$$

Based on certain ideas given in [15], we provide below a technique using which one can construct a normal algorithm of the type $\mathcal{N}_X^{\doteq}$.

Let $\mathcal{A}$ be an alphabet, ξ and μ be the individual generic variables, P and Q denote two words from $\mathcal{A}$, α and β be the auxiliary symbols and * be the delimiter symbol. Let us denote the graphical inverse of a word P as P^{-1}. Then one can construct an inverting normal algorithm $N^{\sim}$ whose scheme would be of the following type:

$$\mathcal{N}^{\sim}: \quad \begin{array}{rcl} \alpha\xi\mu & \rightarrow & \mu\alpha\xi \qquad (\xi, \mu \in \mathcal{A}) \\ \alpha\alpha & \rightarrow & \beta \\ \beta\alpha & \rightarrow & \beta \\ \beta\mu & \rightarrow & \mu\beta \\ \beta & \rightarrow & \cdot \\ & \rightarrow & \alpha \end{array}$$

Now let us consider P∗Q the ∗-system of words from $\mathcal{A}$. One can construct severing normal algorithms $\mathcal{N}^{*]}$ and $\mathcal{N}^{[*}$ which would transform P ∗ Q in the following manner: (i) $\mathcal{N}^{*]}$ (P∗Q) $\doteq$ Q and (ii) $\mathcal{N}^{*]}$(P∗Q) $\doteq$ P. The schemes of both $\mathcal{N}^{*]}$ and $\mathcal{N}^{[*}$ are given below:

$$\mathcal{N}^{*]}: \quad \begin{array}{rcl} \mu * & \rightarrow & * \qquad (\mu \in \mathcal{A}) \\ * & \rightarrow & \cdot \end{array}$$

$$\mathcal{N}^{[*}: \quad \begin{array}{rcl} *\mu & \rightarrow & * \qquad (\mu \in \mathcal{A}) \\ * & \rightarrow & \cdot \end{array}$$

Using the composition theorem, [Refer to theorem 2.3.3.1] one can construct a normal algorithm $\mathcal{N}^{*]\sim}$ such that for any ∗-system P ∗ Q of words from $\mathcal{A}$, the following hold: (i) $\mathcal{N}^{*]\sim}$(P∗Q) ≃ $\mathcal{N}^{\sim}$($\mathcal{N}^{*]}$(P∗Q)) and (ii) $\mathcal{N}^{*]}$(P∗Q) $\doteq$ Q^{-1}. Using union theorem, [Refer to theorem 2.3.3.2 in [49]] one can construct a normal algorithm $\mathcal{N}^{T}$ such that the following hold for any P*Q:

(i) $\mathcal{N}^{T}$(P*Q) ≃ $\mathcal{N}^{[*}$(P∗Q)* $\mathcal{N}^{*]}$ (P∗Q) and (ii) $\mathcal{N}^{T}$(P*Q) $\doteq$ P∗Q^{-1}

Now one can construct a normal algorithm $\mathcal{N}^{(\doteq)}$ which would transform a string P∗Q^{-1} into an empty string only when P and Q are graphically equivalent. Its scheme is given below:

$$\mathcal{N}^{(\doteq)}: \quad \begin{array}{rcl} \mu*\mu & \rightarrow & * \qquad (\mu \in \mathcal{A}) \\ * & \rightarrow & \cdot \end{array}$$

Using the composition theorem, one can construct the desired normal algorithm $\mathcal{N}^{\dot{=}}$ such that the following hold for any P∗Q:

(i) $\mathcal{N}^{\dot{=}}(P*Q) \simeq \mathcal{N}^{(\dot{=})}(\mathcal{N}^{T}(P*Q))$ and
(ii) $\mathcal{N}^{\dot{=}}(P*Q) \doteq \Lambda$ if P is graphically equivalent to Q.

Using the branching theorem, one can construct the normal algorithm $\mathcal{N}_X^{\dot{=}}$ such that the following holds for any P∗Q:

$$\mathcal{N}_X^{\dot{=}}(P*Q) \doteq \mathcal{N}^{I^*}(P*Q) \doteq P \text{ if } \mathcal{N}^{\dot{=}}(P*Q) \doteq \Lambda$$

Now let us consider the following alphabets:

(i) $\mathcal{A}_0$ = { O | } (ii) $\mathcal{A}_1$ = { O | - } (iii) $\mathcal{A}_2$ = { O | - / }
(iv) $\mathcal{A}_3$ = { O | - / ◇ } (v) $\mathcal{D}_1$ = { , } (vi) $\mathcal{D}_2$ = { □ }
(vii) $\mathcal{D}_4$ = { } { } (viii) $\mathcal{A}_{11} = \mathcal{A}_0 \cup \mathcal{D}_1$ (ix) $\mathcal{A}_{15} = \mathcal{A}_{11} \cup \mathcal{D}_2 \cup \mathcal{D}_4$

Given a specific property $\mathcal{P}$ stipulated by means of a formula $\mathcal{B}$(x), one can construct the desired set X consisting of objects from a suitable alphabet $\mathcal{A}$ with the help of the normal algorithms $\mathcal{N}_X^{\in}$ and $\mathcal{N}_X^{\dot{=}}$ in the following manner :

Firstly, one would make a suitable correspondence between the objects of interest from $\mathcal{A}$ and verboids of the form $O||^i O$; $i \geq 1$ from $\mathcal{A}_0$ with the help of the transcription theorem [Refer subsection 2.2.1 in [50]]. By $\{\mathcal{N}_X^{\in}\}$ and $\{\mathcal{N}_X^{\dot{=}}\}$ we mean the transcriptions of the respective normal algorithms $\mathcal{N}_X^{\in}$ and $\mathcal{N}_X^{\dot{=}}$.

Now, the notion of constructive set is defined in the following manner: [REMARK: This definition is a variant of Shanin's notion of a constructive set [22]] .

DEFINITION 9.1.3

By a constructive set we mean the canonically represented verboid of the form $\{\mathcal{N}_X^{\in}\}$ □ $\{\mathcal{N}_X^{\dot{=}}\}$ from the alphabet $\mathcal{A}_{15}$ = { O | } , { □ } where, $\{\mathcal{N}_X^{\in}\}$ decides the preset by identifying the verboidal transcriptions of those constructive objects which satisfy the property $\mathcal{P}$

stipulated by a one-parameter formula $\mathcal{B}(x)$ and $\{\mathcal{N}_X^{\doteq}\}$ is the corresponding regulator of uniqueness in itself of $\{\mathcal{N}_X^{\in}\}$.

Without loss of generality, we can interpret a set process $\{\mathcal{N}_X^{\in}\} \square \{\mathcal{N}_X^{\doteq}\}$ as $\{\mathfrak{R}_X^{\in}\} \square \{\mathfrak{R}_X^{\doteq}\}$ so as to generalize the notion of a constructive set as the one which is decided by a pair of constructive systems $\mathfrak{R}_X^{\in}$ and $\mathfrak{R}_X^{\doteq}$. The successful termination of the set process $\{\mathfrak{R}_X^{\in}\} \square \{\mathfrak{R}_X^{\doteq}\}$ yields the desired set X which is the string of the form {X†,} where X†, is the ,-dilution of all the unique objects decided by the process.

Definition 9.1.4

A set X is *algorithmically enumerable* if one can construct an algorithm $\mathcal{N}_X^E$ over $\mathcal{A} \cup \{O\ |\}$ where $\mathcal{A}$ is an arbitrary alphabet such that for any natural number (a word) n from $\mathcal{A}_0$ and any word P from $\mathcal{A}$, the following hold:

(i) If $!\mathcal{N}_X^E(n)$ then $\mathcal{N}_X^E(n) \in X$ and

(ii) if $P \in X$ then one can find a natural number i for which $!\mathcal{N}_X^E(i)$ and $\mathcal{N}_X^E(i) \doteq P$.

Given any arbitrary alphabet, the set of all words of it is enumerable. The following theorem, which we quote without proof, compares the two concepts of algorithmically decidable sets and algorithmically enumerable sets.

Theorem 9.1.1 [15]

Every decidable set is enumerable, but the converse need not be true. The intersection of a finite number of enumerable (decidable) sets is also enumerable (decidable). The union of a sequence of enumerable sets is enumerable whereas that of decidable sets can fail to be a decidable set.

Based on the definitions 9.1.1 and 9.1.4, the definition 9.1.3 is restated as follows:

Definition 9.1.5

By a constructive set, we mean a word of the form $\{\mathfrak{R}_X^{\in}\} \square \{\mathfrak{R}_X^{\doteq}\}$ from the alphabet $\mathcal{A}_{15}$ such that $\{\mathfrak{R}_X^{\in}\}$ decides (enumerates) the verboidal transcriptions of those constructive objects which satisfy the potentially enumerable property $\mathcal{P}$ stipulated by a formula $\mathcal{B}(x)$ and $\{\mathfrak{R}_X^{\bar{\bar{\cdot}}}\}$ is the corresponding regulator of uniqueness in itself of $\{\mathfrak{R}_X^{\in}\}$.

Definition 9.1.6

Let $\mathcal{P}$ be a potentially enumerable property (PEP) of a set X constructed by $\{\mathfrak{R}_X^{\in}\}\Box\{\mathfrak{R}_X^{\bar{\bar{\cdot}}}\}$. Then X is said to be *finite* if the set process $\{\mathfrak{R}_X^{\in}\}\Box\{\mathfrak{R}_X^{\bar{\bar{\cdot}}}\}$ terminates. On the other hand X is said to be *nonfinite* if the set process is proved to be nonterminating. X is said to be *quasifinite*, if one fails to prove that the set process does not terminate.

Definition 9.1.7

By the *complement* of a set X words from an alphabet $\mathcal{A}$ with respect to the entire set of all words from $\mathcal{A}$, we mean the set $\overline{X}$ of words from $\mathcal{A}$ defined by the condition $P\in\overline{X} \equiv \neg(P\in X)$ such that P does not satisfy the corresponding PEP of the set X.

Definition 9.1.8

Given two PEP's $\mathcal{P}_1$ and $\mathcal{P}_2$ stipulated by formulas $\mathcal{B}(x)$ and $\mathcal{B}(y)$ respectively, the constructive sets X and Y are equivalent if and only if all the elements decided by $\{\mathfrak{R}_X^{\in}\}\Box\{\mathfrak{R}_X^{\bar{\bar{\cdot}}}\}$ satisfy the PEP $\mathcal{P}_2$ and all the elements decided $\{\mathfrak{R}_Y^{\in}\}\Box\{\mathfrak{R}_Y^{\bar{\bar{\cdot}}}\}$ satisfy the PEP $\mathcal{P}_1$.

As outlined by Shanin in [22], various operations on constructive sets and various propositions about them are the corresponding operations and propositions about formulas.

So, the operations of union, and intersection for constructive sets are defined in the following manner:

Definition 9.1.9

Given two PEP's $\mathcal{P}_1$ and $\mathcal{P}_2$ stipulated by $\mathcal{B}(x)$ and $\mathcal{B}(y)$ respectively, the set X is enumerated by $\{\mathfrak{R}_X^{\in}\}\Box\{\mathfrak{R}_X^{\bar{\bar{\cdot}}}\}$ in the strength of $\mathcal{P}_1$ and the set Y by $\{\mathfrak{R}_Y^{\in}\}\Box\{\mathfrak{R}_Y^{\bar{\bar{\cdot}}}\}$ in the strength of $\mathcal{P}_2$ such that the their union (intersection) could be enumerated by $\{\mathfrak{R}^{\in}_{X\cup Y}\}\Box\{\mathfrak{R}^{\bar{\bar{\cdot}}}_{X\cup Y}\}$ (and by $\{\mathfrak{R}^{\in}_{X\cap Y}\}\Box\{\mathfrak{R}^{\bar{\bar{\cdot}}}_{X\cap Y}\}$ respectively) in the strength of the potentially enumerable property $\mathcal{P}_3$ stipulated by $\mathcal{B}(z)$ satisfying the following conditions:

(i) $\supset\forall z\mathcal{B}(z)\vee\mathcal{B}(x)\mathcal{B}(y)$ (for union operation)

(ii) $\supset\forall z\mathcal{B}(z)\&\mathcal{B}(x)\mathcal{B}(y)$ (for intersection operation)

Definition 9.1.10

Let $\mathcal{P}_1$ and $\mathcal{P}_2$ be two PEP's stipulated by $\mathcal{B}(x)$and $\mathcal{B}(y)$ respectively. Then, $\{\Re_X{}^{\in}\}\square\{\Re_X{}^{\dot{=}}\}$ decides (enumerates) the set X in the strength of $\mathcal{P}_1$ and the set Y is decided by the process $\{\Re_Y{}^{\in}\}\square\{\Re_Y{}^{\dot{=}}\}$ in the strength of $\mathcal{P}_2$. By virtue of definition 9.1.1, if $\mathcal{P}_2$ is an enumerable property of words of the basic alphabet $\mathcal{A}$ and if it holds for those and only for those words of X which possess the property $\mathcal{P}_1$, then $\{\Re_Y{}^{\in}\}\square\{\Re_Y{}^{\dot{=}}\}$ decides a particular subset of the set X. In such case, we shall say that the property $\mathcal{P}_2$ is *imbeddable in* $\mathcal{P}_1$. Given a PEP: $\mathcal{P}$, for a every one of its imbeddable property $\mathcal{P}_i$ there corresponds a set which is a subset of the set corresponding to $\mathcal{P}$.

As already mentioned, for a given PEP: $\mathcal{P}$ defined by a formula $\mathcal{B}$ (x), the corresponding set X decided by the process $\{\Re_X{}^{\in}\}\square\{\Re_X{}^{\dot{=}}\}$ is a word of the form {X†,} from the alphabet $\mathcal{A}_{15} = \{O \mid \}$, $\{\square\}$. One can construct a normal algorithm $\mathcal{N}_X{}^{\vee}$ which would find out a constructive natural number n corresponding to every word of the form {X†,} indicating the number of ,-terms in the word, which is in other words known as the cardinal number of the set X.

Definition 9.1.11

Two constructive sets X and Y corresponding to the PEP's : $\mathcal{P}_1$ and $\mathcal{P}_2$ defined by $\mathcal{B}(x)$ and $\mathcal{B}(y)$ are disjoint if one could specify an enumerable property $\mathcal{P}_3$ by a formula $\mathcal{B}(z)$ so that the condition $\supset\forall z\mathcal{B}(z)\neg(\&\mathcal{B}(x)\mathcal{B}(y))$ holds. This means, for any two disjoint constructive sets X and Y the following conditions hold:

(i) $\{\Re^{\in}{}_{X\cap Y}\}\square\{\Re^{\dot{=}}{}_{X\cap Y}\}\dot{=}\Lambda$

(ii) $\left\{\mathcal{N}^{\vee}{}_{\{\Re^{\in}{}_{X\cap Y}\}\square\{\Re^{\dot{=}}{}_{X\cap Y}\}}\right\} \dot{=} \left\{\mathcal{N}^{+}{}_{\{\mathcal{N}^{\vee}{}_X\},\{\mathcal{N}^{\vee}{}_Y\}}\right\}$

(iii) $$\left\{\mathcal{N}^{\vee}_{\{\Re^{\in}{}_{X\cup Y}\}\,\square\,\{\Re^{\dot{=}}{}_{X\cup Y}\}}\right\} \doteq \left\{\mathcal{N}^{+}_{\{\mathcal{N}^{\vee}{}_{X}\},\{\mathcal{N}^{\vee}{}_{Y}\}}\right\}$$

The algorithm $\mathcal{N}^{+}$ of the type shown below is used to add constructive natural numbers.

$\mathcal{N}^{+}$:	Substitution formulas	Formula number
	,O → ,	(0)
	, → ·	(1)

In a similar manner, one can construct a normal algorithm $\mathcal{N}^{-}$ like the one shown below which would subtract a constructive natural number from another:

$\mathcal{N}^{-}$:	Substitution formulas	Formula number
	|,| → ,	(0)
	|,O → |,	(1)
	O,O → O,	(2)
	O,| → ,- O|	(3)
	, → ·	(4)

With the help of the normal algorithm $\mathcal{N}^{\vee}$, $\mathcal{N}^{+}$ and $\mathcal{N}^{-}$ one can construct the following equalities which connect the cardinalities of any two arbitrary sets X and Y:

(i) $$\left\{\mathcal{N}^{\vee}_{\{\Re^{\in}{}_{X\cap Y}\}\,\square\,\{\Re^{\dot{=}}{}_{X\cap Y}\}}\right\} \doteq \left\{\mathcal{N}^{-}_{\left\{\mathcal{N}^{+}_{\{\mathcal{N}^{\vee}{}_{X}\},\{\mathcal{N}^{\vee}{}_{Y}\}}\right\},\left\{\mathcal{N}^{\vee}_{\{\Re^{\in}{}_{X\cup Y}\}\,\square\,\{\Re^{\dot{=}}{}_{X\cup Y}\}}\right\}}\right\}$$

$$\text{(ii)} \left\{ \mathcal{N}^{\vee}_{\{\Re^{\in}{}_{X\cup Y}\}\,\Box\,\{\Re^{\dot{-}}{}_{X\cup Y}\}} \right\} \doteq \left\{ \mathcal{N}^{-}_{\left\{\mathcal{N}^{+}_{\{\mathcal{N}^{\vee}{}_X\},\{\mathcal{N}^{\vee}{}_Y\}}\right\},\ \left\{\mathcal{N}^{\vee}_{\{\Re^{\in}{}_{X\cap Y}\}\,\Box\,\{\Re^{\dot{-}}{}_{X\cap Y}\}}\right\}} \right\}$$

Now, the notion of a power set is interpreted in the following manner: With reference to definition 9.1.10, given a set property $\mathcal{P}_1$ which is potentially enumerable, one can specify an enumerable property $\mathcal{P}_2$ which is imbeddable in $\mathcal{P}_1$ so that the corresponding set of $\mathcal{P}_2$ becomes the subset of the set corresponding to $\mathcal{P}_1$. In what follows, we suggest a method by which one can construct the power set using the idea of property imbeddability.

An enumerable property $\mathcal{P}_2$ is said be imbeddable in a given PEP: $\mathcal{P}_1$ if and only if $\mathcal{P}_2$ holds for those and only those elements of the set described by the property $\mathcal{P}_1$. Let us assume that $\mathcal{P}_1$ and $\mathcal{P}_2$ which are defined by one parameter formulas, say, $\mathcal{B}_1(x)$ and $\mathcal{B}_2(x)$ respectively, are restriction-free. In other words, these enumerable properties are not stipulated with any restriction in deciding, for example, the number of elements which satisfy them. In such a case, the imbedding of $\mathcal{P}_2$ in $\mathcal{P}_1$ is called free imbedding. On the other hand, if $\mathcal{B}_2(x)$ is formulated along with its validity subjected to one or more constraints and $\mathcal{P}_2$ is imbeddable $\mathcal{P}_1$, then the imbedding is called restricted imbedding. For example, if the restriction is about the cardinality of the set to be decided then the corresponding restricted imbedding is called *cardinality restricted imbedding*. Now the power set of a given constructive set is obtained as follows:

Let X_0 be the constructive set decided by $\{\Re_{X_0}{}^{\in}\}\Box\{\Re_{X_0}{}^{\dot{-}}\}$ in the strength of the PEP: $\mathcal{P}_0$ by the formula $\mathcal{B}$. [Note: The restricted variable is not shown here in the logical formula]. Now one can specify enumerable properties of the types $\mathcal{P}_{10}, \mathcal{P}_{11}, \mathcal{P}_{12}, \ldots, \mathcal{P}_{1n}$ where n is the cardinality of the base set X_0. Thus one can specify ${}^{n}C_0$ number of properties of the type $\mathcal{P}_{10}$, ${}^{n}C_1$ number of independent properties of type $\mathcal{P}_{11}$, ${}^{n}C_2$ number of independent properties of the type $\mathcal{P}_{12}$ and so on up to ${}^{n}C_n$ number of properties of the type $\mathcal{P}_{1n}$. In general, one can specify potentially infinite enumerable properties $\mathcal{P}^{k}{}_{ij}$, where i is the ith power of the base set, j is the cardinality index that ranges from 0 to the cardinal number (n_{i-1}) of the (i-1)th power set and k is the index that ranges from 1 to $^{(n_{i-1})}C_j$: $j \geq 0$ for every $\mathcal{P}_{ij}$ and for every $i \geq 1$. [Table 9.1.1].

Based on the above details, we now reformulate the theory of extended topological filters in the constructive logic.

Table 9.1.1: Potentially enumerable properties corresponding to the Power set of a constructive set

Sl.No.	Subset properties	Number of properties	Remarks
1	$\mathcal{P}^1_{10}$	1	Any property which holds for none of the elements of the base set X_0.
2	$\mathcal{P}^1_{11}$, $\mathcal{P}^2_{11}$,..., $\mathcal{P}^k_{11}$,..., $\mathcal{P}^n_{11}$	n	P^k_{11} implies any abstract $\mathcal{P}_0$ imbeddable property that holds only for the kth element of the base set X_0.
3	$\mathcal{P}^1_{12}$, $\mathcal{P}^2_{12}$,..., $\mathcal{P}^k_{12}$,...., $\mathcal{P}^n_{12}$	$^nC_2$	P^k_{12} implies any abstract $\mathcal{P}_0$ that holds only for the kth pair of the base set X_0.
4	$\mathcal{P}^1_{13}$, $\mathcal{P}^2_{13}$,..., $\mathcal{P}^k_{13}$,...., $\mathcal{P}^n_{13}$	$^nC_3$	P^k_{13} implies any abstract $\mathcal{P}_0$-imbeddable property that holds for the kth triple of the set X_0.
	↓	↓	↓
2^n	$\mathcal{P}^1_{1n}$	^nC_n	Any P_0-imbeddable property that holds to all v elements of the base set X_0 .

Definition 9.1.12

Let $\mathcal{P}_0$ be the given PEP in the strength of which $\{\Re_{X_0}{}^{\in}\}\square\{\Re_{X_0}{}^{\overline{\overline{\in}}}\}$ decides the constructive X_0. Let $\mathcal{P}^k_{ij}$ denote any abstract cardinality restricted, $\mathcal{P}_0$-imbeddable enumerable property. Let $\{\mathcal{N}^v{}_{X_0}\} \doteq n$. Then the power set X_1 of the base set X_0 is of the form $\{X_1\dagger,\}$ which is decided by the process $\{\Re_{X_1}{}^{\in}\}\square\{\Re_{X_1}{}^{\overline{\overline{\in}}}\}$ using the property $\mathcal{P}_1$ which is a system of 2^n $\mathcal{P}_0$-imbeddable properties:

$$\mathcal{P}^k_{ij} : 0 \leq j \leq n\ ,\ 1 \leq k \leq {}^nC_j$$

9.2 Constructive Extended Topological Filters

In 1937, Cartan formulated the concepts of filters and ultra filters which were later developed by Bourbaki, Schmidt and Grimeisen. The development of the theory associated with these concepts took place as a part of the study of general topology. But these mathematical tools of general topology have been found wanting in the study of various problems of topological nature in areas like control systems, signal processing, logic and computing, and system theory. This is due to the fact that the general topology deals only with infinite spaces [27].

In 1961, Hammer brought various extensions in general topology such that his theory could be applied to finite sets also. A filter in general, as defined by Hammer, is an ordered dichotomy over a set <accepted elements, rejected elements> [31]. Let us take for instance a normal algorithm $\mathcal{N}$ over an alphabet $\mathcal{A}$. $\mathcal{N}$ is a filter in the sense that it divides the free monoid $\mathcal{A}^*$ into two disjoint sets $\$^{!\mathcal{N}}$ and $\$^{\neg !\mathcal{N}}$. $\$^{!\mathcal{N}}$ is the set of all strings in $\mathcal{A}^*$ to which $\mathcal{N}$ is sa-definite [Refer subsection 7.2] and $\$^{\neg !\mathcal{N}}$ is its compliment with respect to $\mathcal{A}^*$. So the normal algorithmic filter $\mathcal{N}$ is represented by the ordered dichotomy $< \$^{!\mathcal{N}}, \$^{\neg !\mathcal{N}} >$.

Following this notion of a general filter, Thampuran developed the notion of an extended filter, which is a generalization of the concept of a filter due to Cartan [54]. An extended filter over a finite set is a set which consists only of elements from the power set of the given set other than the null set such that every element present in the filter set ensures the presence of every one of its super sets which are elements of the power set.

9.2.1 Definition Of a Constructive Extended Filter

On the same lines of Thampuran, we think of a constructive extended filter over a base set X_0 as a property $\mathcal{P}_F$ described by a formula $\mathcal{B}(f)$ where $\mathcal{P}_F$ is the system of the union of certain cardinality restricted $\mathcal{P}_0$–imbeddable subset properties such that every such property present in the system $\mathcal{P}_F$ ensures the presence of all those cardinality restricted $\mathcal{P}_0$–imbeddable properties which would form a linear chain with it as the basis, by the partial ordering in imbeddability.

Formal definition of constructive extended filter is given below:

Definition 9.2.1.1

By a constructive proper extended filter over a base set X_0, we mean a set F which is decided by the process $\{\Re_F^{\in}\} \Box \{\Re_F^{\doteq}\}$ in the strength of the filter property $\mathcal{P}_F$ depicted by the formula $\mathcal{B}(f)$ such that the following conditions hold for F:

(i) If a set decided by the process $\{\Re^{\in}{}_{X_{1jk}}\} \Box \{\Re^{\doteq}{}_{X_{1jk}}\}$ is a filter element, then every element $\{\Re^{\in}{}_{X_{1j'k'}}\} \Box \{\Re^{\doteq}{}_{X_{1j'k'}}\}$ in the power set $\{\Re^{\in}{}_{X_1}\} \Box \{\Re^{\doteq}{}_{X_1}\}$ where $j \neq j'$ and $k \neq k'$ and for which the element $\{\Re^{\in}{}_{X_{1jk}}\} \Box \{\Re^{\doteq}{}_{X_{1jk}}\}$ is a subset due to the restricted imbedding of the property $\mathcal{P}^{k}{}_{1j}$ in the property $\mathcal{P}^{k'}{}_{1j'}$ is also a filter element.

(ii) $\mathcal{P}^{1}{}_{10}$ does not belong to the system of properties $\mathcal{P}_F$.

The definition of constructive improper filter would be obtained if the condition (ii) in the definition 9.2.1.1, is replaced by the following one:

$\mathcal{P}^{1}{}_{10}$ belongs to the system of property $\mathcal{P}_F$.

However, we are concerned here only with constructive proper extended filters and hereafter we shall call them simply as *constructive extended filters*.

Definition 9.2.1.2

A constructive extended filter (CEF) is called *constructive cartan filter* if it satisfies an additional condition that the intersection of any two filter elements is also a filter element.

9.2.1.1.1 Specific Results Concerning Constructive Cartan Filters

Let us consider a base set X_0 over an alphabet $\mathcal{A}$.
Let $\{\Re_{F1}^{\in}\} \Box \{\Re_{F1}^{\doteq}\}$ and $\{\Re_{F2}^{\in}\} \Box \{\Re_{F2}^{\doteq}\}$ be two constructive cartan filters defined over X_0 in the strength of the filters properties $\mathcal{P}_{F1}$ and $\mathcal{P}_{F2}$. Now if $\mathcal{P}_{F1}$ is $\mathcal{P}_{F2}$–imbeddable, then $\{\Re_{F2}^{\in}\} \Box \{\Re_{F2}^{\doteq}\}$ is said to be *finer than* $\{\Re_{F1}^{\in}\} \Box \{\Re_{F1}^{\doteq}\}$. In other words, $\{\Re_{F1}^{\in}\} \Box \{\Re_{F1}^{\doteq}\}$ is said to be *coarser than* $\{\Re_{F2}^{\in}\} \Box \{\Re_{F2}^{\doteq}\}$.

Let us now consider three cartan filters F_1 and F_2 and F_3 over X_0 described by the PEP's: $\mathcal{P}_{F1}$, $\mathcal{P}_{F2}$ and $\mathcal{P}_{F3}$ respectively. Let us also assume that $\mathcal{P}_{F1}$ is $\mathcal{P}_{F2}$–imbeddable and $\mathcal{P}_{F3}$–imbeddable and $\mathcal{P}_{F2}$ is $\mathcal{P}_{F3}$–imbeddable. Then, F_2 is said to be the interpolant filter of F_1 and F_3.

Given two cartan filters F_i and F_j , the latter for instance is said to be a *just finer* filter of the former only when the following two conditions are satisfied:

(i) $\mathcal{P}_{Fi}$ must be a $\mathcal{P}_{Fj}$ –imbeddable property.

(ii) There is no interpolant filter between F_i and F_j .

Let us consider n cartan filters over X_0 where $\{\Re_{Fi}^{\in}\} \square \{\Re_{Fi}^{\dot{=}}\}$: $1 \le i \le n$ be the ith CEF. These n CEF's are said to form a linear filter chain if and only if for every i^{th} CEF, the $(i+1)^{th}$ CEF is a just finer filter.

Definition 9.2.1.1.1

A constructive cartan filter $\{\Re_{Fi}^{\in}\} \square \{\Re_{Fi}^{\dot{=}}\}$ is defined as an ultra filter if it satisfies the following three conditions:

(i) Cardinalities of the filter elements (subsets) must vary from 1 to n where n is the cardinal number of the base set X_0.

(ii) One and only one of the filter elements should necessarily be of the cardinality 1.

(iii) All those elements of the power set X_1 which contain the filter element of cardinality 1 must also be present in the filter set.

It is not hard to see that any ultra filter F over X_0 does not have a just finer filter. Similarly one can see that the coarsest filter that could be defined over X_0 is the CEF containing the base set X_0 as its only element.

A linear filter chain beginning with the coarsest filter and ending with an ultra filter is called the *maximal length filter chain*. A maximum of n ultra filters of the constructive cartan type could be constructed over a given base set X_0 of cardinality n. For every such ultra filter there correspond (n-1)! maximal length filter chains. This implies that for any base set X_0 of cardinality n, one can construct a maximum of n! maximal length filter chains.

Every ultra filter with itself as the supremum and with the coarsest filter as the infimum, forms an n-level lattice consisting of (n-1)! Maximal length filter chains.

Example 9.2.1.1.1

Let $\mathcal{A}$ be certain alphabet. Every letter of $\mathcal{A}$ can be uniquely transcribed as a (O, |)-link from the alphabet $\mathcal{A}_0$ = {O |} and every word from $\mathcal{A}$ can be uniquely represented as a (O, |)-chain. Now let $\mathcal{P}_0$ be a PEP by which a base set is decided as $\{\Re_{X_0}{}^{\in}\} \square \{\Re_{X_0}{}^{\dot{=}}\} \dot{=} \{O|O, O||O, O|||O\}$. Now one can specify 2^n abstract, cardinality restricted $\mathcal{P}_0$–imbeddable properties such that the power set X_1 is obtained as

$$\{\Re_{X1}{}^{\in}\} \square \{\Re_{X1}{}^{\dot{=}}\} \dot{=} \{\{\}, \{O|O\}, \{O||O\}, \{O|||O\}, \{O|O, O||O\}, \{O|O,O|||O\}, \{O||O,O|||O\}, \{O|O,O||O,O|||O\}\}$$

Now, three ultra filters could be obtained by virtue of three independent $\mathcal{P}_0$–imbeddable ultra filter properties:

(i) $$\left\{\Re_{\underset{\sim}{F}_1}^{\in}\right\} \square \left\{\Re_{\underset{\sim}{F}_1}^{\dot{=}}\right\} \dot{=} \{\{O|O\},\{O|O, O||O\}, \{O|O, O|||O\}, \{O|O, O||O, O|||O\}\}$$

(ii) $$\left\{\Re_{\underset{\sim}{F}_2}^{\in}\right\} \square \left\{\Re_{\underset{\sim}{F}_2}^{\dot{=}}\right\} \dot{=} \{\{O||O\},\{O|O, O||O\}, \{O||O, O|||O\}, \{O|O, O||O, O|||O\}\}$$

(iii) $$\left\{\Re_{\underset{\sim}{F}_3}^{\in}\right\} \square \left\{\Re_{\underset{\sim}{F}_3}^{\dot{=}}\right\} \dot{=} \{\{O|||O\},\{O|O, O|||O\},\{O||O, O|||O\}, \{O|O, O||O, O|||O\}\}$$

The family of all constructive cartan filters over $X_0$is given in table 9.2.1.1.1 and the corresponding lattice structure is shown in figure 9.2.1.1.1.

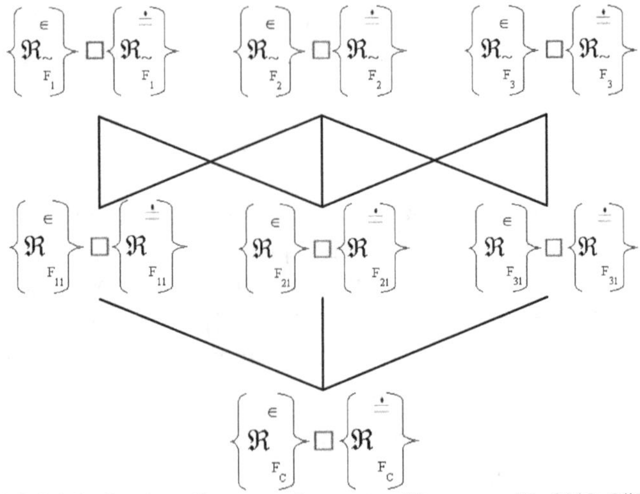

Figure 9.2.1.1.1: Lattice of constructive cartan filters over X={O|O,O||O,O|||O}

Table 9.2.1.1.1: Constructive cartan filters over X = {O|O, O||O, O|||O}

Sl.No	Constructive Cartan Filters
1	$\left\{\underset{F_1}{\overset{\in}{\mathfrak{R}_{\sim}}}\right\}\square\left\{\underset{F_1}{\overset{\dot{=}}{\mathfrak{R}_{\sim}}}\right\}\doteq\{\{O\vert O\},\{O\vert O,O\vert\vert O\},\{O\vert O,O\vert\vert\vert O\},\{O\vert O,O\vert\vert O.O\vert\vert\vert O\}\}$
2	$\left\{\underset{F_2}{\overset{\in}{\mathfrak{R}_{\sim}}}\right\}\square\left\{\underset{F_2}{\overset{\dot{=}}{\mathfrak{R}_{\sim}}}\right\}\doteq\{\{O\vert\vert O\},\{O\vert O,O\vert\vert O\},\{O\vert\vert O,O\vert\vert\vert O\},\{O\vert O,O\vert\vert O.O\vert\vert\vert O\}\}$
3	$\left\{\underset{F_3}{\overset{\in}{\mathfrak{R}_{\sim}}}\right\}\square\left\{\underset{F_3}{\overset{\dot{=}}{\mathfrak{R}_{\sim}}}\right\}\doteq\{\{O\vert\vert\vert O\},\{O\vert O,O\vert\vert\vert O\},\{O\vert\vert O,O\vert\vert\vert O\},\{O\vert O,O\vert\vert O.O\vert\vert\vert O\}\}$
4	$\left\{\underset{F_{11}}{\overset{\in}{\mathfrak{R}}}\right\}\square\left\{\underset{F_{11}}{\overset{\dot{=}}{\mathfrak{R}}}\right\}\doteq\{\{O\vert O,O\vert\vert O\},\{O\vert O,O\vert\vert O.O\vert\vert\vert O\}\}$
5	$\left\{\underset{F_{21}}{\overset{\in}{\mathfrak{R}}}\right\}\square\left\{\underset{F_{21}}{\overset{\dot{=}}{\mathfrak{R}}}\right\}\doteq\{\{O\vert O,O\vert\vert\vert O\},\{O\vert O,O\vert\vert O.O\vert\vert\vert O\}\}$
6	$\left\{\underset{F_{31}}{\overset{\in}{\mathfrak{R}}}\right\}\square\left\{\underset{F_{31}}{\overset{\dot{=}}{\mathfrak{R}}}\right\}\doteq\{\{O\vert\vert O,O\vert\vert\vert O\},\{O\vert O,O\vert\vert O.O\vert\vert\vert O\}\}$
7	$\left\{\underset{F_C}{\overset{\in}{\mathfrak{R}}}\right\}\square\left\{\underset{F_C}{\overset{\dot{=}}{\mathfrak{R}}}\right\}\doteq\{\{O\vert O,O\vert\vert O.O\vert\vert\vert O\}\}$

9.2.1.2 General Results Concerning Constructive Extended Filters

Given a constructive set $\{\Re_{X0}{}^{\in}\}\,\square\,\{\Re_{X0}{}^{\dot{=}}\}$ with the property $\mathcal{P}_0$, its constructive power set $\{\Re_{X1}{}^{\in}\}\,\square\,\{\Re_{X1}{}^{\dot{=}}\}$ possesses a relational structure of a complete lattice in which the lower bound of two subsets is their intersection and the upper bound is their union. A complete lattice is a partially ordered set in which every nonempty subset has a supremum and an infimum.

Example 9.2.1.2.1

Let us consider a set of constructive objects from an alphabet $\mathcal{A}$ which is decided by the process $\{\Re_{X0}{}^{\in}\}\,\square\,\{\Re_{X0}{}^{\dot{=}}\}$ in the strength of the property $\mathcal{P}_0$ such that $\{\Re_{X0}{}^{\in}\}\,\square\,\{\Re_{X0}{}^{\dot{=}}\} \dot{=} \{O|O, O||O, O|||O, O||||O\}$. Then the power set property $\mathcal{P}_1$ consists of 16 properties of the type $\mathcal{P}^k{}_{1j}$: $0 \leq j \leq 4$, $0 \leq k \leq 4C_j$ which are $\mathcal{P}_0$–imbeddable such that 16 constructive subsets of the type $\{\Re^{\in}{}_{X^k{}_{1j}}\}\,\square\,\{\Re_{X^k{}_{1j}}{}^{\dot{=}}\}$ [Refer to table 9.2.1.2.1] form the power set X_1.

Table 9.2.1.2.1 : subsets (S1 to S16) of a constructive set

Sl. No.	Constructive subsets of $\{\Re_{X0}{}^{\in}\}\,\square\,\{\Re_{X0}{}^{\dot{=}}\} \dot{=} \{O\|O, O\|\|O, O\|\|\|O, O\|\|\|\|O\}$
S1	$\left\{\Re^{\in}_{X_{14}{}^{1}}\right\}\square\left\{\Re^{\dot{=}}_{X_{14}{}^{1}}\right\} \dot{=} \{O\|O, O\|\|O, O\|\|\|O, O\|\|\|\|O\}$
S2	$\left\{\Re^{\in}_{X_{13}{}^{1}}\right\}\square\left\{\Re^{\dot{=}}_{X_{13}{}^{1}}\right\} \dot{=} \{O\|O, O\|\|O, O\|\|\|O\}$
S3	$\left\{\Re^{\in}_{X_{13}{}^{2}}\right\}\square\left\{\Re^{\dot{=}}_{X_{13}{}^{2}}\right\} \dot{=} \{O\|O, O\|\|O, O\|\|\|\|O\}$

Contd....

S4	$\left\{\begin{matrix}\in\\ \mathfrak{R}\\ \quad X_{13}^{3}\end{matrix}\right\}\succ\square\left\{\begin{matrix}\doteq\\ \mathfrak{R}\\ \quad X_{13}^{3}\end{matrix}\right\}\succ\ \doteq\ \{O\vert O,\ O\vert\vert\vert O,\ O\vert\vert\vert\vert O\}$
S5	$\left\{\begin{matrix}\in\\ \mathfrak{R}\\ \quad X_{13}^{4}\end{matrix}\right\}\succ\square\left\{\begin{matrix}\doteq\\ \mathfrak{R}\\ \quad X_{13}^{4}\end{matrix}\right\}\succ\ \doteq\ \{O\vert\vert O,\ O\vert\vert\vert O,\ O\vert\vert\vert\vert O\}$
S6	$\left\{\begin{matrix}\in\\ \mathfrak{R}\\ \quad X_{12}^{1}\end{matrix}\right\}\succ\square\left\{\begin{matrix}\doteq\\ \mathfrak{R}\\ \quad X_{12}^{1}\end{matrix}\right\}\succ\ \doteq\ \{O\vert O,\ O\vert\vert O\}$
S7	$\left\{\begin{matrix}\in\\ \mathfrak{R}\\ \quad X_{12}^{2}\end{matrix}\right\}\succ\square\left\{\begin{matrix}\doteq\\ \mathfrak{R}\\ \quad X_{12}^{2}\end{matrix}\right\}\succ\ \doteq\ \{O\vert O,\ O\vert\vert\vert O\}$
S8	$\left\{\begin{matrix}\in\\ \mathfrak{R}\\ \quad X_{12}^{3}\end{matrix}\right\}\succ\square\left\{\begin{matrix}\doteq\\ \mathfrak{R}\\ \quad X_{12}^{3}\end{matrix}\right\}\succ\ \doteq\ \{O\vert O,\ O\vert\vert\vert\vert O\}$
S9	$\left\{\begin{matrix}\in\\ \mathfrak{R}\\ \quad X_{12}^{4}\end{matrix}\right\}\succ\square\left\{\begin{matrix}\doteq\\ \mathfrak{R}\\ \quad X_{12}^{4}\end{matrix}\right\}\succ\ \doteq\ \{O\vert\vert O,\ O\vert\vert\vert O\}$
S10	$\left\{\begin{matrix}\in\\ \mathfrak{R}\\ \quad X_{12}^{5}\end{matrix}\right\}\succ\square\left\{\begin{matrix}\doteq\\ \mathfrak{R}\\ \quad X_{12}^{5}\end{matrix}\right\}\succ\ \doteq\ \{O\vert\vert\vert O,\ O\vert\vert\vert\vert O\}$

S11	$\left\{ \overset{\in}{\mathfrak{R}}_{X_{12}^{6}} \right\} \square \left\{ \overset{\doteq}{\mathfrak{R}}_{X_{12}^{6}} \right\} \doteq \{O\Vert O, O\Vert\Vert O\}$
S12	$\left\{ \overset{\in}{\mathfrak{R}}_{X_{11}^{1}} \right\} \square \left\{ \overset{\doteq}{\mathfrak{R}}_{X_{11}^{1}} \right\} \doteq \{O\vert O\}$
S13	$\left\{ \overset{\in}{\mathfrak{R}}_{X_{11}^{2}} \right\} \square \left\{ \overset{\doteq}{\mathfrak{R}}_{X_{11}^{2}} \right\} \doteq \{O\Vert O\}$
S14	$\left\{ \overset{\in}{\mathfrak{R}}_{X_{11}^{3}} \right\} \square \left\{ \overset{\doteq}{\mathfrak{R}}_{X_{11}^{3}} \right\} \doteq \{O\Vert\vert O\}$
S15	$\left\{ \overset{\in}{\mathfrak{R}}_{X_{11}^{4}} \right\} \square \left\{ \overset{\doteq}{\mathfrak{R}}_{X_{11}^{4}} \right\} \doteq \{O\Vert\Vert O\}$
S16	$\left\{ \overset{\in}{\mathfrak{R}}_{X_{10}^{1}} \right\} \square \left\{ \overset{\doteq}{\mathfrak{R}}_{X_{10}^{1}} \right\} \doteq \{\ \}$

The complete lattice formed by the 16 constructive subsets is shown in figure 9.2.1.2.1.

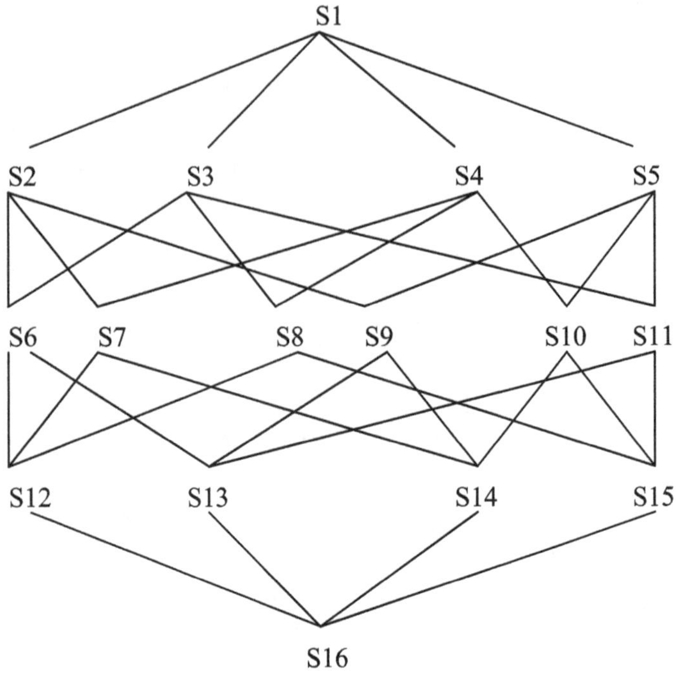

Figure 9.2.1.2.1 : Lattice formed by the subsets of a constructive set

Theorem 9.2.1.2.1

Given a constructive base set $\{\Re_{X0}{}^{\in}\}\Box\{\Re_{X0}{}^{\dot{-}}\}$ with the property $\mathcal{P}_0$, let us denoted by Φ, the family of all constructive extended filters over the base set. Then Φ possesses a relational structure of a complete distributive lattice which is denoted by (Φ , ⊆) where ⊆ is the relation 'coarser than' .

Proof:

The condition for any lattice to be complete is that every one of its elements should have a supremum and an infimum. This means the union and intersection of nonempty elements of the lattice should also be the lattice elements. In the same way we can assert that (Φ, ⊆) is a complete lattice, by proving that the union and intersection of any nonempty family of CEF's are also CEF's. Let us consider n CEF's which are certain elements of the lattice under consideration. Then in the strength of theorem 9.1.1 and definition 9.1.9, one can construct the following processes :

(i) $$\left\{\mathfrak{R}^{\in}{}_{\bigcap_{i=1}^{n}\left[\{\mathfrak{R}^{\in}{}_{Fi}\}\square\{\mathfrak{R}^{\doteq}{}_{Fi}\}\right]}\right\}\square\left\{\mathfrak{R}^{\doteq}{}_{\bigcap_{i=1}^{n}\left[\{\mathfrak{R}^{\in}{}_{Fi}\}\square\{\mathfrak{R}^{\doteq}{}_{Fi}\}\right]}\right\}$$

(ii) $$\left\{\mathfrak{R}^{\in}{}_{\bigcup_{i=1}^{n}\left[\{\mathfrak{R}^{\in}{}_{Fi}\}\square\{\mathfrak{R}^{\doteq}{}_{Fi}\}\right]}\right\}\square\left\{\mathfrak{R}^{\doteq}{}_{\bigcup_{i=1}^{n}\left[\{\mathfrak{R}^{\in}{}_{Fij}\}\square\{\mathfrak{R}^{\doteq}{}_{Fi}\}\right]}\right\}$$

which would enumerate the intersection and union of the n CEF's. The intersection of n CEF's is also CEF due to the following reason: Every element of the constructive set of the intersection of n CEF's is present in all the n CEF's. This is obvious due to the very definition of intersection. By virtue of the definition of a proper extended filter, every such element which is present in all the n CEF's ensures the presence of all of its super sets which are elements of the power set, in all the n CEF's. This in turn implies that all such super sets are present in the set of intersection of all the n CEF's also, thus making it a CEF. A similar reasoning could be made in order to prove that the constructive set of union of all the n CEF's is also a CEF. Thus one can see that the structure $(\Phi\ ,\subseteq)$ is a complete lattice. The distributivity of this lattice can be proved in the following manner: Let us consider three CEF's: F_1 , F_2 and F_3 decided by $\{\mathfrak{R}^{\in}{}_{F1}\}\square\{\mathfrak{R}^{\doteq}{}_{F1}\}$, $\{\mathfrak{R}^{\in}{}_{F2}\}\square\{\mathfrak{R}^{\doteq}{}_{F2}\}$ and $\{\mathfrak{R}^{\in}{}_{F3}\}\square\{\mathfrak{R}^{\doteq}{}_{F3}\}$ respectively. The distributivity is viewed in two ways :

(i) $F_1 \cap (F_2 \cup F_3) \simeq (F_1 \cap F_2) \cup (F_1 \cap F_3)$ and
(ii) $F_1 \cup (F_2 \cap F_3) \simeq (F_1 \cup F_2) \cap (F_1 \cup F_3)$

such that the following equalities hold :

(i) $$\left\{\mathfrak{R}^{\in}{}_{F_1\cap\left(F_2\cup F_3\right)}\right\}\square\left\{\mathfrak{R}^{\doteq}{}_{F_1\cap\left(F_2\cup F_3\right)}\right\}\simeq$$
$$\left\{\mathfrak{R}^{\in}{}_{\left(F_1\cap F_2\right)\cup\left(F_1\cap F_3\right)}\right\}\square\left\{\mathfrak{R}^{\doteq}{}_{\left(F_1\cap F_2\right)\cup\left(F_1\cap F_3\right)}\right\}$$

(ii) $$\left\{\mathfrak{R}^{\in}_{F_1 \cup (F_2 \cap F_3)}\right\} \square \left\{\mathfrak{R}^{\dot{=}}_{F_1 \cup (F_2 \cap F_3)}\right\} \simeq$$

$$\left\{\mathfrak{R}^{\in}_{(F_1 \cup F_2) \cap (F_1 \cup F_3)}\right\} \square \left\{\mathfrak{R}^{\dot{=}}_{(F_1 \cup F_2) \cap (F_1 \cup F_3)}\right\}$$

Now let us consider equality (i). Any element of the set in the left hand side of the equality should either be the element of both $\{\mathfrak{R}^{\in}_{F1}\} \square \{\mathfrak{R}^{\dot{=}}_{F1}\}$ and $\{\mathfrak{R}^{\in}_{F2}\} \square \{\mathfrak{R}^{\dot{=}}_{F2}\}$ or both $\{\mathfrak{R}^{\in}_{F1}\} \square \{\mathfrak{R}^{\dot{=}}_{F1}\}$ and $\{\mathfrak{R}^{\in}_{F3}\} \square \{\mathfrak{R}^{\dot{=}}_{F3}\}$. This proves equality (i). Equality (ii) can be proved in similar terms using the principle of duality.

So, the structure $(\Phi, \subseteq)$ is a complete distributive lattice.

As a generalization of distributivity one can realize the following equalities:

(i) $$\left\{\mathfrak{R}^{\in}_{F \cup (\bigcap_{i=1}^{n} F_i)}\right\} \square \left\{\mathfrak{R}^{\dot{=}}_{F \cup (\bigcap_{i=1}^{n} F_i)}\right\} \simeq$$

$$\left\{\mathfrak{R}^{\in}_{\bigcap_{i=1}^{n} (F \cup F_i)}\right\} \square \left\{\mathfrak{R}^{\dot{=}}_{\bigcap_{i=1}^{n} (F \cup F_i)}\right\}$$

(ii) $$\left\{\mathfrak{R}^{\in}_{F \cap (\bigcup_{i=1}^{n} F_i)}\right\} \square \left\{\mathfrak{R}^{\dot{=}}_{F \cap (\bigcup_{i=1}^{n} F_i)}\right\} \simeq$$

$$\left\{\mathfrak{R}^{\in}_{\bigcup_{i=1}^{n} (F \cap F_i)}\right\} \square \left\{\mathfrak{R}^{\dot{=}}_{\bigcup_{i=1}^{n} (F \cap F_i)}\right\}$$

Definition 9.2.1.2.1

Given a base set X_0 with the PEP: $\mathcal{P}_0$, one can specify an arbitrary system $\mathcal{P}_\sigma$ of $\mathcal{P}_0$ –imbeddable properties by which the process $\{\Re^{\in}{}_{\sigma}\}\square\{\Re^{\dot{-}}{}_{\sigma}\}$ would decide a certain collection of subsets of X_0. Now one can specify a filter property $\mathcal{P}_{\bar{\sigma}}$ – such that $\{\Re^{\in}_{\bar{\sigma}}\}\square\{\Re^{\dot{-}}_{\bar{\sigma}}\}$ would decide a CEF which contains all the elements of the constructive set decided by the process $\{\Re^{\in}{}_{\sigma}\}\square\{\Re^{\dot{-}}{}_{\sigma}\}$ and their corresponding super sets which are the subsets of X_0. Then the CEF: $\{\Re^{\in}_{\bar{\sigma}}\}\square\{\Re^{\dot{-}}_{\bar{\sigma}}\}$ is called the CEF hull of the base $\{\Re^{\in}{}_{\sigma}\}\square\{\Re^{\dot{-}}{}_{\sigma}\}$ and it is the smallest filter that the base could generate.

Theorem 9.2.1.2.2

Let $\{\Re^{\in}{}_{\sigma 1}\}\square\{\Re^{\dot{-}}{}_{\sigma 1}\}$ be a constructive subset of another $\{\Re^{\in}{}_{\sigma 2}\}\square\{\Re^{\dot{-}}{}_{\sigma 2}\}$ where both are subsets of the base set X_0. Then the corresponding CEF hulls are related by the expression:

$$\{\Re^{\in}_{\bar{\sigma}_1}\}\square\{\Re^{\dot{-}}_{\bar{\sigma}_1}\}\subseteq\{\Re^{\in}_{\bar{\sigma}_2}\}\square\{\Re^{\dot{-}}_{\bar{\sigma}_2}\}$$

Proof

The proof is the direct consequence of the definitions 9.2.1.1, and 9.2.1.2.1.

Definition 9.2.1.2.2

A CEF or in general any family of constructive sets is said to have Pairwise Intersection Property (PIP) if and only if any elements of the CEF or any two-member subfamily of the family of sets has a nonempty intersection. Similarly, a CEF or a family of constructive sets is said to have Finite Intersection Property (FIP) if and only if every finite number of elements of the CEF or every finite-member subfamily of the family of sets has a nonempty intersection.

One can easily verify that if a CEF base $\{\Re^{\in}{}_{\sigma}\}\square\{\Re^{\dot{-}}{}_{\sigma}\}$ has either PIP or FIP, then the corresponding CEF hull $\{\Re^{\in}_{\bar{\sigma}}\}\square\{\Re^{\dot{-}}_{\bar{\sigma}}\}$ also has the same property.

Definition 9.2.1.2.3

Let X_0 be a base set and X^k_{1j} be any one of its subsets. Then the complement of X^k_{1j} with respect to X_0 is a set decided by:

$$\left\{ \Re^{\in}_{X_0 - X^k_{1j}} \right\} \square \left\{ \Re^{\doteq}_{X_0 - X^k_{1j}} \right\}$$

by virtue of the property $\mathcal{P}^{k'}_{1j'}$. $\mathcal{P}^{k'}_{1j'}$ holds for all the elements of X_0 other than those which form the set X^k_{1j} by satisfying the property $\mathcal{P}^k_{1j}$. Now, one can specify a filter property $\mathcal{P}_{\overline{F}}$ such that the CEF:

$$\left\{ \Re^{\in}_{\overline{F}} \right\} \square \left\{ \Re^{\doteq}_{\overline{F}} \right\}$$

contains strictly either

$$\left\{ \Re^{\in}_{X^k_{1j}} \right\} \square \left\{ \Re^{\doteq}_{X^k_{1j}} \right\} \text{ or } \left\{ \Re^{\in}_{X_0 - X^k_{1j}} \right\} \square \left\{ \Re^{\doteq}_{X_0 - X^k_{1j}} \right\}$$

in which case it is known as Universal Filter.

Definition 9.2.1.2.4

Let X_0 be a base set and X_1 its power set. Let $\{\Re^{\in}{}_{\sigma}\} \square \{\Re^{\doteq}{}_{\sigma}\}$ be a CEF base set which consists of a single element from X_1. Then the corresponding CEF hull $\{ \Re^{\in}_{\overline{\sigma}} \} \square \{ \Re^{\doteq}_{\overline{\sigma}} \}$ is known as a Principal Filter.

If the single element of the filter base from X_1 happens to be a single element of X_0 then the corresponding principal filter is a universal filter which is also known as ultra filter of the cartan type.

The family of all CEF's over the base set X_0 exhibits a complete distributive lattice $(\Phi, \subseteq)$ where the symbol $\subseteq$ refers to the partial order relation 'coarser than' .

Example 9.2.1.2.2

Let the base set be $\{\Re^{\in}{}_{Y_0}\} \square \{\Re^{\doteq}{}_{X_0}\} \doteq \{O|O, O||O, O|||O\}$ so that the power set is $\{\Re^{\in}{}_{X_1}\} \square \{\Re^{\doteq}{}_{X_1}\} \doteq$ {{}, {O|O}, {O||O}, {O|||O}, {O|O,O||O}, {O|O, O|||O}, {O||O, O|||O}, {O|O,O||O, O|||O}}.

One can construct 18 CEF's over X_0 [Refer to table 9.2.1.2.2] and the lattice Φ formed by these CEF's are shown in figure 9.2.1.2.2.

Table 9.2.1.2.2 : Constructive extended filters (CEF's) over
X_0 = {O|O, O||O, O|||O}

<table>
<tr><th>Sl.No.</th><th>CEFs</th><th>CEF bases</th></tr>
<tr><td>F1</td><td>$\{\Re^{\in}{}_{F1}\} \square \{\Re^{\doteq}{}_{F1}\} \doteq$
{{O|O},{O||O},{O|||O},
{O|O,O||O}, {O|O,O|||O}
{O||O,O|||O}, {O|O,O||O,O|||O}}</td><td>$\{\Re^{\in}{}_{\sigma 1}\} \square \{\Re^{\doteq}{}_{\sigma 1}\} \doteq$
{{O|O},{O||O},{O|||O}}</td></tr>
<tr><td>F2</td><td>$\{\Re^{\in}{}_{F2}\} \square \{\Re^{\doteq}{}_{F2}\} \doteq$
{{O|O},{O||O},{O|O,O||O},
{O|O,O|||O},{O||O,O|||O}
{O|O,O||O,O|||O}}</td><td>$\{\Re^{\in}{}_{\sigma 2}\} \square \{\Re^{\doteq}{}_{\sigma 2}\} \doteq$
{{O|O},{O||O}}</td></tr>
<tr><td>F3</td><td>$\{\Re^{\in}{}_{F3}\} \square \{\Re^{\doteq}{}_{F3}\} \doteq$
{{O|O},{O|||O},{O|O,O||O},
{O|O,O|||O},{O||O,O|||O}
{O|O,O||O,O|||O}}</td><td>$\{\Re^{\in}{}_{\sigma 3}\} \square \{\Re^{\doteq}{}_{\sigma 3}\} \doteq$
{{O|O},{O|||O}}</td></tr>
<tr><td>F4</td><td>$\{\Re^{\in}{}_{F4}\} \square \{\Re^{\doteq}{}_{F4}\} \doteq$
{{O||O},{O|||O},{O|O,O||O},
{O|O,O|||O},{O||O,O|||O}
{O|O,O||O,O|||O}}</td><td>$\{\Re^{\in}{}_{\sigma 4}\} \square \{\Re^{\doteq}{}_{\sigma 4}\} \doteq$
{{O||O},{O|||O}}</td></tr>
<tr><td>F5</td><td>$\{\Re^{\in}{}_{F5}\} \square \{\Re^{\doteq}{}_{F5}\} \doteq$
{{O|O},{O|O,O||O},{O|O,O|||O},
{O||O,O|||O},{O|O,O||O,O|||O}}</td><td>$\{\Re^{\in}{}_{\sigma 5}\} \square \{\Re^{\doteq}{}_{\sigma 5}\} \doteq$
{{O|O},{O||O,O|||O}}</td></tr>
<tr><td>F6</td><td>$\{\Re^{\in}{}_{F6}\} \square \{\Re^{\doteq}{}_{F6}\} \doteq$
{{O||O},{O|O,O||O},{O|O,O|||O},
{O||O,O|||O},{O|O,O||O,O|||O}}</td><td>$\{\Re^{\in}{}_{\sigma 6}\} \square \{\Re^{\doteq}{}_{\sigma 6}\} \doteq$
{{O||O},{O|O,O|||O}}</td></tr>
<tr><td>F7</td><td>$\{\Re^{\in}{}_{F7}\} \square \{\Re^{\doteq}{}_{F7}\} \doteq$
{{O|||O},{O|O,O||O},{O|O,O|||O},
{O||O,O|||O},{O|O,O||O,O|||O}}</td><td>$\{\Re^{\in}{}_{\sigma 7}\} \square \{\Re^{\doteq}{}_{\sigma 7}\} \doteq$
{{O|||O},{O|O,O||O}}</td></tr>
<tr><td>$\overline{F8}$</td><td>$\{\Re^{\in}{}_{F8}\} \square \{\Re^{\doteq}{}_{F8}\} \doteq$
{{O|O},{O|O,O||O},{O|O,O|||O},
{O|O,O||O,O|||O}}</td><td>$\{\Re^{\in}{}_{\sigma 8}\} \square \{\Re^{\doteq}{}_{\sigma 8}\} \doteq$
{{O|O}}</td></tr>
<tr><td>$\overline{F9}$</td><td>$\{\Re^{\in}{}_{F9}\} \square \{\Re^{\doteq}{}_{F9}\} \doteq$
{{O||O},{O|O,O||O},{O||O,O|||O},
{O|O,O||O,O|||O}}</td><td>$\{\Re^{\in}{}_{\sigma 9}\} \square \{\Re^{\doteq}{}_{\sigma 9}\} \doteq$
{{O||O}}</td></tr>
</table>

<table>
<tr><td>$\overline{F10}$</td><td>$\{\mathfrak{R}^{\in}{}_{F10}\} \square \{\mathfrak{R}^{\dot{=}}{}_{F10}\} \dot{=}$
{{O|||O},{O|O,O||O},
{O||O,O|||O},{O|O,O||O,O|||O}}</td><td>$\{\mathfrak{R}^{\in}{}_{\sigma10}\} \square \{\mathfrak{R}^{\dot{=}}{}_{\sigma10}\} \dot{=}$
{{O|||O}}</td></tr>
<tr><td>$\overline{F11}$</td><td>$\{\mathfrak{R}^{\in}{}_{F11}\} \square \{\mathfrak{R}^{\dot{=}}{}_{F11}\} \dot{=}$
{{O|O,O||O}, {O|O,O|||O},
{O||O,O|||O},{O|O,O||O,O|||O}}</td><td>$\{\mathfrak{R}^{\in}{}_{\sigma11}\} \square \{\mathfrak{R}^{\dot{=}}{}_{\sigma11}\} \dot{=}$
{{O|O,O||O},
{O|O,O|||O},{O||O,O|||O}}</td></tr>
<tr><td>F12</td><td>$\{\mathfrak{R}^{\in}{}_{F12}\} \square \{\mathfrak{R}^{\dot{=}}{}_{F12}\} \dot{=}$
{{O|O,O||O}, {O|O,O|||O},
{O|O,O||O,O|||O}}</td><td>$\{\mathfrak{R}^{\in}{}_{\sigma12}\} \square \{\mathfrak{R}^{\dot{=}}{}_{\sigma12}\} \dot{=}$
{{O|O,O||O},
{O|O,O|||O}}</td></tr>
<tr><td>F13</td><td>$\{\mathfrak{R}^{\in}{}_{F13}\} \square \{\mathfrak{R}^{\dot{=}}{}_{F13}\} \dot{=}$
{{O|O,O||O}, {O||O,O|||O},
{O|O,O||O,O|||O}}</td><td>$\{\mathfrak{R}^{\in}{}_{\sigma13}\} \square \{\mathfrak{R}^{\dot{=}}{}_{\sigma13}\} \dot{=}$
{{O|O,O||O},
{O||O,O|||O}}</td></tr>
<tr><td>F14</td><td>$\{\mathfrak{R}^{\in}{}_{F14}\} \square \{\mathfrak{R}^{\dot{=}}{}_{F14}\} \dot{=}$
{{O|O,O|||O}, {O||O,O|||O},
{O|O,O||O,O|||O}}</td><td>$\{\mathfrak{R}^{\in}{}_{\sigma14}\} \square \{\mathfrak{R}^{\dot{=}}{}_{\sigma14}\} \dot{=}$
{{O|O,O|||O},
{O||O,O|||O}}</td></tr>
<tr><td>F15</td><td>$\{\mathfrak{R}^{\in}{}_{F15}\} \square \{\mathfrak{R}^{\dot{=}}{}_{F15}\} \dot{=}$
{{O|O,O||O}, {O|O,O||O,O|||O}}</td><td>$\{\mathfrak{R}^{\in}{}_{\sigma15}\} \square \{\mathfrak{R}^{\dot{=}}{}_{\sigma15}\} \dot{=}$
{{O|O,O||O}}</td></tr>
<tr><td>F16</td><td>$\{\mathfrak{R}^{\in}{}_{F16}\} \square \{\mathfrak{R}^{\dot{=}}{}_{F16}\} \dot{=}$
{{O|O,O|||O}, {O|O,O||O,O|||O}}</td><td>$\{\mathfrak{R}^{\in}{}_{\sigma16}\} \square \{\mathfrak{R}^{\dot{=}}{}_{\sigma16}\} \dot{=}$
{{O|O,O|||O}}</td></tr>
<tr><td>F17</td><td>$\{\mathfrak{R}^{\in}{}_{F17}\} \square \{\mathfrak{R}^{\dot{=}}{}_{F17}\} \dot{=}$
{{O||O,O|||O}, {O|O,O||O,O|||O}}</td><td>$\{\mathfrak{R}^{\in}{}_{\sigma17}\} \square \{\mathfrak{R}^{\dot{=}}{}_{\sigma17}\} \dot{=}$
{{O||O,O|||O}}</td></tr>
<tr><td>F18</td><td>$\{\mathfrak{R}^{\in}{}_{F18}\} \square \{\mathfrak{R}^{\dot{=}}{}_{F18}\} \dot{=}$
{{O|O,O||O,O|||O}}</td><td>$\{\mathfrak{R}^{\in}{}_{\sigma18}\} \square \{\mathfrak{R}^{\dot{=}}{}_{\sigma18}\} \dot{=}$
{{O|O,O||O,O|||O}}</td></tr>
</table>

Figure 9.2.1.2.2 shows the lattice arrangement of 18 CEFs over the constructive set X_0 = {O|O,O||O,O|||O}. Note that there are four universal filters, which satisfy both FIP and PIP.

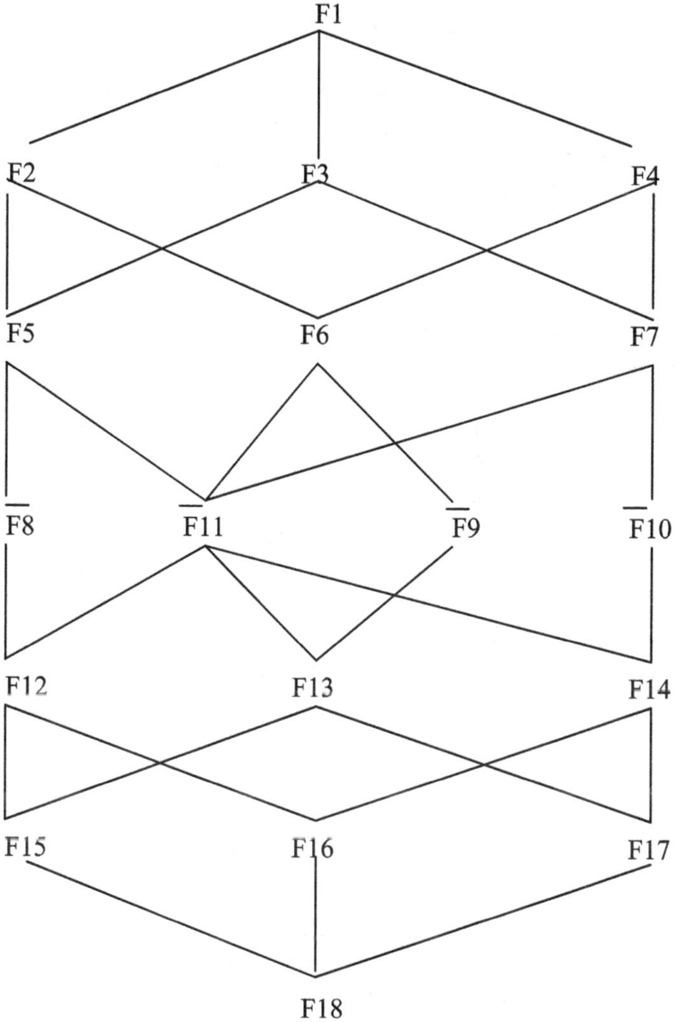

Figure 9.2.1.2.2: Lattice formed by the CEF's over
X_0 = {O|O,O||O,O|||O}

9.3 Description Of Normal Algorithms In Terms Of Constructive Extended Filter Bases

In the beginning of subsection 9.2, it was argued that a normal algorithm $\mathcal{N}$ over an alphabet $\mathcal{A}$ is a filter in the sense that it divides the free monoid $\mathcal{A}^*$ into two disjoint sets $\$^{!\mathcal{N}}$ and $\$^{\neg!\mathcal{N}}$ where $\$^{!\mathcal{N}}$ is the set of all string in $\mathcal{A}^*$ to which $\mathcal{N}$ is sa-definite [Refer to subsection 1.2] and $\$^{\neg!\mathcal{N}}$ is its complement with respect to $\mathcal{A}^*$. So the normal algorithmic filter $\mathcal{N}$ is represented by the ordered dichotomy $< \$^{!\mathcal{N}}, \$^{\neg!\mathcal{N}} >$.

Here we show how a normal algorithm could be visualized in terms of constructive extended filter bases.

With reference to definition 2.2.1, a normal algorithm $\mathcal{N}$ over an alphabet $\mathcal{A}$ consists of an ordered list of substitution formulas of the type $P \rightarrow Q$ where each substitution formula could be viewed as a map of the type $\mathcal{A}^*P\mathcal{A}^* \rightarrow \mathcal{A}^*Q\,\mathcal{A}^*$. The left hand side of the map is a set containing element P which is a subset of the free monoid $\mathcal{A}^*$ and elements for which P is a factor. Similarly the right hand side of the map is a set containing the element Q which is subset of the free monoid $\mathcal{A}^*$and elements for which Q is a factor. We shall denote both the sets $\mathcal{A}^*P\mathcal{A}^*$ and $\mathcal{A}^*Q\mathcal{A}^*$ by $\hat{P}$ and $\hat{Q}$ respectively. Just as the partial order relation 'subset of' indicates the occurrence of a set in another, the partial order relation 'factor of' [Refer to Sl.No. 3 of table 8.1.1] indicates the occurrence of a string of symbols in another string. So, $\hat{P}$ and $\hat{Q}$ could be interpreted as CEF's with their respective bases P and Q. Thus a substitution formula $P \rightarrow Q$ of the normal algorithm $\mathcal{N}$ is viewed as an ordered pair <P, Q> of constructive extended filter bases. This amounts to saying that the normal algorithm $\mathcal{N}$ is a totally ordered list of ordered pairs of constructive extended filter bases.

Normal algorithms are thus seen to have a direct relevance in all potential applications of Hammer's topological techniques in signal processing.

Section 10

Quantifiable Measures Of Constructive Extended Filters In Terms Of Normal Algorithmic Operators

Abstract

Erlandson introduced three different measures of the filtering capabilities of extended filters: (i) the ambiguity of a filter, (ii) the discrimination of a filter and (iii) the resolution of a filter [27]. In addition, he introduced a metric over a space of filters, a measure of how close or far apart two different filters are.

Significantly, Erlandson's measures can be given a constructive interpretation as well. In fact, we could interpret these measures as normal algorithmic operators mapping a metric lattice of extended filters over a constructive set, into the metric space of constructive real numbers. But to describe our interpretation, we need to go into the details of constructive mathematical analysis, starting from the formulation of various constructive numbers, functions and function spaces. This would cause a diversion from the main flow of this book. So, we describe in what follows, the quantifiable measures for CEF's on similar lines of Erlandson, without losing the constructive aspects in them.

10.1 Quantifiable Measures For Constructive Extended Filters

10.1.1 Ambiguity Of A CEF Process

Let us take the lattice $(\Phi, \subseteq)$ formed by a family of CEF's over an alphabet $\mathcal{A}$. Ideally, a filter should not accept both an element and its

E. G. Rajan, *Symbolic Computing - Signal and Image Processing*
ISBN 81-7800-047-4

complement, whereas, such a condition is not stipulated in the definition of a CEF. So, any CEF that accepts both an element and its complement is called an ambiguous filter.

We denote the ambiguity measure of a constructive extended filter F_i of k elements by ψ_a and define it as:

$$\psi_a = \frac{|\{X: X \subseteq F_i \text{ and both } X \text{ and its complement } \bar{X} \text{ are in } F_i\}|}{2^{k-1}}$$

Universal filters are non ambiguous. The coarsest CEF contained in Φ is the least ambiguous filter and the finest CEF in Φ is the most ambiguous filter.

10.1.2 Discrimination Of ACEF Process

Discrimination of a CEF, F_i of k elements, is a measure of the number of elements accepted by it. We denote this measure as ψ_d and define it as:

$$\psi_d = \frac{|F_i|}{2^{k-1}}$$

The finest CEF is the most discriminating filter and the coarsest CEF is the least discriminating filter.

10.1.3 Resolution Of A CEF Process

Resolution is a measure of the smallest size of the elements accepted by a CEF. We define this measure in the following manner:

Let F_i be a CEF and σ_i be its base. Now, we denote the resolution measure of a CEF, F_i

of k elements as ψ_r and define it as : $\psi_r = \dfrac{1}{|\sigma_i|}$.

The finest CEF has a resolution 1/k, where, k is the cardinal number of the CEF and the coarsest CEF has a resolution 1.

10.1.4 Distance Measure Between Two CEF's

Consider two arbitrary CEF's F_i and F_j in a lattice of CEF's. Now the distance between these two CEF's is given by:

$$\psi_\delta = \frac{|F_i \cup F_j| - |F_i \cap F_j|}{|F_i \cup F_j|}$$

Example 10.1.1

Let us recall the example 9.2.1.2.2 and characterize all the 18 CEF's based on their Erlandson's measures. Let $\mathcal{A}$ be an alphabet and X_0 = {O|O,O||O,O|||O} be a base set constructed over $\mathcal{A}$. One can construct 18 extended filters over the set X_0. The complete distributive lattice formed by these 18 CEF's [Figure 9.2.1.2.2] is once again shown here in figure 10.1.1 along with the distance measures indicated at the appropriate places. [Note: We interpret the word O|/O||||||| as the rational number 1/7. A similar interpretation has to be made for any other word of this type.] The remaining measures pertaining to the above example are given in table 10.1.1.

Table 10.1.1: Quantifiable measures of CEF's over X_0={O|O,O||O,O|||O}

<table>
<tr><th>Sl.No.</th><th>$\{\mathcal{N}^{\psi_a}{}_{Fi}\}$</th><th>$\{\mathcal{N}^{\psi_d}{}_{Fi}\}$</th><th>$\{\mathcal{N}^{\psi_r}{}_{Fi}\}$</th></tr>
<tr><td>1</td><td>O|||/O||||</td><td>O||||||/O||||</td><td>O|/O|||</td></tr>
<tr><td>2</td><td>O||/O||||</td><td>O|||||/O||||</td><td>O|/O||</td></tr>
<tr><td>3</td><td>O||/O||||</td><td>O|||||/O||||</td><td>O|/O||</td></tr>
<tr><td>4</td><td>O||/O||||</td><td>O|||||/O||||</td><td>O|/O||</td></tr>
<tr><td>5</td><td>O|/O||||</td><td>O||||/O||||</td><td>O|/O||</td></tr>
<tr><td>6</td><td>O|/O||||</td><td>O||||/O||||</td><td>O|/O||</td></tr>
<tr><td>7</td><td>O|/O||||</td><td>O||||/O||||</td><td>O|/O||</td></tr>
<tr><td>8</td><td>O/O||||</td><td>O|||/O||||</td><td>O|/O|</td></tr>
<tr><td>9</td><td>O/O||||</td><td>O|||/O||||</td><td>O|/O|</td></tr>
<tr><td>10</td><td>O/O||||</td><td>O|||/O||||</td><td>O|/O|</td></tr>
<tr><td>11</td><td>O/O||||</td><td>O|||/O||||</td><td>O|/O|||</td></tr>
<tr><td>12</td><td>O/O||||</td><td>O||/O||||</td><td>O|/O||</td></tr>
<tr><td>13</td><td>O/O||||</td><td>O||/O||||</td><td>O|/O||</td></tr>
<tr><td>14</td><td>O/O||||</td><td>O||/O||||</td><td>O|/O||</td></tr>
<tr><td>15</td><td>O/O||||</td><td>O||/O||||</td><td>O|/O|</td></tr>
<tr><td>16</td><td>O/O||||</td><td>O||/O||||</td><td>O|/O|</td></tr>
<tr><td>17</td><td>O/O||||</td><td>O||/O||||</td><td>O|/O|</td></tr>
<tr><td>18</td><td>O/O||||</td><td>O|/O||||</td><td>O|/O|</td></tr>
</table>

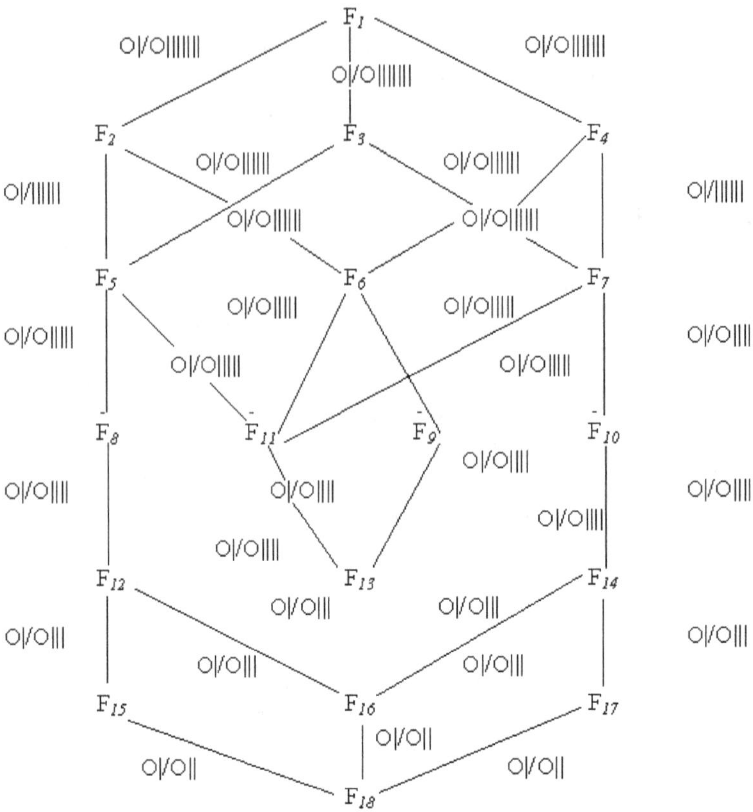

Figure 10.1.1: Same as figure 3.2.1.2.2

10.2 Combinatorial Theorems Involving Quantifiable Measures Of CEF's

Certain observations were made while computing Erlandson's measures for various CEF's over base sets whose cardinal numbers are less than or equal to three.

Those observations are stated here in the form of the following theorems:

Theorem 10.2.1

Let X_0 be the base set whose cardinal number is k. Then the following statements are valid:

(i) The finest filter is the most ambiguous filter over X_0 .
(ii) The coarsest filter is the least ambiguous filter over X_0 .
(iii) All the universal filters are non-ambiguous filter over X_0 .
(iv) All the CEF's which are coarser than universal filters over X_0 whose $k \leq 3$ are non-ambiguous filters.
(v) Ambiguity creeps in certain CEF's which are coarser than universal filters over X_0 whose $k > 3$.

Proof

(i) It is obvious that the cardinal number of the power set X_1 of the base set X_0 is 2^k. The finest filter contains all the elements of X_1 other than the null set. This means that the finest filter allows maximum number of subsets along with their complements too, thus possessing the highest measure of ambiguity.

(ii) The coarsest filter contains the base set X_0 as its only element. This shows that it is the least ambiguous (non-ambiguous) filter.

(iii) A universal filter by virtue of its definition satisfies pair wise intersection property. This rules out the presence of any pair of elements of a universal filter which are complement to each other. So the universal filters are non-ambiguous.

(iv) Refer to table 10.2.1. All the CEF's: F_{12} to F_{18} are non-ambiguous.

(v) Let us consider $X_0 \doteq \{O|O, O||O, O|||O, O||||O\}$ whose $k = 4$. One can construct CEF's which are ambiguous and coarser than the universal filters similar to the one given below

$$\{\Re^{\in}{}_{Fi}\} \square \{\Re^{\doteq}{}_{Fi}\} \doteq \{\{O|O,O||O\},\{O|||O,O||||O\},\{O|O,O||O,O|||O\} \{O|O,O||O\},\{O||||O\} \{O|O,O|||O,O||||O\}, \{O||O,O|||O,O||||O,\ O|O,O||O,O|||O,O||||O\}\}$$

The number of ambiguous filters which are coarser than the universal filters increases when base sets of higher cardinalities are considered.

Theorem 10.2.2

Let X_0 be the base set whose cardinal number is k. Then CEF's whose cardinal numbers are greater than 2^{k-1} do not posses pair wise intersection property (PIP).

Proof

All CEF's whose cardinal numbers are greater than 2^{k-1} are ambiguous and ambiguous filters do not possess PIP.

Corollary

All those CEF's which possess PIP would be of cardinalities less than or equal to 2^{k-1} . This is the direct consequence of theorem 10.2.2 .

Theorem 10.2.3

The discrimination measure of a family of CEF's over a base set X_0 of cardinality k

ranges from $\frac{1}{2^{k-1}}$ to $\frac{2^k-1}{2^{k-1}}$ in steps of $\frac{1}{2^{k-1}}$.

Proof

As defined earlier, the discrimination ψ_d of a CEF, F_i is given by

$$\psi_d = \frac{|F_i|}{2^{k-1}}$$

Now the complete distributive lattice formed by the family of CEF's over a given base set of cardinality k, consists of linear chains of CEF's. Each linear chain contains 2^{k-1} CEF's which are linked by the relation "*just finer than*". The distance measure between any two CEF's, of which one is just finer than the other is $\frac{1}{2^{k-1}}$.

This is true for all linear chains contained in the lattice. Hence the theorem is proved.

Theorem 10.2.4

For base sets with $k \geq 3$, every universal filter which satisfies both FIP and PIP, yields a universal filter of resolution 1/k and which satisfies only PIP, when the base element of the former is replaced by its complement with respect to X_0 .

Proof

The universal filters over a base set X_0, which satisfy both FIP and PIP are ultra filters of cartan type whose single element bases consist of elements from X_0. Let us consider one such filter $\tilde{F}_i$ whose base consists of any one of the k elements of X_0. By virtue of the definition 9.2.1.1.1., the remaining $(2^{k-1}-1)$ elements of $\tilde{F}_i$ must contain this base element. If this base element is replaced by its complement set which is a subset of X_0 consisting of (k-1) elements of X_0, then the finite intersection property does not hold for the resulting filter. On the other hand, the complement set has a nonempty intersection with each of the $(2^{k-1}-1)$ element of $\tilde{F}_i$. So, the resulting filter is a universal filter, which satisfies only PIP. Let us denote this resulting filter by $\tilde{F}_{ic}$. The base of $\tilde{F}_{ic}$ will then consist of k elements, in which (k-1) elements would be the super sets of cardinality 2 of the base element of $\tilde{F}_i$ and the remaining one element would be the complement set of the base element of $\tilde{F}_i$. For a base set X_0 with k=1 there is only one universal filter and the question of complement set of its base does not arise at all. For a base set X_0 with k=2 there are two universal filters whose bases are complements to each other. So the question of getting a universal filter of the type $\tilde{F}_{ic}$ does not arise at all. For a base set X_0 with k=3 there are three universal filters and only one universal filter of the type $\tilde{F}_{ic}$ would result when any of the bases of the three $\tilde{F}_i$'s is complemented [Refer to table 9.2.1.2.2] . For a base set X_0 with k>3 each of the k universal filters of the cartan type ultra filters would yield a unique and independent universal filter of the type $\tilde{F}_{ic}$ with the resolution 1/k when its base element is complemented.

The following theorem due to Erlandson, characterizes a certain kind of universal filters in terms of 'resolution'.

Theorem 10.2.5 [27]

Given a base set X_0 with $k \geq 3$ and k being an old number, one can construct a universal filter $\bar{F}_i$ with ${}^kC_{[k/2]}$ elements.

[Note: [k/2] denotes the next integer greater than the result of dividing k by 2. Similarly (k/2) denotes the next integer less than the result of dividing k by 2.]

Proof:

The proof is omitted here. [Refer to [27] for detailed proof.]

Part IV

Abstract

This part provides a compressive introduction to symbolic processing of digital image using Cellular Logic Algorithms. A cellular logic algorithm is essentially a realization of a Cellular Automaton by a Generalised Markov Algorithm. The notion of a Generalised Markov Algorithm has been already described at the end of section 1 of the first part of this book. With images treated as arrays of symbols, which we refer as *Array Configurations*, from an alphabet $\mathcal{A}$, our concern is to consider the realization of various pattern generating and image processing operations in terms of pattern matching and substitution operations using cellular automata rules.

Symbolic Image Processing

Section 11

Cellular Automata And Their Realizations

11.1 Why Do We Model Digital Images As Cellular Automata Configurations ?

Traditionally, an image processing operation in spatial domain is expressed as a transformation g(x,y) = T[f(x,y)], where f(x,y) is the input image, g(x,y) is the output image and T is the transformation operator on f, defined over some neighborhood of (x,y).

Regardless of the nature of operations, however, the general approach is to scan a given 2-D array by a 3x3 window and update all the pixel values with the computed ones, the computations involving the coefficients of the window and those of the image pixels scanned by it. But, there are occasions when one can carry out a required operation using a simple *pattern matching and updating* technique instead of computing update values from an expression involving the window coefficients and the corresponding image pixel values. For example, let us take the case of *edge detection,* which is an operation of locating the pixels that form a transition between two regions of distinct gray-level properties in an image. Numerous edge detection algorithms are available in the literature among which use of *Sobel Operators* has become by far one of the most popular edge detection techniques because of their advantages in computational speed. Alternatively, the pattern-directed edge detection technique that is given in section 14, makes use of a simple nonnumerical operation of assigning the gray value 0 to a pixel if it along with its neighbors forms a particular homogeneous pattern inside a 3 x 3 window. By using this edge detection technique, we could achieve a considerable increase in the computational speed as compared to that observed in obtaining a gradient image using Sobel operators.

E. G. Rajan, *Symbolic Computing - Signal and Image Processing*
ISBN 81-7800-047-4

All these amount to say that pattern-directed array processing techniques play an important role in the image processing practice where high-throughput image understanding systems are deemed. Digital images are represented as symbolic array configurations, and are processed using pattern-directed schemes of Generalized Markov Algorithms. A pattern-directed scheme of this kind essentially consists of a finite number of *Search* and *Substitute* rules called *Conjoint Substitution Formulas.* Since the notion of a conjoint substitution formula is closely related to that of pattern substitution using neighborhood principles, it is then reasonable to treat an image as an input configuration to a *Cellular Automaton,* and realize filtering operations on the image in terms of cellular automata evolutions carried out by Generalized Markov Algorithms. In this section, we discuss some of the salient features of cellular automata and their generalizations.

11.2 The Notion Of a Cellular Automaton

The concept of *Cellular Automata* was originally introduced by von Neumann and Ulam, under the name *cellular spaces,* as a possible idealization of a biological systems, with a particular purpose of modeling biological self-reproduction [25], [26]. Later, this concept has been reinterpreted, for various purposes, under different names like *tessellation automata, homogeneous structures, cellular structures* and *iterative arrays.*

The term *cellular automaton,* in general, denotes a regular uniform lattice, usually infinite in extent, with a discrete variable at each site. The state of a cellular automaton, at a time instant, is determined by the corresponding *configuration,* that is, by the array of values (numerical) of these variables at that time instant. We are concerned here only with the following three types of cellular automata: (i) one-dimensional cellular automata, (ii) two-dimensional cellular automata and (iii) three-dimensional cellular automata, and we denote their configurations respectively as (i) linear array configuration, (ii) square array configuration and (iii) cube array configuration.

A cellular automaton evolves in discrete time steps, with the value of the variable at one site being affected by the values of the variables at sites in its neighborhood on the previous time step. By *neighborhood of a site* we mean the site itself along with all or some of its immediately adjacent sites. The site values corresponding to a configuration at a particular time step, say t, are updated, all at once, based on the values in their neighborhood, according to as definite set of updating rules. The resulting configuration at time step t+1, is the evolved version of the one at time step t.

Updating rules are classified in the following manner. An updating rule which involves the neighborhood values of the just previous time step only, is referred as a *local rule* or a *first order rule,* whereas the one which involves the neighborhood values of the previous two time steps is called a *second order rule.* All updating rules beyond second order rules are called *higher order rules.* A cellular automaton, which evolves purely according to a fixed set of local rules is called a *first order cellular automaton.* Second and higher order cellular automata are to be understood in the same manner. We are concerned here only with *first order cellular automaton.*

11.3 One-Dimensional Cellular Automata

A one dimensional N-ary valued cellular automaton **C** consists of a 1-D array of cells. Each cell takes on any of N given values, and all the values are simultaneously updated at a particular stage of evolution according to a rule involving the values contained in certain neighboring cells. The evolutions of a cellular automaton are assumed to take place in successive stages. The value of a cell i at a particular stage of evolution t, is an element from a set of numbers X = {0, 1, … , N-1 }, and it is denoted by $\xi^{(t)}_i$. A numerical sequence corresponding to the values contained in the linear array of cells at a stage t, is called a *configuration* of **C**. From a given configuration, a new configuration is evolved by updating the given cell values in accordance with a rule that decides the new value of each cell based on its old value and those of some of its neighbors. By the *r-neighborhood* of a cell, we mean the cell itself together with (r-1)/2 adjacent cells to its immediate left (r-1)/2 adjacent cells to its immediate right; r are is always assumed to be odd.

For example, a 3-neighborhood of a cell i of a cellular automaton **C** is a structure formed by the cell i and its immediate left and right neighbors as shown below:

i-1	i	i+1

At a state t, let $\xi^{(t)}_{i-1}$, $\xi^{(t)}_{i}$ and $\xi^{(t)}_{i+1}$ be the values held by the 3-neighborhood of i. Now, let us consider an updating rule ϕ that applies to all 3-neighborhoods and let us apply it to the configuration at stage t. Then, the value of ith cell $\xi^{(t)}_{i}$ is updated as $\xi^{(t+1)}_{i}$ where,

$$\xi^{(t+1)}_{i} = \phi\,(\,\xi^{(t)}_{i-1}\,,\xi^{(t)}_{i}\,,\xi^{(t)}_{i+1}\,)\ .$$

All the cell values in the configuration are updated simultaneously in this manner. For the sake of illustration, let us take the case of a one-dimensional three-neighborhood cellular automaton whose cell variables take on values from the set X = {0, 1}. An updating rule ϕ, in this case, would be a Boolean function of the sites within the neighborhood . As an example, let us consider A Boolean function ϕ, where $\phi : \xi^{(t+1)}_{i} = \xi^{(t)}_{i-1} \oplus \xi^{(t)}_{i+1}$ is a modulo two rule. According to this rule, the value of a particular cell is simply the sum modulo two of the values of its two neighboring cells on the previous time step.

This rule can also be viewed as a map as shown below:

$\xi^{(t)}_{i-1}$	$\xi^{(t)}_{i}$	$\xi^{(t)}_{i+1}$		$\xi^{(t+1)}_{i}$	
0	0	0	→	0	← LSB
0	0	1	→	1	
0	1	0	→	0	
0	1	1	→	1	
1	0	0	→	1	
1	0	1	→	0	
1	1	0	→	1	
1	1	1	→	0	← MSB

MSB LSB
↓ ↓

Now we see that the 8-bit word 01011010 given in the last column of the above map is the binary representation of the decimal number 90. We call this binary representation as *rule 90.* Thus one can generate a total of 256 rules (Boolean Functions) for a binary valued, three-neighborhood one-dimensional cellular automaton [26]. In general, one can generate a total of $N^{N^{r}}$ rules for an N-ary valued, r-neighborhood one-dimensional cellular automaton.

Example 11.3.1

Let us see now, how a 3-neighborhood one-dimensional cellular automaton governed by the rule 90, evolves from a single seed input configuration (see figure 11.3.1(a)) and from an input configuration with values 0 and 1, randomly placed in it (see figure 11.3.1(b)). The Boolean function corresponding to the rule number 90 is

$$\xi^{(t+1)}{}_{i} = \xi^{(t)}{}_{i-1} \oplus \xi^{(t)}{}_{i} \oplus \xi^{(t)}{}_{i+1}$$

Single seed input															
13 evolutions ↓	**0**	**0**	**0**	**0**	**0**	**0**	**0**	**1**	**0**	**0**	**0**	**0**	**0**	**0**	**0**
	0	0	0	0	0	0	1	0	1	0	0	0	0	0	0
	0	0	0	0	0	1	0	0	0	1	0	0	0	0	0
	0	0	0	0	1	0	1	0	1	0	1	0	0	0	0
	0	0	0	1	0	0	0	0	0	0	0	1	0	0	0
	0	0	1	0	1	0	0	0	0	0	1	0	1	0	0
	0	1	0	0	0	1	0	0	0	1	0	0	0	1	0
	0	0	1	0	1	0	1	0	1	0	1	0	1	0	0
	0	1	0	0	0	0	0	0	0	0	0	0	0	1	0
	0	0	1	0	0	0	0	0	0	0	0	0	1	0	0
	0	1	0	1	0	0	0	0	0	0	0	1	0	1	0
	0	0	0	0	1	0	0	0	0	0	1	0	0	0	0
	0	0	0	1	0	1	0	0	0	1	0	1	0	0	0
	0	0	1	0	0	0	1	0	1	0	0	0	1	0	0

Figure 11.3.1 (a): Pattern generated by a cellular automaton with rule number 90 that evolves from an input configuration with a seed value 1 placed in it at a chosen cell.

Input with disordered cell values															
13	**0**	**1**	**1**	**0**	**1**	**0**	**1**	**1**	**0**	**1**	**0**	**1**	**0**	**1**	**0**
evolutions	0	1	1	0	0	0	1	1	0	0	0	0	0	0	0
	0	1	1	1	0	1	1	1	1	0	0	0	0	0	0
	0	1	0	1	0	1	0	0	1	1	0	0	0	0	0
	0	0	0	0	0	0	1	1	1	1	1	0	0	0	0
	0	0	0	0	0	1	1	0	0	0	1	1	0	0	0
	0	0	0	0	1	1	1	1	0	1	1	1	1	0	0
	0	0	0	1	1	0	0	1	0	1	0	0	1	1	0
	0	0	1	1	1	1	1	0	0	0	1	1	1	1	0
	0	1	1	0	0	0	1	1	0	1	1	0	0	1	0
	0	1	1	1	0	1	1	1	0	1	1	1	1	0	0
	0	1	0	1	0	1	0	1	0	1	0	0	1	1	0
	0	0	0	0	0	0	0	0	0	0	1	1	1	1	0
↓	0	0	0	0	0	0	0	0	0	1	1	0	0	1	0

Figure 11.3.1 (b): Pattern generated by a cellular automaton with rule number 90 that evolves from an input confuguration with values 0 and 1, randomly placed in it.

Examples of patterns generated by finite number of evolutions of various ternary valued 1-D cellular automata starting from the seed value 1 and also from configurations with disordered cell values 0 and 1 are respectively shown in figure 11.3.2 (a) and in figure 11.3.2 (b). Figure 11.3.2 (c) shows a pattern generated by a 1-D cellular automaton from disordered sites with multiple values

Rule number: 90; Single seed value: 1; length: 500; evolutions: 300

Rule number: 150; Single seed value: 1; length: 500: evolutions: 300

Figure 11.3.2 (a): Patterns generated by 1-D Cellular Automata from a seed value 1

Rule number: 170; Random site values: 0,1; length: 500; evolutions: 300

Rule number: 204; Random site values: 0,1; length: 500; evolutions: 300
Figure 11.3.2 (b): Patterns due to 1-D cellular automata from disordered sites

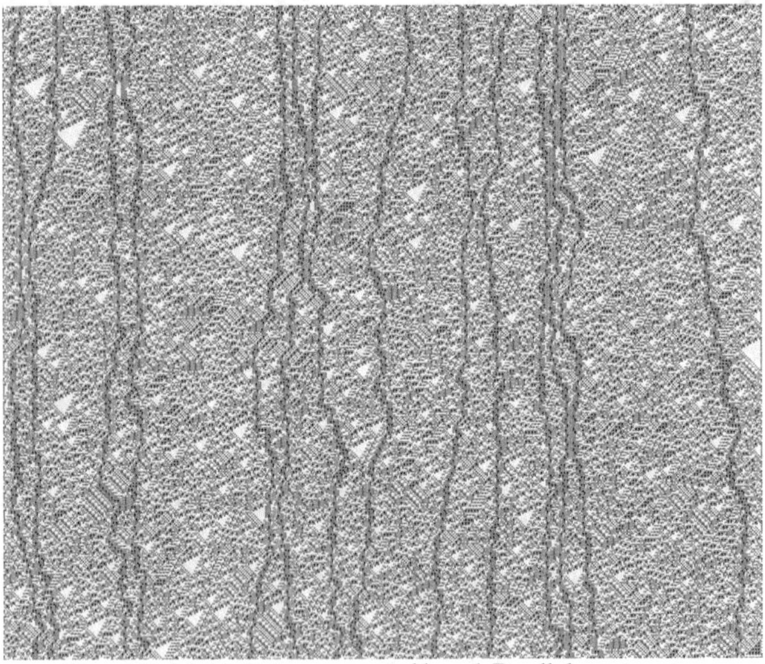

Figure 11.3.2 (c) Pattern generated by a 1-D cellular automaton from disordered sites with multiple values

The initial configuration of the pattern shown in figure 11.3.2 (c) consists of 500 cells. Each cell is entitled to take up any of the 16 values ranging from 0 to 15. The 3-neighbourhood updating rule is one of the 15^{15^3} rules. The cellular automaton evolves 450 times, and all the 450 configurations along with the initial configuration make the pattern shown in the figure.

This cellular automaton could be seen to exhibit a diffusion process denoted by the random walk phenomenon shown in the figure in the form of fourteen streaks starting from initial configuration and ending at the 450th configuration.

11.4 Filter Automata

A new class of automata that use newly computed cell values as soon as they are available was introduced in 1986 by Park, Steiglitz and Thurston [26]. They are called *Filter Automata.* They are analogous to *Infinite Impulse Response (IIR) Digital Filters,* whereas the usual one dimensional cellular automata described in the previous subsection 11.3 correspond to *Finite Impulse Response (FIR) Digital Filters.* In this subsection we provide a brief idea of filter automata as they have a direct relevance in formulating techniques for realizing IIR digital filters using one dimensional cellular automata.

11.4.1 The Notion Of a Filter Automaton

Let us consider a one dimensional r-neighborhood cellular automaton. By the r-neighborhood of a cell, we mean the cell itself together with (r–1)/2 adjacent cells to its immediate left and (r–1)/2 adjacent cells to its immediate right. In the case of the usual cellular automaton, the next value of a cell i is a function of the previous values in the neighborhood. On the other hand, in a filter automaton, the next state rule is of the form:

$$\xi^{(t+1)}_i = \phi\left(\xi^{(t+1)}_{i-(r-1)/2}, \xi^{(t+1)}_{i-(r-1)/2+1}, \ldots, \xi^{(t+1)}_{i-1}, \xi^{(t)}_{i}, \xi^{(t)}_{i+1}, \ldots, \xi^{(t)}_{i+(r-1)/2}\right)$$

Note that the next state values of a cell i is computed using the newly updated values of $\xi^{(t+1)}_{i-(r-1)/2}, \xi^{(t+1)}_{i-(r-1)/2+1}, \ldots, \xi^{(t+1)}_{i-1}$ instead of $\xi^{(t)}_{i-(r-1)/2}, \xi^{(t)}_{i-(r-1)/2+1}, \ldots, \xi^{(t)}_{i-1}$. This is exactly analogous to the operation of an IIR digital filter.

Definition 11.4.1

A cellular automaton is called *totalistic* if the next state value of a cell i is calculated as the sum of all the values in the prescribed neighborhood. For example, a one dimensional r-neighborhood cellular automaton is called totalistic only when the updating rule is of the form.

$$\xi_i^{(t+1)} = \sum_{j=-r/2}^{r/2} \xi^{(t)}_{i-j}$$

Definition 11.4.2

A one dimensional binary valued r-neighborhood filter automaton is called *parity-rule filter automaton* only when its updating rule is of the form

$$\xi_i^{(t+1)} = \begin{cases} 1, & \text{when the number of 1's in the neighborhood is even but not zero} \\ 0, & \text{otherwise} \end{cases}$$

More theoretical details about parity-rule filter automata and their applications can be found in [26]. An example pattern generated by 20 evolutions of a filter automaton from an input configuration of length 50 using rule number 90 is shown in figure 11.4.1. Figure 11.4.2 shows the patterns generated by 1-D, three neighborhood, binary valued, second order filter automata with updating rules ranging from 0 to 255.

```
000000000001011000000010001110000000101100000011000
000000000010110000000100011100000001011000000110000
000000000101100000001000111000000010110000001100000
000000001011000000010001110000000101100000011000000
000000010110000000100011100000001011000000110000000
000000101100000001000111000000010110000001100000000
000001011000000010001110000000101100000011000000000
000010110000000100011100000001011000000110000000000
000101100000001000111000000010110000001100000000000
001011000000010001110000000101100000011000000000000
010110000000100011100000001011000000110000000000000
010011111110111000111111101001111110011111111111111
011000000010001110000000101100000011000000000000001
```

Figure 11.4.1: Evolution of a filter automaton

The following 256 patterns are due to a 1-D, binary valued, three neighborhood, second order filter automata evolving 45 times from a starting configuration containing 50 disordered sites using rules ranging from 0 to 255.

 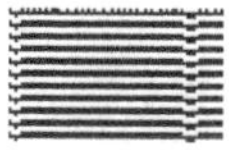  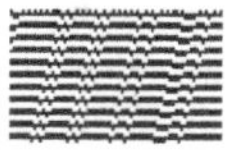

0 1 2 3

 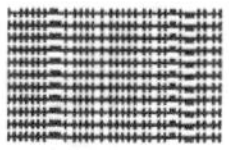  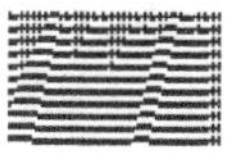

4 5 6 7

   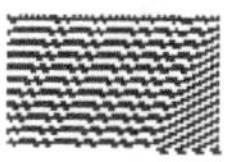

8 9 10 11

 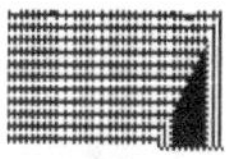  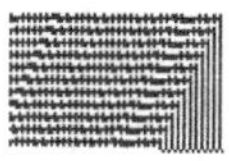

12 13 14 15

 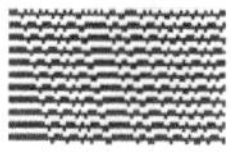  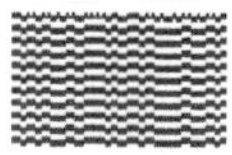

16 17 18 19

 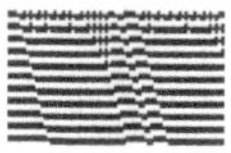  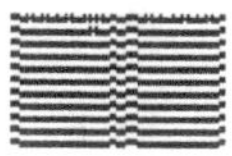

20 21 22 23

   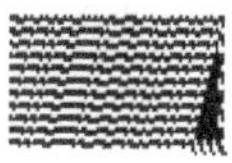

24 25 26 27

   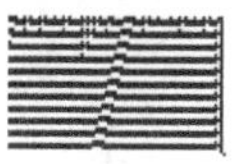

28 29 30 31

 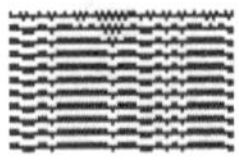 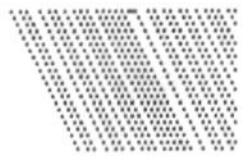 

32 33 34 35

 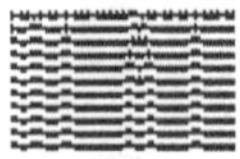  

36 37 38 39

 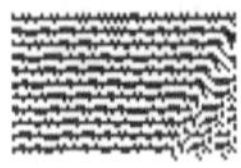  

40 41 42 43

 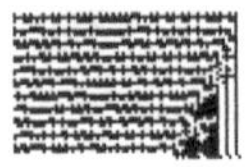  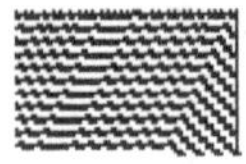

44 45 46 47

 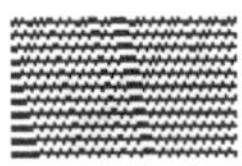  

48 49 50 51

   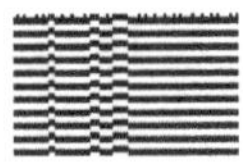

52 53 54 55

 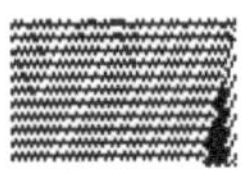  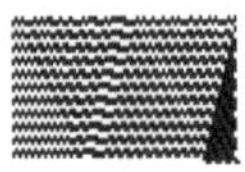

56 57 58 59

   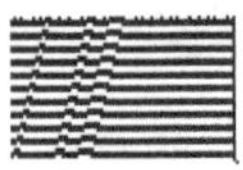

60 61 62 63

64
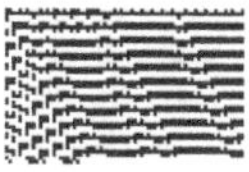
65

66
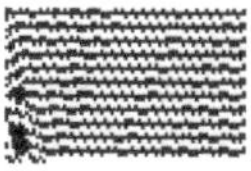
67

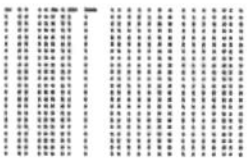
68
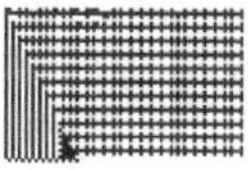
69

70

71

72
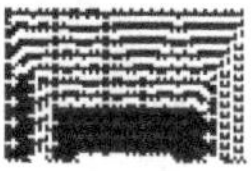
73

74

75

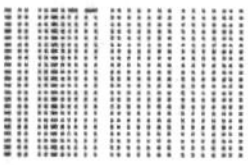
76
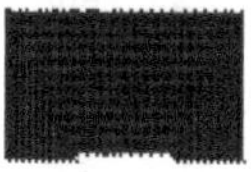
77
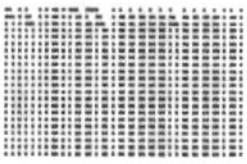
78
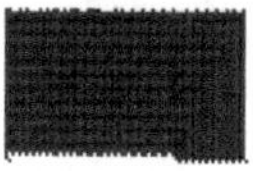
79

80
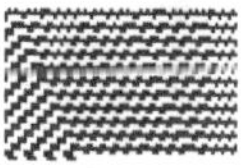
81

82
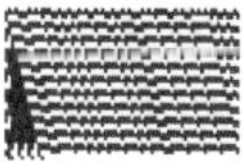
83

84
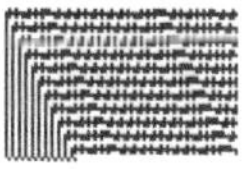
85

86
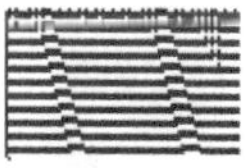
87

88

89

90
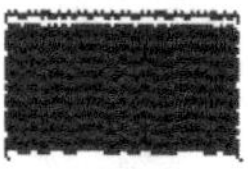
91

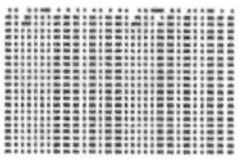
92
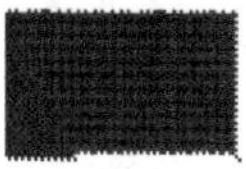
93
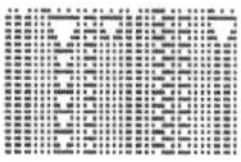
94
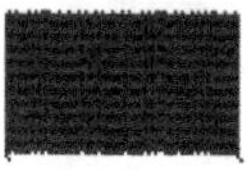
95

96
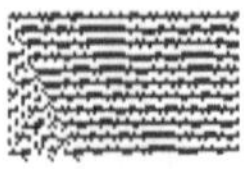
97
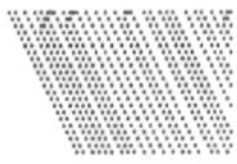
98

99
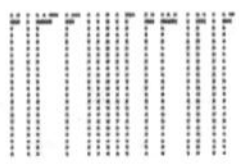
100

101

102

103

104

105

106

107

108
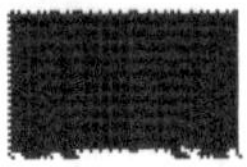
109

110
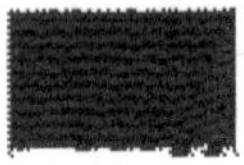
111

112

113

114
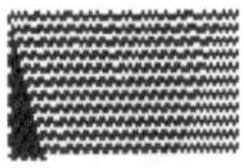
115

116
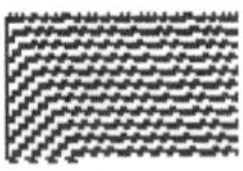
117

118
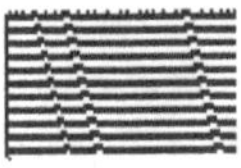
119

120
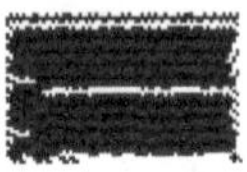
121

122
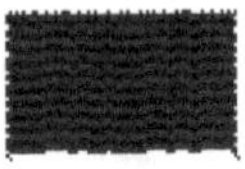
123

124
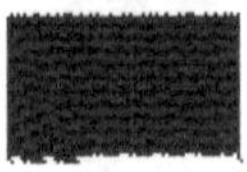
125
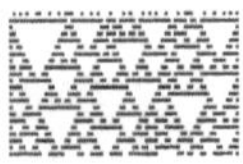
126
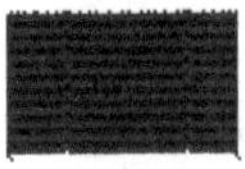
127

128

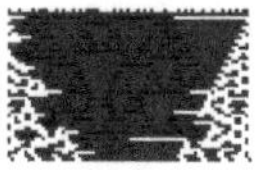
129

130

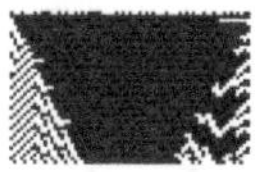
131

132

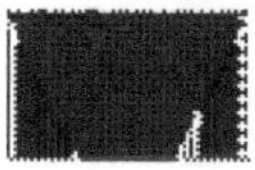
133

134

135

136

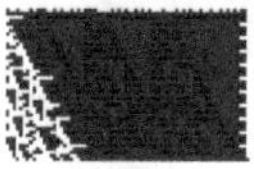
137

138

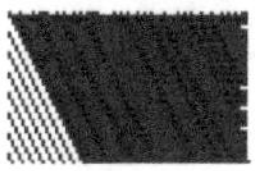
139

140

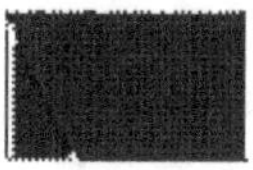
141

142

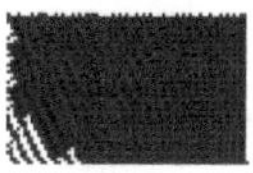
143

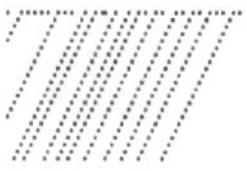
144

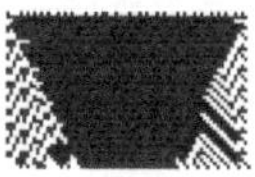
145

146

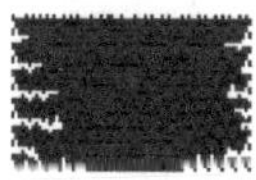
147

148

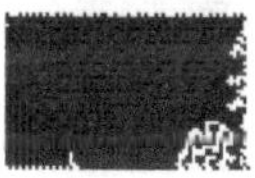
149

150

151

152

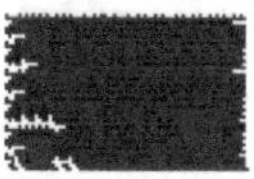
153

154

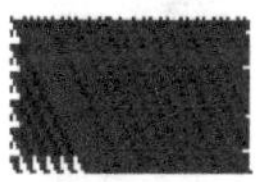
155

156

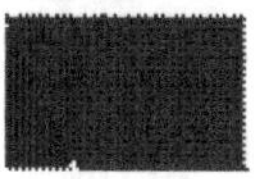
157

158

159

160
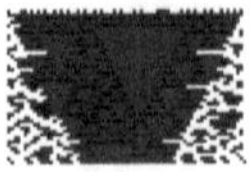
161

162

163
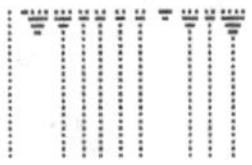
164
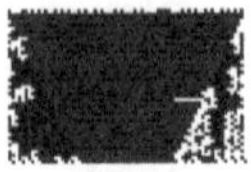
165

166

167

168
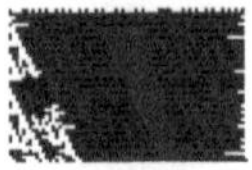
169

170
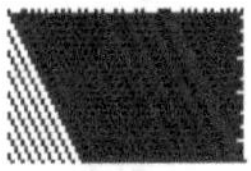
171
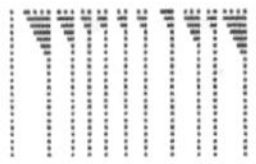
172
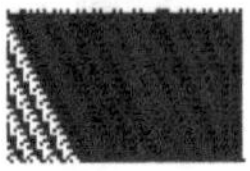
173

174
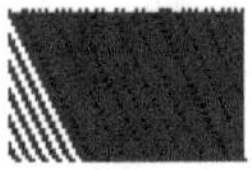
175

176
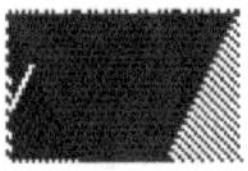
177

178
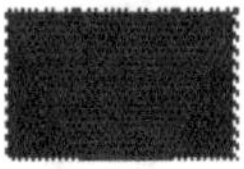
179

180

181

182

183

184
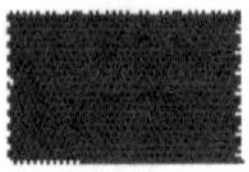
185

186
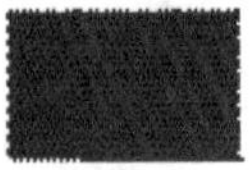
187

188

189

190

191

192

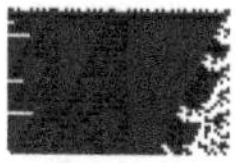

193

194

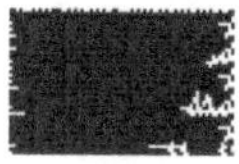

195

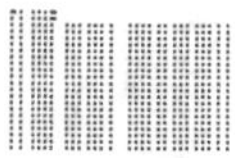

196

197

198

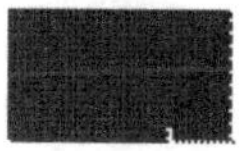

199

200

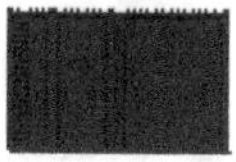

201

202

203

204

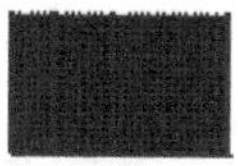

205

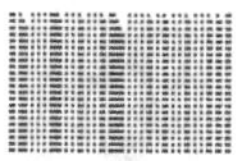

206

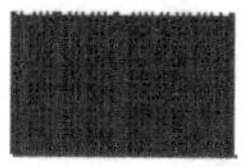

207

208

209

210

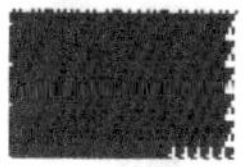

211

212

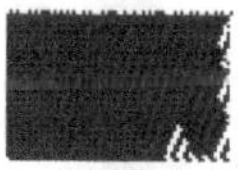

213

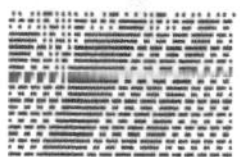

214

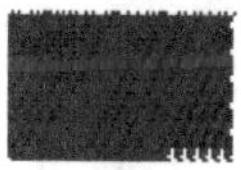

215

216

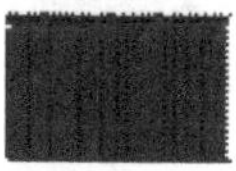

217

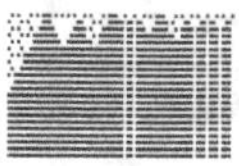

218

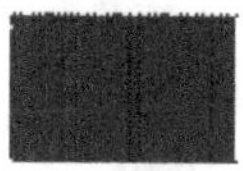

219

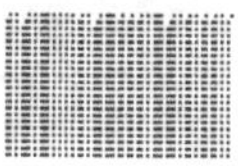

220

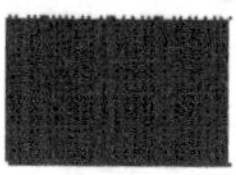

221

222

223

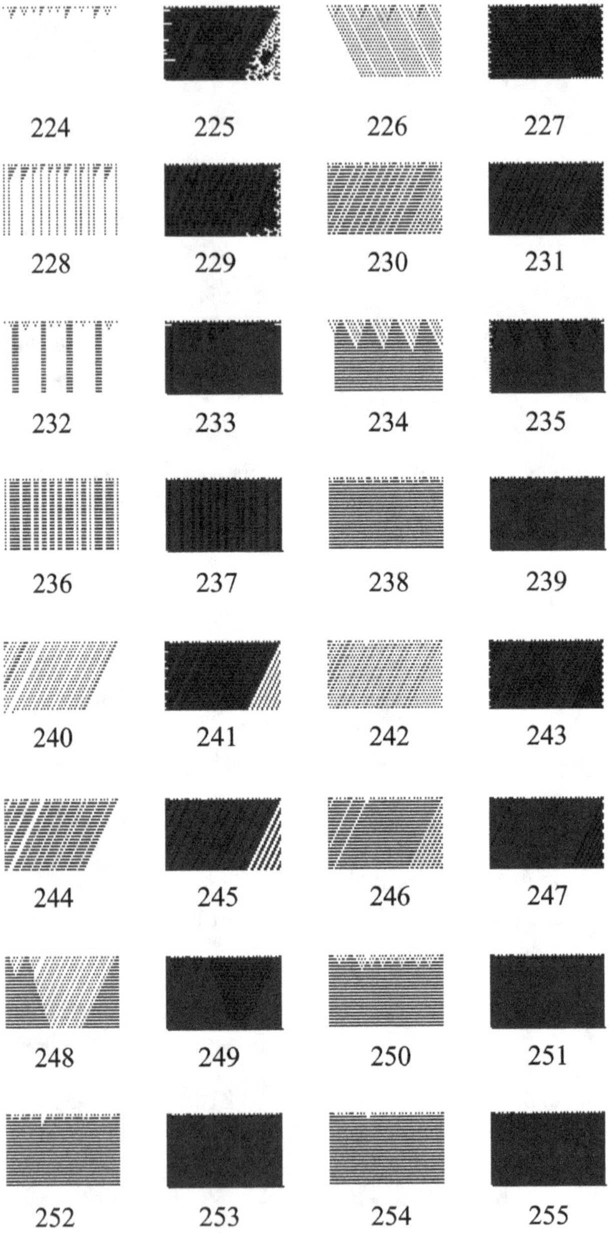

Figure 11.4.2: Patterns generated by 2nd order filter automata

11.5 Two Dimensional Cellular Automata

As defined in [26], a two dimensional N-ary valued cellular automaton **C** consists of 2-D array of cells. Each cell takes on any of the N given values, and all the values are simultaneously updated at a particular stage of evolution according to a rule involving the values contained in certain surrounding cells. Though one can think of several possible 2-D arrays and neighborhood structures, we are concerned here only with square arrays with 5 and 9-neighborhood structures as shown in figure 11.5.1.

	i-1,j	
i, j-1	i, j	i, j+1
	i+1,j	

i-1,j-1	i-1,j	i-1,j+1
i,j-1	i,j	i,j+1
i+1,j-1	i+1,j	i+1,j+1

Figure 11.5.1: 5 and 9-neighborhood structures

Let us consider a square array and let (i,j) be one of its cells. Then the value, $\xi^{(t)}_{i,j}$, held by the cell (i,j) at a stage t is an element from a set of numbers X = { 0, 1, ... , N-1 } . Now, the value held by the cell (i,j) could be updated in accordance with a 5-neighborhood or a 9-neighborhood rule. A 5-neighborhood cellular automaton evolves according to a rule ϕ:

$$\xi^{(t+1)}_{i,j} = \phi\left(\xi^{(t)}_{i,j}, \xi^{(t)}_{i,j+1}, \xi^{(t)}_{i+1,j}, \xi^{(t)}_{i,j-1}, \xi^{(t)}_{i-1,j} \right)$$

Similarly, a 9-neighborhood cellular automaton evolves according to a rule ϕ:

$$\xi^{(t+1)}_{i,j} = \phi\Big(\xi^{(t)}_{i,j}, \xi^{(t)}_{i,j+1}, \xi^{(t)}_{i+1,j+1}, \xi^{(t)}_{i+1,j}, \xi^{(t)}_{I+-1,j-1}$$
$$\xi^{(t)}_{i,j-1}, \xi^{(t)}_{i-1,j-1}, \xi^{(t)}_{i-1,j}, \xi^{(t)}_{i-1,j+1} \Big)$$

One can construct a total of N^{N^5} local rules for a five-neighborhood N-ary valued two-dimensional cellular automaton, and N^{N^9} rules for a nine-neighborhood N-ary valued two-dimensional cellular automaton.

For example, let us take the case of a binary valued five-neighborhood two-dimensional cellular automaton. A local rule in this case, can be viewed as a 32-bit word as shown in the table 11.5.1. This table displays 2^{32} local rules ϕ_0 , ϕ_1 , ϕ_2 , ... The column under ϕ_i is to be treated as the local rule ϕ_i .

Table 11.5.1: Local rules of binary valued 5-neighborhood cellular automata

COMBI-NATIONS	LOCAL RULES								
	ϕ_0	ϕ_1	ϕ_2	ϕ_3	ϕ_4	... ...	$\phi_{2^{32}-3}$	$\phi_{2^{32}-2}$	$\phi_{2^{32}-1}$
11111	0	0	0	0	0	... ...	1	1	1
11110	0	0	0	0	0	... ...	1	1	1
11101	0	0	0	0	0	... ...	1	1	1
11100	0	0	0	0	0	... ...	1	1	1
↓	↓	↓	↓	↓	↓	... ...	↓	↓	↓
00010	0	0	0	0	1	... ...	1	1	1
00001	0	0	1	1	0	... ...	0	1	1
00000	0	1	0	1	0	... ...	1	0	1

In the same manner, an updating rule in the case of a nine-neighborhood automaton, can be viewed as a 512-bit word, and there are 2^{512} such local rules for us to choose from.

Example 11.5.1

Let us consider a 2-D, 5-neighborhood binary valued cellular automaton characterized by the rule $\phi_{2222772222}$. The 32-bit word corresponding to this rule is 00001101010001110011101111111110. Let the configuration of this automaton at a particular stage of evolution t be:

0 1 1 0 0
0 1 0 1 0
0 0 1 0 0
0 0 1 1 0
0 1 0 0 0

Then the configuration of this automaton at the next evolution t+1 would be:

0 0 0 0 0
0 1 0 1 0
0 1 0 1 0
0 1 0 1 0
0 0 0 0 0

Examples of patterns generated by finite number of evolutions of various ternary valued 2-D cellular automata starting from the seed value 2, are shown in figure 11.5.2. Figure 11.5.2 (a) shows a pattern obtained after 112 stages of evolution using the five neighborhood updating rule $01(12)^{120}1$. Here $(12)^{120}$ denotes a string 12 repeated 120 times. Figure 11.5.2 (b) shows a pattern obtained using a nine neighborhood cellular automaton.

Figure 11.5.2 (a): Pattern generated by a 2-D five neighborhood cellular automaton

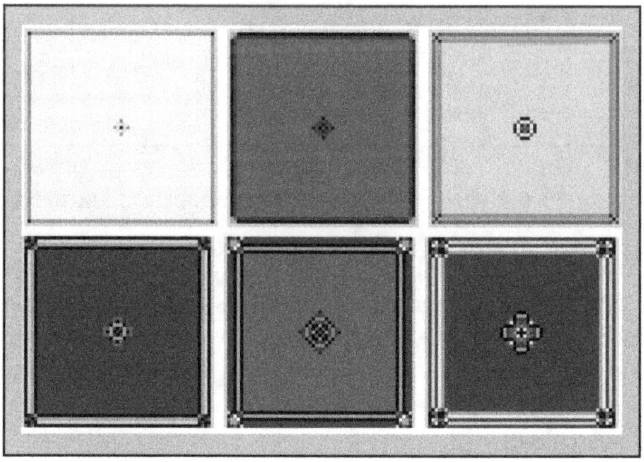

Figure 11.5.2 (b): Pattern generated by a 2-D nine neighborhood 2-D cellular automaton

11.6 Three Dimensional Cellular Automata

Analogous to a two dimensional cellular automaton, a three dimensional N-ary valued cellular automaton **C** consists of a 3-D array of cells. Each cell takes on any of the N given values, and all the values are simultaneously updated at a particular stage of evolution according to a rule involving the values contained in certain surrounding cells. Though it is possible to have several 3-D neighborhood structures, we are concerned here only with two types, seven and nine neighborhood structures, which are shown in figures 11.6.1 (a) and 11.6.1 (b).

(k-1)th plane

	i,j,k-1	

kth plane

	i-1,j,k	
i,j-1,k	i,j,k	i,j+1,k
	i+1,j,k	

(k+1)th plane

	i,j,k+1	

Figure 11.6.1 (a): A 3-D 7-neighborhood structure

(k-1)th plane

i-1, j-1, k-1		i-1, j+1, k-1
i+1, j-1, k-1		i+1, j+1, k-1

kth plane

	i, j, k,	

(k+1)th plane

i-1, j-1, k+1		i-1, j+1, k+1
i+1, j-1, k+1		i+1, j+1, k+1

Figure 11.6.1 (b) A 3-D 9-neighborhood structure

Let us consider a 3-D array and let (i,j,k) be one of its cells. Then the value, $\xi^{(t)}_{i,j,k}$, held by the cell (i,j,k) at a stage t is an element from a set of numbers X = { 0 , 1, … , N-1 } . Now, the value held by the cell (i,j,k) could be updated in accordance with a 7-neighborhood or a 9-neighborhood rule. A 3-D, 7-neighborhood cellular automaton evolves according to a rule ϕ:

$$\xi^{(t+1)}_{i,j,k}=\phi\left(\xi^{(t)}_{i,j,k}, \xi^{(t)}_{i,j,k+1}, \xi^{(t)}_{i,j+1,k}, \xi^{(t)}_{i+1,j,k}, \xi^{(t)}_{i,j,k-1}, \xi^{(t)}_{i,j-1,k}, \xi^{(t)}_{i-1,j,k}\right)$$

Similarly, a 3-D 9-neighborhood cellular automaton evolves according to a rule

$$\xi^{(t+1)}_{i,j,k}=\phi\big(\xi^{(t)}_{i,j,k},\ \xi^{(t)}_{i+1,j+1,k-1},\ \xi^{(t)}_{i+1,j-1,k-1},\ \xi^{(t)}_{i+1,j-1,k+1},$$
$$\xi^{(t)}_{i+1,j+1,k+1},\ \xi^{(t)}_{i-1,j+1,k+1},\ \xi^{(t)}_{i-1,j+1,k-1},\ \xi^{(t)}_{i-1,j-1,k-1},\ \xi^{(t)}_{i-1,j-1,k+1}\big)$$

One can construct a total of N^{N^7} local rules for a seven-neighborhood N-ary valued three-dimensional cellular automaton, and N^{N^9} rules for a nine-neighborhood N-ary valued three-dimensional cellular automaton.

Example 11.6.1

Let us consider a 3-D 9-neighborhood binary valued cellular automaton characterized by the rule $\phi_{999999999}$. The 512-bit word corresponding to this rule transforms an input 5x5x5, 3-D array configuration with a seed value 1 at the centre (i.e., third row and third column of third plane) into

```
0 0 0 0 0      0 0 0 0 0      0 0 0 0 0
0 0 1 0 0      0 1 1 1 0      0 0 1 0 0
0 1 1 1 0      0 1 0 1 0      0 1 1 1 0
0 1 1 1 0      0 1 1 1 0      0 1 1 1 0
0 0 0 0 0      0 0 0 0 0      0 0 0 0 0
```

These are the second, third and fourth planes of the evolved pattern respectively. The first and last planes, which have zero value at all locations, are not shown here for brevity.

An example of patterns generated for two stages of evolutions of a 6-ary valued 3-D, 27-neighborhood cellular automaton with a sum modulo-7 rule, starting from single seed input 5, is shown in figure 11.6.2.

```
00000    00000  00000  00000  00000
00000    00000  00000  00000  00000
00000    00000  00500  00000  00000
00000    00000  00000  00000  00000
00000    00000  00000  00000  00000
```

Input seed

0 0 0 0 0	0 0 0 0 0	0 0 0 0 0	0 0 0 0 0	0 0 0 0 0
0 0 0 0 0	0 5 5 5 0	0 5 5 5 0	0 5 5 5 0	0 0 0 0 0
0 0 0 0 0	0 5 5 5 0	0 5 5 5 0	0 5 5 5 0	0 0 0 0 0
0 0 0 0 0	0 5 5 5 0	0 5 5 5 0	0 5 5 5 0	0 0 0 0 0
0 0 0 0 0	0 0 0 0 0	0 0 0 0 0	0 0 0 0 0	0 0 0 0 0

After First Evolution

5 3 1 3 5	3 6 2 6 3	1 2 3 2 1	3 6 2 6 3	5 3 1 3 5
3 6 2 6 3	6 5 4 5 6	2 4 6 4 2	6 5 4 5 6	3 6 2 6 3
1 2 3 2 1	2 4 6 4 2	3 6 2 6 3	2 4 6 4 2	1 2 3 2 1
3 6 2 6 3	6 5 4 5 6	2 4 6 4 2	6 5 4 5 6	3 6 2 6 3
5 3 1 3 5	3 6 2 6 3	1 2 3 2 1	3 6 2 6 3	5 3 1 3 5

After Second Evolution

Figure 11.6.2: Patterns generated by 3-D cellular automata from seed value 5

11.7 The Concept Of Growing Configuration Of A Cellular Automaton

This concept has been introduced here with the purpose of reducing computation time involved in implementing especially 2-D and 3-D cellular automata, which evolve from single-site seed configurations. Usually, an initial configuration of a 2-D cellular automaton is treated as a square array of 0's, say of the size NxN, but with a nonzero value at the center of the array. This nonzero value $\xi^{(t)}_{N/2,\,N/2}$ acts as the seed to a 2-D cellular automaton, and it grows as per a 5- or 9-neighborhood rule. Note that the first evolution is obtained only after (N-2) X (N-2) computations if we follow the traditional methods.

Here as per our method, an array of 0's of size 5x5, with a nonzero value at the center, is treated as the initial configuration of a 2-D cellular automaton. Thus the number of site-values to be processed turns out to be just 9. After the first evolution, the resulting array size is increased to 7x7 and it is treated as the input configuration for the second evolution. This technique of increasing the size of a configuration before causing an evolution is referred here as Growing Configuration. For example, let us consider the following type-1 square array configuration of size 11x11, with the seed value N at the center.

O O O O O O O O O O O
O O O O O O O O O O O
O O O O O O O O O O O
O O O O O O O O O O O
O O O O O O O O O O O
O O O O O N O O O O O
O O O O O O O O O O O
O O O O O O O O O O O
O O O O O O O O O O O
O O O O O O O O O O O
O O O O O O O O O O O

In this case, the first evolution is usually obtained, only after processing 81 site-values as per an updating rule. The maximum growth of the seed N that one could expect in the first evolution would be as shown below.

O O O O O O O O O O O
O O O O O O O O O O O
O O O O O O O O O O O
O O O O O O O O O O O
O O O O N N N O O O O
O O O O N N N O O O O
O O O O N N N O O O O
O O O O O O O O O O O
O O O O O O O O O O O
O O O O O O O O O O O
O O O O O O O O O O O

As a matter of fact, this growth can be effectively obtained from the following square array configuration of size 5x5, with the seed value N at the center, instead of from the 11x11 array considered above. The total number of site-values to be processed in this case is just 9.

O O O O O
O O O O O
O O N O O
O O O O O
O O O O O

The configuration obtained after the first evolution would be of the form

```
O O O O O
O N N N O
O N N N O
O N N N O
O O O O O
```

The grown configuration after the first evolution, which is used as input to the second evolution, would then be of the form

```
O O O O O O O
O O O O O O O
O O N N N O O
O O N N N O O
O O N N N O O
O O O O O O O
O O O O O O O
```

In the same manner, the second evolution could be obtained from this grown configuration after processing 25 site-values as per the updating rule. The grown configuration with a maximum growth at this second stage of evolution would be as shown below.

```
O O O O O O O O O
O O O O O O O O O
O O N N N N N O O
O O N N N N N O O
O O N N N N N O O
O O N N N N N O O
O O N N N N N O O
O O O O O O O O O
O O O O O O O O O
```

Thus, irrespective of the nature of the 2-D cellular automaton and the type of its updating rule, we have the initial square array configuration of size 5x5, and this configuration grows after every evolution.

11.8 The Notion Of a Generalized Cellular Logic Scheme

With a view to reduce space occupied by various cellular automata rules, and to provide a generalized mechanism of rule-writing, we introduce here the notion of a generalized cellular logic scheme.

As described earlier, an r-neighborhood cellular automaton rule is nothing but a look-up table consisting of an ordered list of N^r patterns in one column with corresponding N^r values in the other column. For a large value of N, specifying the individual entries of the corresponding look-up table is a tedious and error-prone job [25]. Moreover, the look-up table would occupy considerable amount of space. So, what we can do is to adhere to a structured approach to rule writing, or to have a language for expressing a rule in whatever terms we find most suitable, and a mechanism for interpreting our needs and translating them into a look-up table. In practice, we can use any extensible programming language for interpreting our needs, but, we can not get them translated without a set of specialized primitives of the language for realizing them in a particular machine.

The notion of a generalized cellular logic scheme, on the other hand, does not require any specialized primitives of a high-level language. It mainly deals with the relational aspects of cell values in a specified neighborhood, and pattern directed symbol-rewriting techniques. The term pattern is to be understood here as a group of cell values in a particular neighborhood arranged in a manner described by a relational expression or a logical sentence. Any extensible programming language can be used for constructing logical sentences corresponding to various updating rules. More importantly, a logical sentence will not generate the look-up table of the corresponding rule. On the other hand, it will generate a minimal set of pattern-directed rules required for the processing of a cellular automaton configuration. Needless to say, we treat an ordered list of such a minimal set of pattern-directed rules as the scheme of a Generalized Markov Algorithm.

A simple example would illustrate this notion. Let us take the case of a two-dimensional binary-valued cellular automaton and a five-neighborhood rule described by the following expression: if

$$\left(\xi^{(t)}_{i,j},\ \xi^{(t)}_{i,j+1},\ \xi^{(t)}_{i+1,j},\ \xi^{(t)}_{i,j-1},\ \xi^{(t)}_{i-1,j}\right)_1$$

is odd, then $\xi^{(t)}_{i,j}$ is 1 ; otherwise it is 0.

The term $\left(\xi^{(t)}_{i,\, j},\ \xi^{(t)}_{i,\, j+1},\ \xi^{(t)}_{i+1,\, j},\ \xi^{(t)}_{i,\, j-1},\ \xi^{(t)}_{i-1,\, j}\right)_1$ refers to the number of 1s in a sub array under the five neighborhood structure. This expression refers to a Generalized Markov Algorithm consisting of the following sixteen pattern-directed rules.

$\mathcal{N}^{PAR}$: Substitution formulas	Formula number
00001→1	00
00010→1	01
00100→1	02
00111→1	03
01000→1	04
01011→1	05
01101→1	06
01110→1	07
10000→1	08
10011→1	09
10101→1	10
10110→1	11
11001→1	12
11010→1	13
11100→1	14
11111→1	15

The functional expression

$$\xi^{(t)}_{i,j} = \xi^{(t)}_{i,j} \oplus \xi^{(t)}_{i,j+1} \oplus \xi^{(t)}_{i+1,j} \oplus \xi^{(t)}_{i,j-1} \oplus \xi^{(t)}_{i-1,j}$$

which is usually used to describe the updating rules discussed above will, on the other hand, generate the following look-up table with thirty two entries in it.

00000→0	01000→1	10000→1	11000→0
00001→1	01001→0	10001→0	11001→1
00010→1	01010→0	10010→0	11010→1
00011→0	01011→1	10011→1	11011→0
00100→1	01100→0	10100→0	11100→1
00101→0	01101→1	10101→1	11101→0
00110→0	01110→1	10110→1	11110→0
00111→1	01111→0	10111→0	11111→1

It is clear from the above, that relational pattern-directed approach to cellular automata realizations would be a convenient and more efficient means of doing array processing. We call this a Generalized Cellular Logic Scheme.

Section 12

Normal Algorithmic Realization Of Cellular Automata

With subsets of a free monoid treated as sets of configurations of cellular automata, the notion of a normal algorithm admits to be treated as a kind of means of realizing various cellular automata. As a concrete step in this direction, we provide in this section certain techniques of realizing cellular automata using normal algorithms. More specifically, we workout a method of characterizing all one-dimensional, N-ary valued three neighborhood cellular automata by means of a normal algorithm $\mathcal{N}^{1N3CA}$ over an appropriate alphabet, and all two-dimensional, N-ary valued five and nine neighborhood cellular automata by means of a normal algorithm $\mathcal{N}^{2NRCA}$, where R = 5 or 9.

12.1 One Dimensional Normal Algorithmic Cellular Automata

As defined in section 11, a one dimensional N-ary valued cellular automaton **C** consists of a line of sites, with each site taking on any of the N possible values, updated in discrete time steps according to a deterministic rule involving a local neighborhood of sites around it. The value of a site i at time step t is denoted by $\xi^{(t)}_i$ and is a symbol chosen from an alphabet A={0,1, …, N-1}. A sequence of such symbols from the alphabet $\mathcal{A}$, denoting the values of the sites at a time step t, is called a *Configuration* of **C**. Now, the symbols present in a configuration could be rewritten in accordance with a local rule, so that a new configuration evolves.

By the neighborhood of a site, we mean the site itself together with r adjacent sites to its immediate left and r adjacent sites to its immediate right. For example, a three neighborhood of a site i of a cellular automaton **C** is the triple formed by i and its immediate left and right neighbors. The triple corresponds to the word $\xi^{(t)}_{i-1}\ \xi^{(t)}_i\ \xi^{(t)}_{i+1}$ in the configuration at a time step t. Now, when a rule ϕ is applied to the

E. G. Rajan, *Symbolic Computing - Signal and Image Processing*
ISBN 81-7800-047-4

configuration at time step t, the value of an ith site $\xi^{(t)}{}_i$, is updated as $\xi^{(t+1)}{}_i$ by rewriting the word $\xi^{(t)}{}_{i-1}\ \xi^{(t)}{}_i\ \xi^{(t)}{}_{i+1}$ corresponding to its neighborhood triple, as the word $\xi^{(t+1)}{}_i\ \xi^{(t)}{}_{i+1}$.

The problem of our immediate concern now, is the retrieval of information about the previous value of the ith site after the updating, and its use in rewriting the word $\xi^{(t)}{}_i\ \xi^{(t)}{}_{i+1}\ \xi^{(t)}{}_{i+2}$ corresponding to the next immediate triple formed by the ith, (i+1)[th] and (i+2)[th] sites. What is usually done is that the value of the site i at time step t is stored before it is updated and retrieved for use in the updating of the right adjacent site value. However, we solve this problem in the following manner.

Let us consider a word $\xi^{(t)}{}_{i-1}\ \xi^{(t)}{}_i\ \xi^{(t)}{}_{i+1}$ which is present in a configuration of a three neighborhood automaton **C**, at a time step t. Now, we rewrite this word, according to a substitution formula of the type:

$$\xi^{(t)}{}_{i-1}\xi^{(t)}{}_i\ \xi^{(t)}{}_{i+1} \rightarrow \xi^{(t+1)}{}_i\ \xi^{(t)}{}_i\xi^{(t)}{}_{i+1}$$

so that the ith site value is updated and at the same time its previous value is preserved for further use in the updating of the (i+1)[th] site value. Thus at time step (t+1), a new configuration evolves as a result of an exhaustive updating of all the site values other than the first and the last ones of the configuration at time step t. Successively, we flank with the symbol 0, both the left and the right ends of this new configuration at time step (t+1), so that its length is preserved.

The above argument is valid for the normal algorithmic realization of any N-ary valued (2r+1)–neighborhood cellular automaton.

In what follows, we make use of the above technique and construct a normal algorithm $\mathcal{N}^{1N3CA}$ for realizing N-ary valued 3-neighbourhood cellular automata. We need the following alphabets:

Alphabet of terminals: $\mathcal{A}$ = {0 1 2 3 4 5 6 7 8 9}
Alphabet of nonterminals: $\mathcal{E}$ = {α}

Site variables are denoted by ξ, η and μ , and they take on values from $\mathcal{A}$. The scheme of $\mathcal{N}^{1N3CA}$ given below is constructed over the union of $\mathcal{A}$ and $\mathcal{E}$. $\mathcal{N}^{1N3CA}$ is a composition of two normal algorithms $\mathcal{N}^1$ and $\mathcal{N}^2$.

Formula number	Substitution Formulas	Remarks
$\mathcal{N}^1$:		
(00)	$\xi^{(t)}\eta^{(t)}\alpha\mu^{(t)} \rightarrow \eta^{(t+1)}\eta^{(t)}\mu^{(t)}\alpha$	This formula is used to preserve the value $\eta^{(t)}$ of the site i at time step t and at the same time update it with $\eta^{(t+1)}$ according to a rule
(01)	$\xi^{(t)}\eta^{(t)}\alpha \rightarrow\cdot\ 0$	This formula is used to flank with 0, the right end of a finite length configuration after one evolution is complete.
(02)	$\alpha\xi^{(t)} \rightarrow \xi^{(t)}\alpha$	This formula is used to shift the auxiliary variable α to the right in a configuration.
(03)	$\rightarrow \alpha$	This formula is used to introduce the symbol α in the beginning of a configuration.
$\mathcal{N}^2$:		
(04)	$\rightarrow\cdot\ 0$	This formula is used to flank with 0, the left end of a configuration after one evolution is complete.

Example 12.1

Let us consider the case of a binary valued three neighborhood cellular automaton **C** which can be realized normal algorithmically over the union of the alphabets $\mathcal{A} = \{0\ 1\}$ and $\mathcal{E} = \{\alpha\}$.

At a time step t, let $\mathbf{C}^{(t)}$ be the configuration of **C**, and $\xi^{(t)}_{i-1}\ \xi^{(t)}_{i}\ \xi^{(t)}_{i+1}$ be the word corresponding to the values of a neighborhood triple formed by an ith site and its neighbors. A three neighborhood triple can hold 2^3 possible combinations of symbols from the alphabet $\mathcal{A}$. An updating rule ϕ in this case, is a system of eight substitution formulas with their left parts consisting of the eight words of length 3 from $\mathcal{A}$ and their right parts consisting of single letters from $\mathcal{A}$. If we arrange all the eight words as per the increasing order of their numerical counterparts, then we can code a rule ϕ as a word L of length 8 from the alphabet $\mathcal{A}$. In fact, one can generate 2^8 updating rules as shown in table 12.1.

Table 12.1 Coded rules of a 3-neighborhood binary valued Normal algorithmic cellular automaton

COMBI-NATIONS	CODED RULES								
	ϕ_0	ϕ_1	ϕ_2	ϕ_3	ϕ_4	…	…	ϕ_{253}	ϕ_{254}	ϕ_{255}
111	0	0	0	0	0	…	…	1	1	1
110	0	0	0	0	0	…	…	1	1	1
101	0	0	0	0	0	…	…	1	1	1
100	0	0	0	0	0	…	…	1	1	1
011	0	0	0	0	0	…	…	1	1	1
010	0	0	0	0	1	…	…	1	1	1
001	0	0	1	1	0	…	…	0	1	1
000	0	1	0	1	0	…	…	1	0	1

Let us take a finite length configuration $\mathbf{C}^{(t)} = 0010100$ and apply rule ϕ_3 to it. This configuration consists of seven symbols, and it can be factored into five triples 001, 010, 101, 010 and 100 from left to right. The new configuration that evolves as the result of the application of rule ϕ_3 is $\mathbf{C}^{(t+1)} = 0100000$.

Let us see now, how this new configuration could be obtained by means of the normal algorithm $\mathcal{N}^{123CA}$.

Remarks :

(i) $\mathcal{N}^{123CA}(C^{(t)}) \simeq \mathcal{N}^2(\mathcal{N}^1(C^{(t)}))$

(ii) The 0th formula of the scheme of $\mathcal{N}^1$ represents a set of 8 substitution formulas:

$\mathcal{N}^{123CA}$:

Formula Number	Substitution Formulas	Remarks
$\mathcal{N}^1$:		
	$00\alpha0 \rightarrow 100\alpha$	
	$00\alpha1 \rightarrow 101\alpha$	
	$01\alpha0 \rightarrow 010\alpha$	
	$01\alpha1 \rightarrow 011\alpha$	A set of eight formulas corresponding to the updating rule ϕ_3 .
	$10\alpha0 \rightarrow 000\alpha$	
	$10\alpha1 \rightarrow 001\alpha$	
	$11\alpha0 \rightarrow 010\alpha$	
	$11\alpha1 \rightarrow 011\alpha$	
	$\xi\eta\alpha \rightarrow \cdot 0$	$\xi, \eta \in A$
	$\alpha\xi \rightarrow \xi\alpha$	
	$\rightarrow \alpha$	
$\mathcal{N}^2$:	$\rightarrow \cdot 0$	

$\mathcal{N}^1$: $0010100 \vdash \alpha0010100 \vdash 0\alpha010100 \vdash 00\alpha10100 \vdash 101\alpha0100 \vdash 1010\alpha100 \vdash 10001\alpha00 \vdash 100010\alpha0 \vdash 1000000\alpha \vdash \cdot 100000$

$\mathcal{N}^2$: $100000 \vdash \cdot 0100000$

12.2 Two Dimensional Normal Algorithmic Cellular Automata

As already explained in section 11, a two dimensional N-ary valued cellular automaton **C** consists of a lattice of sites, with each site taking on any of the N possible values, updated in discrete time steps according to a deterministic rule involving a local neighborhood of sites surrounding it.

Though one can think of several possible lattices and neighborhood structures for two dimensional cellular automata, we are concerned here, only with the square lattices with five and nine neighborhood structures shown in figure 12.2.1.

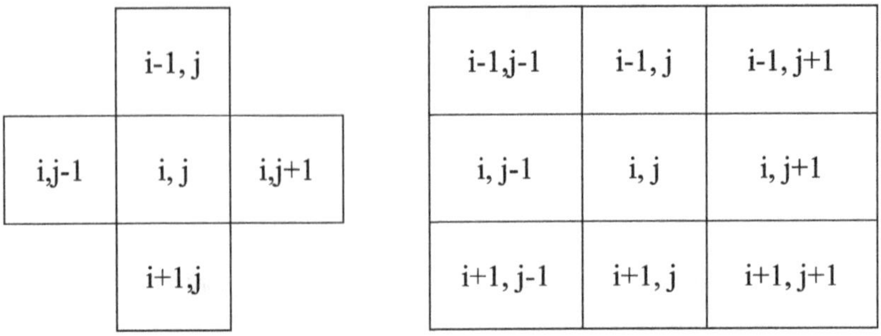

5-neighborhood structure 9-neighborhood structure

Figure 12.2.1: Neighborhood structures

The value of a site i,j at a time step t is denoted by $\xi^{(t)}_{i,j}$ and is a symbol chosen from an alphabet $\mathcal{A} = \{0, 1, \ldots, N\text{-}1\}$. Now, the symbol present in each site of a square lattice could be rewritten in accordance with a local rule which involves the values of either four or eight of its neighboring sites also, so that a new square lattice configuration evolves.

A five-neighborhood cellular automaton evolves according to a rule ϕ, where

$$\xi^{(t+1)}_{i,j} = \phi\,[\xi^{(t)}_{i,j},\ \xi^{(t)}_{i,j+1},\ \xi^{(t)}_{i+1,j},\ \xi^{(t)}_{i,j-1},\ \xi^{(t)}_{i-1,j}].$$

A nine-neighborhood cellular automaton evolves according to a rule ϕ, where

$$\xi^{(t+1)}_{i,j} = \phi\,[\,\xi^{(t)}_{i,j}, \xi^{(t)}_{i,j+1}, \xi^{(t)}_{i+1,j+1}, \xi^{(t)}_{i+1,j}, \xi^{(t)}_{i+1,j-1}, \xi^{(t)}_{i,j-1}, \xi^{(t)}_{i-1,j-1}, \xi^{(t)}_{i-1,j}, \xi^{(t)}_{i-1,j+1}]$$

Let us recall from earlier discussions, that a normal algorithm $\mathcal{N}$ over an alphabet $\mathcal{A}$ is applicable only to one-dimensional strings consisting of symbols from $\mathcal{A}$ and not to two-dimensional arrays of symbols from $\mathcal{A}$. This primarily causes difficulty in constructing a normal algorithm for realizing a two-dimensional cellular automaton. However, as a first step to overcome this difficulty, we represent an array of symbols in the form of a one-dimensional string, in the following manner. Let us consider at a time step t, a finite, square lattice configuration of n rows of symbols from an alphabet $\mathcal{A}$, each row consisting of n number of symbols.

Now, we represent this array as:

$$) \xi^{(t)}_{1,1}\ \xi^{(t)}_{1,2}\ \xi^{(t)}_{1,3} \ldots\ \xi^{(t)}_{1,n}\ \&\ \xi^{(t)}_{2,1}\ \xi^{(t)}_{2,2}\ \xi^{(t)}_{2,3} \ldots \xi^{(t)}_{2,n}\ \& \ldots$$
$$\ldots \&\ \xi^{(t)}_{i,1}\ \xi^{(t)}_{i,2}\ \xi^{(t)}_{i,3} \ldots\ \xi^{(t)}_{i,n}\ \& \ldots \ldots \&\ \xi^{(t)}_{n,1}\ \xi^{(t)}_{n,2}\ \xi^{(t)}_{n,3} \ldots \xi^{(t)}_{n,n}$$

where the symbols) and & are called *delimiters*, that is, separating symbols, and they are not in the alphabet $\mathcal{A}$. Let us take for example, a square lattice of five rows with each row consisting of five sites.

$$\begin{matrix} \xi^{(t)}_{1,1} & \xi^{(t)}_{1,2} & \xi^{(t)}_{1,3} & \xi^{(t)}_{1,4} & \xi^{(t)}_{1,5} \\ \xi^{(t)}_{2,1} & \xi^{(t)}_{2,2} & \xi^{(t)}_{3,3} & \xi^{(t)}_{2,4} & \xi^{(t)}_{2,5} \\ \xi^{(t)}_{3,1} & \xi^{(t)}_{3,2} & \xi^{(t)}_{3,3} & \xi^{(t)}_{3,4} & \xi^{(t)}_{3,5} \\ \xi^{(t)}_{4,1} & \xi^{(t)}_{4,2} & \xi^{(t)}_{4,3} & \xi^{(t)}_{4,4} & \xi^{(t)}_{4,5} \\ \xi^{(t)}_{5,1} & \xi^{(t)}_{5,2} & \xi^{(t)}_{5,3} & \xi^{(t)}_{5,4} & \xi^{(t)}_{5,5} \end{matrix}$$

Then the one-dimensional equivalent string corresponding to an array configuration of this lattice at a time step t, would be of the form:

$$P =)\xi^{(t)}_{1,1}\ \xi^{(t)}_{1,2}\ \xi^{(t)}_{1,3}\ \xi^{(t)}_{1,4}\ \xi^{(t)}_{1,5}\ \&\ \xi^{(t)}_{2,1}\ \xi^{(t)}_{2,2}\ \xi^{(t)}_{2,3}\ \xi^{(t)}_{2,4}\ \xi^{(t)}_{2,5}\ \&$$
$$\xi^{(t)}_{3,1}\ \xi^{(t)}_{3,2}\ \xi^{(t)}_{3,3}\ \xi^{(t)}_{3,4}\ \xi^{(t)}_{3,5}\ \&\ \xi^{(t)}_{4,1}\ \xi^{(t)}_{4,2}\ \xi^{(t)}_{4,3}\ \xi^{(t)}_{4,4}\ \xi^{(t)}_{4,5}\ \&$$
$$\xi^{(t)}_{5,1}\ \xi^{(t)}_{5,2}\ \xi^{(t)}_{5,3}\ \xi^{(t)}_{5,4}\ \xi^{(t)}_{5,5}$$

Having thus represented a two-dimensional array configuration as a one-dimensional string P, our next step would be to find out a method for applying five or nine-neighborhood updating rules to it.

In the traditional sense, the five neighborhood of a site, say, (3,3) of the array configuration of P is viewed as the 5-tuple formed by the site (3,3) and its immediate surrounding neighbors (3,4), (4,3), (3,2) and (2,3). Then, the word consisting of the symbols corresponding to the values of this 5-tuple at a time step t, is $\xi^{(t)}_{3,3}\,\xi^{(t)}_{3,4}\,\xi^{(t)}_{4,3}\,\xi^{(t)}_{3,2}\,\xi^{(t)}_{2,3}$. Now, the fact that this word does not occur in the string P either fully or in parts, poses some difficulty in making use of this word in a substitution formula that implements a five-neighborhood rule. However, we overcome this difficulty in the following manner.

Let us consider the word $\xi^{(t)}_{2,2}\,\xi^{(t)}_{2,3}\,\xi^{(t)}_{2,4}\,\xi^{(t)}_{3,2}\,\xi^{(t)}_{3,3}\,\xi^{(t)}_{3,4}\,\xi^{(t)}_{4,2}\,\xi^{(t)}_{4,3}\,\xi^{(t)}_{4,4}$ which occurs in P, in parts, as triples. This word contains all the symbols corresponding to the values of the 5-tuple and also certain other symbols which are called *quiescent symbols* (i.e., inactive symbols) as far as the five-neighborhood rule is concerned.

Now a substitution formula of the type

$$\lfloor \xi^{(t)}_{2,2}\xi^{(t)}_{2,3}\xi^{(t)}_{2,4}\rfloor \lfloor \xi^{(t)}_{3,2}\ \xi^{(t)}_{3,3}\ \xi^{(t)}_{3,4}\rfloor \lfloor \xi^{(t)}_{4,2}\ \xi^{(t)}_{4,3}\ \xi^{(t)}_{4,4}\rfloor \rightarrow \xi^{(t+1)}_{3,3}$$

could be used in updating the values of the site (3,3) . The symbols $\lfloor$ and $\rfloor$ denote respectively the left and the right parentheses. They are introduced here in order to show distinctly the triples, which occur in P at three different places. We refer to the above substitution formula as a *Conjoint Substitution Formula,* based on the fact that it is a composition of three simple substitution formulas:

(i) $\xi^{(t)}_{2,2}\ \xi^{(t)}_{2,3}\ \xi^{(t)}_{2,4} \rightarrow \xi^{(t+1)}_{3,3}$

(ii) $\xi^{(t)}_{3,2}\ \xi^{(t)}_{3,3}\ \xi^{(t)}_{3,4} \rightarrow \Lambda$ and

(iii) $\xi^{(t)}_{4,2}\ \xi^{(t)}_{4,3}\ \xi^{(t)}_{4,4} \rightarrow \Lambda$

By the term *Conjoint Substitution,* we mean the testing of a given string for the occurrences of certain words listed in an order of precedence and substituting them, in case all of them occur, by their values, in the same order. Now, the nine-neighborhood of the site (3,3) is the 9-tuple formed by the site (3,3) and its neighbors (3,4), (4,4), (4,3), (4,2), (3,2), (2,2), (2,3) and (2,4). On the same lines that we saw earlier, the word $\xi^{(t)}_{2,2}\ \xi^{(t)}_{2,3}\ \xi^{(t)}_{2,4}\ \xi^{(t)}_{3,2}\ \xi^{(t)}_{3,3}\ \xi^{(t)}_{3,4}\ \xi^{(t)}_{4,2}\ \xi^{(t)}_{4,3}\ \xi^{(t)}_{4,4}$ which occurs in P, in parts, as triples, can be used in a conjoint substitution formula that implements a nine-neighborhood rule.

So far we have seen that the value of a site (i,j) in a square array configuration at a time step t, could be updated according to a rule, by rewriting the word corresponding to its five or nine-neighborhood in the one-dimensional equivalent string. The problem that we face now, is the retrieval of information about the previous value of the site (i,j) after the updating, and its use in the updating of the values of the sites (i,j+1), (i+1,j-1), (i+1,j) and (i+1,j+1). We solve this problem in the following manner:

Let us consider the one-dimensional equivalent word:

$$P =)\ \xi^{(t)}_{1,1}\ \xi^{(t)}_{1,2}\ \xi^{(t)}_{1,3}\ \xi^{(t)}_{1,4}\ \xi^{(t)}_{1,5}\ \&\ \xi^{(t)}_{2,1}\ \xi^{(t)}_{2,2}\ \xi^{(t)}_{2,3}\ \xi^{(t)}_{2,4}\ \xi^{(t)}_{2,5}\ \&\ \xi^{(t)}_{3,1}\ \xi^{(t)}_{3,2}\ \xi^{(t)}_{3,3}\ \xi^{(t)}_{3,4}\ \xi^{(t)}_{3,5}\ \&\ \xi^{(t)}_{4,1}\ \xi^{(t)}_{4,2}\ \xi^{(t)}_{4,3}\ \xi^{(t)}_{4,4}\ \xi^{(t)}_{4,5}\ \&\ \xi^{(t)}_{5,1}\ \xi^{(t)}_{5,2}\ \xi^{(t)}_{5,3}\ \xi^{(t)}_{5,4}\ \xi^{(t)}_{5,5}$$

corresponding to the finite array configuration :

$$\begin{matrix} \xi^{(t)}_{1,1} & \xi^{(t)}_{1,2} & \xi^{(t)}_{1,3} & \xi^{(t)}_{1,4} & \xi^{(t)}_{1,5} \\ \xi^{(t)}_{2,1} & \xi^{(t)}_{2,2} & \xi^{(t)}_{2,3} & \xi^{(t)}_{2,4} & \xi^{(t)}_{2,5} \\ \xi^{(t)}_{3,1} & \xi^{(t)}_{3,2} & \xi^{(t)}_{3,3} & \xi^{(t)}_{3,4} & \xi^{(t)}_{3,5} \\ \xi^{(t)}_{4,1} & \xi^{(t)}_{4,2} & \xi^{(t)}_{4,3} & \xi^{(t)}_{4,4} & \xi^{(t)}_{4,5} \\ \xi^{(t)}_{5,1} & \xi^{(t)}_{5,2} & \xi^{(t)}_{5,3} & \xi^{(t)}_{5,4} & \xi^{(t)}_{5,5} \end{matrix}$$

and rewrite P as

$$) \xi^{(t)}_{1,1} \xi^{(t)}_{1,2} \xi^{(t)}_{1,3} \xi^{(t)}_{1,2} \xi^{(t)}_{1,3} \xi^{(t)}_{1,4} \xi^{(t)}_{1,3} \xi^{(t)}_{1,4} \xi^{(t)}_{1,5} \,\&\, \xi^{(t)}_{2,1} \xi^{(t)}_{2,2} \xi^{(t)}_{2,3} \xi^{(t)}_{2,2} \xi^{(t)}_{2,3} \xi^{(t)}_{2,4} \xi^{(t)}_{2,3} \xi^{(t)}_{2,4} \xi^{(t)}_{2,5} \,\&\, \xi^{(t)}_{3,1} \xi^{(t)}_{3,2} \xi^{(t)}_{3,3} \xi^{(t)}_{3,2} \xi^{(t)}_{3,3} \xi^{(t)}_{3,4} \xi^{(t)}_{3,3} \xi^{(t)}_{3,4} \xi^{(t)}_{3,5} \,\&\, \xi^{(t)}_{2,1} \xi^{(t)}_{2,2} \xi^{(t)}_{2,3} \xi^{(t)}_{2,2} \xi^{(t)}_{2,3} \xi^{(t)}_{2,4} \xi^{(t)}_{2,3} \xi^{(t)}_{2,4} \xi^{(t)}_{2,5} \,\&\, \xi^{(t)}_{3,1} \xi^{(t)}_{3,2} \xi^{(t)}_{3,3} \xi^{(t)}_{3,2} \xi^{(t)}_{3,3} \xi^{(t)}_{3,4} \xi^{(t)}_{3,3} \xi^{(t)}_{3,4} \xi^{(t)}_{3,5} \,\&\, \xi^{(t)}_{4,1} \xi^{(t)}_{4,2} \xi^{(t)}_{4,3} \xi^{(t)}_{4,2} \xi^{(t)}_{4,3} \xi^{(t)}_{4,4} \xi^{(t)}_{4,3} \xi^{(t)}_{4,4} \xi^{(t)}_{4,5} \,\&\, \xi^{(t)}_{3,1} \xi^{(t)}_{3,2} \xi^{(t)}_{3,3} \xi^{(t)}_{3,2} \xi^{(t)}_{3,3} \xi^{(t)}_{3,4} \xi^{(t)}_{3,3} \xi^{(t)}_{3,4} \xi^{(t)}_{3,5} \,\&\, \xi^{(t)}_{4,1} \xi^{(t)}_{4,2} \xi^{(t)}_{4,3} \xi^{(t)}_{4,2} \xi^{(t)}_{4,3} \xi^{(t)}_{4,4} \xi^{(t)}_{4,3} \xi^{(t)}_{4,4} \xi^{(t)}_{4,5} \,\&\, \xi^{(t)}_{5,1} \xi^{(t)}_{5,2} \xi^{(t)}_{5,3} \xi^{(t)}_{5,2} \xi^{(t)}_{5,3} \xi^{(t)}_{5,4} \xi^{(t)}_{5,3} \xi^{(t)}_{5,4} \xi^{(t)}_{5,5}$$

Let us call this string P'. Now, let us take the case of updating the values of all the sites according to a rule ϕ . The first site value that could be updated in P' is $\xi^{(t)}_{2,2}$, and the string that results after this updating would be :

$$) \xi^{(t+1)}_{2,2} \xi^{(t)}_{1,2} \xi^{(t)}_{1,3} \xi^{(t)}_{1,4} \xi^{(t)}_{1,3} \xi^{(t)}_{1,4} \xi^{(t)}_{1,5} \,\&\, \xi^{(t)}_{2,2} \xi^{(t)}_{2,3} \xi^{(t)}_{2,4} \xi^{(t)}_{2,3} \xi^{(t)}_{2,4} \xi^{(t)}_{2,5} \,\&\, \xi^{(t)}_{3,2} \xi^{(t)}_{3,3} \xi^{(t)}_{3,4} \xi^{(t)}_{3,3} \xi^{(t)}_{3,4} \xi^{(t)}_{3,5} \,\&\, \xi^{(t)}_{2,1} \xi^{(t)}_{2,2} \xi^{(t)}_{2,3} \xi^{(t)}_{2,2} \xi^{(t)}_{2,3} \xi^{(t)}_{2,4} \xi^{(t)}_{2,3} \xi^{(t)}_{2,4} \xi^{(t)}_{2,5} \,\&\, \xi^{(t)}_{3,1} \xi^{(t)}_{3,2} \xi^{(t)}_{3,3} \xi^{(t)}_{3,2} \xi^{(t)}_{3,3} \xi^{(t)}_{3,4} \xi^{(t)}_{3,3} \xi^{(t)}_{3,4} \xi^{(t)}_{3,5} \,\&\, \xi^{(t)}_{4,1} \xi^{(t)}_{4,2} \xi^{(t)}_{4,3} \xi^{(t)}_{4,2} \xi^{(t)}_{4,3} \xi^{(t)}_{4,4} \xi^{(t)}_{4,3} \xi^{(t)}_{4,4} \xi^{(t)}_{4,5} \,\&\, \xi^{(t)}_{3,1} \xi^{(t)}_{3,2} \xi^{(t)}_{3,3} \xi^{(t)}_{3,2} \xi^{(t)}_{3,3} \xi^{(t)}_{3,4} \xi^{(t)}_{3,3} \xi^{(t)}_{3,4} \xi^{(t)}_{3,5} \,\&\, \xi^{(t)}_{4,1} \xi^{(t)}_{4,2} \xi^{(t)}_{4,3} \xi^{(t)}_{4,2} \xi^{(t)}_{4,3} \xi^{(t)}_{4,4} \xi^{(t)}_{4,3} \xi^{(t)}_{4,4} \xi^{(t)}_{4,5} \,\&\, \xi^{(t)}_{5,1} \xi^{(t)}_{5,2} \xi^{(t)}_{5,3} \xi^{(t)}_{5,2} \xi^{(t)}_{5,3} \xi^{(t)}_{5,4} \xi^{(t)}_{5,3} \xi^{(t)}_{5,4} \xi^{(t)}_{5,5}$$

Thc second and third site values that could be updated successively in P' are $\xi^{(t)}_{2,3}$ and $\xi^{(t)}_{2,4}$ and the string that results after these updating would be :

$$) \xi^{(t+1)}_{2,2} \xi^{(t+1)}_{2,3} \xi^{(t+1)}_{2,4} \,\&\&\&\, \xi^{(t)}_{2,1} \xi^{(t)}_{2,2} \xi^{(t)}_{2,3} \xi^{(t)}_{2,2} \xi^{(t)}_{2,3} \xi^{(t)}_{2,4} \xi^{(t)}_{2,3} \xi^{(t)}_{2,4} \xi^{(t)}_{2,5} \,\&\, \xi^{(t)}_{3,1} \xi^{(t)}_{3,2} \xi^{(t)}_{3,3} \xi^{(t)}_{3,2} \xi^{(t)}_{3,3} \xi^{(t)}_{3,4} \xi^{(t)}_{3,3} \xi^{(t)}_{3,4} \xi^{(t)}_{3,5} \,\&\, \xi^{(t)}_{4,1} \xi^{(t)}_{4,2} \xi^{(t)}_{4,3} \xi^{(t)}_{4,2} \xi^{(t)}_{4,3} \xi^{(t)}_{4,4} \xi^{(t)}_{4,3} \xi^{(t)}_{4,4} \xi^{(t)}_{4,5} \,\&\, \xi^{(t)}_{3,1} \xi^{(t)}_{3,2} \xi^{(t)}_{3,3} \xi^{(t)}_{3,2} \xi^{(t)}_{3,3} \xi^{(t)}_{3,4} \xi^{(t)}_{3,3} \xi^{(t)}_{3,4} \xi^{(t)}_{3,5} \,\&\, \xi^{(t)}_{4,1} \xi^{(t)}_{4,2} \xi^{(t)}_{4,3} \xi^{(t)}_{4,2} \xi^{(t)}_{4,3} \xi^{(t)}_{4,4} \xi^{(t)}_{4,3} \xi^{(t)}_{4,4} \xi^{(t)}_{4,5} \,\&\, \xi^{(t)}_{5,1} \xi^{(t)}_{5,2} \xi^{(t)}_{5,3} \xi^{(t)}_{5,2} \xi^{(t)}_{5,3} \xi^{(t)}_{5,4} \xi^{(t)}_{5,3} \xi^{(t)}_{5,4} \xi^{(t)}_{5,5}$$

After an exhaustive updating of all the remaining six possible sites (3,2), (3,3),(3,4),(4,2),(4,3) and (4,4) in P' , in this manner, we have $)\xi^{(t+1)}_{2,2} \xi^{(t+1)}_{2,3} \xi^{(t+1)}_{2,4} \,\&\&\&\, \xi^{(t+1)}_{3,2} \xi^{(t+1)}_{3,3} \xi^{(t+1)}_{3,4} \,\&\&\&\, \xi^{(t+1)}_{4,2} \xi^{(t+1)}_{4,3} \xi^{(t+1)}_{4,4}$. We see that a new 3X3 square array configuration evolves as shown below,

$$\begin{matrix} \xi^{(t+1)}_{2,2} & \xi^{(t+1)}_{2,3} & \xi^{(t+1)}_{2,4} \\ \xi^{(t+1)}_{3,2} & \xi^{(t+1)}_{3,3} & \xi^{(t+1)}_{3,4} \\ \xi^{(t+1)}_{4,2} & \xi^{(t+1)}_{4,3} & \xi^{(t+1)}_{4,4} \end{matrix}$$

as the result of applying a local rule just once to all the nine possible site values in the 5x5 square array configuration.

Lastly, as we have done in the case of one-dimensional cellular automata, we flank with the symbol 0 all the four sides of the newly evolved 3x3 square array configuration in order to maintain its array size. The resulting pattern would appear as shown below:

$$\begin{array}{ccccc} 0 & 0 & 0 & 0 & 0 \\ 0 & \xi^{(t+1)}{}_{2,2} & \xi^{(t+1)}{}_{2,3} & \xi^{(t+1)}{}_{2,4} & 0 \\ 0 & \xi^{(t+1)}{}_{3,2} & \xi^{(t+1)}{}_{3,3} & \xi^{(t+1)}{}_{3,4} & 0 \\ 0 & \xi^{(t+1)}{}_{4,2} & \xi^{(t+1)}{}_{4,3} & \xi^{(t+1)}{}_{4,4} & 0 \\ 0 & 0 & 0 & 0 & 0 \end{array}$$

The above argument is valid for the normal algorithmic realization of any N-ary valued five or nine-neighborhood two-dimensional cellular automaton. **The proof ends.**

In what follows, we construct a normal algorithm $\mathcal{N}^{22RCA}$ for realizing a binary valued, R-neighborhood (R=5 or 9), two dimensional cellular automata. We need the following alphabets:

Alphabet of terminals: $\mathcal{A} = \{\ 0\ 1\ \}$
Alphabet of nonterminals: $\mathcal{E} = \{\ \alpha\ \beta\ \Gamma\ \sigma\ \}$
Alphabet of delimiters: $\mathcal{D}_1 = \{\ )\ \}$, $\mathcal{D}_2 = \{\ \&\ \}$

Site variables are denoted by ξ, η, μ and ϕ, and they take on values from $\mathcal{A}$. The variable ζ ranges over the union of the alphabets $\mathcal{A}$ and $\mathcal{D}_2$. The symbols $\llcorner$ and $\lrcorner$ denote the left and the right parentheses respectively.

The scheme of $\mathcal{N}^{22RCA}$ given below, is constructed over the union of the alphabets $\mathcal{A}$, $\mathcal{E}$, $\mathcal{D}_1$, and $\mathcal{D}_2$. $\mathcal{N}^{21RCA}$ is a composition of four normal algorithms $\mathcal{N}^1$, $\mathcal{N}^2$, $\mathcal{N}^3$ and $\mathcal{N}^4$.

Formula Number	Substitution Formulas	Remarks
$\mathcal{N}^1$:		
(00)	$\sigma Q\alpha \rightarrow Q\alpha$	Q is a word from $\mathcal{A} \cup D_2$. $\|Q\|$=3(NSIZE)-6 and NSIZE is the width of the given square array configu-ration.
(01)	$\&R\alpha\& \rightarrow \&R\&R\&\sigma\alpha$	R is a word from $\mathcal{A} \cup \mathcal{D}_2$. $\|R\|$=6(NSIZE)-11.
(02)	$\xi\eta\mu\alpha\phi \rightarrow \xi\eta\mu\eta\mu\phi\alpha$	
(03)	$\alpha\zeta \rightarrow \zeta\alpha$	
(04)	$\alpha \rightarrow \cdot$	
(05)	$) \rightarrow)\,\alpha$	
$\mathcal{N}^2$:		
(06)	$\lfloor\alpha\xi^{(t)}{}_{2,2}\xi^{(t)}{}_{2,3}\,\xi^{(t)}{}_{2,4}\rfloor$ $\lfloor\beta\xi^{(t)}{}_{3,2}\,\xi^{(t)}{}_{3,3}\,\xi^{(t)}{}_{3,4}\rfloor$ $\lfloor\Gamma\xi^{(t)}{}_{4,2}\xi^{(t)}{}_{4,3}\xi^{(t)}{}_{4,4}\rfloor \rightarrow \xi^{(t+1)}{}_{3,3}\lfloor\alpha\rfloor\lfloor\beta\rfloor\lfloor\Gamma\rfloor$	The symbol $\lfloor$ denotes the left parenthesis and the symbol $\rfloor$ the right parenthesis.
(07)	$\alpha\&\beta\&\Gamma\& \rightarrow \&\alpha\Gamma\&$	
(08)	$\alpha\beta\Gamma Q\& \rightarrow \alpha Q\&\beta\Gamma$	Q is a word from $\mathcal{A} \cup \mathcal{D}_2$, and $\| Q \|$ = 3 (NSIZE)-6.
(09)	$\beta\Gamma Q\& \rightarrow \beta Q\&\Gamma$	Q is a word $\mathcal{A} \cup \mathcal{D}_2$, and $\|Q\|$=3(NSIZE)-6.
(10)	$\alpha\&\beta\&\Gamma \rightarrow \cdot\, 0\&0^{NSIZE}$	0^{NSIZE} is a string of NSIZE 0's.
(11)	$) \rightarrow)\alpha\beta\Gamma$	
$\mathcal{N}^3$:		
(12)	$) \rightarrow \cdot\,)0^{NSIZE}\&0$	
$\mathcal{N}^4$:		
(13)	$) \rightarrow$	
(14)	$\& \rightarrow$	

A five neighborhood cellular automaton, as we have seen already, evolves according to a rule ϕ, where, for any site (i, j) we have:

$$\xi^{(t+1)}_{i,j} = \phi\ [\xi^{(t)}_{i,j}, \xi^{(t)}_{i,j+1}, \xi^{(t)}_{i+1,j}, \xi^{(t)}_{i,j-1}, \xi^{(t)}_{i-1,j}].$$

Similarly, a nine-neighborhood cellular automaton evolves according to a rule ϕ, where, for any site (i, j) the following holds:

$$\xi^{(t+1)}_{i,j} = \phi\ [\ \xi^{(t)}_{i,j}, \xi^{(t)}_{i,j+1}, \xi^{(t)}_{i+1,j+1}, \xi^{(t)}_{i+1,j}, \xi^{(t)}_{i+1,j-1}, \xi^{(t)}_{i,j-1}, \xi^{(t)}_{i-1,j-1}, \xi^{(t)}_{i-1,j}, \xi^{(t)}_{i-1,j+1}\ ].$$

A five-neighborhood 5-tuple, $\xi^{(t)}_{i,j}, \xi^{(t)}_{i,j+1}, \xi^{(t)}_{i+1,j}, \xi^{(t)}_{i,j-1}, \xi^{(t)}_{i-1,j}$ holds 2^5possible combinations of symbols from the alphabet $\mathcal{A}$. An updating rule ϕ in this case, is a system of 32 substitution formulas with their left parts consisting of the eight words of length 5 from $\mathcal{A}$ and their right parts consisting of single letters from $\mathcal{A}$. If we arrange all the thirty two words as per the increasing order of their numerical counterparts, then we code a rule ϕ as a word L of length 32 from the alphabet $\mathcal{A}$. In fact, one can generate 2^{32} updating rules as shown in table 11.4.1.

In the same manner, a nine-neighborhood 9-tuple

$$\xi^{(t)}_{i,j},\xi^{(t)}_{i,j+1},\xi^{(t)}_{i+1,j+1},\xi^{(t)}_{i+1,j},\xi^{(t)}_{i+1,j-1},\xi^{(t)}_{i,j-1},\xi^{(t)}_{i-1,j-1},\xi^{(t)}_{i-1,j},\xi^{(t)}_{i-1,j+1}$$

holds 2^9 possible combinations of symbols from the alphabet $\mathcal{A}$. An updating rule ϕ in this case, in a system of 512 substitution formulas with their left parts consisting of the 512 words of length 9 from $\mathcal{A}$ and their right parts consisting of single letters from $\mathcal{A}$. If we arrange all the 512 words as per the increasing order of their numerical counterparts, then we can code a rule ϕ as a word L of length 512 from the alphabet $\mathcal{A}$. In fact, one can generate 2^{512} updating rules.

Example 12.2

Let us consider the following binary valued square array configuration of width NSIZE=5, of a two-dimensional cellular automaton, at a time step t:

```
0 1 1 0 0
0 1 0 1 0
0 0 1 0 0
0 0 1 1 0
0 1 0 0 0
```

and apply the five-neighborhood rule $\phi_{222772222}$ to it. The code word L corresponding to this rule is: 00001101010001110011101111111110.

The one-dimensional string corresponding to this square array configuration is : P =)01100&01010&00100&00110&01000 .

$\mathcal{N}^1$:

)01100&01010&00100&00110&01000
⊢)α01100&01010&00100&00110&01000
⊢)0α1100&01010&00100&00110&01000
⊢)01α100&01010&00100&00110&01000
⊢)011α00&01010&00100&00110&01000
⊢)011110α0&01010&00100&00110&01000
⊢)011110100α&01010&00100&00110&01000
⊢)011110100&α01010&00100&00110&01000
⊢)011110100&0α1010&00100&00110&01000
⊢)011110100&01α010&00100&00110&01000
⊢)011110100&010α10&00100&00110&01000
⊢)011110100&010101α0&00100&00110&01000
⊢)011110100&010101010α&00100&00110&01000
⊢)011110100&010101010&α00100&00110&01000
⊢)011110100&010101010&0α0100&00110&01000
⊢)011110100&010101010&00α100&00110&01000
⊢)011110100&010101010&001α00&00110&01000
⊢)011110100&010101010&001010α0&00110&01000
⊢)011110100&010101010&001010100α&00110&01000
⊢)011110100&010101010&001010100&010101010&001010100σα &00110&01000
⊢)011110100&010101010&001010100&010101010&001010100σ& α00110&01000
⊢)011110100&010101010&001010100&010101010&001010100σ& 0α0110&01000
⊢)011110100&010101010&001010100&010101010&001010100σ& 00α110&01000
⊢)011110100&010101010&001010100&010101010&001010100σ &001α10&01000
⊢)011110100&010101010&001010100&010101010&001010100σ &001011α0&01000

⊢)011110100&010101010&001010100&010101010&001010100σ
&001011110α&01000

⊢)011110100&010101010&001010100&010101010&001010100
&001011110α&01000

⊢)011110100&010101010&001010100&010101010&001010100
&001011110α&001010100&001011110σα&01000

⊢)011110100&010101010&001010100&010101010&001010100
&001011110&001010100&001011110σ&α01000

⊢)011110100&010101010&001010100&010101010&001010100
&001011110&001010100&001011110σ&0α1000

⊢)011110100&010101010&001010100&010101010&001010100
&001011110&001010100&001011110σ&01α000

⊢)011110100&010101010&001010100&010101010&001010100
&001011110&001010100&001011110σ&010α00

⊢)011110100&010101010&001010100&010101010&001010100
&001011110&001010100&001011110σ&010100α0

⊢)011110100&010101010&001010100&010101010&001010100
&001011110&001010100&001011110σ&010100000α

⊢)011110100&010101010&001010100&010101010&001010100
&001011110&001010100&001011110&010100000α

⊢)011110100&010101010&001010100&010101010&001010100
&001011110&001010100&001011110&010100000

$\mathcal{N}^2$:

⊢)011110100&010101010&001010100&010101010&001010100
&001011110&001010100&001011110&010100000

⊢)αβΓ011110100&010101010&001010100&010101010&001010100
&001011110&001010100&001011110&010100000

⊢)α011110100&βΓ010101010&001010100&010101010&001010100
&001011110&001010100&001011110&010100000

⊢)α011110100&β010101010&Γ001010100&010101010&001010100
&001011110&001010100&001011110&010100000

⊢)1α110100&β101010&Γ010100&010101010&001010100
&001011110&001010100&001011110&010100000

⊢)10α100&β010&Γ100&010101010&001010100
&001011110&001010100&001011110&010100000

⊢)101α&β&Γ&010101010&001010100
&001011110&001010100&001011110&010100000

⊢)1010&0αβΓ010101010&001010100
&001011110&001010100&001011110&010100000

⊢)1010&0α010101010&βΓ001010100
&001011110&001010100&001011110&010100000
⊢)1010&0α010101010&β001010100
&Γ001011110&001010100&001011110&010100000
⊢)1010&01α101010&β010100
&Γ011110&001010100&001011110&010100000
⊢)1010&010α010&β100&Γ110&001010100&001011110&010100000
⊢)1010&0101α&β&Γ&001010100&001011110&010100000
⊢)1010&01010&0αβΓ001010100&001011110&010100000
⊢)1010&01010&0α001010100&βΓ001011110&010100000
⊢)1010&01010&0α001010100&β001011110&Γ010100000
⊢)1010&01010&01α010100&β011110&Γ100000
⊢)1010&01010&010α100&β110&Γ000
⊢)1010&01010&0101α&β&Γ
⊢)1010&01010&01010&00000

$\mathcal{N}^3$:

)1010&01010&01010&00000
⊢)00000&01010&01010&01010&00000

$\mathcal{N}^4$:

)00000&01010&01010&01010&00000
⊢ 0000001010010100101000000

The new square array configuration that have evolved now, is shown below:

$$\begin{matrix} 0 & 0 & 0 & 0 & 0 \\ 0 & 1 & 0 & 1 & 0 \\ 0 & 1 & 0 & 1 & 0 \\ 0 & 1 & 0 & 1 & 0 \\ 0 & 0 & 0 & 0 & 0 \end{matrix}$$

12.3 Three Dimensional Normal Algorithmic Cellular Automata

As described in section 11.6 of this book, a three-dimensional, N-ary valued cellular automaton **C** consists of a 3-D array of cells. Each cell takes on any of the N given values, and all the values are simultaneously updated at a particular stage of evolution according to a rule involving the values contained in certain surrounding cells. Though it is possible to have several 3-D neighborhood structures, we are concerned here only with two types, 7 and 9-neighborhood structures, which are shown respectively in figure 12.3.1 (a) and 12.3.1 (b).

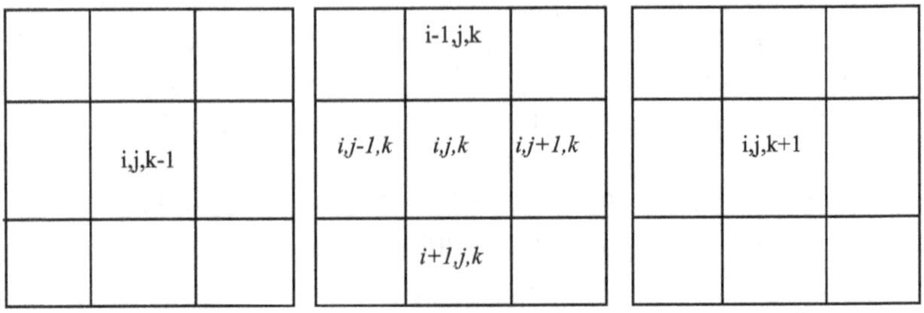

(k-1)th plane kth plane (k+1)th plane

Figure 12.3.1 (a): A 3-D 7-neighborhood structure

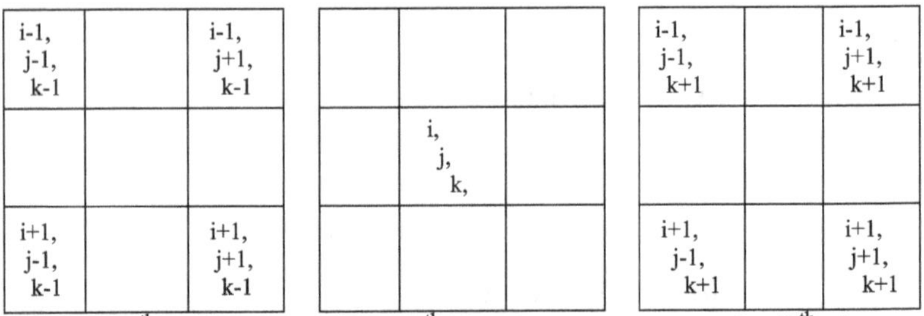

(k-1)th plane kth plane (k+1)th plane

Figure 12.3.1 (b) A 3-D 9-neighborhood structure

Let us consider a 3-D array and let (i,j,k) be one of its cells. Then the value, $\xi^{(t)}_{i,j,k}$, held by the cell (i,j,k) at a stage t is an element from a set of numbers X = { 0, 1, …, N-1 }. Now, the value held by the cell (i,j,k) could be updated in accordance with a 7-neighborhood or a 9-neighborhood rule. A 3-D 7-neighborhood cellular automaton evolves according to a rule ϕ.

$$\xi^{(t+1)}_{i,j,k} = \phi\left(\xi^{(t)}_{i,j,k}, \xi^{(t)}_{i,j,k+1}, \xi^{(t)}_{i,j+1,k}, \xi^{(t)}_{i+1,j,k}, \xi^{(t)}_{i,j,k-1}, \xi^{(t)}_{i,j-1,k}, \xi^{(t)}_{i-1,j,k} \right)$$

Similarly, a 3-D 9-neighborhood cellular automaton evolves according to a rule

$$\xi^{(t+1)}_{i,j,k} = \phi\left(\xi^{(t)}_{i,j,k}, \xi^{(t)}_{i+1,j+1,k-1}, \xi^{(t)}_{i+1,j-1,k-1}, \xi^{(t)}_{i+1,j-1,k+1}, \xi^{(t)}_{i+1,j+1,k+1}, \xi^{(t)}_{i-1,j+1,k+1}, \xi^{(t)}_{i-1,j+1,k-1}, \xi^{(t)}_{i-1,j-1,k-1}, \xi^{(t)}_{i-1,j-1,k+1}\right)$$

Let us recall from earlier discussions, that in order to construct a normal algorithm $\mathcal{N}$ for realizing a two-dimensional cellular automaton, we had to represent its 2-D array of symbols in the form of a one-dimensional string. In the same manner, a three-dimensional cellular automaton can be realized by means of a normal algorithm only when its 3-D array configuration is represented in the form of a one-dimensional string. One way of representing a 3-D array configuration in the form of a 1-D string is as described below.

Let us consider at a time step t, a finite, cube lattice configuration of n planes, each plane consisting of n rows, and each row containing n symbols from an alphabet $\mathcal{A}$. Now, we represent this 3-D array as:

$$
\begin{aligned}
P =)&\xi^{(t)}_{1,1,1}\xi^{(t)}_{1,2,1} \cdots \xi^{(t)}_{1,j,1} \cdots \xi^{(t)}_{1,n,1}\& \xi^{(t)}_{2,1,1}\xi^{(t)}_{2,2,1} \cdots \xi^{(t)}_{2,j,1} \cdots \xi^{(t)}_{2,n,1}\&\ldots \\
\ldots.\ &\xi^{(t)}_{i,1,1}\xi^{(t)}_{i,2,1} \cdots \xi^{(t)}_{i,j,1} \cdots \xi^{(t)}_{i,n,1}\& \ldots \&\xi^{(t)}_{n,1,1}\xi^{(t)}_{n,2,1} \cdots \xi^{(t)}_{n,j,1} \cdots \xi^{(t)}_{n,n,1}\,\square \\
&\xi^{(t)}_{1,1,2}\xi^{(t)}_{1,2,2} \cdots \xi^{(t)}_{1,j,2} \cdots \xi^{(t)}_{1,n,2}\ \&\ \xi^{(t)}_{2,1,2}\xi^{(t)}_{2,2,2} \cdots \xi^{(t)}_{2,j,2} \cdots \xi^{(t)}_{2,n,2}\&\ldots \\
\ldots\&\ &\xi^{(t)}_{i,1,2}\xi^{(t)}_{i,2,2} \cdots \xi^{(t)}_{i,j,2} \cdots \xi^{(t)}_{i,n,2}\&\ldots \&\ \xi^{(t)}_{n,1,2}\xi^{(t)}_{n,2,2} \cdots \xi^{(t)}_{n,j,2} \cdots \xi^{(t)}_{n,n,2}\,\square \\
&\xi^{(t)}_{1,1,k}\xi^{(t)}_{1,2,k} \cdots \xi^{(t)}_{1,j,k} \cdots \xi^{(t)}_{1,n,k}\ \&\ \xi^{(t)}_{2,1,k}\xi^{(t)}_{2,2,k} \cdots \xi^{(t)}_{2,j,k} \cdots \xi^{(t)}_{2,n,k}\ \&\ldots \\
\ldots\&\ &\xi^{(t)}_{i,1,k}\xi^{(t)}_{i,2,k} \cdots \xi^{(t)}_{i,j,k} \cdots \xi^{(t)}_{i,n,k}\&\ldots \&\ \xi^{(t)}_{n,1,k}\xi^{(t)}_{n,2,k} \cdots \xi^{(t)}_{n,j,k} \cdots \xi^{(t)}_{n,n,k}\,\square \\
&\xi^{(t)}_{1,1,n}\xi^{(t)}_{1,2,n} \cdots \xi^{(t)}_{1,j,n} \cdots \xi^{(t)}_{1,n,n}\ \&\ \xi^{(t)}_{2,1,n}\xi^{(t)}_{2,2,n} \cdots \xi^{(t)}_{2,j,n} \cdots \xi^{(t)}_{2,n,n}\&\ldots \\
\ldots\&\ &\xi^{(t)}_{i,1,n}\xi^{(t)}_{i,2,n} \cdots \xi^{(t)}_{i,j,n} \cdots \xi^{(t)}_{i,n,n}\&\ldots\&\xi^{(t)}_{n,1,n}\xi^{(t)}_{n,2,n} \cdots \xi^{(t)}_{n,j,n} \cdots \xi^{(t)}_{n,n,n}
\end{aligned}
$$

where the symbols) & and $\square$ are called delimiters (separating symbols) and they are not in the alphabet A. Having thus represented a three-dimensional array configuration as a one-dimensional string P, our next step would be to find out a method for applying seven or nine-neighborhood updating rules to it.

In the case of a seven neighborhood structure, the seven neighborhood of a site, say, (i,j,k) of the array configuration of P is viewed as the 7-tuple formed by the sites (i,j,k-1), (i-1,j,k), (i,j-1,k), (i,j,k), (i,j+1,k), (i+1,j,k), (i,j,k+1).

Similarly in the case of nine neighborhood structure, the nine neighborhood of a site, say (i,j,k) of the array configuration of P is viewed as the 9-tuple formed by the sites (i-1,j-1,k-1), (i-1,j+1,k-1), (i+1,j-1,k-1), (i+1,j+1,k-1), (i,j,k), (i-1,j-1,k+1), (i-1,j+1,k+1), (i+1,j-1,k+1) and (i+1,j+1,k+1) .

Now, let us consider the word:

$$\xi^{(t)}_{i-1,j-1,k-1}\ \xi^{(t)}_{i-1,j,k-1}\ \xi^{(t)}_{i-1,j+1,k-1}\ \xi^{(t)}_{i,j-1,k-1}\ \xi^{(t)}_{i,j,k-1}\ \xi^{(t)}_{i,j+1,k-1}\ \xi^{(t)}_{i+1,j-1,k-1}$$
$$\xi^{(t)}_{i+1,j,k-1}\ \xi^{(t)}_{i+1,j+1,k-1}\ \xi^{(t)}_{i-1,j-1,k}\ \xi^{(t)}_{i-1,j,k}\ \xi^{(t)}_{i-1,j+1,k}\ \xi^{(t)}_{i,j-1,k}\ \xi^{(t)}_{i,j,k}\ \xi^{(t)}_{i,j+1,k}$$
$$\xi^{(t)}_{i+1,j-1,k}\ \xi^{(t)}_{i+1,j,k}\ \xi^{(t)}_{i+1,j+1,k}\ \xi^{(t)}_{i-1,j-1,k+1}\ \xi^{(t)}_{i-1,j,k+1}\ \xi^{(t)}_{i-1,j+1,k+1}\ \xi^{(t)}_{i,j-1,k+1}$$
$$\xi^{(t)}_{i,j,k+1}\ \xi^{(t)}_{i,j+1,k+1}\ \xi^{(t)}_{i+1,j-1,k+1}\ \xi^{(t)}_{i+1,j,k+1}\ \xi^{(t)}_{i+1,j+1,k+1}$$

which occurs in P, in parts, as 9-tuples. This word contains addition to the symbols of the 7-tuple and the 9-tuple corresponding to the seven and nine neighborhood structures discussed above, certain other symbols also, which are called quiescent symbols (that is, inactive symbols) as far as the seven and nine neighborhood rules are concerned. Now the following conjoint substitution formula:

$$\lfloor\ \xi^{(t)}_{i-1,j-1,k-1}\ \xi^{(t)}_{i-1,j,k-1}\ \xi^{(t)}_{i-1,j+1,k-1}\ \xi^{(t)}_{i,j-1,k-1}\ \xi^{(t)}_{i,j,k-1}\ \xi^{(t)}_{i,j+1,k-1}\ \xi^{(t)}_{i+1,j-1,k-1}$$
$$\xi^{(t)}_{i+1,j,k-1}\ \xi^{(t)}_{i+1,j+1,k-1} \rfloor \lfloor\ \xi^{(t)}_{i-1,j-1,k}\ \xi^{(t)}_{i-1,j,k}\ \xi^{(t)}_{i-1,j+1,k}\ \xi^{(t)}_{i,j-1,k}\ \xi^{(t)}_{i,j,k}\ \xi^{(t)}_{i,j+1,k}$$
$$\xi^{(t)}_{i+1,j-1,k}\ \xi^{(t)}_{i+1,j,k}\ \xi^{(t)}_{i+1,j+1,k} \rfloor \lfloor \xi^{(t)}_{i-1,j-1,k+1}\ \xi^{(t)}_{i-1,j,k+1}\ \xi^{(t)}_{i-1,j+1,k+1}\ \xi^{(t)}_{i,j-1,k+1}$$
$$\xi^{(t)}_{i,j,k+1}\ \xi^{(t)}_{i,j+1,k+1}\ \xi^{(t)}_{i+1,j-1,k+1}\ \xi^{(t)}_{i+1,j,k+1}\ \xi^{(t)}_{i+1,j+1,k+1} \rfloor \rightarrow \xi^{(t+1)}_{i,j,k}$$

could be used in updating the value of the site (i,j,k). The symbols $\lfloor$ and $\rfloor$ denote respectively the left and the right parentheses.

Based on the details give above, one can construct a normal algorithm for realizing all seven and nine neighborhood 3-D cellular automata. The actual construction of the normal algorithm is left here as an exercise to the reader.

Example 12.3.1

Let us consider a 3-D, 9-neighborhood binary valued cellular automaton characterized by the rule $\phi_{999999999}$. The 512-bit word corresponding to this rule transforms an input 5x5x5 3-D array configuration with a seed value 1 at the center (that is, third row and third column of the third plane) into

```
0 0 0 0 0      0 0 0 0 0      0 0 0 0 0
0 0 1 0 0      0 1 1 1 0      0 0 1 0 0
0 1 1 1 0      0 1 0 1 0      0 1 1 1 0
0 1 1 1 0      0 1 1 1 0      0 1 1 1 0
0 0 0 0 0      0 0 0 0 0      0 0 0 0 0
```

These are the second, third and fourth planes of the evolved pattern respectively. The first and last planes, which have zero value at all locations, are not shown here for brevity.

12.4 Computer Implementation Of Cellular Automata

In order to develop efficient programs for various computer implementation purposes, one need not have to code the substitution formulas of the relevant normal algorithms directly in the form they have been arranged in their corresponding schemes. Wherever possible, one can exploit their special features to economize on the number of intermediate transformations between input and output.

For example, the normal algorithm $\mathcal{N}^{1N3CA}$ given in subsection 12.1 consists of four substitution formulas, whereas one can make use of the single substitution formula

$$\xi^{(t)}\,\eta^{(t)}\,\mu^{(t)} \rightarrow \eta^{(t+1)}$$

which coding the scheme. Basically, the pattern $\xi^{(t)}\,\eta^{(t)}\,\mu^{(t)}$ is identified in a given one dimensional configuration, say, $C^{(t)}$ and the symbol $\eta^{(t)}$ is rewritten as $\eta^{(t+1)}$ in a duplicate string of $C^{(t)}$.

Similarly, the algorithm $\mathcal{N}^{2NRCA}$ discussed in subsection 12.2 could be coded with the help of a single conjoint substitution formula:

$$\llcorner\, \xi^{(t)}_{i-1,\,j-1}\ \xi^{(t)}_{i-1,j}\ \xi^{(t)}_{i-1,j+1} \,\lrcorner\ \llcorner\, \xi^{(t)}_{i,\,j-1}\,\xi^{(t)}_{i,\,j}\,\xi^{(t)}_{i,\,j+1} \,\lrcorner\ \xi^{(t)}_{i+1,j-1}\ \xi^{(t)}_{i+1,\,j}\,\xi^{(t)}_{i+1,\,j+1} \,\lrcorner \rightarrow \xi^{(t+1)}_{i,\,j}$$

The pattern corresponding to the left part of the above substitution formula is identified in a given 2-D array configuration and the symbol $\xi^{(t)}_{i,\,j}$ is rewritten as $\xi^{(t+1)}_{i,\,j}$ in a duplicate 2-D array configuration.

In the same manner, we see that a 3-D cellular automata algorithm $\mathcal{N}^{3NRCA}$ could be coded with the help of a single conjoint substitution formula:

$$\lfloor \xi^{(t)}_{i-1,j-1,k-1}\ \xi^{(t)}_{i-1,j,k-1}\ \xi^{(t)}_{i-1,j+1,k-1}\ \xi^{(t)}_{i,j-1,k-1}\ \xi^{(t)}_{i,j,k-1}\ \xi^{(t)}_{i,j+1,k-1}\ \xi^{(t)}_{i+1,j-1,k-1}$$
$$\xi^{(t)}_{i+1,j,k-1}\ \xi^{(t)}_{i+1,j+1,k-1} \rfloor \lfloor \xi^{(t)}_{i-1,j-1,k}\ \xi^{(t)}_{i-1,j,k}\ \xi^{(t)}_{i-1,j+1,k}\ \xi^{(t)}_{i,j-1,k}\ \xi^{(t)}_{i,j,k}\ \xi^{(t)}_{i,j+1,k}$$
$$\xi^{(t)}_{i+1,j-1,k}\ \xi^{(t)}_{i+1,j,k}\ \xi^{(t)}_{i+1,j+1,k} \rfloor \lfloor \xi^{(t)}_{i-1,j-1,k+1}\ \xi^{(t)}_{i-1,j,k+1}\ \xi^{(t)}_{i-1,j+1,k+1}\ \xi^{(t)}_{i,j-1,k+1}$$
$$\xi^{(t)}_{i,j,k+1}\ \xi^{(t)}_{i,j+1,k+1}\ \xi^{(t)}_{i+1,j-1,k+1}\ \xi^{(t)}_{i+1,j,k+1}\ \xi^{(t)}_{i+1,j+1,k+1} \rfloor \rightarrow \xi^{(t+1)}_{i,j,k}$$

The pattern corresponding to the left part of the above substitution formula is identified in a given 3-D array configuration and symbol $\xi^{(t)}_{i,j,k}$ is rewritten as $\xi^{(t+1)}_{i,j,k}$ in a duplicate 3-D array configuration.

In the section that follows, we provide methods for generating 1-D, 2-D and 3-D patterns using the techniques discussed here, and describe procedures for constructing cellular automata rules using either look-up tables or logical expressions.

Section 13

Pattern Generation

A cellular automaton evolves in discrete time steps, with the value of the variable at one site being affected by the values of the variables at sites in its neighborhood on the previous time step. The site-values corresponding to a configuration at a particular time step, say t, are updated, all at once, based on the values in their neighborhood, according to a definite set of updating rules. The resulting configuration at time step t+1, is the evolved version of the one at time step t. The initial configurations of a cellular automaton are broadly classified into two types: (1) Single-site seed configuration and (2) multi-site (say L sites) arbitrary configurations. The pattern generated by a cellular automaton evolving from a single-site seed configuration or from a multi-site arbitrary configuration, indicates the behavior of the automaton.

As already discussed in earlier sections, an N-ary valued r-neighborhood cellular automaton accommodates at most N^{N^r} updating rules. Note that we can have, in this case, at most (N-1) type-1 and (N^L-N) type-2 initial configurations. This amounts to saying that one can construct at most $N^{N^r}(N^L-1)$, N-ary valued r-neighborhood cellular automata.

Cellular automata are classified under four types: (1) cellular automata that evolve after a finite number of time steps from almost all initial states to a unique homogeneous state, in which all sites have the same value, (2) cellular automata that serve as filters which generate stable structures or periodic structures with small periods from particular initial site value sequences. (3) cellular automata that evolve from almost all possible initial states to aperiodic, that is, chaotic patterns. (4) cellular automata that evolve from several disordered initial configurations yield, after a finite number of time steps, either zero-valued configurations or stable and periodic structures or propagating structures.

E. G. Rajan, *Symbolic Computing - Signal and Image Processing*
ISBN 81-7800-047-4

In this section, we describe methods for generating patterns using cellular automata of the above four types. The realization of all these various cellular automata is hereby understood to be carried out using Generalised Markov Algorithms. Given below are certain high-throughput pattern generating techniques.

13.1 Pattern Generation Using 1-D, 3-Neighborhood Cellular Automata

As described in section 12, a one dimensional N-ary valued cellular automaton **C** consists of a 1-D array of cells. Each cell takes on any of N given values, and all the values are simultaneously updated at a particular stage of evolution according to a fixed rule. From a given configuration, a new configuration is evolved by updating the given cell values in accordance with a rule that decides the new value of each cell based on its old value and those of its left and right neighbors.

At a stage t, let $\mathbf{C}^{(t)}$ be finite-length configuration of a 1-D cellular automaton, and let $\xi^{(t)}_{i-1}, \xi^{(t)}_{i}$ and $\xi^{(t)}_{i+1}$ be the values held by the 3-neighborhood of an ith cell. First, let us store $\mathbf{C}^{(t)}$ in a file, say, PATTERN. Now, let us consider a 3-neighbourhood updating rule ϕ and let us apply it to the configuration $\mathbf{C}^{(t)}$. Then, the value of ith cell $\xi^{(t)}_{i}$ is updated as $\xi^{(t+1)}_{i}$ where,

$$\xi^{(t+1)}_{i} = \phi\,(\,\xi^{(t)}_{i-1}\,,\,\xi^{(t)}_{i}\,,\,\xi^{(t)}_{i+1}\,)$$

Note that the first and the last cell in the configuration do not have respectively the left and right neighbors, and so, their values, that is, zero or a nonzero number would remain unchanged throughout. So, all the cell values in the configuration, leaving the first and the last ones are updated, one by one, in this manner. Let us call this resulting configuration, denoted by the symbol $\mathbf{C}^{(t+1)}$ as the first evolution, and let us write it in the file PATTERN just below $\mathbf{C}^{(t)}$. The second evolution $\mathbf{C}^{(t+2)}$ could also be obtained in a similar manner by applying the same rule ϕ to $\mathbf{C}^{(t+1)}$. Now, $\mathbf{C}^{(t+2)}$ is written in the file PATTERN, just below $\mathbf{C}^{(t+1)}$.

By having a control over the number of evolutions, we thus can generate a pattern using the 1-D cellular automaton.

13.2 Pattern Generation Using 2-D, Five And Nine Neighborhood Cellular Automata

A two dimensional N-ary valued cellular automaton **C** consists of a 2-D array of cells. Each cell takes on any of the N given values, and all the values are simultaneously updated at a particular stage of evolution according to a rule involving the values contained in certain surrounding cells. We are concerned here only with square arrays with five and nine neighborhood structures.

	i-1,j	
i,j-1	i,j	i,j+1
	i+1,j	

i-1,j-1	i-1,j	i-1,j+1
i,j-1	i,j	i,j+1
i+1,j-1	i+1,j	i+1,j+1

Figure 13.2.1 (Same as figure 12.3.1)

Let us consider a square array and let (i,j) be one of its cells. Then the value $\xi^{(t)}_{i,j}$, held by the cell (i,j) at a stage t is an element from a set of numbers X = { 0, 1, …., N-1 }. Now, the value held by the cell (i,j) could be updated in accordance with a five neighborhood or a nine neighborhood rule.

A 5-neighbourhood rule ϕ is of the form

$$\xi^{(t+1)}_{i,\,j} = \phi\left(\xi^{(t)}_{i,\,j}\,,\ \xi^{(t)}_{i,\,j+1}\,,\ \xi^{(t)}_{i+1,\,j}\,,\ \xi^{(t)}_{i,\,j-1}\,,\ \xi^{(t)}_{i-1,\,j}\right)$$

Similarly, a 9-neighborhood rule ϕ is of the form

$$\xi^{(t+1)}_{i,\,j} = \phi\left(\xi^{(t)}_{i,\,j}\,,\ \xi^{(t)}_{i,\,j+1}\,,\ \xi^{(t)}_{i+1,\,j+1}\,,\ \xi^{(t)}_{i+1,\,j}\ \ \xi^{(t)}_{i+1,\,j-1}\ \ \xi^{(t)}_{i,\,j-1}\,,\ \xi^{(t)}_{i-1,\,j-1}\,,\ \xi^{(t)}_{i-1,\,j}\ \ \xi^{(t)}_{i-1,\,j+1}\right)$$

At a stage t, let $C^{(t)}$ be a finite-size square array configuration of a 2-D cellular automaton, and let $\xi^{(t)}_{i,j}$, $\xi^{(t)}_{i,\,j+1}$, $\xi^{(t)}_{i+1,\,j}$, $\xi^{(t)}_{i,\,j-1}$ and $\xi^{(t)}_{i-1,\,j}$ be the values held by the 5-neighborhood of an ith cell. First, let us store $C^{(t)}$ in a file, say PATTERN. Now, let us consider a 5-neighborhood updating rule ϕ and let us apply it to the square array configuration $C^{(t)}$. Then, the value of ith cell $\xi^{(t)}_{i,j}$ is updated as $\xi^{(t+1)}_{i,j}$. Note that the cells in the first and the last row, and the cells in the first and the last column of the array configuration do not form 5-neighborhoods, and so, their values, that is, 0, would remain unchanged throughout. So, all the cell values in the square array configuration, leaving the ones in the first row and column and the last row and column and updated, one by one, in this manner. Let us call this resulting array, denoted by the symbol $C^{(t+1)}$ as the first evolution. $C^{(t+1)}$ can be stored in a different file, or in the file PATTERN itself so that $C^{(t)}$ is rewritten as $C^{(t+1)}$. The second evolution $C^{(t+1)}$ could also be obtained in a similar manner by applying the same rule ϕ to $C^{(t+1)}$. Now, $C^{(t+2)}$ is written in the file PATTERN so that $C^{(t+1)}$ is rewritten as $C^{(t+2)}$. By having a control over the number of evolutions, we thus obtain the desired 2-D pattern corresponding to a particular updating rule. The technique that has been discussed for generating patterns using 2-D, 5-neighborhood cellular automata, is valid also for generating patterns using 2-D, 9-neighborhood cellular automata.

13.3 Pattern Generation Using 3-D, Seven And Nine Neighborhood Cellular Automata

A three-dimensional N-ary valued cellular automaton **C** consists of a 3-D array of cells. Each cell takes on any of the N given values, and all the values are simultaneously updated at a particular stage of evolution according to a rule involving the values contained in certain surrounding cells. We are concerned here only with cube lattice configurations and the following 7- and 9-neighborhood structures.

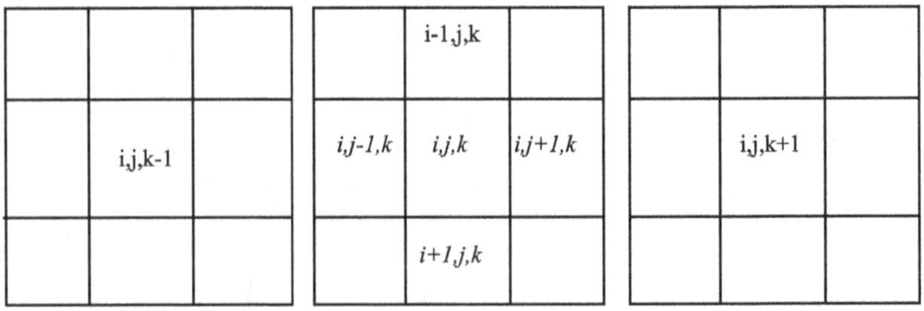

(k-1)[th] plane   k[th] plane   (k+1)[th] plane

Figure 13.3.1 (a): A 3-D 7-neighborhood structure

i-1, j-1, k-1		i-1, j+1, k-1
i+1, j-1, k-1		i+1, j+1, k-1

(k-1)th plane

	i, j, k,	

kth plane

i-1, j-1, k+1		i-1, j+1, k+1
i+1, j-1, k+1		i+1, j+1, k+1

(k+1)th plane

Figure 13.3.1 (b) A 3-D 9-neighborhood structure

Let us consider a 3-D cube lattice configuration array and let (i,j,k) be one of its cells. Then value $\xi^{(t)}_{i,j,k}$, held by the cel (i,j,k) at a stage t is an element from a set of numbers X = { 0, 1, ...N-1 } . Now, the value held by the cell (i,j,k) could be updated in accordance with a 7-neighborhood or a 9-neighborhood rule.

A 3-D, 7-neighborhood rule ϕ is of the form

$$\xi^{(t+1)}_{i,j,k} = \phi\left(\xi^{(t)}_{i,j,k}, \xi^{(t)}_{i,j,k+1}, \xi^{(t)}_{i,j+1,k}, \xi^{(t)}_{i+1,j,k}, \xi^{(t)}_{i,j,k-1}, \xi^{(t)}_{i,j-1,k}, \xi^{(t)}_{i-1,j,k}\right)$$

Similarly, a3-D, 9-neighbourhood rule ϕ is of the form

$$\xi^{(t+1)}_{i,j,k} = \phi\left(\xi^{(t)}_{i,j,k}, \xi^{(t)}_{i+1,j+1,k-1}, \xi^{(t)}_{i+1,j-1,k-1}, \xi^{(t)}_{i+1,j-1,k+1}, \xi^{(t)}_{i+1,j+1,k+1}, \xi^{(t)}_{i-1,j+1,k+1}, \xi^{(t)}_{i-1,j+1,k-1}, \xi^{(t)}_{i-1,j-1,k-1}, \xi^{(t)}_{i-1,j-1,k+1}\right)$$

At a stage t, let $\mathbf{C}^{(t)}$ be a finite-size cube lattice configuration of a 3-D cellular automaton, and let $\xi^{(t)}_{i,j,k}$, $\xi^{(t)}_{i,j,k+1}$, $\xi^{(t)}_{i,j+1,k}$, $\xi^{(t)}_{i+1,j,k}$, $\xi^{(t)}_{i,j,k-1}$, $\xi^{(t)}_{i,j-1,k}$ and $\xi^{(t)}_{i-1,j,k}$ be the values held by the 7-neighborhood of an ith cell. First, let us store the initial configuration $\mathbf{C}^{(t)}$ in a file, say, PATTERN.

Now, let us consider a 7-neighborhod updating rule ϕ and let us apply it to the initial configuration $\mathbf{C}^{(t)}$. Then, the value of ith cell $\xi^{(t)}_{i,j,k}$ is updated as $\xi^{(t+1)}_{i,j,k}$. Note that the cells in the first and the last planes, and the cells in the first row and column and the last row and column of all the intermediate planes of the cube lattice configuration do not form 7-neighborhood, and so, their values, that is, 0, would remain unchanged throughout. So, all the cell values in the cube lattice configuration, leaving the ones in the first and the last planes, the ones in the first row and column and the last row and column of all the intermediate planes are updated, one by one, in this manner. Let us call this resulting configuration, denoted by the symbol $\mathbf{C}^{(t+1)}$ as the first evolution. $\mathbf{C}^{(t+1)}$ can be stored in a different file, or in the file PATTERN itself so that $\mathbf{C}^{(t)}$ is rewritten as $\mathbf{C}^{(t+1)}$. The second evolution $\mathbf{C}^{(t+2)}$, could also be obtained in a similar manner by applying the same rule ϕ to $\mathbf{C}^{(t+1)}$. Now, $\mathbf{C}^{(t+2)}$ is written in the file PATTERN, so that $\mathbf{C}^{(t+1)}$ is written as $\mathbf{C}^{(t+2)}$.

By having a control over the number of evolutions, we thus can obtain the desired 3-D pattern corresponding to a particular evolution.

The technique that has been discussed above for generating patterns using 3-D 7-neighbourhood cellular automata, is valid also for generating patterns using 3-D, 9-neighborhood cellular automata.

13.4 Logical Pattern Generating System (A Software Package - LPGS)

Logical Pattern Generating System is a PC compatible software package consisting of a number of routines that generate designs of different types such as textures, motifs, mosaics, fractals, geometric and spirographic patterns.

In what follows, we provide a comprehensive description of the algorithms, and structure of various menus and relevant technical details involved in the development of this package. LPGS has been deployed in the Visual Studio.Net environment.

Figure 13.4.1 shows the opening menu of the software package "*Logical Pattern Generating System*" (LPGS). The fast algorithms of this package have been developed in the framework of *Cellular Logic Array Processing*.

Note: The techniques and the software details that are discussed in this section have been reproduced here with the permission from M/s Pentagram Research, Hyderabad, Andhra Pradesh, India.

Figure 13.4.1: Opening menu of LPGS
(Courtesy by Pentagram Research Center, Hyderabad)

13.4.1 About Logical Pattern Generating System

Logical Pattern Generation System version 1.0 is a collection of a number of pattern generating tools developed using Visual C++, and it works in Windows 95 environment.

The algorithms pertaining to most of the routines in this package have been developed in the novel logico-mathematical framework Cellular Logic Array Processing (CLAP). As discussed so far in detail, this nontraditional paradigm advocates pattern-directed *Search And Replace* (SAR) techniques, and so, it guarantees speed and precision.

Hardware required

LPGS version 1.0 will run on any IBM compatible PC, which has at least 16 MB RAM and 4GB hard disk. A high-resolution color monitor is recommended for a fine image display. The operating system should be Windows 95 or Windows NT.

Other platforms

LPGS version 2.0 runs on Silicon Graphics workstation with the operating system IRIX 6.1 and above. LPGS version 3.0 runs on SOLARIS OS based SUN workstations like SUN SPARC machines.

Potential users

Textile printers would find this package to be very useful for modern fabric manufacturing. Automated printing industries, Tile printers, Pattern designers, Wall paper printers, Handloom fabric designers, Silk sari weavers, Greeting card printers, Artists, Painters, Garment and fashion designers and Carpet manufacturers could use this package effectively.

LPGS has been designed and developed by experts in the field of Computer Graphics, and so, academic and training institutions in fashion technology would benefit from using this package. The main menu is open and students can include their own DLL files. This package is compatible to all Microsoft products, highly user friendly and supported by on-line help.

Technical details of LPGS

LPGS has three modules: (i) Pattern Generation, (ii) Pattern Processing and (iii) Pattern Design. Patterns are geometric representations of various mathematical formulae. The concepts of Cellular Automata, Linden Mayer Systems, Array Grammars, Complex and Trigonometric functions, and various image processing tools have been used while developing the routines contained in this package.

The routines in LPGS are compatible to all standard Microsoft products. The structure of the package is organized in the following manner:

13.4.2 Menu Structure Of LPGS

This package consists of an opening menu with eleven items displayed in the menu bar. This subsection provides a detailed report on each item and on every item in the respective popup menu.

File and Edit menu

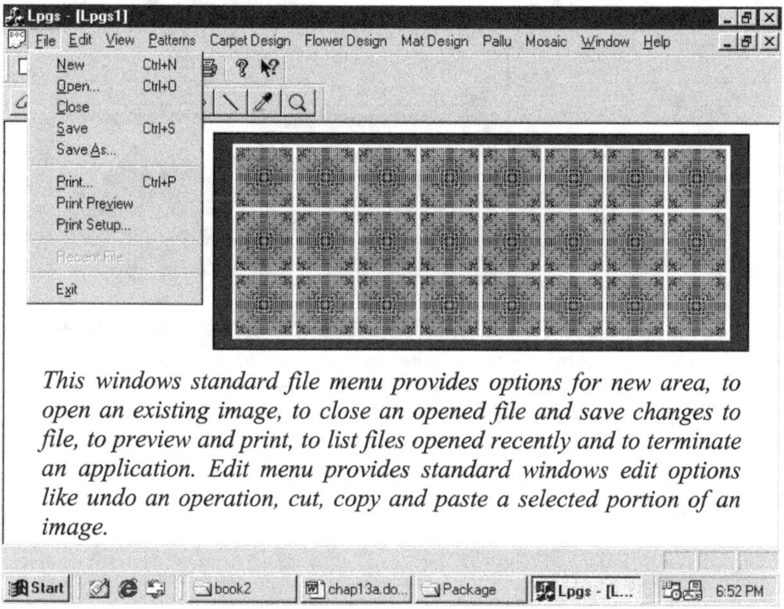

This windows standard file menu provides options for new area, to open an existing image, to close an opened file and save changes to file, to preview and print, to list files opened recently and to terminate an application. Edit menu provides standard windows edit options like undo an operation, cut, copy and paste a selected portion of an image.

View menu

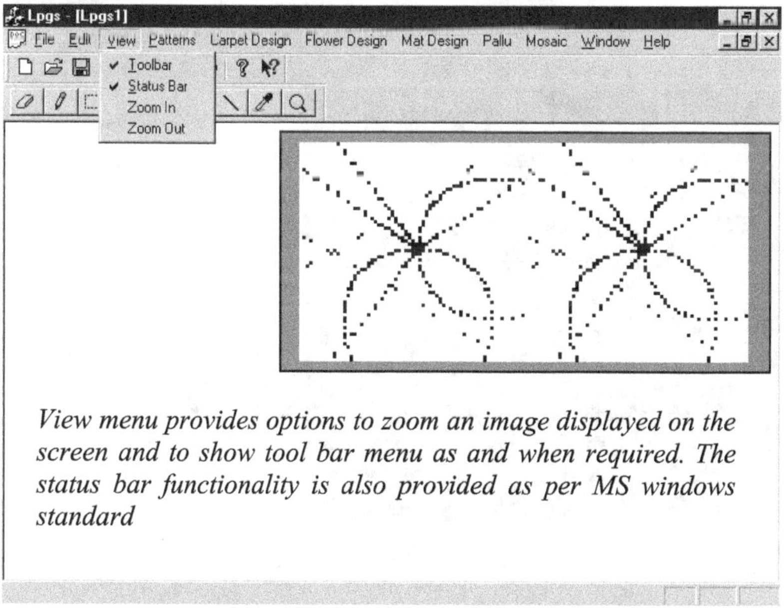

View menu provides options to zoom an image displayed on the screen and to show tool bar menu as and when required. The status bar functionality is also provided as per MS windows standard

Patterns Menu

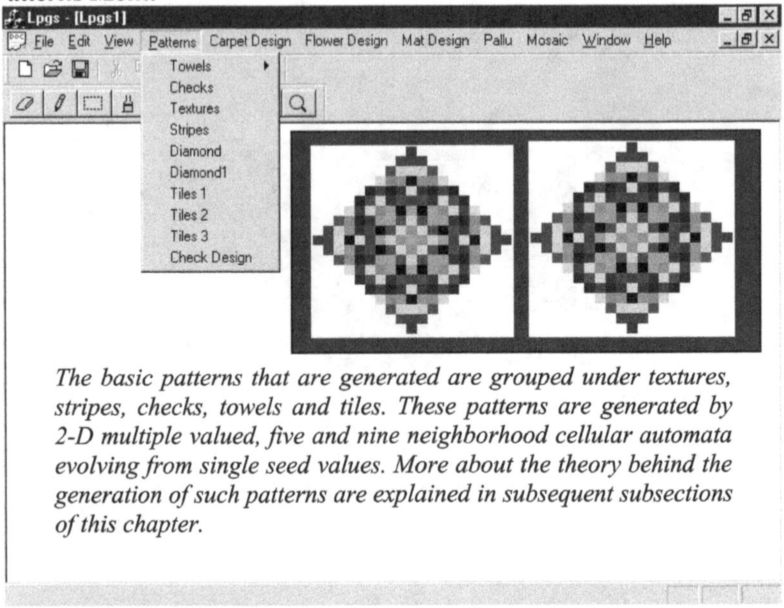

Tile designs

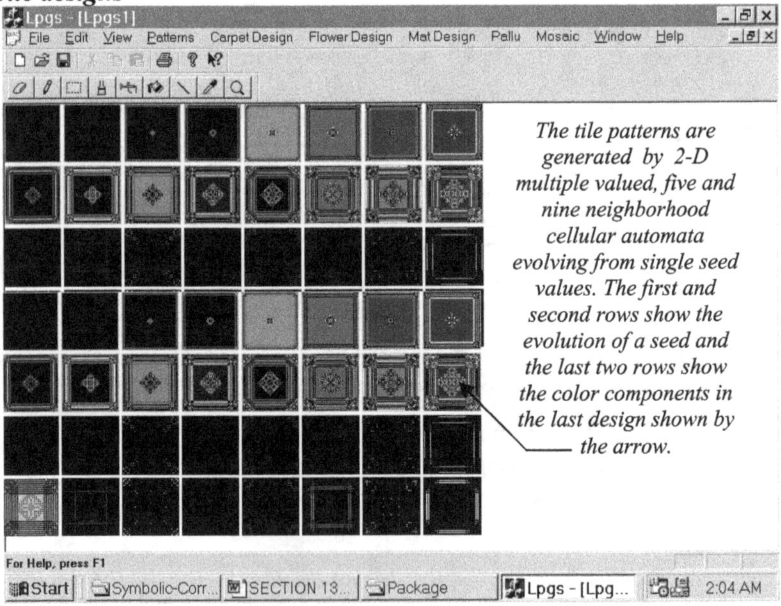

Carpet Design Menu

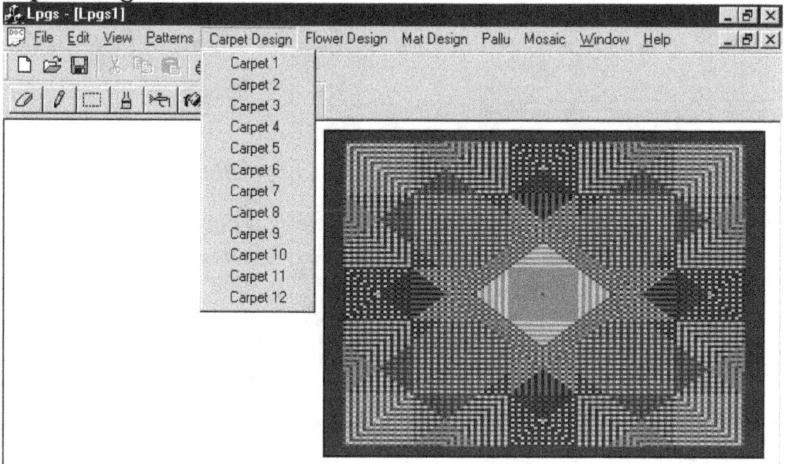

These 2-D cellular automata programs generate patterns that are suitable for carpet designs. Each program generates infinitely large number of patterns.

Flower Design Menu

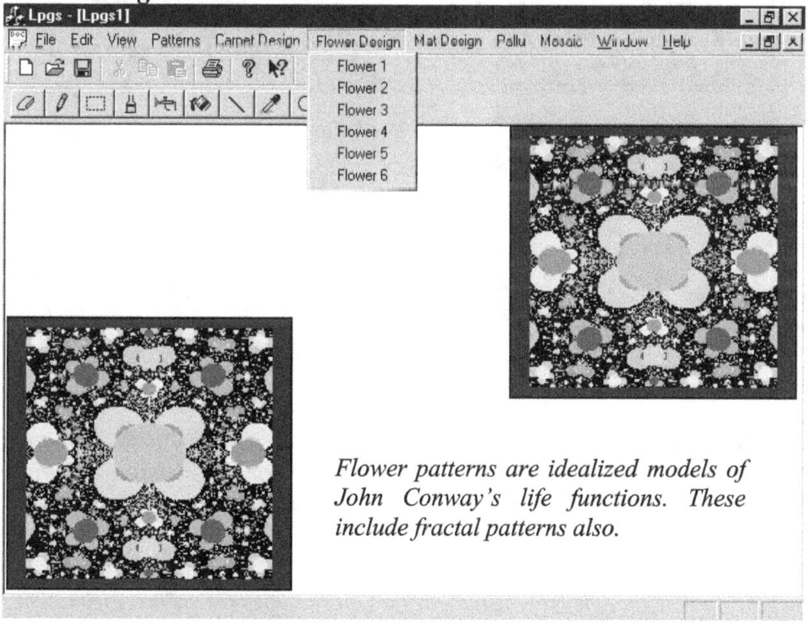

Flower patterns are idealized models of John Conway's life functions. These include fractal patterns also.

Mat Design Menu

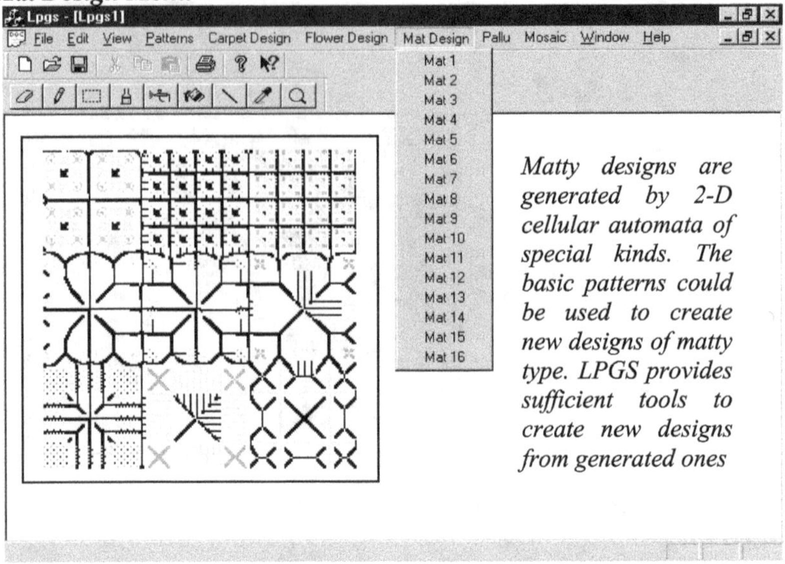

Pallu Menu

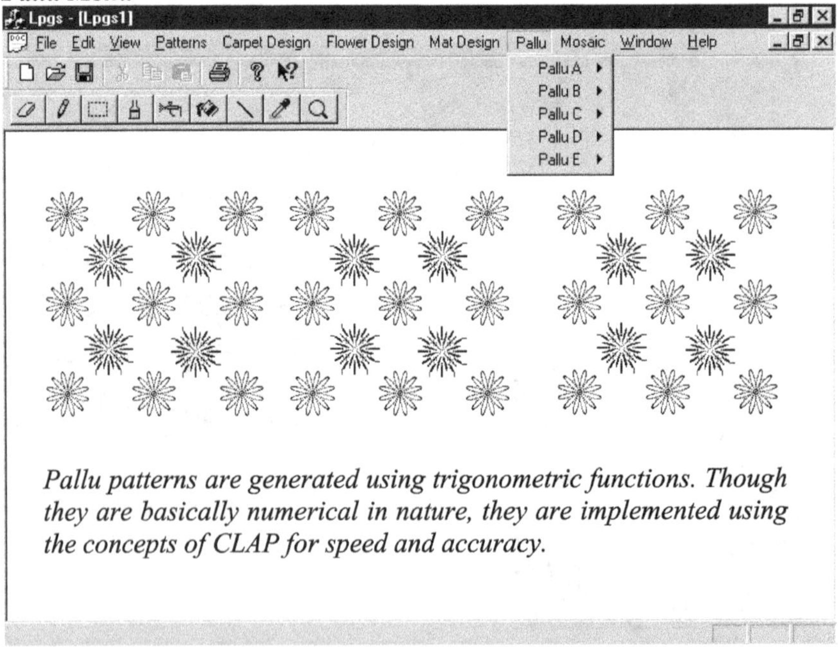

Mosaic Menu

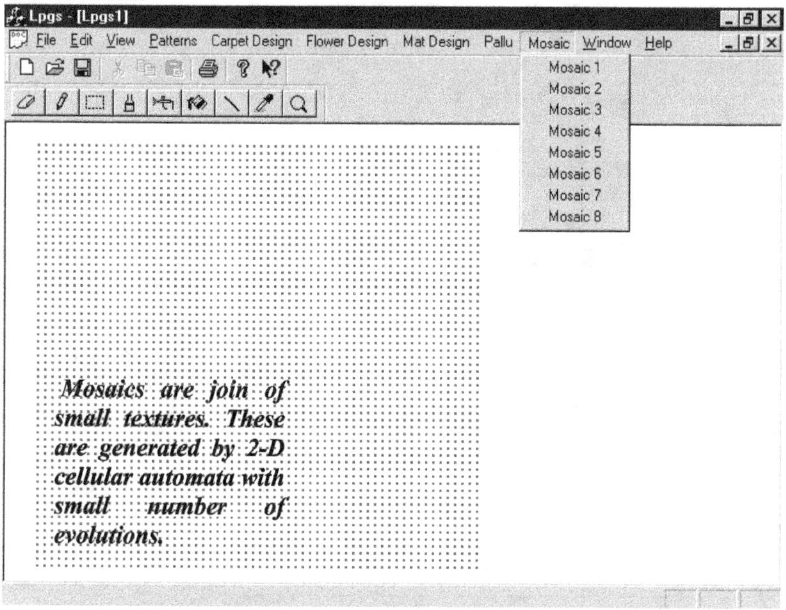

Large mosaic design

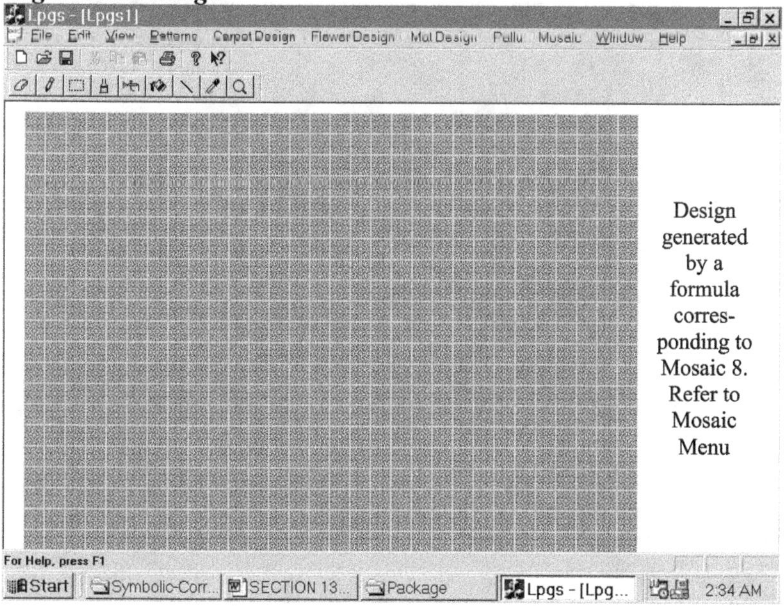

Windows Menu

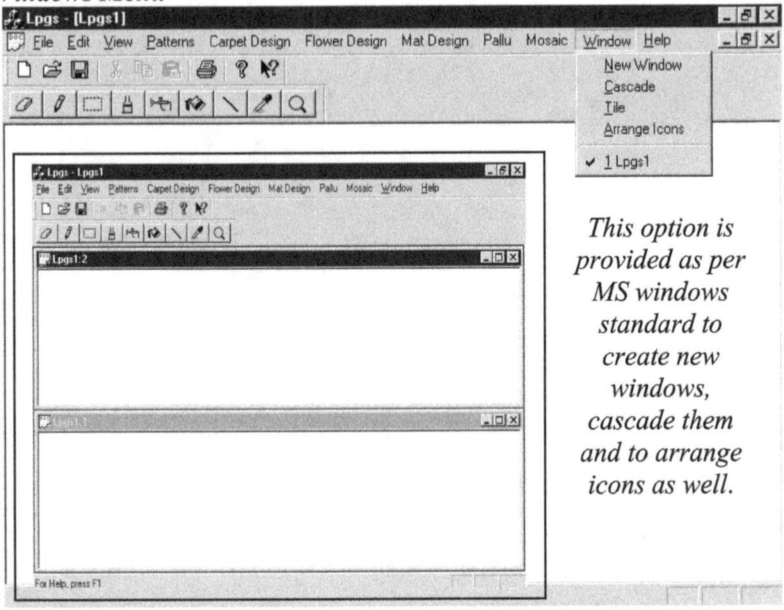

This option is provided as per MS windows standard to create new windows, cascade them and to arrange icons as well.

Help Menu

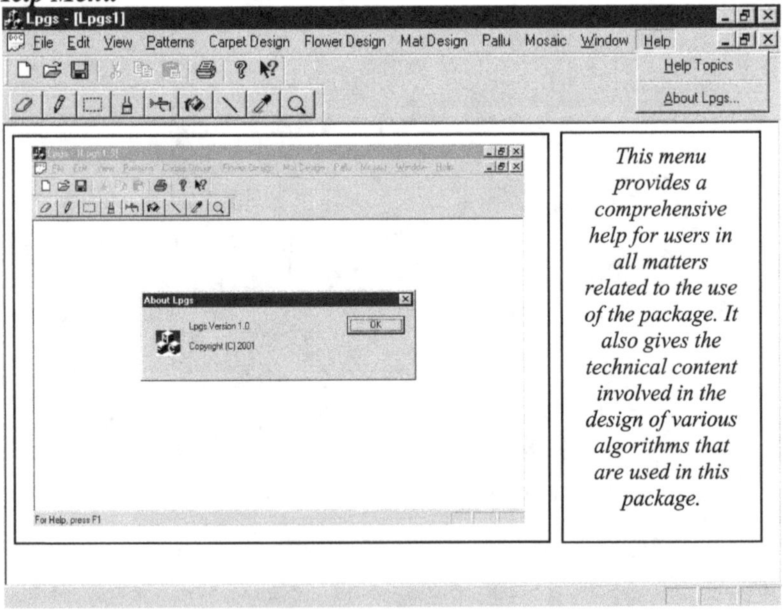

This menu provides a comprehensive help for users in all matters related to the use of the package. It also gives the technical content involved in the design of various algorithms that are used in this package.

Section 14

Image Processing

In our discussions so far in the last three sections, our attention has primarily been on the role of cellular automata and normal algorithms in the generation of patterns and pattern-like-images. We now look at their role in implementing image processing operations. In this role the image to be processed forms the initial configuration from which a cellular automaton evolves and produces the desired processed image as its final configuration. Thus, apart from generating patterns from initial states, normal algorithmic cellular automata could also be used for processing digital images. In what follows, we provide techniques for implementing morphological operations, and for implementing operations such as segmentation, binarization, and edge detection on digital images.

14.1 Fast Algorithms For Processing 2-D Images

Note that most of the traditional image processing operations involve numerical computations, and so their implementation in a number crunching digital computer purely in terms of pattern-directed algorithms, would lead to unwarranted complexity and consumption of more CPU time. Consequently, wherever it is necessary, we make use of these numerical operations as such in our fast operating pattern-directed algorithms so that the algorithms together with a digital computer form a high throughput image processing system.

14.1.1 Morphological Operations On Binary, Gray-Level And Color Images

The fundamental operations of mathematical morphology are the two dual operations of *Dilation* and *Erosion*. The operation of dilation is commutative, whereas that of erosion is not. These two operations have been defined separately for binary and gray-level images.

E. G. Rajan, *Symbolic Computing - Signal and Image Processing*
ISBN 81-7800-047-4

Dilation And Erosion Of Binary Images

Let us consider a set of numbers E to denote the row and column positions of the pixels in binary images A and B. Let us treat the image B as the *Structuring Element.*

Then the dilation of A by B is defined as the Minkowski addition, $A \oplus B = \{x \mid \text{for some } a \in A \text{ and } b \in B, x = a+b\}$, and, the erosion of A by B is defined as the Minkowski subtraction, $A \theta B = \{x \mid \text{for every } b \in B, x+b \in A\}$.

Dilation And Erosion Of Gray-Level And Color Images

For any two gray-level digital images A and B, the ***dilation*** is defined as the Minkowski addition,

$$\mathcal{D}(A,B) = A \oplus B = \text{EXTSUP}_{(x,y) \in DB}[A_{x,y} + B(x,y)],$$

where D_B is the domain of the image B, and EXTSUP is an operation of *supremum* over the union of the domains. The operation of ***erosion*** is defined using the Minskowski subtraction $A \theta B = \text{INF}_{(x,y) \in DB}[A_{-x,-y} + B(x,y)]$ as $\mathcal{E}(A,B) = \text{INF}_{(x,y) \in DB}[A_{-x,-y} - B(x,y)]$, where D_B is the domain of the image B, and INF is an operation of *infimum* over the intersection of the domains.

Following these definitions for both binary, gray-level and color digital images [13], the morphological filtering operations of ***Closing*** and ***Opening*** are defined in the following manner.

The closing of A by B is represented as AoB and defined as $AoB = (A \oplus B) \theta B$. The opening of A by B is represented as $A \bullet B$ and defined as $A \bullet B = (A \theta B) \oplus B$.

In the case of binary valued images A and B, the morphological operations $A \oplus B = \{x \mid \text{for some } a \in A \text{ and } b \in B, x = a+b\}$, and $A \theta B = \{x \mid \text{for every } b \in B, x+b \in A\}$ are simulated here, by a two dimensional, 9-neighbourhood binary valued cellular automaton characterized by two updating rules, one for dilation and another for erosion. The dilation rule has the code $0(1)^{511}$ and it consists of the following 512 conjoint substitution formulas:

Formula Number	Substitution Formulas
001	$\lfloor 000 \rfloor \lfloor 000 \rfloor \lfloor 000 \rfloor \rightarrow 0$
002	$\lfloor 001 \rfloor \lfloor 000 \rfloor \lfloor 000 \rfloor \rightarrow 1$
:::::	:::::
:::::	:::::
511	$\lfloor 110 \rfloor \lfloor 111 \rfloor \lfloor 111 \rfloor \rightarrow 1$
001	$\lfloor 111 \rfloor \lfloor 111 \rfloor \lfloor 111 \rfloor \rightarrow 1$

The erosion rule has the code $(0)^{511}1$ and it consists of the following set of 512 substitution formulas:

Formula Number	Substitution Formulas
001	$\lfloor 000 \rfloor \lfloor 000 \rfloor \lfloor 000 \rfloor \rightarrow 0$
002	$\lfloor 001 \rfloor \lfloor 000 \rfloor \lfloor 000 \rfloor \rightarrow 0$
:::::	:::::
:::::	:::::
511	$\lfloor 110 \rfloor \lfloor 111 \rfloor \lfloor 111 \rfloor \rightarrow 0$
001	$\lfloor 111 \rfloor \lfloor 111 \rfloor \lfloor 111 \rfloor \rightarrow 1$

Fast Algorithm For Dilating / Eroding Binary Images

In view of the special form of the above two groups of substitution formulas their practical implementation is rather simple. In the case of dilation, if the left part of the first substitution formula is encountered, a 0 is substituted, and if it is not encountered a 1 is substituted. Likewise in the case of erosion, if the left part of the last substitution formula is encountered then a 1 is substituted, otherwise a 0 is substituted. Note that this algorithm does not involve even a single numerical operation.

Example 14.1.1.1

Figure 14.1.1.1 (a) shows a random noise pattern of size 75X75. The binary image of figure 14.1.1.1 (b), of size 75x75, is masked by this noise pattern and the result is shown in figure 14.1.1.1 (c). Figure 14.1.1.1 (d) shows the result of applying one pass of the opening operation implemented in terms of normal algorithmic cellular automata. The opening is done with a 3X3 square structure element consisting of 1's in all the cells.

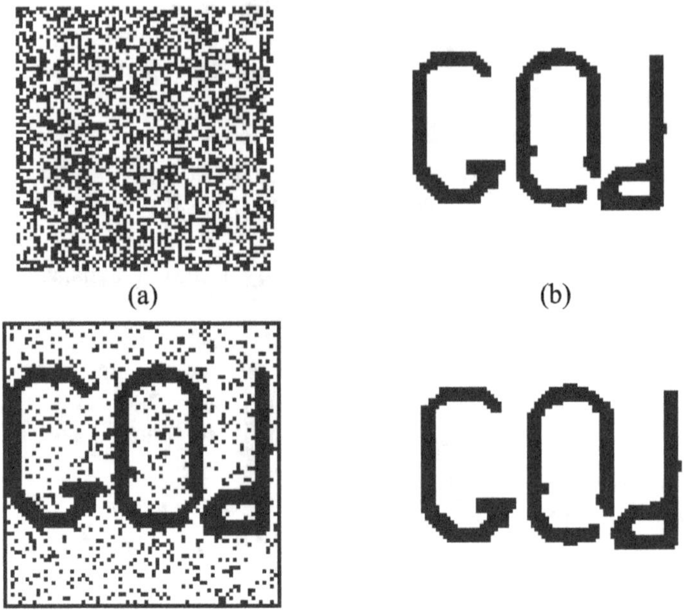

(a) (b)

(c) (d)

Figure 14.1.1.1: Opening of an image

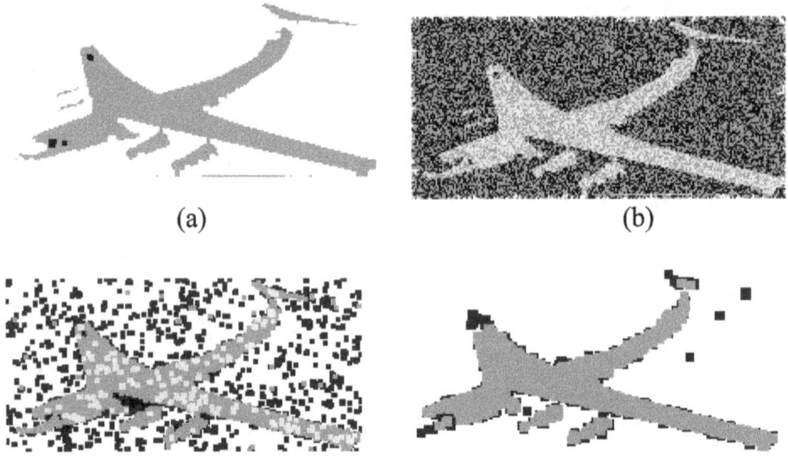

(a) (b)

Opening with 3x3 structuring element (c)

Opening with 5x5 structuring element (d)

Figure 14.1.1.2: Opening of noisy binary image

Figure 14.1.1.2 (a) shows a binary image of size 222X105. Figure 14.1.1.2 (b) shows the image masked by noise pattern. Figure 14.1.1.2 (c) shows the result of applying one pass of the opening operation with a 3X3 square structure element consisting of 1's in all the cells, and figure 14.1.1.2 (d) shows the result of applying one pass of the opening operation with 5X5 square structuring element.

Fast Algorithms For Dilating / Eroding Gray-Level And Color Images

Unlike what has been done in the case of binary dilation and erosion, the operations of gray-level dilation and erosion can not be simulated directly and exclusively by a 2-dimensional cellular automaton. The algorithm is described in a summarized form using pseudo code as given below. Here the term *pixel* is also referred as *pel.*

Algorithm For Erosion

```
Repeat sliding the structuring element over the image
{subtract pels of structuring element from the corresponding pels of the
   image find the minimum, k, among all of them if all the structuring
         element pels are less than the corresponding image pels then
             replace the central pel in the image with k; else replace it
                  with 0}
until the structuring element spans whole of the image
```

Algorithm For Dilation

```
Repeat sliding the structuring element over the image
{add pels of structuring element to the corresponding pels of the image
    find the maximum, k, among all of them if at least one of the image
      pels that are spanned by structuring element is non-zero then
        replace the central pel in the image with k; else replace it with 0}
until the structuring element spans whole of the image
```

Note:

The above algorithms are applicable to RGB color images also. The procedure for dilation or erosion is carried out independently for Red, Green and Blue components of the image and the results displayed simultaneously. Try it out with the programs given in the demonstration CD provided with this book.

Original 256-level
Bitmap gray image
(a)

Image dilated with a 3X3
structuring element
(b)

Image eroded with 3X3
structuring element
(c)

Image closed with 3X3
structuring element
(d)

Figure 14.1.1.3: Closing operation on a gray image by a 3X3 structuring element

Figure 14.1.1.3 (a) shows a 256-level gray image of size 384X288. This gray image is dilated with a 3X3 square structuring element consisting of all 0's and the result is shown in figure 14.1.1.3 (b). The same structuring element has been used to erode the gray image and the result is shown in figure 14.1.1.3 (c). Figure 14.1.1.3 (d) shows the result of applying *one pass closing operation* to the original gray image with the 3X3 structuring element consisting of all 0's.

Morphological Filters And Their Properties

The operations of closing and opening are called morphological filters. Closing and opening are idempotent operators. That is, closing or opening of an already closed or opened image with the same structuring element will not produce any change in the image. This leads to an interesting study on what are known as *Valid Filters*.

Let us denote the morphological operations of erosion and dilation, by the binary digits 0 and 1 respectively. Now, the binary strings 10 and 01 for instance, represent the secondary operations, viz. closing and opening respectively. Each morphological filter is a composition of finite number of primary operations and the filter is denoted by a string of binary digits.

The main idea of any image processing operation is to retain the original size of the features of images. This calls for morphological filtering of images using equal number of dilation and erosion operations. This means that the number of 1s and 0s in the filter representations must be equal and thus the length of a filter string is always even. However, there are occasions wherein one would not mind sacrificing the size information of an image in the context of other priorities. In such cases, one could as well use filters whose representations are of unequal number of 0s and 1s.

For example, the filter 10011 has three 1s and two 0s. That is, the string 10011 represents the morphological filtering of an image by the sequence of operations *dilation-erosion-erosion-dilation-dilation*. Note that this filter will not preserve the size of the various features in the given image.

The important property of the morphological operators of closing and opening are idempotent. That is, consecutive repetition of closing or opening is futile. Any image closed more than once is no different from an image closed once, and the same goes for the opening operation. For example, filtering of an image with 1010 produces the same effect as that with 10. Hence, the filter 1010 is termed as an *Invalid Filter*. A filter which is not invalid is called a *Valid Filter*. Note that the filter 10101 is invalid because 10101 is the same as 101. The filter 10010 is valid but the filter 100101 is invalid because 100101 is the same as 1001.

All morphological operations employ only valid filters. It is essential to identify invalid filters because they hinder the overall performance of the image processing system, consuming more time to perform simpler operations. For better understanding of the concept of idempotence let us take an example. Consider a filter with string length L of 6. The possible filters are 64 (i.e., $2^6 = 64$). Now, the filters which do not change the size of the features are 20 (i.e., ${}^6C_3=20$). These filters are listed below:

0 0 0 1 1 1   0 0 1 0 1 1   0 0 1 1 0 1   0 0 1 1 1 0
0 1 0 0 1 1   0 1 0 1 0 1   0 1 0 1 1 0   0 1 1 0 0 1
0 1 1 0 1 0   0 1 1 1 0 0   1 0 0 0 1 1   1 0 0 1 0 1
1 0 0 1 1 0   1 0 1 0 0 1   1 0 1 0 1 0   1 0 1 1 0 0
1 1 0 0 0 1   1 1 0 0 1 0   1 1 0 1 0 0   1 1 1 0 0 0

Of the above listed filters the idempotent (invalid) filters can be identified and separated. Those filters in which the closing (01) or opening (10) operation is repeated consecutively at least once are:

0 1 0 1 0 1   0 1 0 1 1 0   0 1 1 0 1 0
1 0 0 1 0 1   1 0 1 0 0 1   1 0 1 0 1 0

These filters possess different degrees of idempotence. The degree of idempotence is defined as the number times the closing or opening operation is consecutively repeated. The filters 010101 and 101010 are third degree idempotent filters whereas the filters 010110, 011010, 100101 and 101001 are second degree idempotent filters. Note that the result of filtering an image using 010101 is same as that using the filter 01 and the result due to 010110 is same as that due to 0110.

Structuring Elements – Primary And Higher Order Structures

One can visualize 16 convex polygons in a 9-neighborhood structure as shown below in figure 14.1.1.4. These are called primary structures and these are generally used as structuring elements for morphological processing of digital images. For convenience, all the 16 polygons have been labeled in five categories, A, B, C, D and E. The cells of a 3x3 neighborhood structure are labeled as shown below.

1	2	3
4	5	6
7	8	9

Cell numbering of a 3x3 neighborhood structure

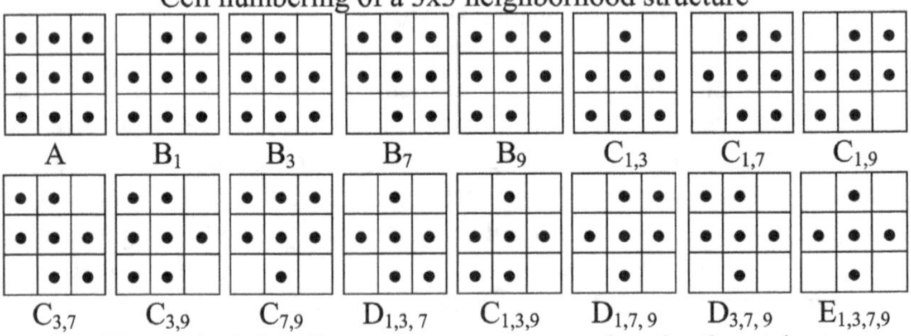

Figure 14.1.1.4: Sixteen convex patterns in a 3 x 3 matrix

Structuring elements are not confined to 3x3 neighborhood alone. One can visualize structuring elements in neighborhoods of size 5x5 or 7x7 or even more. One should be clear in the concept that a structuring element is essentially a digital image and so it admits the possibility of being represented in large neighborhoods. Note that the number of structuring elements that could be generated depends on the size of the neighborhood. For instance, one can generate 81 structuring elements in the neighborhood of size 5x5. Figure 14.1.1.5 shows the cell numbering of a 5x5 neighborhood structure and structuring elements in the A and B categories.

	11	2	33	3
11				33
4		5		6
77				99
7	77	8	99	9

A

	11	2	33	3
11				33
4		5		6
77				99
7	77	8	99	9

B_1

		2	33	3
				33
4		5		6
77				99
7	77	8	99	9

B_{11}

1	11	2	33	
11				33
4		5		6
77				99
7	77	8	99	9

B_3

1	11	2		
11				
4		5		6
77				99
7	77	8	99	9

B_{33}

1	11	2	33	3
11				33
4		5		6
77				99
	77	8	99	9

B_7

1	11	2	33	3
11				33
4		5		6
				99
		8	99	9

B_{77}

1	11	2	33	3
11				33
4		5		6
77				99
7	77	8	99	

B_9

1	11	2	33	3
11				33
4		5		6
77				
7	77	8		

B_{99}

Figure 14.1.1.5: A and B type structuring elements in 5x5 neighborhood

Figure 14.1.1.6 shows the image of a lioness and a cub and also the structuring element chosen from the menu. Figure 14.1.1.7 shows the edge map, which resulted by subtracting from the original image, the image which is eroded with a structuring element $D_{1,1,7,7,9,9}$.

Figure 14.1.1.7: Structuring element chosen from menu

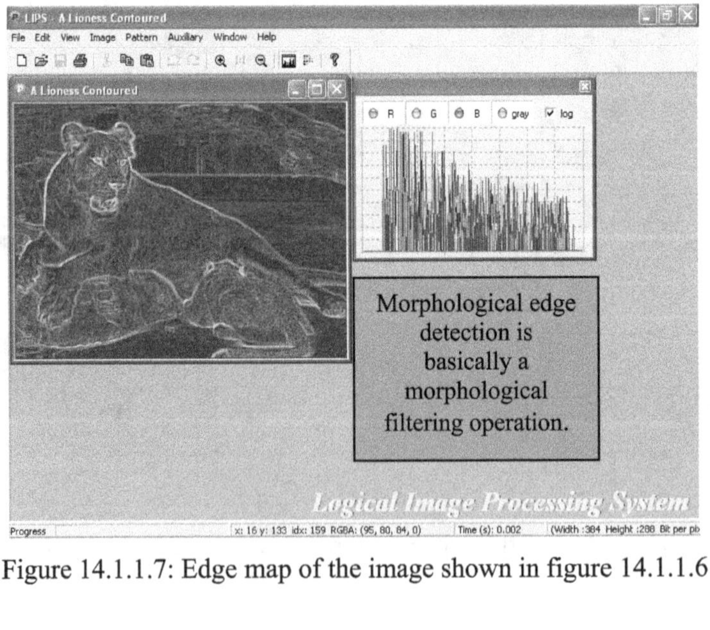

Figure 14.1.1.7: Edge map of the image shown in figure 14.1.1.6

14.1.2 Fast Algorithms For Traditional Image Processing Operations On Two Dimensional Binary, Gray And Color Images

Binarization Of Gray And Color Images

The given digital image of size say NXN, is scanned by a 3X3 window. On each move, the 3X3 sub image covered by the window is examined to see whether the central pixel value lies in between a specified gray region including its lower and upper threshold values. If it is found to lie in that region, then the central cell is assigned a particular gray value. If not, it is assigned the value 0. This procedure is continued till the entire image is scanned. The overall effect is that the entire gray-level image is transformed into an image having only two values.

Example 14.1.2.1

Figure 14.1.2.1 (a) shows a 32 gray level image of size 213X159, digitized from a picture of a human brain. From the histogram on can observe that the gray levels from 0 to 17 could be quantized as one level, and those from 18 to 31 as another level in order to binarize the image. Figure 14.1.2.1 (b) shows the binarized input image.

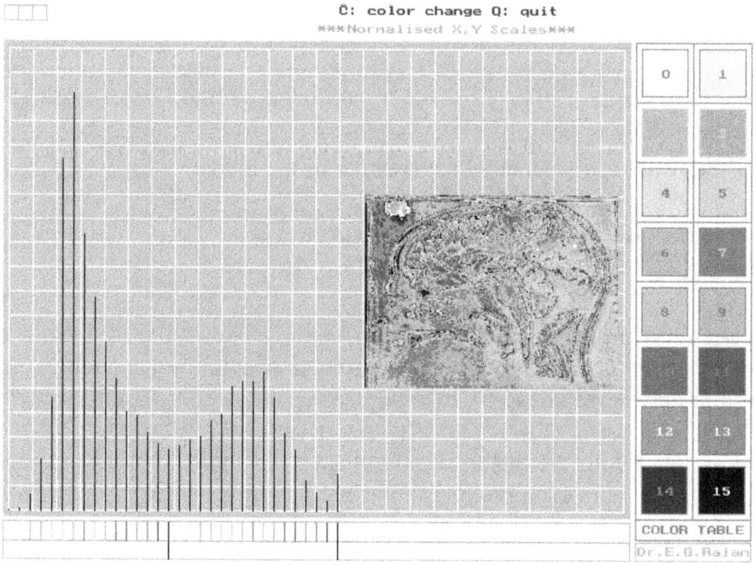

Figure 14.1.2.1 (a): Image of a human brain

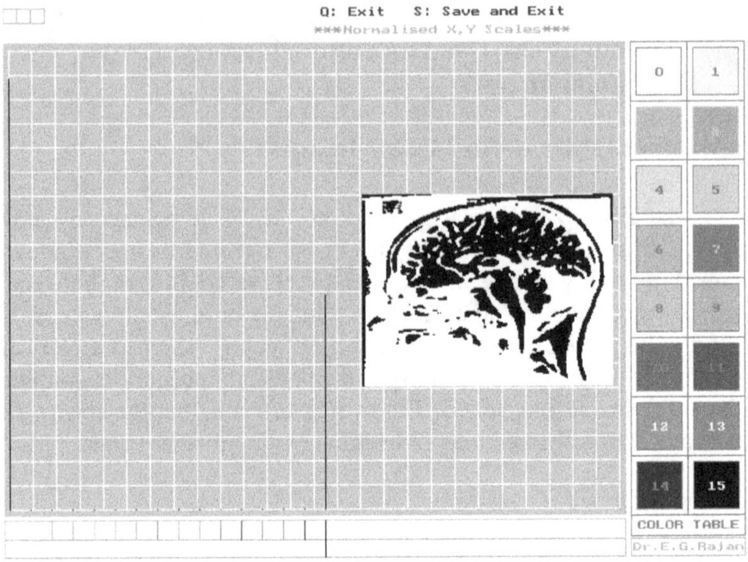

Figure 14.1.2.1(b): Binarized version of the image shown in (a)

Algorithm For Binarization

Repeat sliding a 3X3 empty window over the image
{check whether the central pixel value lies in between a specified lower and upper threshold values. If it is found to lie in that region, then the central cell is assigned a particular gray value. If not, it is assigned the value 0.}
until the structuring element spans whole of the image.

Detection Of Edges In a Digital Image Consisting Of Various Uniform Gray Levels

Among the various types of edge detection algorithms that are available now, those which make use of neighborhood principles, detect edges in a multiple gray level image by locating edge points at places where abrupt changes in gray levels occur. We too make use of the neighborhood principle, but with the difference that instead of locating abrupt changes in gray levels we locate boundaries of regions over which gray levels do not change. This is done in the following manner. The given digital image of size say NXN, is scanned by a 3X3 window. On each move, the 3X3 sub image covered by the window is examined to see whether some or all of its pixels form a convex region of a single gray level, containing at least one pixel from each row and column. Note that such regions canbe formed in sixteen different ways as shown in the figure 14.1.2.2.

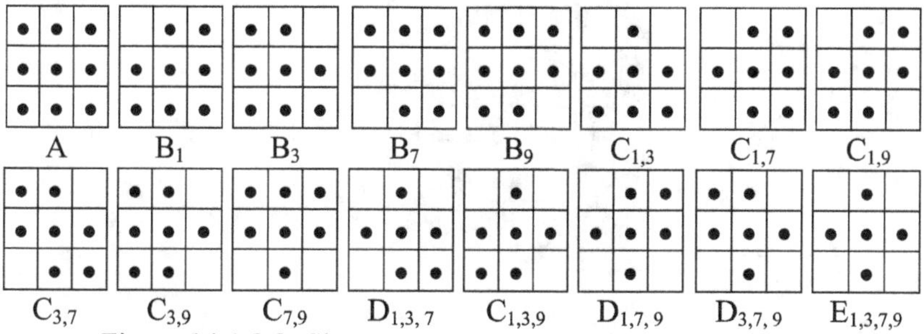

Figure 14.1.2.2: Sixteen convex patterns in a 3X3 window

Of these, the sixteenth one is covered in the rest. To identify whether any of these regions has been encountered or not, it is therefore adequate to check for the sixteenth one alone. If the sub image is found to contain the sixteenth pattern of figure 14.1.2.2, then its central cell is assigned the 0 gray level. This procedure is continued till the entire image is scanned. The overall effect is that the boundaries of various single gray level regions in the given image are retained and the interior parts are erased thus giving us the edge detected version of the original image.

This procedure is given below in the form of a pseudo code, which can be easily translated into any computer language.

Fast Algorithm For Detecting Edges Of Single Gray Level Regions Of Digital Images

Repeat sliding the 5-neighbourhood structure over the image;
{if all the five pixel values of the sub image covered by the scanning
   structure are identical then replace the central pixel value with 0, else
      slide the 5-neighbourhood structure}
until the structuring element spans whole of the image.

Figure 14.1.2.3 shows an image consisting of uniform regions and its edge detected version obtained using the algorithm given above.

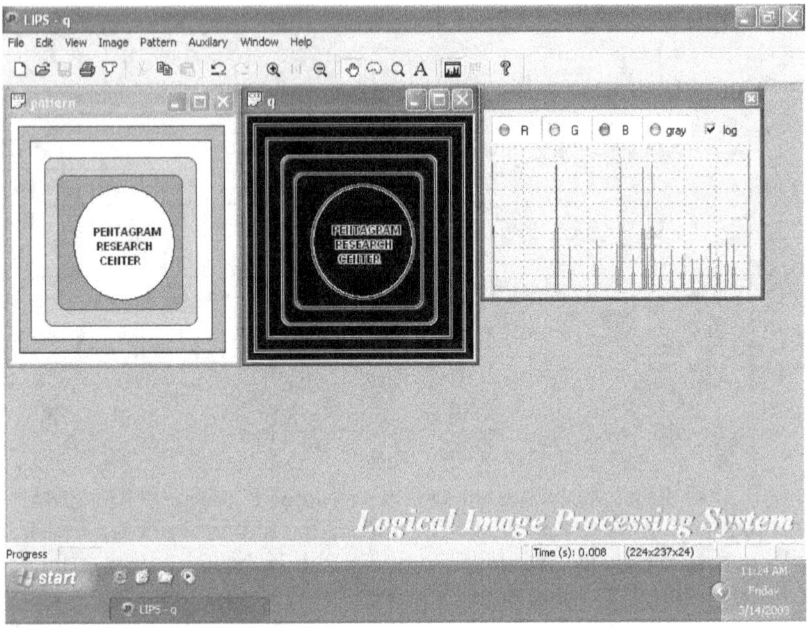

Figure 14.1.2.3: Original image of uniform regions and its edge map

Detection Of Edges In a Digital Image Consisting Of Regions That Appear To Be Uniform

The technique of detecting the edges of various single gray-level regions is easily extended to detecting the edges of regions that appear to be single gray or color level regions. A region that appears to have uniform gray or color levels may actually contain several adjacent gray or color levels. That they appear to be same is the result of visual quantization done by the observer.

The process of partitioning a given gray-level image into regions each of which appears to an observer to have a single gray-level is called segmentation.

So, the central idea behind this extension is that the given image is first segmented using a threshold-based-quantization scheme and then the boundaries of the quantized regions are detected. We proceed as follows. Similar to what is done in the previous case, the given digital image is scanned by the five-neighborhood structure.

On each move, the 3X3 sub image covered by this window is examined to see whether the gray-distance, say D, that is the difference between the maximum and the minimum gray-values corresponding to that subimage, is less than or equal to a threshold value, say T. If D is less than or equal to T, then the central cell is assigned the gray-value 0; otherwise the original value contained in the central cell is left as it is. This procedure is continued till the entire image is scanned. The overall effect is that the boundaries of various regions in the given image, that appear to be uniform, are retained and their interior parts are erased thus giving us the edge detected version of the original image.

Algorithm For Detecting Edges Of Various Regions That Appear To Be Uniform

Repeat sliding the 5-neighbourhood structure over the image;
{find the maximum gray value G_max; find the minimum gray value
G_min; if the difference between these two values D is less than or
equal to a threshold value T then replace the central pixel value with
0, else slide the five neighborhood structure.}
until the structuring element spans whole of the image.

The Turbo C code of this algorithm is provided here for the benefit of the reader.

```
/*****************************************************************************/
/* This program is used to detect various contours in a digital image. Concept introduced and   */
/* program developed by Dr. E. G. Rajan. The reader can develop programs for implementing  */
/* other operations also based on the coding technique provided here.                        */
/*****************************************************************************/

# include<stdio.h>
# include<math.h>
# include<stdlib.h>
# include<graphics.h>
# include<process.h>
# include<dos.h>
# include<conio.h>
# include<alloc.h>
# define MAX(A,B) A>B? A:B
# define MIN(A,B) A<B? A:B
int boxy,flash=0,xscale,yscale,l,e,m,n;
int Y_RES,gray,scale,gd,gm;
unsigned WIDTH,HEIGHT,size,th,MAXGRAY,max,min,g1,g2,k,k1,k2;
unsigned i,j,j1,j2,j3,j4,j5,abc,a,b;
unsigned char *A,*C,*D,*E,*F;
char *ptr,z,fname[8];
FILE *xyz;
```

```
main()
{
 ptr=&fname[0];
 detectgraph(&gd,&gm);
 if(gd==9)
 Y_RES=480;
 else
 Y_RES=350;
  boxy=Y_RES/20+15;
  printf(" Give the WIDTH of the file\n");
   scanf("%u", &WIDTH);
   printf(" Give the HEIGHT of the file\n");
   scanf("%u", &HEIGHT);
   printf(" Give the maximum gray value in the image\n");
   scanf("%u", &MAXGRAY);
   max_gray();
   printf(" Give the threshold value\n");
   scanf("%u", &th);
   size = (unsigned) WIDTH * (unsigned) HEIGHT;
   getchar();
   printf(" Enter the file name\n");
   gets(ptr);
/*********************************************************/
              initgraph(&gd,&gm,"");
              a = (520 - WIDTH);
              b = (Y_RES - HEIGHT)/2;
              j=b-1;
              A=(unsigned char *)calloc(size,sizeof(char));
              E=(unsigned char *)calloc(size,sizeof(char));
              C=(unsigned char *)calloc(MAXGRAY,sizeof(char));
              D=(unsigned char *)calloc(MAXGRAY,sizeof(char));
              F=(unsigned char *)calloc(MAXGRAY,sizeof(char));
               nofile();
               graph();
               col_box();
                        xyz=fopen(ptr,"rt");
                        for(i=0;i<size;i++)
                        {
                         fscanf(xyz," %d",&A[i]);
                         abc = a + (i % WIDTH);
                         if(!(i%WIDTH))
                         j++;
                         putpixel(abc,j,A[i]);
                        }
                        fclose(xyz);
   setcolor(14);
   outtextxy(320,5,"Original Image");
/*****************************************************************/
    for(i=0;i<MAXGRAY;i++)
    {C[i]=0;D[i]=0;F[i]=0;}
    for(j=0;j<size;j++)
    { k1=A[j];
              if(C[k1]==255)D[k1]=D[k1]+1;
              if(D[k1]==255)F[k1]=F[k1]+1;
              C[k1]=C[k1]+1;
    }
              max=0;
```

```
for(i=0;i<MAXGRAY;i++)
{
 max=(max>F[i])? max:F[i];
}
g1=0;g2=0;gray=0;
for(i=0;i<MAXGRAY;i++)
{
 if((F[i]==max)&&(D[i]>g1))g1=D[i]+max;
}
for(i=0;i<MAXGRAY;i++)
{
 if((F[i]==max)&&(D[i]==g1)&&(C[i]>g2)){g2=C[i]+g1;gray=i;}
}
j=b-1;
if(MAXGRAY<=(a-5))xscale=(a-5)/MAXGRAY;
else xscale=MAXGRAY/(a-5);
(unsigned) k2 = (unsigned) max * 255 + (unsigned) g1 * 255 + g2;
if(k2<360)
{
yscale=360/k2;scale=0;
}
else
{
yscale=k2/360+1;scale=1;
}
 setcolor(15);
 for(i=0;i<MAXGRAY;i++)
 {
  line(5+i*xscale,420,5+i*xscale,
     (420-((unsigned) F[i]*255+(unsigned) D[i]*255+C[i])/yscale));
 }
 k=0,
 for(i=0;i<MAXGRAY;i++)
 {
  setcolor(k);
   {
   line(5+i*xscale,445,5+i*xscale,430);
   if((i>14)&&((i+1)%16==0))
    {
    line(5+i*xscale,445,5+i*xscale,460);
    }
   }  k=k+1;
 }
 setcolor(12);
 outtextxy(266,20,"***");
 outtextxy(460,20,"***");
 setcolor(3);
 outtextxy(292,20,"Normalised X,Y Scales");
 printf("(max_freq,gray_value):(");
 printf("%u",k2);printf(",");printf("%u",gray);printf(")");
/***************************************************************/
 process();
 getch();
 setcolor(0);
 outtextxy(320,5,"Original Image");
 setcolor(14);
 outtextxy(315,5,"Processing ...!");
```

```
for(j=0;j<size;j++) E[j]=A[j];
j1=0; j2=WIDTH; j3=j2+WIDTH;
for(j=0;j<(HEIGHT-2);j++)
{
        for(i=0;i<(WIDTH-2);i++)
        {
        if(A[j1+1]!=0 &&   /* Checks for the presence */
          A[j2]!=0 &&     /* of the five neighborhood */
          A[j2+1]!=0 &&   /* structure.             */
          A[j2+2]!=0 &&
          A[j3+1]!=0)
           {
             max=(A[j1+1] > A[j2])? A[j1+1]:A[j2];
             max=(max > A[j2+1])? max:A[j2+1];
             max=(max > A[j2+2])? max:A[j2+2];
             max=(max > A[j3+1])? max:A[j3+1];


             min=(A[j1+1] < A[j2])? A[j1+1]:A[j2];
             min=(min < A[j2+1])? min:A[j2+1];
             min=(min < A[j2+2])? min:A[j2+2];
             min=(min < A[j3+1])? min:A[j3+1];

                     if((max-min)<=th)
                     E[j2+1]=0;
             }
                   j1++;
                   j2++;
                   j3++;
        }
        j1+=2;
        j2+=2;
        j3+=2;
}
j = b-1;
for(i=0;i<size;i++)
{
        abc = a + (i % WIDTH);
        if(!(i%WIDTH))
        j++;
        putpixel(abc,j,E[i]);
}
        setcolor(0);
        outtextxy(315,5,"Processing ...!");
        setcolor(14);
        outtextxy(315,5,"Contoured Image");
/******************************************************************/
  for(i=0;i<MAXGRAY;i++)
  {C[i]=0;D[i]=0;F[i]=0;}
  for(j=0;j<size;j++)
  { k1=E[j];
        if(C[k1]==255)D[k1]=D[k1]+1;
        if(D[k1]==255)F[k1]=F[k1]+1;
        C[k1]=C[k1]+1;
  }

        max=0;
```

```
        for(i=0;i<MAXGRAY;i++)
        {
         max=(max>F[i])? max:F[i];
        }
        g1=0;g2=0;gray=0;
        for(i=0;i<MAXGRAY;i++)
        {
         if((F[i]==max)&&(D[i]>g1))g1=D[i]+max;
        }
        for(i=0;i<MAXGRAY;i++)
        {
         if((F[i]==max)&&(D[i]==g1)&&(C[i]>g2)){g2=C[i]+g1;gray=i;}
        }

        j=b-1;
        if(MAXGRAY<=(a-5))xscale=(a-5)/MAXGRAY;
        else xscale=MAXGRAY/(a-5);
        (unsigned) k2 = (unsigned) max * 255 + (unsigned) g1 * 255 + g2;
        if(k2<360)
        {
        yscale=360/k2;scale=0;
        }
        else
        {
        yscale=k2/360+1;scale=1;
        }
         setcolor(10);
         for(i=0;i<MAXGRAY;i++)
         {
          outtextxy(2+i*xscale,
            (420-((unsigned) F[i]*255+(unsigned) D[i]*255+C[i])/yscale),"ø");
         }
         k=0;
         for(i=0;i<MAXGRAY;i++)
         {
          setcolor(k);
           {
            line(5+i*xscale,445,5+i*xscale,430);
            if((i>14)&&((i+1)%16==0))
             {
              line(5+i*xscale,445,5+i*xscale,460);
             }
           }   k=k+1;
         }
        printf("\n(max_freq,gray_value):(");
        printf("%u",k2);printf(",");
        printf("%u",gray);printf(")");
/***********************************************************/
   quit_msg();
   getch();
        setcolor(0);
        outtextxy(315,5,"Contoured Image");
        setcolor(14);
        outtextxy(272,5,"Q: Exit   S: Save and Exit");
        z=getch();
                if((z=='s')||(z=='S'))
```

```
                    {
                    setcolor(0);
                     outtextxy(272,5,"Q: Exit   S: Save and Exit");
                     setcolor(14);
                     outtextxy(302,5,"Enter the file name");
          setcolor(0);
          outtextxy(266,20,"***");
          outtextxy(460,20,"***");
          outtextxy(292,20,"Normalised X,Y Scales");
                     gets(ptr);
                     setcolor(0);
                     outtextxy(302,5,"Enter the file name");
                     setcolor(14);
                     outtextxy(262,5,"Please Wait ! Writing Output");
                     xyz=fopen(ptr,"wt");
                     for(i=0;i<size;i++)
                     fprintf(xyz," %d",E[i]);
                     }
                     fclose(xyz);
closegraph();
clrscr();
free(A);free(C);free(D);free(E);
exit(0);
}
/****************************************************************************/
/* This subroutine is for displaying a graticule background with fixed major divisions. This   */
/* should be used with the col_box subroutine. Two rectangles below the graticule and one */
/*  below the color box would be displayed. The name plate bearing " Dr.E.G.Rajan " would */
/*  also be displayed.                                                                       */
/****************************************************************************/
graph()
          {
          setfillstyle(SOLID_FILL,EGA_DARKGRAY);
          bar(0,34,530,425);
          setcolor(3);
          rectangle(0,429,530,445);
          rectangle(0,445,530,460);
          rectangle(535,445,633,460);
          setcolor(2);
          outtextxy(537,9*boxy+98,"Dr.E.G.Rajan");
          setcolor(0);
          for(i=0;i<27;i++)
          { line(5+i*20,420,5+i*20,40); }
          for(i=1;i<=21;i++)
          { line(5,i*20,525,i*20); }
          }
/***********************************************/
/* This subroutine is for displaying all the 16 EGA colors.  */
/* Append this after the main(). Declare  boxy  as a global  */
/* integer variable, that is before the main.   Include the   */
/* following snippet right in the beginning of the main.      */
/*                    detectgraph(&gd,&gm);                   */
/*                    if(gd==9) Y_RES=480;                    */
/*                    else     Y_RES=200;                     */
/*                    boxy=Y_RES/20+15;                       */
/***********************************************/
```

```
col_box()
  {          setfillstyle(SOLID_FILL,0);
/*BLACK*/  bar(540,boxy, 540+boxy,2*boxy);
           setcolor(7);
           rectangle(540,boxy, 540+boxy,2*boxy);
           settextstyle(DEFAULT_FONT,HORIZ_DIR,1);
           outtextxy(540+boxy/2-2,boxy+boxy/2-2,"0");
           setfillstyle(SOLID_FILL,1);
/*BLUE*/   bar(540+boxy+10,boxy, 540+2*boxy+10,2*boxy);
           setcolor(7);
           rectangle(540+boxy+10,boxy, 540+2*boxy+10,2*boxy);
           settextstyle(DEFAULT_FONT,HORIZ_DIR,1);
           outtextxy(540+boxy+10+boxy/2-2,boxy+boxy/2-2,"1");
           setfillstyle(SOLID_FILL,2);
/*GREEN*/  bar(540,2*boxy+10, 540+boxy,3*boxy+10);
           setcolor(8);
           rectangle(540,2*boxy+10,540+boxy,3*boxy+10);
           settextstyle(DEFAULT_FONT,HORIZ_DIR,1);
           outtextxy(540+boxy/2-2,2*boxy+10+boxy/2-2,"2");
           setfillstyle(SOLID_FILL,3);
/*CYAN*/   bar(540+boxy+10,2*boxy+10, 540+2*boxy+10,3*boxy+10);
           setcolor(8);
           rectangle(540+boxy+10,2*boxy+10, 540+2*boxy+10,3*boxy+10);
           settextstyle(DEFAULT_FONT,HORIZ_DIR,1);
           outtextxy(540+boxy+10+boxy/2-2,2*boxy+10+boxy/2-2,"3");
           setfillstyle(SOLID_FILL,4);
/*RED*/    bar(540,3*boxy+20, 540+boxy,4*boxy+20);
           setcolor(7);
           rectangle(540,3*boxy+20, 540+boxy,4*boxy+20);
           settextstyle(DEFAULT_FONT,HORIZ_DIR,1);
           outtextxy(540+boxy/2-2,3*boxy+20+boxy/2-2,"4");
           setfillstyle(SOLID_FILL,5);
           bar(540+boxy+10,3*boxy+20, 540+2*boxy+10,4*boxy+20);
           setcolor(7);
           rectangle(540+boxy+10,3*boxy+20, 540+2*boxy+10,4*boxy+20);
           settextstyle(DEFAULT_FONT,HORIZ_DIR,1);
           outtextxy(540+boxy+10+boxy/2-2,3*boxy+20+boxy/2-2,"5");
           setfillstyle(SOLID_FILL,6);
           bar(540,4*boxy+30, 540+boxy,5*boxy+30);
           setcolor(7);
           rectangle(540,4*boxy+30,540+boxy,5*boxy+30);
           settextstyle(DEFAULT_FONT,HORIZ_DIR,1);
           outtextxy(540+boxy/2-2,4*boxy+30+boxy/2-2,"6");
           setfillstyle(SOLID_FILL,7);
           bar(540+boxy+10,4*boxy+30, 540+2*boxy+10,5*boxy+30);
           setcolor(7);
           rectangle(540+boxy+10,4*boxy+30, 540+2*boxy+10,5*boxy+30);
           setcolor(8);
           settextstyle(DEFAULT_FONT,HORIZ_DIR,1);
           outtextxy(540+boxy+10+boxy/2-2,4*boxy+30+boxy/2-2,"7");
           setfillstyle(SOLID_FILL,8);
           bar(540,5*boxy+40, 540+boxy,6*boxy+40);
           setcolor(7);
           rectangle(540,5*boxy+40, 540+boxy,6*boxy+40);
           settextstyle(DEFAULT_FONT,HORIZ_DIR,1);
           outtextxy(540+boxy/2-2,5*boxy+40+boxy/2-2,"8");
           setfillstyle(SOLID_FILL,9);
```

```
bar(540+boxy+10,5*boxy+40, 540+2*boxy+10,6*boxy+40);
setcolor(7);
rectangle(540+boxy+10,5*boxy+40, 540+2*boxy+10,6*boxy+40);
settextstyle(DEFAULT_FONT,HORIZ_DIR,1);
outtextxy(540+boxy+10+boxy/2-2,5*boxy+40+boxy/2-2,"9");
setfillstyle(SOLID_FILL,10);
bar(540,6*boxy+50, 540+boxy,7*boxy+50);
setcolor(7);
rectangle(540,6*boxy+50,540+boxy,7*boxy+50);
settextstyle(DEFAULT_FONT,HORIZ_DIR,1);
outtextxy(540+boxy/2-6,6*boxy+50+boxy/2-2,"10");
setfillstyle(SOLID_FILL,11);
bar(540+boxy+10,6*boxy+50, 540+2*boxy+10,7*boxy+50);
setcolor(7);
rectangle(540+boxy+10,6*boxy+50, 540+2*boxy+10,7*boxy+50);
settextstyle(DEFAULT_FONT,HORIZ_DIR,1);
outtextxy(540+boxy+10+boxy/2-6,6*boxy+50+boxy/2-2,"11");
setfillstyle(SOLID_FILL,12);
bar(540,7*boxy+60, 540+boxy,8*boxy+60);
setcolor(7);
rectangle(540,7*boxy+60, 540+boxy,8*boxy+60);
setcolor(0);
settextstyle(DEFAULT_FONT,HORIZ_DIR,1);
outtextxy(540+boxy/2-6,7*boxy+60+boxy/2-2,"12");
setfillstyle(SOLID_FILL,13);
bar(540+boxy+10,7*boxy+60, 540+2*boxy+10,8*boxy+60);
setcolor(7);
rectangle(540+boxy+10,7*boxy+60, 540+2*boxy+10,8*boxy+60);
setcolor(0);
settextstyle(DEFAULT_FONT,HORIZ_DIR,1);
outtextxy(540+boxy+10+boxy/2-6,7*boxy+60+boxy/2-2,"13");
setfillstyle(SOLID_FILL,14);
bar(540,8*boxy+70, 540+boxy,9*boxy+70);
setcolor(7);
rectangle(540,8*boxy+70,540+boxy,9*boxy+70);
settextstyle(DEFAULT_FONT,HORIZ_DIR,1);
outtextxy(540+boxy/2-6,8*boxy+70+boxy/2-2,"14");
setfillstyle(SOLID_FILL,15);
bar(540+boxy+10,8*boxy+70, 540+2*boxy+10,9*boxy+70);
setcolor(7);
rectangle(540+boxy+10,8*boxy+70, 540+2*boxy+10,9*boxy+70);
setcolor(0);
settextstyle(DEFAULT_FONT,HORIZ_DIR,1);
outtextxy(540+boxy+10+boxy/2-6,8*boxy+70+boxy/2-2,"15");
setcolor(7);
outtextxy(541,9*boxy+80,"COLOR TABLE");
rectangle(535,boxy-5, 540+2*boxy+15,9*boxy+92);
line(540+boxy+5,boxy-5, 540+boxy+5,9*boxy+75);
line(535,9*boxy+75, 540+2*boxy+15,9*boxy+75);
line(535,2*boxy+5, 540+2*boxy+15,2*boxy+5);
line(535,3*boxy+15, 540+2*boxy+15,3*boxy+15);
line(535,4*boxy+25, 540+2*boxy+15,4*boxy+25);
line(535,5*boxy+35, 540+2*boxy+15,5*boxy+35);
line(535,6*boxy+45, 540+2*boxy+15,6*boxy+45);
line(535,7*boxy+55, 540+2*boxy+15,7*boxy+55);
line(535,8*boxy+65, 540+2*boxy+15,8*boxy+65);
}
```

```
quit_msg()
  {
            flash=0;
            while(flash==0)
                      {
                      setcolor(11);
                      settextstyle(5,0,3);
                      outtextxy(500,20,"Hit a key to quit");
                      sleep(1);
                      setcolor(0);
                      settextstyle(5,0,3);
                      outtextxy(500,20,"Hit a key to quit");
                      sleep(1);
                      if(!kbhit()) flash=0;
                      else
                      flash=1;
                      }
  }
/****************************************/
/* Subroutine for file error in opening or writing */
/****************************************/
nofile()
            {
            if((fopen(ptr,"rt")==NULL))
            {
             perror("\n\n");
             printf("Hit a key to quit");
             getch();
             closegraph();
             exit(1);
            }
            }
/****************************************/
process()
  {
            flash=0;
            while(flash==0)
                      {
                      setcolor(11);
                      settextstyle(5,0,3);
                      outtextxy(548,20,"Hit a key !");
                      sleep(1);
                      setcolor(0);
                      settextstyle(5,0,3);
                      outtextxy(548,20,"Hit a key !");
                      sleep(1);
                      if(!kbhit()) flash=0;
                      else
                      flash=1;
                      }
    }
/****************************************/
max_gray()
    {
          if((MAXGRAY>= 0)&&(MAXGRAY< 8)){MAXGRAY= 8;}
          else
          if((MAXGRAY>= 8)&&(MAXGRAY< 16)){MAXGRAY= 16;}
```

```
        else
        if((MAXGRAY>= 16)&&(MAXGRAY< 32)){MAXGRAY= 32;}
        else
        if((MAXGRAY>= 32)&&(MAXGRAY< 64)){MAXGRAY= 64;}
        else
        if((MAXGRAY>= 64)&&(MAXGRAY<128)){MAXGRAY=128;}
        else
        if((MAXGRAY>=128)&&(MAXGRAY<256)){MAXGRAY=256;}
    }
/*****************************************************************************/
```

Figure 14.1.2.4 shows the complex RGB color image of a baboon and figure 14.1.2.5 shows its contoured version.

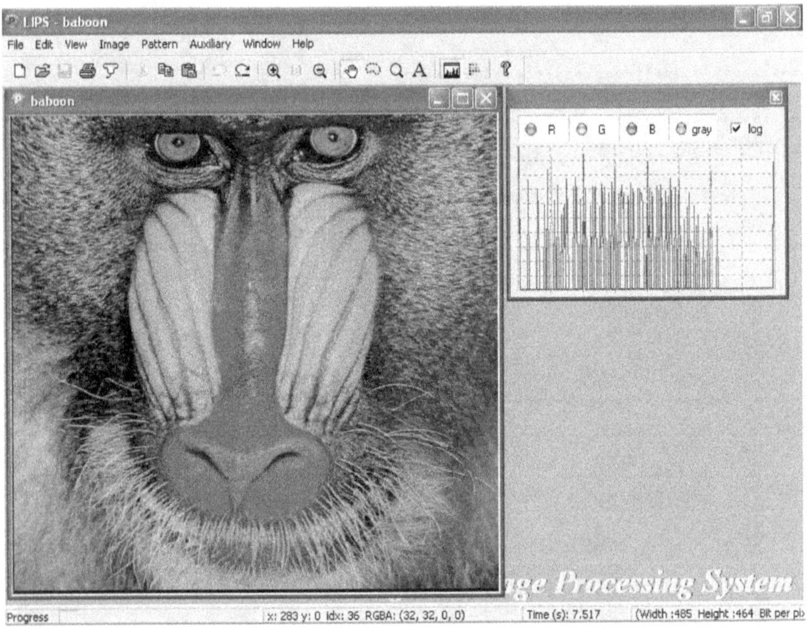

Figure 14.1.2.4: Image of a baboon

The contouring algorithm was applied to the image shown in figure 14.1.2.4 with the threshold of 80. Note that each pixel in an RGB 24 bit color image has three values corresponding to the red, green and blue components. The algorithm checks for the following conditions:

1. Image is raster scanned and nonzero five neighborhood is verified for each pixel.

2. All red components of the five pixels are examined and the maximum and minimum values of the red components are found. The same is repeated for green and blue components too. The variance in the colors are calculated independently and examined whether they are less than the given threshold value.
3. If it is true then the value of zero is assigned to its red, green and blue components; else the scanning window is moved further.

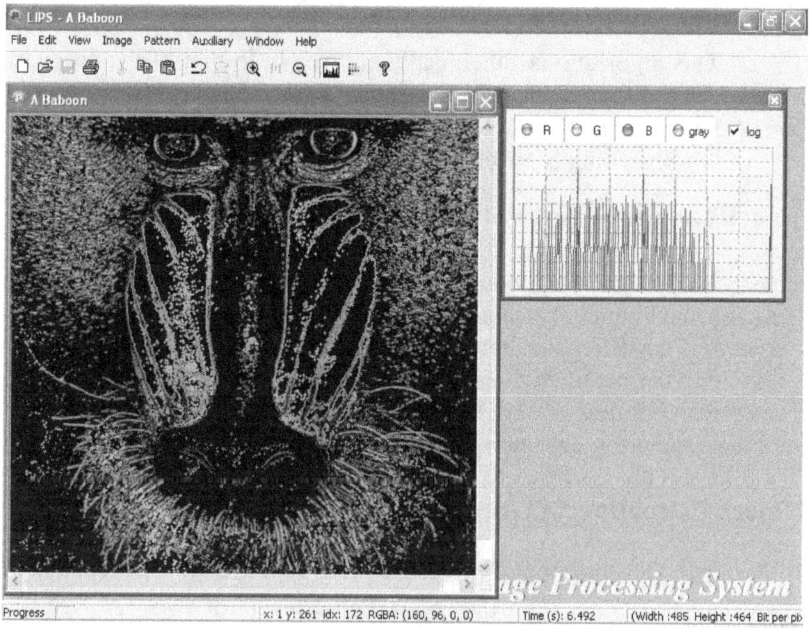

Figure 14.1.2.5: Contoured image

For example let us consider a situation where the five pixels have certain typical values as shown below.

	<R=140 G=68 B=95>	
<R=138 G=74 B=101>	<R=139 G=71 B=99>	<R=141 G=75 B=103>
	<R=144 G=67 B=100>	

Now, the maximum color value could be seen to be 144 and the minimum 138, and the color difference of red is 6. Similarly, the color difference of green is 8 and that of blue is 8. If we set a threshold of say 10, then all the differences are less than 10, and thus the five neighborhood region is viewed as the region of uniform color. Note that this technique is the same as the one meant for contouring gray images.

Segmentation Of Gray And Color Images

This algorithm is functionally equivalent to that of the previous one except for the change that instead of assigning the value 0 to the central cell when D≤T, it assigns the value (G_min+(D/2)). The pseudo code of this algorithm is as follows:

Algorithm For Segmentation

Repeat sliding the 5-neighbourhood structure over the image
{find the maximum gray-value G_max; find the minimum gray value
G_min; if the difference between these two values D is less than or
equal to the specified threshold value T then replace the central pixel
value with (G_min+(D/2)), else slide the 5-neighbourhood structure }
until the structuring element spans whole of the image.

Object Extraction In Gray And Color Images

The algorithm for solid object extraction is somewhat similar to that of segmentation. Here the given digital image of size, say NXN is scanned by a window of specified size. On each move, if the number of pixels contained in the sub image covered by the window that lie outside the specified gray range, is more than half the total pixels in the window, then the central pixel in the window is replaced with a zero, otherwise it is left untouched. This way solid objects, bigger than the specified size and lying in the required gray range are extracted. Figure 14.1.2.6 shows a 32 gray level human brain image of size 213X159. One could infer from the histogram details that the gray matter of the brain is actually described by pixel values from 18 to 31. The remaining matter, on the other hand, is described by pixel values from 0 to 17. So a window of size 1X1 is made use of to extract the region corresponding to the gray matter separately from the original imagery, and this separated portion is shown in figure 14.1.2.7. One can clearly visualize the extracted image as well as its corresponding histogram.

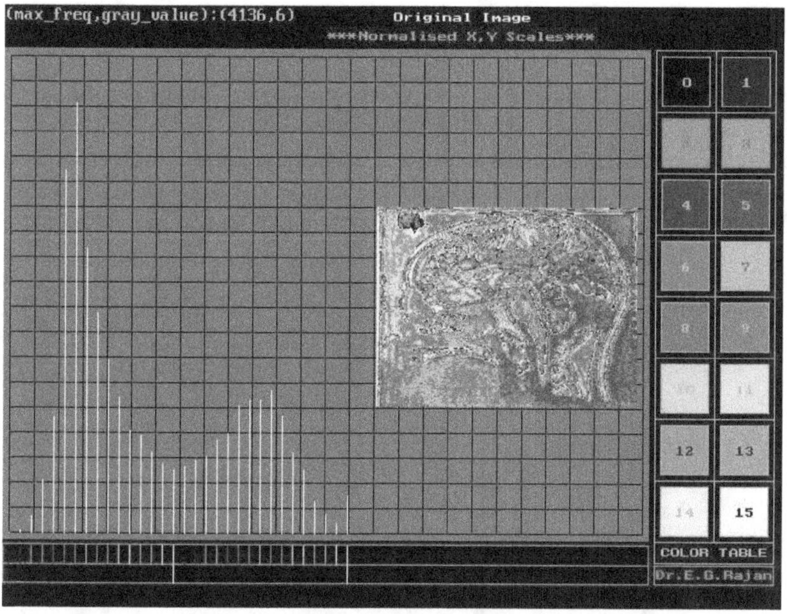

Figure 14.1.2.6: Pseudocolored image of a human brain

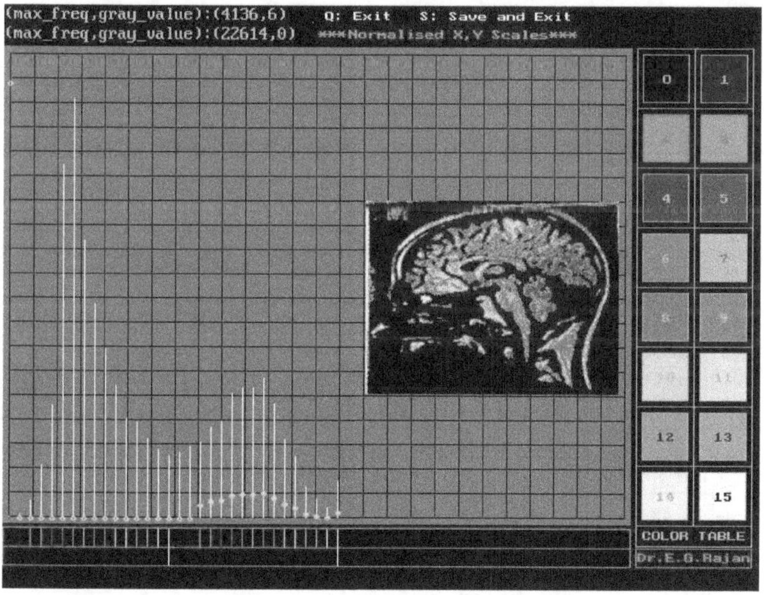

Figure 14.1.2.7: Image after the spatial features extracted

Skeletonization And Thinning Of Gray and Color Images

Skeletonization is a converse operation when compared to contouring. In the case of contouring, we remove the central pixel in order to detect the boundary pixels. On the other hand, we remove the boundary pixels in order to skeletonize a digital image. Let us consider figure 14.1.2.8, which shows a square, a rhombus and an arbitrary image.

*	*	*	*	*
*	*	*	*	*
*	*	*	*	*
*	*	*	*	*
*	*	*	*	*

		*		
	*	*	*	
*	*	*	*	*
	*	*	*	
		*		

	*	*	*	
*	*	*	*	*
*	*	*	*	*
*	*	*	*	
*	*	*		

Figure 14.1.2.8: Sample images

Now the operations of thinning and skeletonization are to be understood in the following manner:

Thinning Process

*	*	*	*	*
*	*	*	*	*
*	*	*	*	*
*	*	*	*	*
*	*	*	*	*

		*		
	*	*	*	
*	*	*	*	*
	*	*	*	
		*		

	*	*	*	
*	*	*	*	*
*	*	*	*	*
*	*	*	*	
*	*	*		

↓ ↓ ↓

	*	*	*	
	*	*	*	
	*	*	*	

		*		
	*	*	*	
		*		

	*	*	*	
	*	*	*	
	*	*		

↓ ↓ ↓

		*		

		*		

		*		

Skeletonization Process

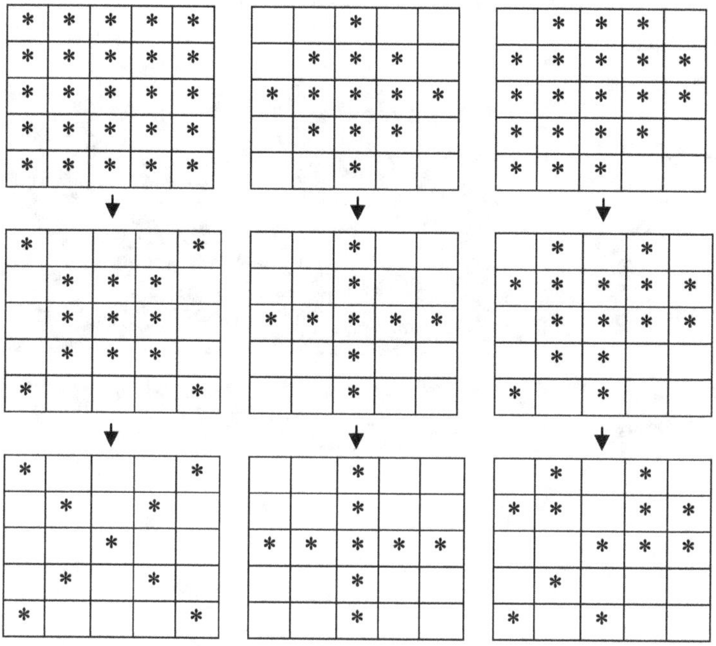

Note that there are differences between the thinned images and the skeletonized images. Thinning refers to iterated boundary removal and skeletonization refers to iterated boundary removal with the exception that the corner pixels are kept in tact.

Algorithm For Skeletonization And Thinning

Repeat sliding the 5-neighbourhood structure over the image
{find the maximum gray-value G_max; find the minimum gray value
G_min; if the difference between these two values D is less than or
equal to the specified threshold value T then retain the central pixel
and remove the boundary pixels; else slide the 5-neighbourhood structure } until the structuring element spans whole of the image. Repeat this procedure till there is no boundary left for removal. The resulting final image is the thinned version of the original image. On the other hand, if the corner pixels are also retained along with the central pixel then the resulting final image is the skeletonized version. Figure 14.1.2.9 shows an image and its skeletonized and thinned versions.

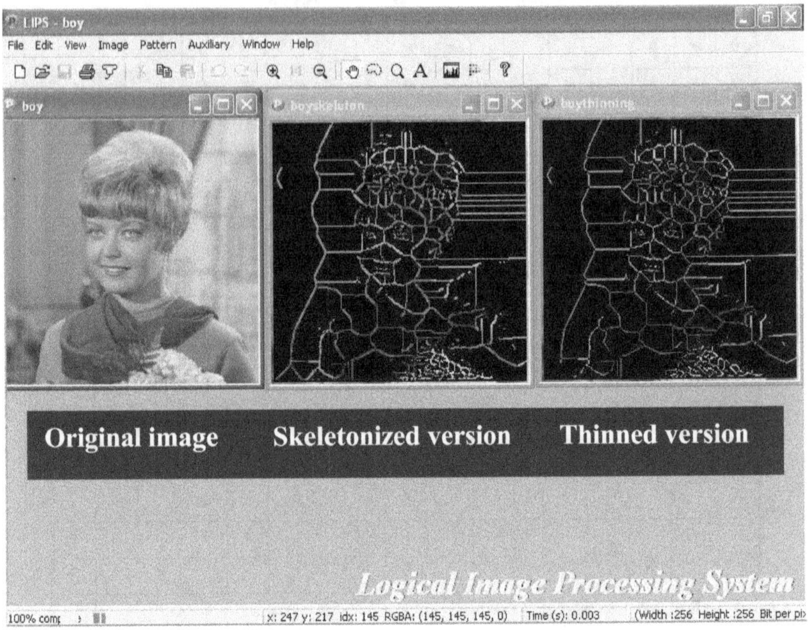

Figure 14.1.2.9: Image with its skeletonized and thinned versions

Having thus studied some basic algorithms for processing two dimensional digital images we now proceed to study the notion of three dimensional digital images and their processing using fast algorithms.

14.2 Fast Algorithms For Processing 3-D Images

14.2.1 Visualization Of 3-D Digital Images On a 2-D Rectangular Grid Monitor

Here, the term *3-D digital image* refers to an actual 3-D data, and not to an image obtained by stereo photographic methods. The perspective view of a 3-D image is presented on a 2-D display screen as it is carried out in the case of geometric drawing. The Z-axis which provides depth information about a 3-D image is considered here as a line that makes an angle of 45° with both X and Y axes and goes into the screen.

A 3-D object image is displayed frame behind frame in Z direction, each frame being shifted by one pixel in both X and Y directions. All the rules of geometric drawing have been incorporated in the display procedures such that operations like hiding lines and surfaces are automatically taken care of. As is done in the case of geometric drawing, finer details of a 3-D image are also visualized on a 2-D monitor in the following manner. Plan, elevation, side views, rear and bottom views of a given 3-D digital image are displayed as projections on the respective planes. While displaying various views, the unseen pixels are automatically hidden. For instance, let us consider the case of elevation. In this case, the pixels of the 0th plane are displayed first. Next, the nonzero pixels of the first plane are shown with a 45° shift, keeping the pixels of the 0th plane in tact for which the corresponding pixels of the first plane happen to be 0s. This procedure is continued till all the planes are displayed. This way the unseen pixels are automatically hidden. Same procedure is used to display all other views. Full section views along the three mutually orthogonal planes are displayed by slicing the image along the required planes.

14.2.2 Morphological Operations On Binary Gray And Color 3-D Images

Operationally 3-D morphological operations are identical to those of 2-D, with the difference that the image is traced with a 3-D structuring element here, where as in the 2-D case a 2-D structuring element is used to scan the image. So, the algorithms described in section 14.1.1 for 2-D images will hold good for 3-D object images as well.

14.2.3 Traditional Image Processing Operations On Three Dimensional Object Digital Images

A 3-D digital image is normally viewed as an array of pixel values arranged in a 3-D grid of Z^3 space. By *edge* and *surface*, we refer to what are conventionally understood as edge and surface of a physical object. In addition to this, as defined in the case of 2-D images, the term edge is also viewed here, as the boundary between two regions of different quantized gray levels. Given a 3-D digital image, we detect its edges using an extended version of the techniques given in the previous section. First, let us consider a scanning empty window consisting of three planes k-1, k and k+1, and of size 3x3x3, as shown in figure 14.2.3.1.

We refer to this empty window as a 27-neighbourhood structure in figure 14.2.3.2..

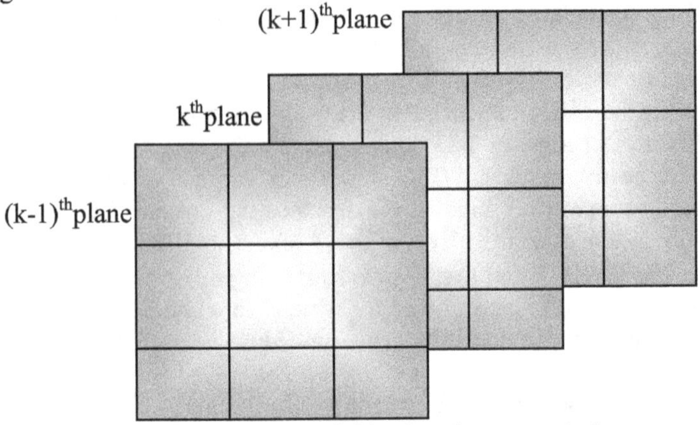

Figure 14.2.3.1: 27-neighborhood empty window

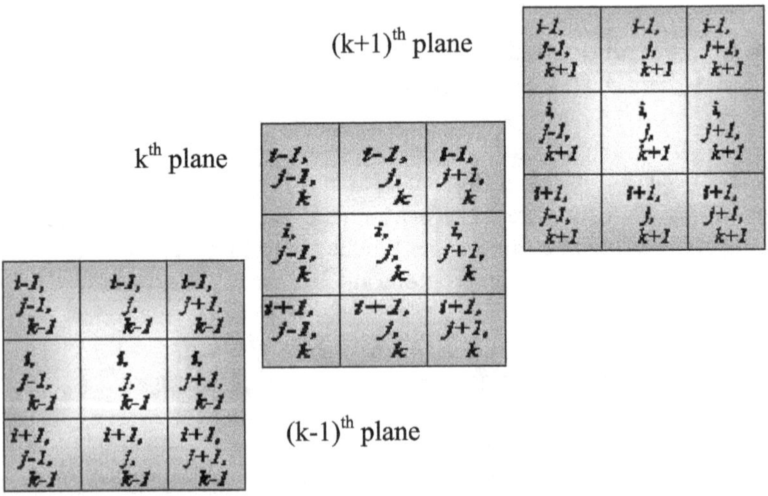

Figure 14.2.3.2: 27-neighborhood structure

Algorithm For Detecting Edges And Surfaces Of Single Gray Level Regions Of a 3-D Image

The given digital image of size, say, NXNXN is plane-wise raster-scanned by the above 3X3X3 window. On each move, the 3X3X3 sub image covered by the above window is examined to see whether some or all of its pixels form a 3-D convex region of a single gray level, containing at least one pixel from each row and column. Note that such regions can be formed in 256 different ways, and that a bounded single-gray-level subgrid region of Z^3 space can be uniquely decomposed into a set-theoretic combination of these 256 convex 3-D solid regions. Figure 14.2.3.2 shows the first convex 3-D solid pattern and figure 14.2.3.3 the 256th convex 3-D solid pattern. Of these, the 256th 3-D pattern is covered in the rest. To identify whether any of these patterns has been encountered or not, it is therefore adequate to check for the 256th one alone.

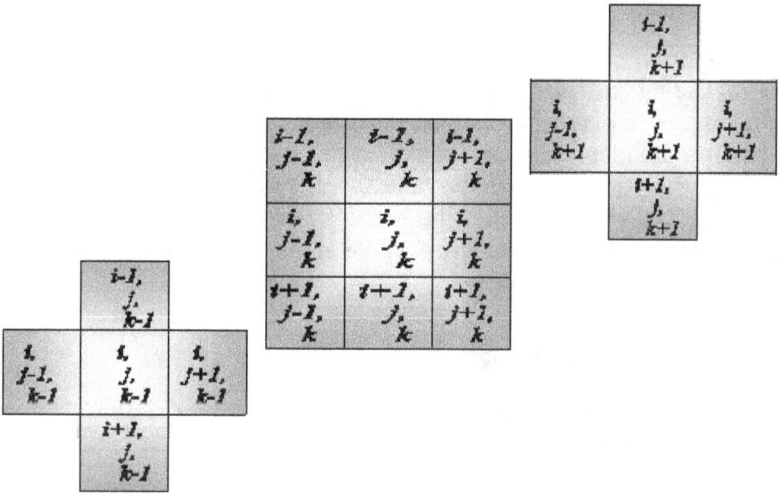

Figure 14.2.3.3: 256th convex pattern

However, one can scan a given 3-D object digital image by a seven-neighborhood window, which is shown in figure 14.2.3.3, and carry out certain image processing operations. If the condition that the subimage covered by this seven-neighborhood window has to contain nonzero pixels is satisfied, then one of the following two operations is carried out: (i) gray-value 0 is assigned to all the seven cells, that is, to (i,j,k-1), (i-1,j,k), (i,j-1,k), (i,j,k), (i,j+1,k), (i+1,j,k) and (i,j,k+1); (ii) gray-value 0 is assigned only to the central cell, that is to (i,j,k). The first operation is carried out in order to detect the edges of the given 3-D image, and the second operation is carried out for detecting the surfaces of the image. Now, if the condition is not satisfied, then the 7-neighbourhood window is moved further. This procedure is continued till the entire 3-D image is scanned. The overall effect is that either the edges or the surfaces of various single gray level 3-D solid regions in the given image are retained, depending on the type of operation carried out, and the remaining interior parts are erased thus giving us the required processed form of the original 3-D digital image. Figure 14.2.3.4 shows image of cube with size 50X50X25 and its edge detected version

Remark

This technique is applicable only to those images that do not have surfaces coplanar to any of the surfaces of the 3-D, 7-neighbourhood window.

Algorithm

Repeat sliding the 7-neighbourhood window over the image
{if all the seven pixel values of the sub image covered by the scanning
window are identical then assign the value 0 to all the seven cells for
edge detection or assign the value 0 only to the central cell for
surface detection; else slide the 7-neighbourhood window}
until the structuring element spans whole of the 3-D image

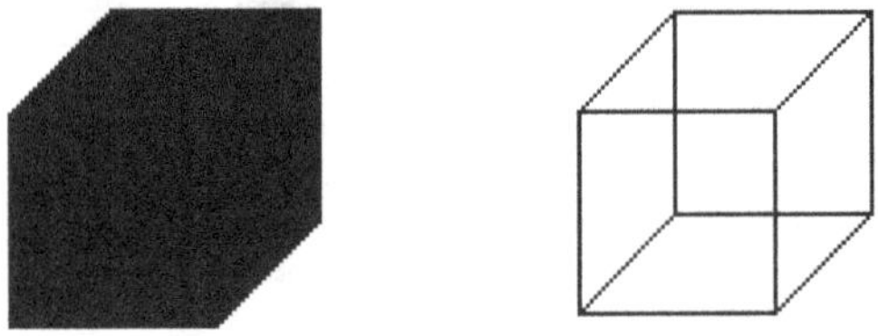

Figure 14.2.3.4: Solid cube with size 50X50X25 and its edge detected version

Edge And Surface Detection Of Regions That Appear To Be Uniform In a 3-D Image

Similar to what is done in the case of 2-D digital images, we first segment the given 3-D digital image using a threshold-based-quantization scheme and then extract the boundaries of the quantized regions. We proceed in the following manner. The given 3-D digital image is plane-wise raster-scanned by the seven-neighborhood window. On each move, the 3X3X3 sub grid covered by this window is examined to see whether the gray-distance, say D, corresponding to that sub image is less than or equal to a threshold value, say T. If D is less than or equal to T, then the gray-value 0 is assigned either to all the seven cells or only to the central cell, depending on the requirement whether edge detection or surface detection has to be carried out in the given image. For D greater than T, the original values contained in these cells are left undisturbed. This procedure is continued till the entire image is scanned. The overall effect is that the edges or surfaces of various 3-D solid regions in the given image that appear to be uniform, are retained and their remaining interior parts are erased thus giving us the edge or surface detected version of the original image.

Algorithm For Detecting Edges And Surfaces Of Solid Regions That Appear To Be Uniform In a 3-D Digital Image

Repeat sliding the 7-neighbourhood window over the image
{find the maximum gray-value G_max; find the minimum gray-value
G_min; if the difference between these two values D is less than or
equal to the specified threshold value T then assign the value 0 to all
the seven cells for edge detection or assign the value 0 only to the
central cell for surface detection, else slide the 7-neighbourhood
window} until the structuring element spans whole of the 3-D image

Figure 14.2.3.5 shows the 4-level 3-D gray digital image of a cube of size 50X50X25 and its edge detected version. The algorithm uses a threshold of 2.

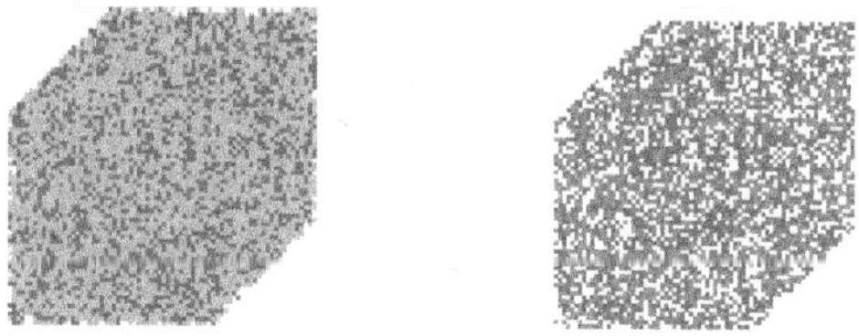

Figure 14.2.3.5: 3-D gray image of a cube and its edge detected version

14.3 LIPS – Logical Image Processing System (A Software Package)

Logical Image Processing System (LIPS) is a PC compatible software package consisting of a number of routines that are used as image processing tools in different environments. In what follows, we provide a comprehensive description of the algorithms and structure of various menus and relevant technical details involved in the development of the package. LIPS has been developed in Visual Studio environment.

Figure 14.3.1 shows the opening menu of the software package "*Logical Image Processing System*" (LIPS). The fast algorithms of this package have been developed in the framework of cellular logic array processing.

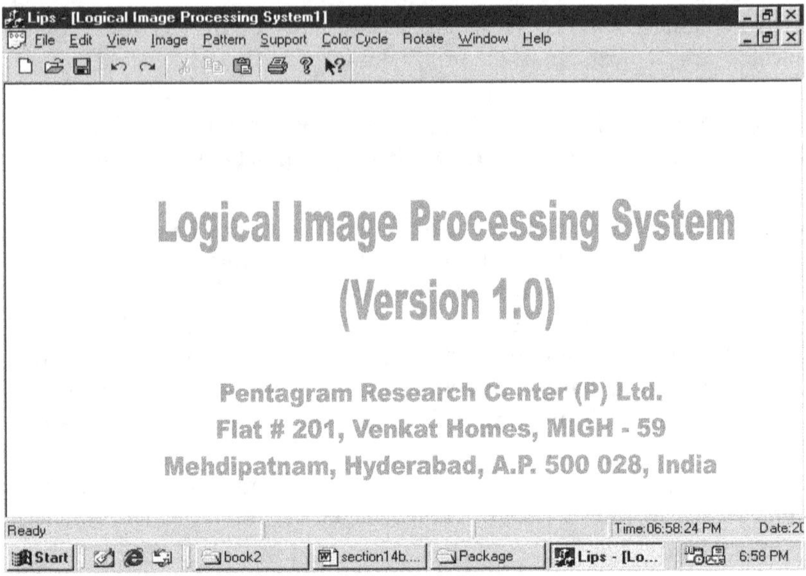

Figure 14.3.1: Opening menu of LIPS
(Courtesy by Pentagram Research Center, Hyderabad)

14.3.1 ABOUT LOGICAL IMAGE PROCESSING SYSTEM

Logical Image Processing System version 1.0 is a collection of a number of image processing tools developed using Visual C++, and it works in Windows 95 environment. The algorithms pertaining to most of the routines in this package have been developed in a novel logico-mathematical framework called Cellular Logic Array Processing (CLAP). This nontraditional paradigm advocates pattern-directed *Search And Replace* (SAR) techniques, and so, it guarantees speed and precision.

Hardware required

LIPS version 1.0 will run on any IBM compatible PC, which has at least 16 MB RAM and 4 GB hard disk. A high resolution color monitor is recommended for a good display. The operating system should be Windows 95 or Windows NT.

Other platforms

LIPS version 2.0 runs on Silicon Graphics workstation with the operating system IRIX 6.1 and above. LIPS version 3.0 runs on SOLARIS OS based SUN workstation

Potential users

Research laboratories would find this package to be very useful for field applications. Automated factories, Remote Sensing and GIS application centers, Vision based guided and autonomous mobile systems and robots manufacturers, Forest resources evaluation centers, Geological survey and mapping agencies, Radiologists and medical imaging experts, Intelligence agencies which make use of remotely sensed imageries, Nondestructive testing laboratories and Space surveillance agencies could use this package. LIPS has been designed and developed by experts in the field of Computer Vision and Pattern Recognition, and so, academic institutions would benefit from using this package. The main menu is open and students can include their own DLL files. This package is compatible to all Micro Soft products, highly user-friendly and supported by on-line help.

Technical details of LIPS

LIPS has three modules: (i) Image Processing, (ii) Pattern Recognition and Analysis and (iii) Pattern Generation. A digital image is treated here as a square array configuration of a cellular automaton and the operation on it as a cellular automaton parallel updating rule. Most of the algorithms used in this package have been developed based on this idea only. The term Pattern Recognition refers here to the detection of local features like straight lines, curves, break points, angles, textures in an image. The main tool used in developing the pattern recognition algorithms is Rajan Transform which is a fast algorithm similar to Decimation-In-Frequency FFT algorithm. Pattern generation is carried out using complex mathematical formulas.

LIPS routines

The routines in LIPS are compatible to all standard Microsoft products. The structure of the package is organized in the following manner:

14.3.2 Menu Structure Of LIPS

This package consists of an opening menu with ten items displayed in the menu bar. This subsection provides a detailed report on each item and on every item in the respective popup menu.

File and Edit menu

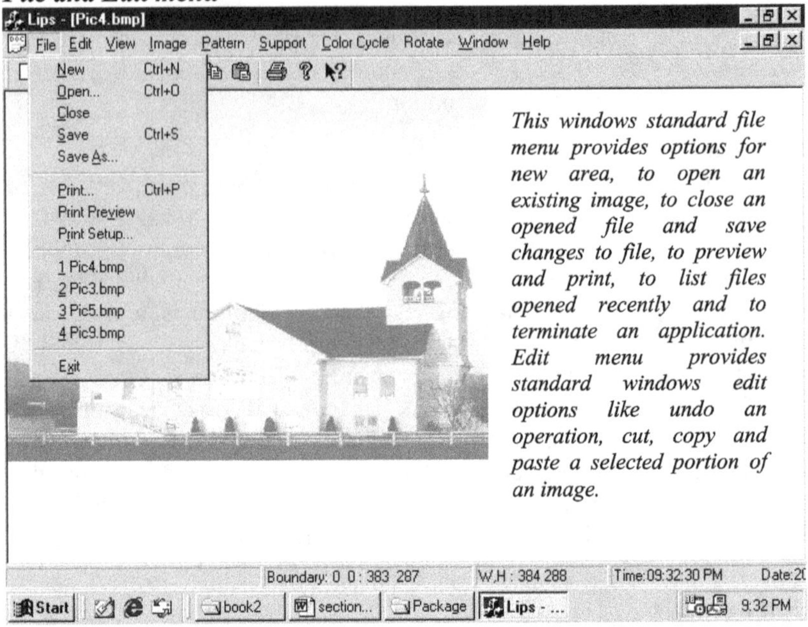

This windows standard file menu provides options for new area, to open an existing image, to close an opened file and save changes to file, to preview and print, to list files opened recently and to terminate an application. Edit menu provides standard windows edit options like undo an operation, cut, copy and paste a selected portion of an image.

View menu

Image menu (Sample image of a ship)

Resulting image after applying absolute operator

Sample image with histogram details (RGB) from support menu

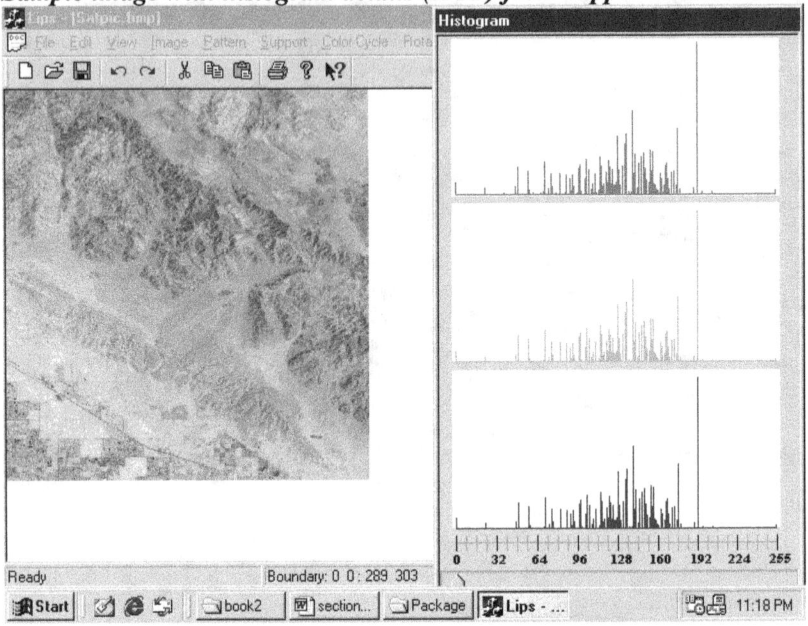

Sample gray image of a lioness (Originally an RGB color image)

Histogram of a sample RGB color image

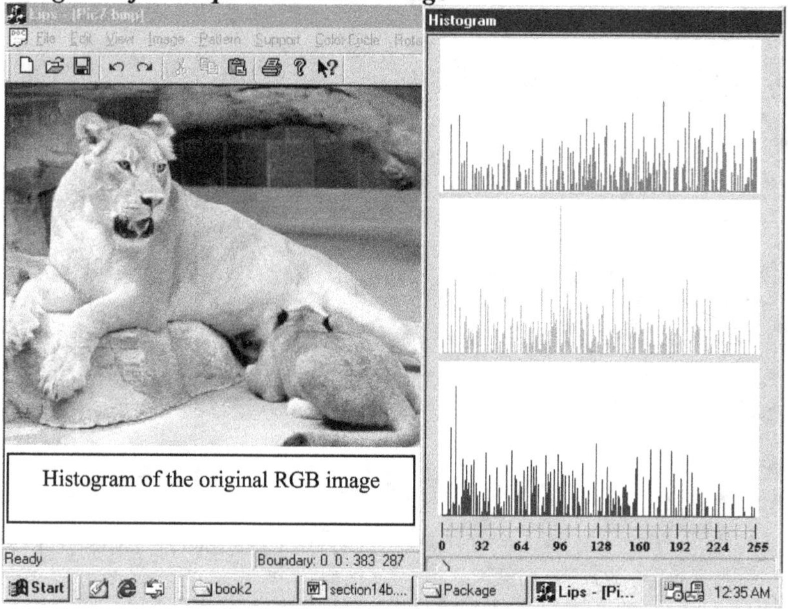

Color (green) filtered image

Cascading of two different images

Help menu

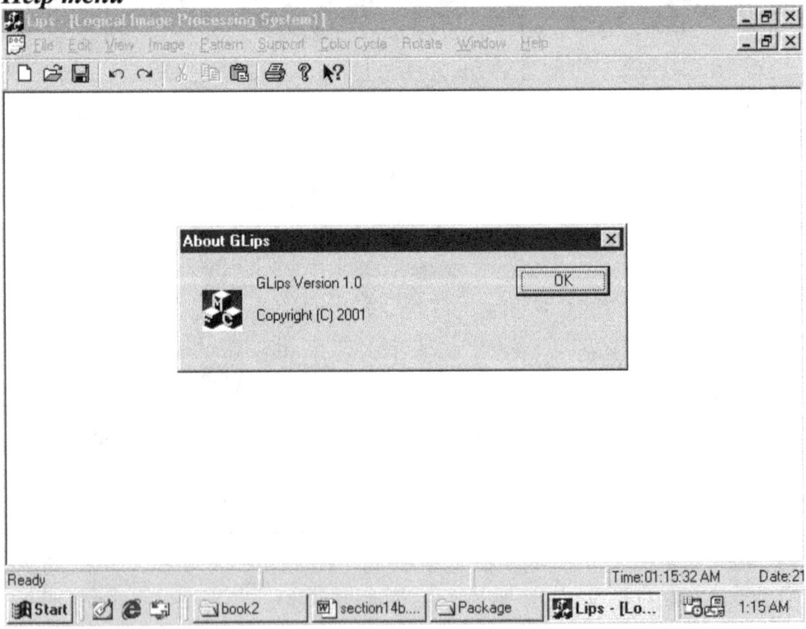

Section 15

Cellular Logic Array Processing Of Digital Images On a Hexagonal Grid

15.1 Introduction

Sthanislaw Ulam and von Neumann did pioneering work in early fifties on what are currently known as digital computers. Digital computers are serial machines operating on packets of binary bits. A modern digital computer can solve highly complex mathematical problems like partial differential equations. Ulam and von Neumann were already aware of such possibilities. Yet they were also aware of the fact that no serial machine could be most natural and powerful as that of a biological species. In fact they were influenced by the biological systems, which neither approximate continuous systems nor use arithmetical operations in solving problems. Von Neumann tried to simulate the least complex discrete systems that are capable of *self reproduction* in a digital computer, and Ulam could actually approximate this problem using the idea of what are called *cellular spaces*. A modern name to these cellular spaces is *cellular automata*. As we have seen in the previous sections, cellular automata are idealized models of discrete space-time physical processes in the form of certain arrays of cells whose values change with every stage of their evolutions by means of an updating rule. We also know that one can as well consider any type of array in which the cells could be arranged. In this section we are going to see a special kind of cellular automata whose cells are arranged in a hexagonal array and examine their use in processing digital images represented in a hexagonal grid.

15.2 Hexagonal Lattices From Square Lattices

Let us consider a square lattice as shown in figure 15.2.1, and see how we can go about realizing a hexagonal cell arrangement from the square lattice. The first cell (0,0) of the hexagonal lattice [Refer to figure

E. G. Rajan, *Symbolic Computing - Signal and Image Processing*
ISBN 81-7800-047-4

15.2.2] could be seen to coincide with the cell (0,0) of the square lattice. The second cell (0,1) of the hexagonal lattice coincides with the cell (0,2) of the square lattice, and the third cell (0,2) of the hexagonal lattice is the same as the cell (0,4) of the square lattice. Similarly, the cells (1,0) and (1,1) are respectively the same as the cells (2,1) and (2,3). Unlike the square lattice, we see that a cell in a hexagonal lattice is determined by the corresponding row and the zig-zag column. Hereafter, we shall refer to the zig-zag column as zig-zag only. In general, a cell (i,j) of the hexagonal lattice corresponds to the cell (2i,2j) if i is even, or to the cell (2i,2j+1) if i is odd.

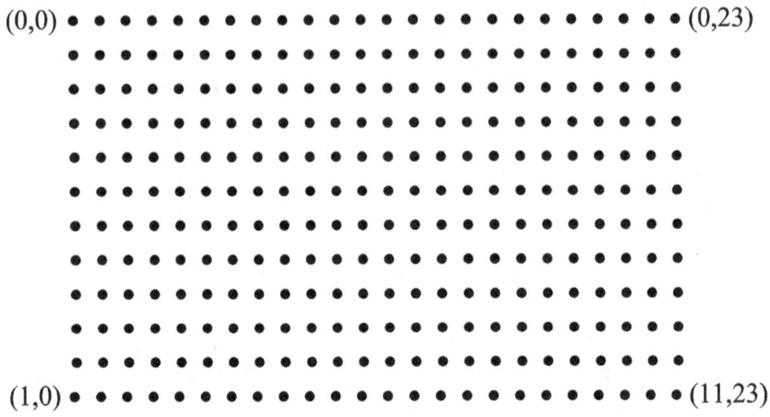

Figure 15.2.1: Rectangular grid of pixels

Figure 15.2.2: Hexagonal grid of pixels

Similar to what has been described in section 11, a two dimensional N-ary valued cellular automaton **C** could be thought of as a 2-D array of cells arranged in a hexagonal grid. Each cell takes on any of the N given values, and all the values are simultaneously updated at a particular stage of evolution according to a rule involving the values contained in certain surrounding cells. Though one can think of several possible neighborhood structures in a hexagonal grid, we are concerned here only with three structures as shown in figures 15.2.3(a), 15.2.3(b) and 15.2.3(c).

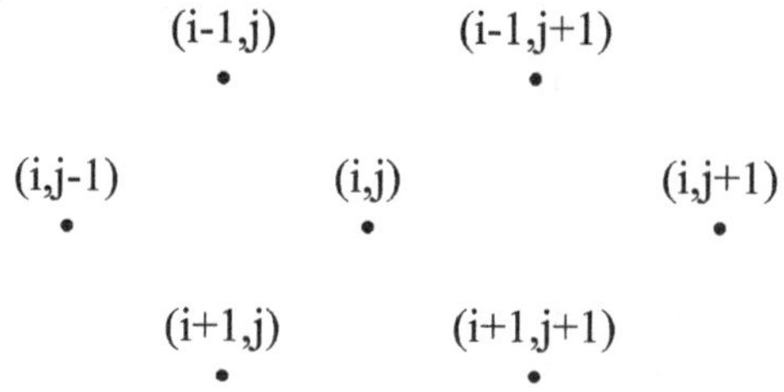

(a): 7-neighborhood structure

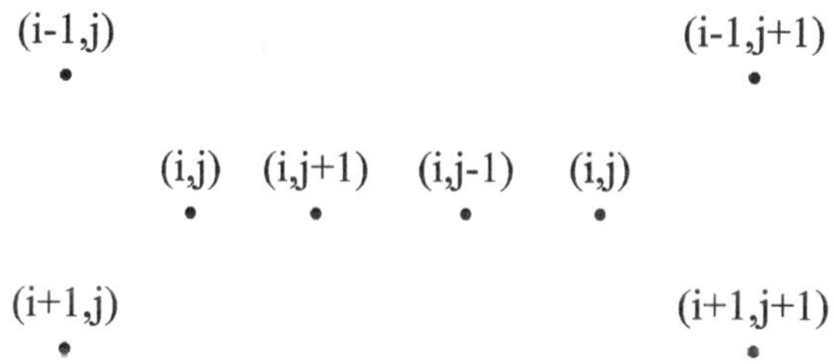

(b) : 4-neighborhod structure # 1 (c) : 4-neighborhood structure # 2

Figure 15.2.3: neighborhood structures in a hexagonal lattice

Let us consider a hexagonal lattice and let (i,j) be one of its cells. Then the value $\xi^{(t)}_{i,j}$ held by the cell (i,j) at a stage t is an element from a set of numbers X = {0,1,2, …., N-1} . Now the value held by the cell (i,j) could be updated in accordance with the 7-neighborhood or one of the 4-neighborhood rules. A 7-neighborhood cellular automaton evolves according to a rule ϕ:

$$\xi^{(t+1)}_{i,j} = \phi\left(\xi^{(t)}_{i,j}, \xi^{(t)}_{i,j+1}, \xi^{(t)}_{i+1,j+1}, \xi^{(t)}_{i+1,j}\ \xi^{(t)}_{i,j-1}, \xi^{(t)}_{i-1,j}\ \xi^{(t)}_{i-1,j+1} \right)$$

Similarly, a 4-neighborhood cellular automaton evolves according to a rule ϕ_1 or ϕ_2 depending on the type of structure that is used.

$$\xi^{(t+1)}_{i,j} = \phi_1\left(\xi^{(t)}_{i,j}, \xi^{(t)}_{i,j+1}, \xi^{(t)}_{i+1,j}, \xi^{(t)}_{i-1,j}\right)$$
$$\xi^{(t+1)}_{i,j} = \phi_2\left(\xi^{(t)}_{i,j}, \xi^{(t)}_{i+1,j+1}, \xi^{(t)}_{i,,j-1}, \xi^{(t)}_{i-1,j+1}\right)$$

One can construct a total of N^{N^7} local rules for a seven neighborhood N-ary valued two-dimensional cellular automaton, and N^{N^4} rules for a four neighborhood N-ary valued two-dimensional cellular automata.

For example, let us take the case of a binary valued four neighborhood two-dimensional cellular automaton in a hexagonal lattice. A local rule in this case, can be viewed as a 16-bit word as shown in the table 15.2.1. This table displays 2^{16} local rules ϕ_0, ϕ_1, ϕ_2, …… The column under ϕ_i is to be treated as the local rule ϕ_i.

Table 15.2.1: Local rules of binary valued four neighborhood cellular automata

COMBI-NATIONS	LOCAL RULES									
	ϕ_0	ϕ_1	ϕ_2	ϕ_3	ϕ_4	...	...	$\phi_{2^{16}-3}$	$\phi_{2^{16}-2}$	$\phi_{2^{16}-1}$
1111	0	0	0	0	0	...	...	1	1	1
1110	0	0	0	0	0	...	...	1	1	1
1101	0	0	0	0	0	...	...	1	1	1
1100	0	0	0	0	0	...	...	1	1	1
↓	↓	↓	↓	↓	↓	...	...	↓	↓	↓
0010	0	0	0	0	1	...	...	1	1	1
0001	0	0	1	1	0	...	...	0	1	1
0000	0	1	0	1	0	...	...	1	0	1

In the same manner, an updating rule in the case of a seven neighborhood automaton can be viewed as a 128-bit word, and there are 2^{128} such local rules for us to choose from.

```
0     0     0     0     0     0     0     0     0
   0     0     0     0     0     0     0     0     0
0     0     0     1     1     1     1     0     0
   0     0     1     1     1     1     1     0     0
0     0     1     1     1     1     1     1     0
   0     1     1     1     1     1     1     1     0
0     0     1     1     1     1     1     1     0
   0     0     1     1     1     1     1     0     0
0     0     0     1     1     1     1     0     0
   0     0     0     0     0     0     0     0     0
0     0     0     0     0     0     0     0     0
```

Figure 15.2.4: Example pattern generated from a seed 1 [Refer to example 15.2.1]

Example 15.2.1

Let us consider a 2-D, 4-neighborhood binary valued cellular automaton characterized by the rule $\phi_{216\text{-}2}$. The 16-bit word corresponding to this rule is 00001101010001110011101111111110. the seed value is 1, and the configuration obtained after three evolutions using the above rule is shown in figure 15.2.4.

15.3 High Throughput Processing Of Digital Images In a Hexagonal Lattice

Here our study would be primarily focused on the role of cellular automata in the processing of digital images in a hexagonal lattice. As mentioned in section 14, an image to be processed forms the initial configuration from which a cellular automaton evolves and produces the desired processed image as its final configuration. Whatever techniques that have been described in section 14 for implementing morphological operations and traditional image processing operations such as *segmentation, binarization,* and *edge detection* are also valid for processing digital images in hexagonal lattices with the only differences in the type of scanning window structures.

Figure 15.3.1 shows the digital image of a motor car. This image is an RGB formatted one displayed in the usual rectangular lattice of pixels.

Figure 15.3.1: RGB color image of a motor car

The image shown in figure 15.3.1 is zoomed and shown in a rectangular array of pixels in figure 15.3.2. Now, on the lines of the technique given in subsection 15.2, the image is re-represented over a hexagonal lattice of pixels and shown in figure 15.3.3.

The following observations could be made from the figures 15.3.2 and 15.3.3.

1. The curves (refer to the tyres of the car) in the hexagonal representation has much better visual appeal than its rectangular counterpart.
2. The diagonal lines in the hexagonal lattice are seen to be more linear than the ones in the rectangular lattice.
3. The only drawback in the hexagonal representation is that the vertical and horizontal lines are diluted in resolution and they do not give a better visual appeal. However, this can be disregarded due to the fact that a digital image rarely consists of vertical and horizontal lines.

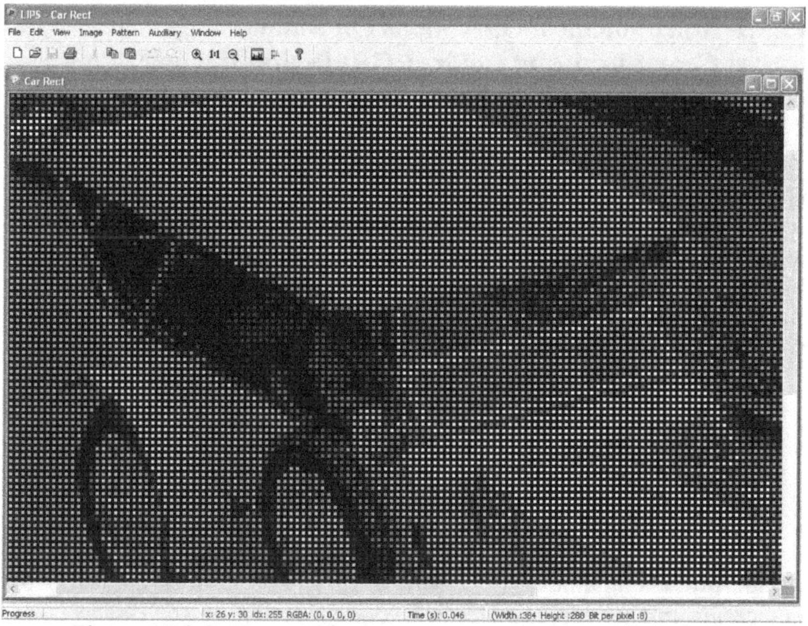

Figure 15.3.2: Zoomed image over rectangular grid of pixels

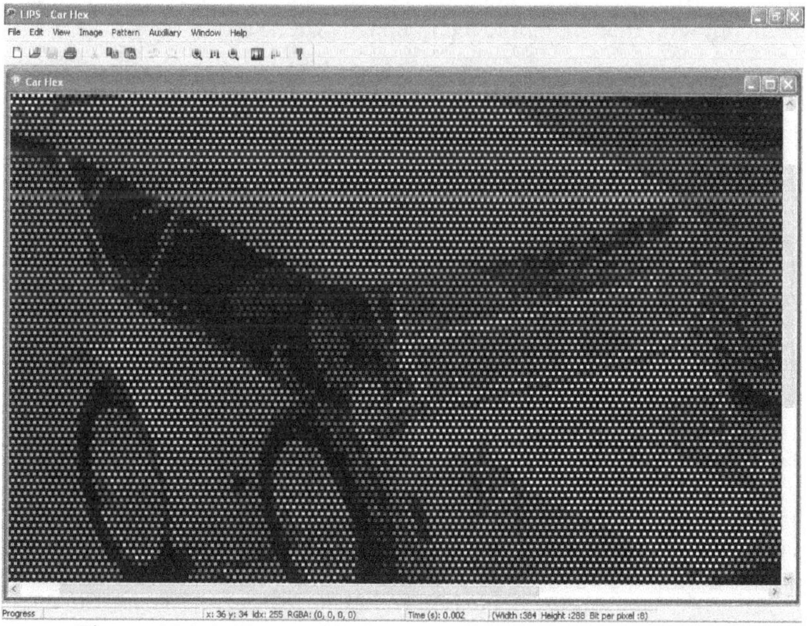

Figure 15.3.2: Zoomed image over hexagonal grid of pixels

15.3.1 Morphological Operations On Binary Gray Level And Color (RGB) Digital Images

Dilation and *erosion* are the fundamental operations of mathematical morphology, and more theoretical details about these operations could be had from [13] and [35]. The operation of dilation is commutative, whereas that of erosion is not. These two operations together with their cellular logic implementations have been described in section 14. What is more important to be noted here is that the structuring elements and the images are to be represented on hexagonal lattices.

15.3.2 Fast Algorithms For Traditional Image Processing Operations

In most of the cases, we make use of the 7-neighborhood structure as the scanning window. All the algorithms described in section 14 for processing images represented on square lattices are valid for processing images represented on hexagonal lattices also. However, we discuss here the operation to edge detection since it often sets an example in the formulation and understanding of the various techniques and methodologies that are employed in image processing.

15.3.2.1. Detection Of Edges Of a Digital Image Represented On a Hexagonal Lattice

The given digital image of size, N rows and N zigzags, is scanned by the 7-neighborhood window.

On each move the subimage covered by the window is examined to see whatever some or all of its pixels form a convex region of an admissible gray range. Note that such regions can be formed in 18 different ways as shown in figure 15.3.2.1.1.

1• •2

6• 7• •3

5• •4

Of these, five are basis patterns. $D_{1,3,5}$ is contained in $C_{1,3}$, $C_{1,5}$ and $C_{3,5}$. $D_{2,4,6}$ is contained in $C_{2,4}$, $C_{2,6}$ and $C_{4,6}$. The basis pattern $C_{1,4}$ is contained in B_1 and B_4. The basis pattern $C_{2,5}$ is contained in B_2 and B_5. The basis pattern $C_{3,6}$ is contained in B_3 and B_6. Figure 15.3.2.1.2 shows the lattice formed by these 18 convex patterns.

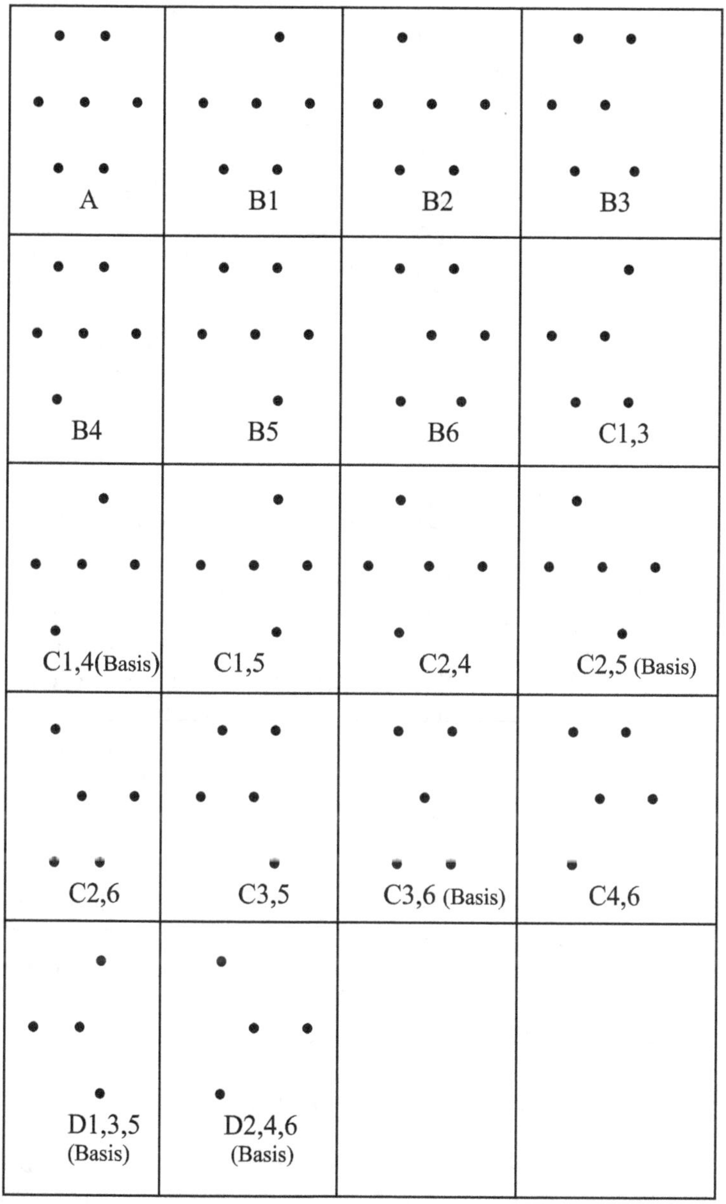

Figure 15.3.2.1.1: Eighteen convex patterns in a 3x3 hexagonal window

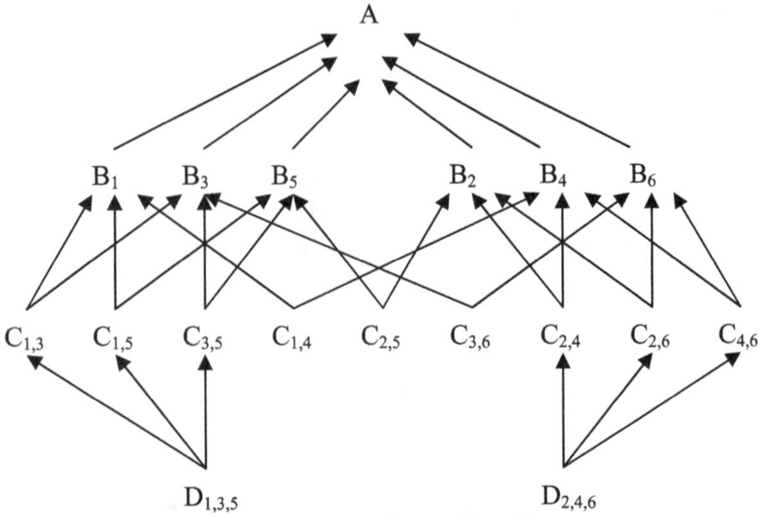

Figure 15.3.2.1.2: Lattice formed by 18 convex patterns

If the subimage is found to contain any one of the five basis patters $C_{1,4}$, $C_{2,5}$, $C_{3,6}$, $D_{1,3,5}$, $D_{2,4,6,}$ then the central cell is assigned the 0 gray level. This procedure is continued till the entire image is scanned. The overall effect is that the boundaries of various regions of an admissible gray range in the given image are retained and the interior parts are erased thus giving us the edge detected version of the original image. This procedure is given below in the form of a pseudo code, which can be easily translated into any computer language.

```
Repeat sliding the 7-neighborhood hexagonal structure over the image
  { check for the presence of one of the five basis patterns inside the
      window; if at least one of these five patterns is seen then find G_max
        and G_min; if the difference D is les than or equal to T, a threshold,
      then replace the central pixel value with 0, else slide the window to
    the next pixel } until the entire image is scanned.
```

15.3.2.2. Other Traditional Operations

All other image processing operations could also be carried out in hexagonal lattice by scanning a given image by an appropriate hexagonal window. Note that the algorithms for processing hexagonal lattice based images are the same as those of rectangular lattice based images.

Section 16

On The Notion Of a Geometric Filter And Its Relevance In the Neighborhood Processing Of Digital Images

The purpose of this section is to introduce certain structural concepts of constructive image processing in an algebraic framework based on Markov's constructive mathematical logic. The prerequisite for reading this section is a considerable amount of working knowledge of the material provided in the third part of this book. As outlined in section13, with subsets of a free monoid treated as sets of configurations of cellular automata, the notion of a Generalized Markov Algorithm (GMA) admits to be treated as a kind of means of realizing various cellular automata. Moreover, we worked out in section 13, a method of characterizing all one dimensional, N-ary valued three neighborhood cellular automata by means of a normal algorithm $\mathcal{N}^{1N3CA}$ over an appropriate alphabet and all two dimensional, N-ary valued five neighborhood cellular automata by means of a normal algorithm $\mathcal{N}^{2N5CA}$.

It is in this connection that we admit here, for the study of constructive image processing systems, an extended theory Th($\mathfrak{I}$) of the constructive theory for signal processing Th($\mathfrak{R}$) . Note that Th($\mathfrak{R}$) has been defined by five closed formulas they are $Я_{\omega|}$-provable [See subsection 7.2].

16.1 What Is Constructive Image Processing?

Here, the term *Constructive Image Processing* refers to the symbolic processing of digital images by *Generalized Markov Algorithms*, irrespective of the fact whether sample (pixel) values of images are expressed as numbers or patterns of symbols.

E. G. Rajan, *Symbolic Computing - Signal and Image Processing*
ISBN 81-7800-047-4

Definition 16.1.1

By constructive image processing system, we mean an ordered pair < $\mathfrak{I}$, X >, where, $\mathfrak{I}$ represents a GMA, and X a subset of $(\mathcal{A}^*)^n$, n being the dimension of a digital grid.

A Generalized Markov Algorithm is a totally ordered list of computable mappings of the type $(\mathcal{A}^*)^n \rightarrow \mathcal{A}^*$ that are actually realized in terms of mappings of the type $(\mathcal{A} \cup \mathcal{E})^* \rightarrow \mathcal{A}^*$. Let us denote here the class of image processing GMAs by $C_{\mathfrak{I}}$. Now, the constructive theory Th($\mathfrak{I}$) consists of five closed formulas which are Я$_{\omega|}$-provable. Note that the input image is represented by a cellular automaton configuration $\mathbf{C}^t$ and the output image as $\mathbf{C}^{t+1}$. $\mathcal{N}$ represents a normal algorithmic cellular automaton.

Th($\mathfrak{I}$) :

(i) Fmω|.1 $\supset\neg\neg!\mathcal{N}\lfloor C^t\rfloor!\ \mathcal{N}\lfloor C^t\rfloor$

(ii) Fmω|.2 $\supset\mathcal{N}\lfloor C^t\rfloor \doteq C^{t+1}!\mathcal{N}\lfloor C^t\rfloor$

(iii) Fmω|.3 $\supset\forall xyz\mathfrak{I}_1\lfloor z\mathfrak{I}_1\lfloor y\mathfrak{I}_1\lfloor x(x : y \Rightarrow z)\ \{\mathcal{N}_i\}\rfloor\,[C^t]^{\mathcal{T}}\rfloor\ [C^{t+1}]^{\mathcal{T}}\rfloor \doteq \mathfrak{I}_1\lfloor z\mathfrak{I}_1\lfloor y\mathfrak{I}_1\lfloor x(x : y \Rightarrow z)\ \{\mathcal{N}_j\}\rfloor\,[C^t]^{\mathcal{T}}\rfloor\ [C^{t+1}]^{\mathcal{T}}\rfloor\,\{\mathcal{N}_i\} \simeq \{\mathcal{N}_j\}$

(iv) Fmω|.4 $\supset\forall XYZ\ \&\&\ \mathcal{N}_i\lfloor X\rfloor \doteq Y\ \mathcal{N}_i\lfloor Y\rfloor \doteq Z\ \mathcal{N}_k\lfloor X\rfloor \doteq Z\mathcal{N}_j\lfloor \mathcal{N}_i\lfloor X\rfloor\,\rfloor \doteq \mathcal{N}_k\ \lfloor X\rfloor$

(v) Fmω|.5 $\supset\forall XYZ\ \&\&\ \mathcal{N}_i\lfloor X\rfloor \doteq Y\ \mathcal{N}_j\lfloor X\rfloor \doteq Z\ \mathcal{N}_k\lfloor X\rfloor \doteq YZ\mathcal{N}_i\lfloor X\rfloor\,\mathcal{N}_j\lfloor X\rfloor \doteq \mathcal{N}_k\ \lfloor X\rfloor$

Thus, with $C_{\mathfrak{I}}$ as a model of the theory Th($\mathfrak{I}$), we now have a formal basis for the study of the structural properties of $C_{\mathfrak{I}}$-type constructive image processing systems. Most of the properties of the $C_{\mathfrak{R}}$-type constructive signal processing systems that are given in table 8.1 are valid for $C_{\mathfrak{I}}$-type constructive image processing systems also. The verification is left to the reader as an exercise.

Recollect from section 8.2 that we have made use of Lyndon's homomorphism theorem for characterizing the first order properties of the model $C_{\mathfrak{R}}$. This theorem along with its limitations could be applied to the model $C_{\mathfrak{I}}$ also.

So, it is reasonable to go in for certain logical tools similar to ultra filters and ultra products which could be used in getting the first order equivalents of certain higher order properties of the model $C_{\mathfrak{I}}$. It is in this context we introduce here the notion of *Geometric Filters,* which appears to bear a direct relevance to the notion of Thampuran's *Extended Topological Filters* [Refer to subsection 9]. In fact, this is a variant of the notion of extended topological filters. We first formulate the notion of geometric filter and then study their structural properties in the framework of a lattice of filters.

16.2 The Notion Of Geometric Filters (G-Filters)

The processing of images based on well-defined mathematical techniques has remained a subject of interest for many years. In particular, mathematical theories associated with the processing, enhancement, analysis and recognition of sensed imageries have received significant amount of attention and effort. So far with one or two notable exceptions, there is no construct or theory that defines how to accomplish complex image processing tasks such as pattern recognition. Nevertheless some attempts have been made to mathematically describe various collections of image processing methodologies with a rigorous mathematical frame work, for example, that of Serra's mathematical morphology. In spite of these efforts, the wide variety of existing methodologies associated with image processing have yet to be consolidated under one rigorous unifying mathematical structure.

The term *mathematical structure* refers to the 3-tuple <X,.O, R>, where X is a set of mathematical objects, O is a set of operations and R is a set of relations. A mathematical structure with binary operations alone would fall under the algebraic structures of monoids, groups, rings, integral domains and fields. Alternatively, a mathematical structure with binary relations alone falls under the category of formal relational structures like that of lattices. The central idea on which the proposed *Image Algebra* is based, is that of treating an image as a construct made up of certain convex polygons or polyhedrons according as the image being 2-D or 3-D, and treating an image processing operation as a filtering by means of what we call as *Geometric Filters* (G-filters). In this section, we discuss the concept of geometric filters and of the algebra of G-filters. Let us consider 3 x 3 matrix of pixels in a 2-D array as shown in figure 16.2.1(b). The smallest convex polygon that could be formed inside the matrix is also shown in figure 16.2.1(a).

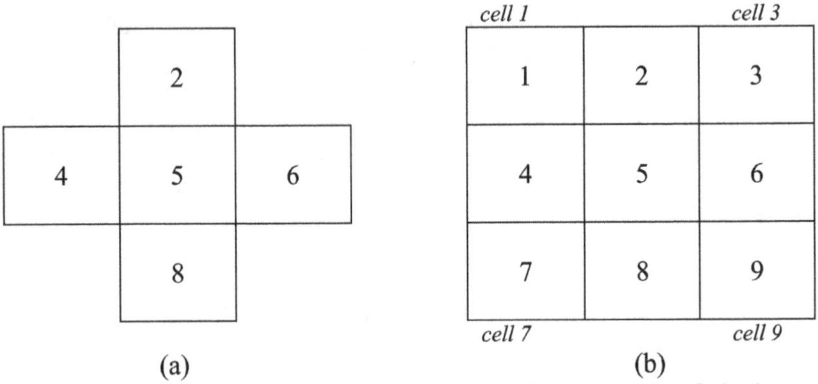

Figure 16.2.1: Smallest convex polygon and 3 x 3 matrix of pixels

Note that such convex polygons can be formed in sixteen different ways as labeled in figure 16.2.2. The suffixes denote the cell that are dropped.

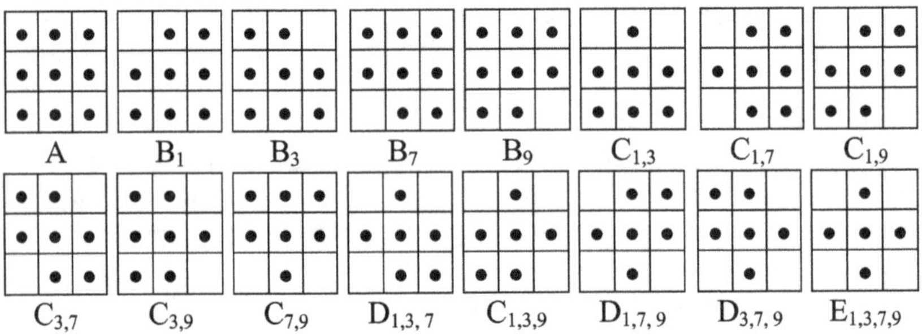

Figure 16.2.2 : Sixteen convex patterns in a 3 x 3 matrix

In the same manner, one can construct 256 unique convex polyhedrons in a 3 x 3 x 3 matrix of pixels of a cubic array. They are classified under nine groups such as A, B, C, D, E, F, G, H and I. The polyhedrons A and I are shown below in figure 16.2.3.

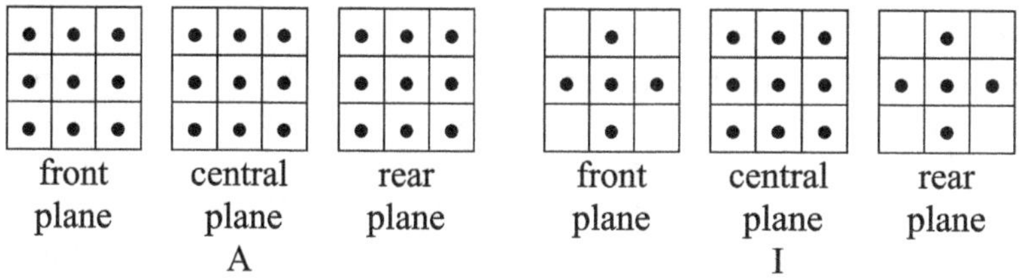

Figure 16.2.3 : Cubic array of size 3 x 3 x 3

Definition 16.2.1

A geometric filter (G-filter) is a set of 2D / 3D convex polygons/ polyhedrons satisfying the following conditions.

(i) The set does not contain a convex null, i.e., a convex polygon/polyhedron consisting exclusively of *don't care pixel values.*

(ii) Every convex polygon / polyhedron in the set ensures the presence of all of its proper envelopes. An envelope of a convex polygon/polyhedron is also a convex polygon/polyhedron that contains it. Every convex polygon / polyhedron is an envelope of itself. If a convex polygon/polyhedron has an envelope with more number of corners, then the envelope is said to be proper.

For example, the set $F = \{A, B_1, B_7, C_{1,7}\}$ is a G-filter defined over the set of sixteen convex patterns.

16.3 The Algebra Of G-Filters

The relational mathematical structure in which the G-filters are studied is a lattice $\Phi = < X, \leq >$ where X is a set of G-filters and $\leq$ is the partial order relation '*finer than*'. For example, the filter $F_1 = \{A, B_1, B_7, B_9, C_{1,7}\}$ is finer than that of $F_2 = \{A, B_1, B_7, C_{1,7}\}$.

All the 2D convex polygons form a lattice with A as their supremum and E as their infimum. The binary relation involved here is the partial order relation of *inclusion* [Refer 16.2.4]. Note that there are five levels in the lattice. All the elements in a level constitute a group, which is viewed as an immediate subgroup of the group of elements in the just higher level. It is not hard to see from this lattice that there are 24 linear chains consisting of a proper envelopes starting from E. Each chain exhibits a linear hierarchy of generating A from E. For example consider the chain {E, $D_{1,3,7}$, $C_{1,3}$, B_1, A}. E is a convex polygon without the cells 1, 3, 7 and 9. Assuming *equally likelihood* in recovering any of these four cells, $D_{1,3,7}$ is generated with the probability 1/4. From $D_{1,3,7}$ once can generate $C_{1,3}$ with the probability 1/3. Next, B_1 could be generated from $C_{1,3}$ with the probability 1/2 and finally A is recovered from B_1 with certainty.

This amounts to saying that the probability of generating A from E along this chain is 1/24 and the sum of all the probabilities of generating A from E along these 24 independent chains is 1.

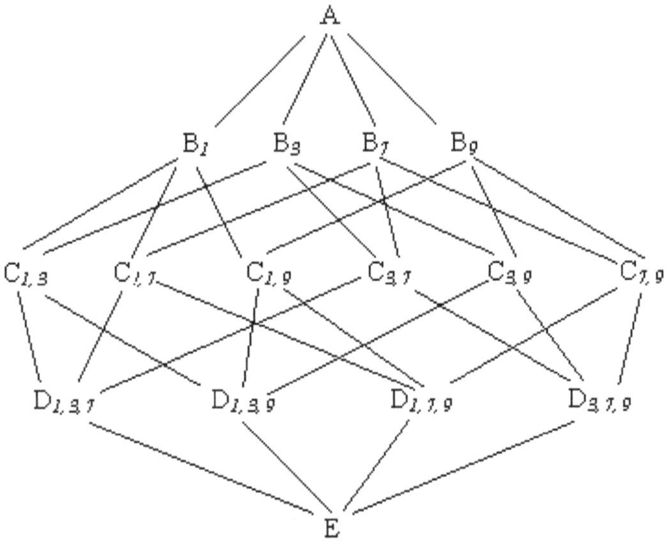

Figure 16.3.1 : Lattice formed by 16 convex polygons

Definition 16.3.1

We propose here the notion of hierarchical G-filter over the set of 16 convex polygons. A G-filter is called hierarchical only when it satisfies the following conditions. That is, the absence of even one element of a group in a level ensures the absence of all families in all the lower levels.

Theorem 16.3.1

One can construct a total of 95 hierarchical G-filters using a 3x3 cell structure.

Proof:

As seen earlier, there are four corner cells in a 3 X 3 cell structure and we construct

$$\sum_{i=0}^{4} 4C_i = 16$$

convex patterns in the following manner. The first group A contains $^4C_0$ that is, one polygon which is the 3 x 3 cell structure itself. The group B contains $^4C_1$ that is, 4 polygons B_1 (without cell 1), B_2 (without cell 2), B_3 and B_4. Similarly the group C contains $^4C_2$ that is, 6 polygons $C_{1,3}$ (without cells 1 and 3), $C_{1,7}$, $C_{1,9}$, $C_{3,7}$, $C_{3,9}$ and $C_{7,9}$. In this manner, the elements of group D and E could be identified. Now, the first G-filter F_1 contains the polygons E in the set, and as per the definition of a G-filter, F_1 should contain all of its fifteen proper envelopes. It is easy to see the cardinality of the set to be 16. Now, the absence of E in the set would yield a coarse G-filter F_2 with 15 remaining elements. Then by dropping one element at a time from the group D we can generate four hierarchical G-filters with cardinality 14. Next, in order to get a filter with a cardinality 13, we leave out E and any two elements in group D. We see here $^4C2$ such possibilities. Subsequently we construct $^4C_3$ filters with cardinality 12 by dropping E and any three elements of group D. Lastly we generate one filter with cardinality 11 by dropping E and all the elements of group D. Next, we generate $^6C_1$ filters with cardinality 10 by dropping E, all elements in group D and any one element in group C. This procedure is repeated for the remaining groups also. Ultimately we obtain the total number of hierarchical G-filters as:

$$2+2\sum_{i=1}^{4} 4\ C_i + \sum_{i=1}^{6} 6\ C_i = 95$$

Theorem 16.3.2

One can construct a total of

$$2+2\sum_{i=1}^{8} 8C_i + 2\sum_{i=1}^{28} 28C_i + 2\sum_{i=1}^{56} 56C_i + \sum_{i=1}^{70} 70C_i$$ Hierarchical G-filters in a 3x3x3 cell structure.

Proof:

Same as the proof of theorem 16.2.1

Symmetric Properties

Table 16.3.1 : Binary representation of permutation groups

Cell1	Cell3	Cell7	Cell9	Group	Remarks
0	0	0	0	A	3X3 cell structure itself
1	0	0	0	B_1	Corner cell 1 dropped
0	1	0	0	B_3	Corner cell 3 dropped
0	0	1	0	B_7	Corner cell 7 dropped
0	0	0	1	B_9	Corner cell 9 dropped
1	1	0	0	$C_{1,3}$	Corner cell 1, 3 dropped
0	1	1	0	$C_{3,7}$	Corner cell 3, 7 dropped
0	0	1	1	$C_{7,9}$	Corner cell 7, 9 dropped
1	0	0	1	$C_{1,9}$	Corner cell 1, 9 dropped
1	0	1	0	$C_{1,7}$	Corner cell 1, 7 dropped
0	1	0	1	$C_{3,9}$	Corner cell 3, 9 dropped
1	1	1	0	$D_{1,3,7}$	Corner cell 1, 3, 7 dropped
0	1	1	1	$D_{3,7,9}$	Corner cell 3, 7, 9 dropped
1	0	1	1	$D_{1,7,9}$	Corner cell 1, 7, 9 dropped
1	1	0	1	$D_{1,3,9}$	Corner cell 1, 3, 9 dropped
1	1	1	1	E	All corner cells dropped

From the table we see that there are six groups of patterns that exhibit cyclic permutation. The group A consists of only one element, which exhibits rotational symmetry with respect to the central cell. So, permuting its corresponding binary word 0000 does not have any meaning. Now take the case of group B. From the above table we observe that all the four elements of this group form a cyclic group with the generator B_1. Note that the binary string 1000 corresponds to the generator B_1 and by permuting this word cyclically we are able to generate other words corresponding to other elements of the group B. The number of cyclic permutations that are required to generate all the words from the generator word is 4, and this is called the cycle length of the permutation group. We extend this approach to the group C to find that this is a permutation group with two disjoint subgroups. Both the subgroups are cyclic groups, one with the cycle length 4 and the other with the cycle length 2. It is not hard to see that the group D is also a cyclic group with cycle length 4 and the group E is also unique like A, exhibiting rotational symmetry.

The next theorem quantifies the number of cyclic groups present in the various permutation groups formed of 256 convex polygons in a 3x3x3 cell structure.

Theorem 16.3.3

Consider the permutation groups A, B, C, D, E, F, G, H and I. Each group element is represented by an eight bit word. Now, every permutation group contains

$$Q\left(\frac{{}^{n}C_{i}}{n}\right)$$

number of independent cyclic groups with cycle length n and one cyclic group of cycle length

$$R\left(\frac{{}^{n}C_{i}}{n}\right) \text{, where } \quad Q\left(\frac{{}^{n}C_{i}}{n}\right) \quad \text{and} \quad R\left(\frac{{}^{n}C_{i}}{n}\right)$$

represent the quotient and the remainder respectively.

16.4 G-Filters Over Hexagonal Lattices

To construct hexagonal G-filters, we first start from a hexagonal grid and study various convex polygons in it. The hexagonal grid structure deals symmetrically with G-filters, and it does not have ambiguous diagonal configurations. It is not hard to see that this structure is based on the richest possible rotation group on a grid. So the associated algorithms also turn out to be much simpler. In what follows, we provide the definition of hexagonal grid G-filters, and outline their potential in all relevant applications of pattern generation and digital image processing.

Let us consider a 7-neighborhood hexagonal array of pixels as shown in figure 16.4.1 as A. Note that there are eighteen convex polygons inside this 7-neighborhood. The suffixes denote the cells that are dropped. Of these, the polygons $C_{1,4}$, $C_{2,5}$, $C_{3,6}$, $C_{1,3,5}$ and $D_{2,4,6}$, form the basis patterns.

<table>
<tr><td>1 2
6 7 3
5 4
A</td><td>2
6 7 3
5 4
B_1</td><td>1
6 7 3
5 4
B_2</td><td>1 2
6 7
5 4
B_3</td></tr>
<tr><td>1 2
6 7 3
5
B_4</td><td>1 2
6 7 3
4
B_5</td><td>1 2
7 3
5 4
B_6</td><td>2
6 7
5 4
$C_{1,3}$</td></tr>
<tr><td>2
6 7 3
5
$C_{1,4}$</td><td>2
6 7 3
4
$C_{1,5}$</td><td>1
6 7 3
5
$C_{2,4}$</td><td>1
6 7 3
4
$C_{2,5}$</td></tr>
<tr><td>1
7 3
5 4
$C_{2,6}$</td><td>1 2
6 7
4
$C_{3,5}$</td><td>1 2
7
5 4
$C_{3,6}$</td><td>1 2
7 3
5
$C_{4,6}$</td></tr>
<tr><td>2
6 7
4
$D_{1,3,5}$</td><td>1
7 3
5
$D_{2,4,6}$</td><td></td><td></td></tr>
</table>

Figure 16.4.1: Convex patterns in a 7-neighborhood hexagonal window

It is not hard to see from figure 16.4.1 that the entire set of eighteen polygons could by visualized as a set of five subsets, each subset consisting of certain polygons starting from A. They are (i) { A, B_1 , B_2 , B_4 , $C_{1,4}$ }, (ii) {A, B_2 , B_5 , $C_{2,5}$ }, (iii) {A, B_3 , B_6 , $C_{3,6}$ }, (iv) {A, B_1 , B_3 , B_5 , $C_{1,3}$, $C_{1,5}$, $C_{3,5}$, $C_{1,3,5}$ } and (v) {A, B_2 , B_4, B_6 , $C_{2,4}$, $C_{2,6}$, $C_{4,6}$, $C_{2,4,6}$ } .

Definition 16.4.1

A geometric filter (G-filters) over a hexagonal lattice is a set of 2D convex polygons satisfying the following conditions:

1. The set does not contain a convex null, that is, a convex polygon consisting exclusively of don't care pixel values.

2. Every convex polygon in the set ensures the presence of all of its proper envelopes. An envelope of a convex polygon is also a convex polygon that contains it. Every convex polygon is an envelope of itself. If a convex polygon has an envelope with more number of corners, then the envelope is said to be proper.

For example, the set F = { A, B_3 , B_4 , B_6 , $C_{3,6}$ } is a G-filter defined over the set of eighteen convex patterns.

16.5 The Algebra Of Hexagonal G-Filters

As outlined is subsection 16.3, the relational mathematical structure in which the hexagonal G-filters are studied is a lattice $\Phi = < S, \leq >$ where X is a set of hexagonal G-filters and $\leq$ is the partial order relation '*finer than*'.

For example, the filter F_1={A, B_1, B_3, B_5, $C_{1,3}$, $C_{1,5}$, $C_{3,5}$, $D_{1,3,5}$} is finer than that of F_2={A, B_1, B_3, B_5, $C_{1,3}$, $C_{1,5}$, $C_{3,5}$}. Unlike the 2D convex polygons in a square lattice, the eighteen polygons in a hexagonal lattice form a lattice with A as its supremum and $C_{1,4}$, $C_{2,5}$, $C_{3,6}$, $D_{1,3,5}$ and $D_{2,4,6}$ as its infima. As usual, the binary relation involved here is the partial order relation of *inclusion* [Refer to figure 16.5.1].

Note that there are four levels in each lattice. All the elements in a level constitute a group, which is viewed as an immediate subgroup of the group of elements in the just higher level. It is not hard to see from this lattice that there are six linear chains consisting of proper envelopes starting from $D_{1,3,5}$, six linear chains starting from $D_{2,4,6}$, two linear chains starting from $C_{1,4}$, two linear chains starting from $C_{2,5}$ and two linear chains starting from $C_{3,6}$.

Thus a total of eighteen linear chains could be seen in the lattice. Each chain exhibits a linear hierarchy of generating A from one of the infima.

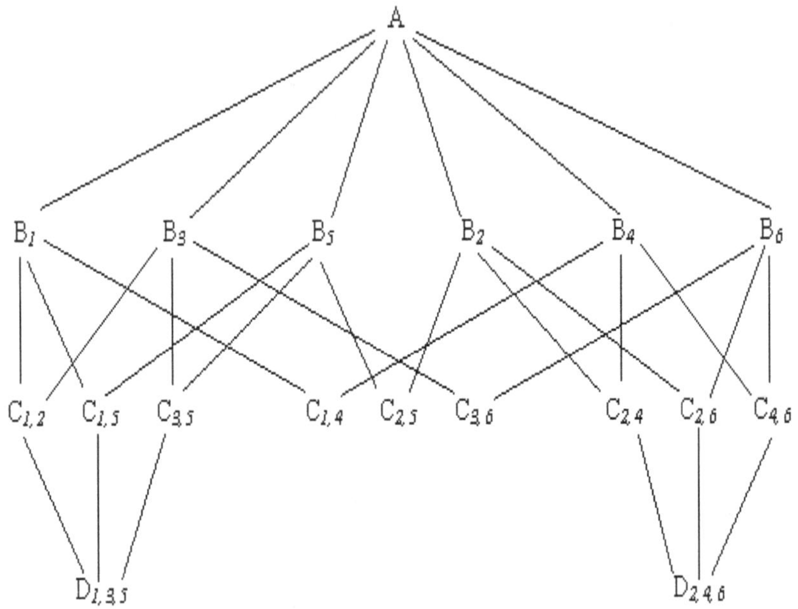

Figure 16.5.1 : Lattices formed by 18 convex polygons

Definition 16.5.1

We extend here the notion of a hierarchical G-filter over the set of 18 convex polygons. A G-filter is called hierarchical only when it satisfies the following conditions. That is, the absence of even one element of a group in a level ensures the absence of all families in all the lower levels.

Rotational Symmetric Properties

Table 16.5.1 : Binary representation of permutation groups

Cells 1	2	3	4	5	6	Group	Remarks
0	0	0	0	0	0	A	7 - cell structure itself
1	0	0	0	0	0	B_1	corner cell 1 dropped
0	1	0	0	0	0	B_2	corner cell 2dropped
0	0	1	0	0	0	B_3	corner cell 3 dropped
0	0	0	1	0	0	B_4	corner cell 4 dropped
0	0	0	0	1	0	B_5	corner cell 5 dropped
0	0	0	0	0	1	B_6	corner cell 6 dropped
1	0	1	0	0	0	$C_{1,3}$	corner cells 1,3 dropped
0	1	0	1	0	0	$C_{2,4}$	corner cells 2,4 dropped
0	0	1	0	1	0	$C_{3,5}$	corner cells 3,5 dropped
0	0	0	1	0	1	$C_{4,6}$	corner cells 4,6 dropped
1	0	0	0	1	0	$C_{1,5}$	corner cells 1,5 dropped
0	1	0	0	0	1	$C_{2,6}$	corner cells 2,6 dropped
1	0	0	1	0	0	$C_{1,4}$	corner cells 1, 4 dropped
0	1	0	0	1	0	$C_{2,5}$	corner cells 2, 5 dropped
0	0	1	0	0	1	$C_{3,6}$	corner cells 3, 6 dropped
1	0	1	0	1	0	$D_{1,3,5}$	corner cells 1, 3, 5 dropped
0	1	0	1	0	1	$D_{2,4,6}$	corner cells 2, 4, 6 dropped

From the table we see that there are five groups of patterns that exhibit cyclic permutation. The group A consists of only one element, which exhibits rotational symmetry with respect to the central cell. Now take the case of group B. From the above table we observe that all the six elements of this group form a cyclic group with the generator B_1. Note that the binary string 100000 corresponds to the generator B_1 and by permuting this word cyclically we are able to generate other words corresponding to other elements of the group B. The number of cyclic permutations that are required to generate all the words from the generator word is 6, and this is the cycle length of the permutation group.

We extend this approach to the group C and find that this is a permutation group with two disjoint subgroups. Both the subgroups are cyclic groups, one with the cycle length 6 and the other with the cycle length 3. It is not hard to see that the group D is also a cyclic group with cycle length 2 exhibiting rotational symmetry. Note that these cyclic groups have larger cycle lengths when compared to the ones corresponding to the square lattice discussed in section 16.3, thus exhibiting their better rotational symmetries.

16.6 Quantifiable Measures Of G-Filters

We propose here three measures of filtering capabilities of G-filters : (i) ambiguity of a G-filter (ii) discrimination of a G-filter and (iii) resolution of a G-filter. Note that these measures are not the extended concepts of Erlandson's measures which have been already described in section 10.

16.6.1 Ambiguity Of a G-Filter

A geometric filter is, in general, said to be ambiguous if the set consists of elements that constitute more than one linear chain of polygons / polyhedrons. The measure of ambiguity is given by the formula $\Psi_a (F) = x / L$, where x is the number of linear chains in the set and L is the total number of linear chains in the lattice of polygons / polyhedrons.

For example in the 3 X 3 array of pixels, the filter $\{A, B_1, B_9, C_{1,3}, D_{1,3,7}\}$ consists of 2 linear chains of 2D polygons, $\{A, B_1, C_{1,3}, D_{1,3,7}\}$ and $\{A, B_9\}$. So the measure of its ambiguity is given by 2 / 24.

16.6.2 Discrimination Of a G-Filter

The discrimination of a G-filter is a measure of the number of elements accepted by it. We denote this measure as Ψ_d and define it as $\Psi_d(F) = y / 2^n$ where n is the number of corners in the window and y is the number of elements contained in the filter set.

For example, the discrimination of G-filter described earlier has the discrimination of 5 / 16.

16.6.3 Resolution Of a G-Filter

Resolution is a measure of the number of elements of the lowest level that are present in the set, and it is given by the formula $\Psi_r = z / M$, where z is the number of elements in the lowest level and M is the total number of elements in that level.

For example, the resolution measure of the G-filter mentioned above is 1/4 .

16.7 Use Of G-Filters In Image Processing

In section 14 and 15, our attention has primarily been on processing digital images with the help of fast algorithms. The logic behind most of these algorithms could be seen to make use of the convex polygons in a 3 x 3 or 3 x 3 x 3 window or in a 7-neighborhood hexagonal window.

For example let us take the algorithm for edge detection. As given in section 14, the given digital image of size, say, N x N is scanned by a 3 x 3 window. On each move, the 3 x 3 sub image covered by the window is examined to see whether some or all of its pixels form a convex region of a single gray level, containing at least one pixel from each row and column. Note that such regions can be formed in sixteen different ways as shown in figure 16.7.1. Of these, the sixteenth one, that is the polygon E is covered in the rest. So, to identify whether any of these regions has been encountered or not, it is adequate to check for the presence of polygon E alone.

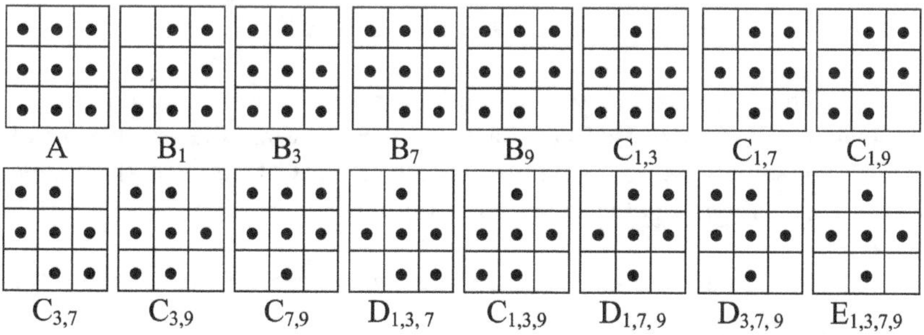

Figure 16.7.1: Sixteen convex patterns in a 3 x 3 matrix

If the subimage is found to contain to polygon E, then its central cell is assigned the 0 gray level. This procedure is continued till the entire image is scanned. The overall effect is that the boundaries of various single gray level regions in the given image are retained and the interior parts are erased thus giving us the edge detected version of the original image.

It is not hard to see that the entire operation of contouring is carried out with the help of a G-filter {A, B_3, B_7, $C_{3,7}$, B_9, $C_{3,9}$, $C_{7,9}$, $D_{3,7,9}$, B_1, $C_{1,3}$, $C_{1,7}$, $D_{1,3,7}$, $C_{1,9}$, $D_{1,3,9}$, $D_{1,7,9}$, E}, whose base is {E}. By *base* of a G-filter, we mean the set of infima corresponding to all linear chains in the filter set.

In the same manner, one can verify the operation of contouring 3-D digital images by the base 1 of the G-filter consisting of 256 convex polyhedrons. It is interesting to note that in our 3-D edge and surface detection algorithm given in subsection 14.2, we have not made use of the base 1 but the convex polyhedron consisting of the central cell and the central cells of all six faces of the 3 x 3 x 3 cubic structure. This is shown in figure 16.7.2.

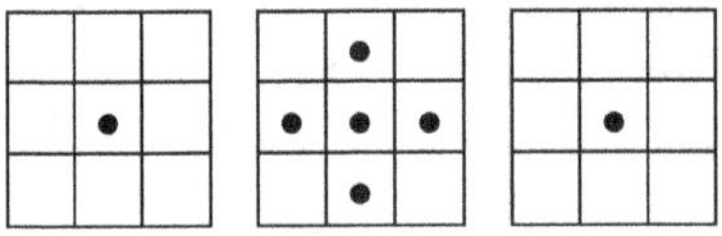

Figure 16.7.2 : 3-D edge and surface detection operation

As regards the use of 2-D hexagonal G-filters, it is obvious that these are applicable to images represented on hexagonal grid of the type described in the previous section. In the case of edge detection, we make use of five G-filters with the base $C_{1,4}$, $C_{2,5}$, $C_{3,6}$, $D_{1,3,5}$ and $D_{2,4,6}$.

Thus we come to an understand that with digital image represented in terms of certain basis convex patterns, the processing of such representations could be carried out using G-filters. In short, one could view *Image Algebra* as the *Algebra of G-filters.*

In the next section we introduce the concept of *Pextrum* and the *Pextral Coding* of digital images.

Section 17

Pextral Coding Of Digital Images

Abstract

This section is concerned with the problem of coding 2D and 3D digital images for the purposes of data compression and subsequent high-throughput transmission.

17.1 Introduction

For more than twenty years, various image coding techniques have been developed and many of such classical techniques provide high compression ratios. Among them *segmentation based* image coding techniques have been considered promising for the reasons that these techniques mimic *Human Visual Systems* (HVS) for the processing of contours and textures in the given image. These techniques, which are also called contour-texture oriented techniques, usually segment an image into homogeneous regions surrounded by contours and use different methods for coding the extracted contours and segmented regions. There are different possible ways of performing segmentation, contour coding and region coding.

This section describes a novel segmentation based image coding technique, which guarantees a large but lossy compression.

17.2 The Notion Of Pextral Codes

In general, pextral codes could be thought of as *iconic representations* of 2D / 3D digital images. More formally, a pextral code is a finite sequence of what are called *Pextral Icons.* A 2D pextral icon is a convex polygon formed of pixels in a nine neighborhood enclosing the

E. G. Rajan, *Symbolic Computing - Signal and Image Processing*
ISBN 81-7800-047-4

central pixel as shown in figure 17.2.1 (b). The smallest convex polygon that can be formed in this nine neighborhood structure is shown in figure 17.2.1 (a).

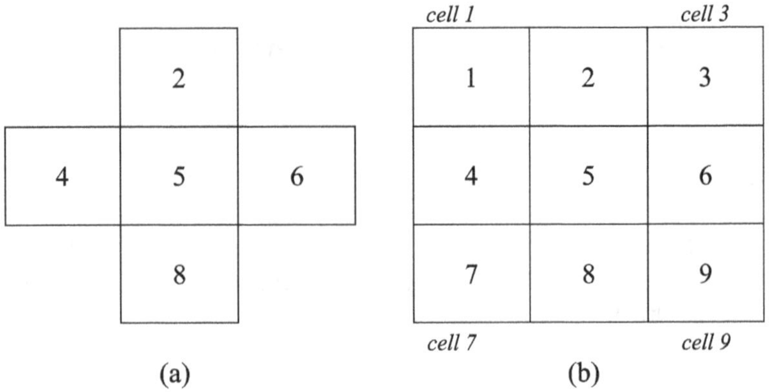

Figure 17.2.1 : Smallest convex polygon and 3 x 3 matrix of pixels

A given digital image of size say NxN is scanned by this nine neighborhood window. On every move the 3x3 subimage covered by the window is examined to see whether some or all of its pixels form a convex polygon consisting of uniform gray values. As detailed in earlier sections, one can construct such convex polygons in 16 different ways as labeled in figure 17.2.2. The suffixes denote the cells that are dropped.

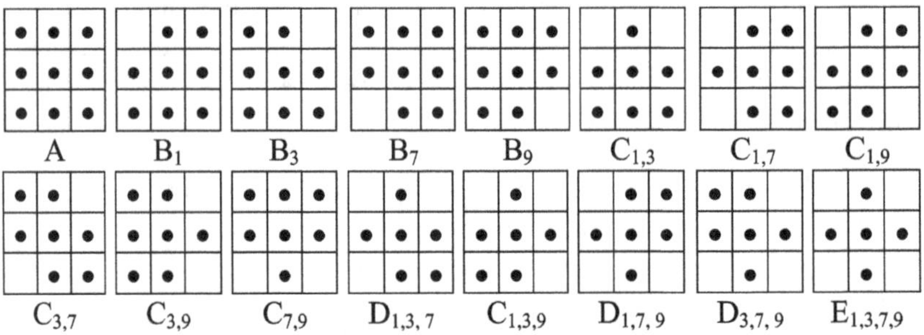

Figure 17.2.2: Sixteen convex patterns in a 3 x 3 matrix

With reference to figure 17.2.2, every polygon is a unique geometrical pattern encountered during scanning. All the sixteen geometrical patterns are coded in terms of four bit binary words as shown in table 17.2.1. These binary codes are divided into five permutation groups.

First, we observe that the binary words in group B are arranged in a cyclic order. In other words, with 0001 as the generator, all other words are obtained just by causing cyclic permutations in it. Group D elements could also be seen to follow the cyclic permutation pattern. Alternatively, we see in group C, two such independent subgroups exhibiting cyclic permutations. Moreover, group C elements show the property of complements. That is, there are three pairs of elements with their complements. For example, C_{19} = 1001 is the complement of $C_{3,7}$ = 0110. Refer to table 1 for identifying the other two pairs.

Table 17.2.1: Binary representation of sixteen polygons

Cell1	Cell3	Cell7	Cell9	Group	Remarks
0	0	0	0	A	3X3 cell structure itself
1	0	0	0	B_1	Corner cell 1 dropped
0	1	0	0	B_3	Corner cell 3 dropped
0	0	1	0	B_7	Corner cell 7 dropped
0	0	0	1	B_9	Corner cell 9 dropped
1	1	0	0	$C_{1,3}$	Corner cell 1, 3 dropped
0	1	1	0	$C_{3,7}$	Corner cell 3, 7 dropped
0	0	1	1	$C_{7,9}$	Corner cell 7, 9 dropped
1	0	0	1	$C_{1,9}$	Corner cell 1, 9 dropped
1	0	1	0	$C_{1,7}$	Corner cell 1, 7 dropped
0	1	0	1	$C_{3,9}$	Corner cell 3, 9 dropped
1	1	1	0	$D_{1,3,7}$	Corner cell 1, 3, 7 dropped
0	1	1	1	$D_{3,7,9}$	Corner cell 3, 7, 9 dropped
1	0	1	1	$D_{1,7,9}$	Corner cell 1, 7, 9 dropped
1	1	0	1	$D_{1,3,9}$	Corner cell 1, 3, 9 dropped
1	1	1	1	E	All corner cells dropped

The point of interest here is that it is enough to use just three elements of group C together with a complementation operator to aid an effective compression of digital image. In general, it is sufficient to have the following elements to act as the bases for coding 2D digital images.

Code	Group Generator	Operation	Remarks
0000	A		Unique element
1000	B	Cyclic permutation	Group contains 4 elements
1100	C	Cyclic permutation	Group contains 4 elements
1010	C	Cyclic permutation	Group contains 2 elements
1110	D	Cyclic permutation	Group contains 4 elements
1111	E		Unique element

17.3 Pextral Coding Of Binary Images

Given a binary image we code it in terms of the 16 convex patterns. For instance, consider the picture shown in figure 17.3.1. The pextral code of this image is shown in figure 17.3.2.

0	0	0	0	0	0	0	0	0	0	0	0
0	0	0	0	1	0	0	0	0	0	0	0
0	0	0	0	1	1	1	0	0	0	0	0
0	0	0	1	1	1	1	1	1	1	0	0
0	0	0	1	1	1	1	1	1	1	0	0
0	0	1	1	1	1	1	1	1	1	0	0
0	0	1	1	1	1	1	1	1	1	0	0
0	0	1	1	1	1	1	1	1	1	1	0
0	1	1	1	1	1	1	1	1	1	0	0
0	0	0	1	1	1	1	1	1	1	0	0
0	0	0	0	0	0	0	0	0	1	0	0
0	0	0	0	0	0	0	0	0	0	0	0

Figure 17.3.1: A sample binary image

0	0	0	0	0	0	0	0	0	0
0	0	0	0	0	0	0	0	0	0
0	0	0	B_1	A	B_3	0	0	0	0
0	0	0	A	A	A	A	A	0	0
0	0	B_1	A	A	A	A	A	0	0
0	0	A	A	A	A	A	A	0	0
0	0	A	A	A	A	A	A	B_3	0
0	0	B_7	A	A	A	A	A	0	0
0	0	0	0	0	0	0	0	0	0
0	0	0	0	0	0	0	0	0	0

Figure 17.3.2: Array representation of pextral code of the given image

It is not hard to see that one can reconstruct the original image from this code. Moreover, we use arithmetic descriptors to avoid redundant patterns, if any, which would improve data compression. In our previous example, the code length could be further reduced as $0^{23}B_1$ A B_3 0^7 A^5 0^4 B_1 A^5 0^4 A^6 0^4 A^6 B_3 0^3 B_7 A^5 0^{23} . The larger the image size, the more it is compressed. In addition, it is but logical to say that the contour information of a binary image alone could describe the entire image, provided the image has no contours inside it. This amounts to saying that the pextral code of a given binary image is nothing but the code consisting of pextral icons corresponding to contours alone. In this manner, a very high amount of compression could be achieved.

Next, we discuss a method of coding 3D digital binary images in terms of pextral icons.

17.4 Pextral Coding Of 3D Binary Images

The method of coding 2D digital binary images in terms of 2D polygons can be further extended to coding of 3D binary images also. A 3D image is scanned by a 3x3x3 window with 27 cells in it. The window is shown in figure 17.4.1. It has 8 corner cells, and one can construct 256 unique convex polyhedrons inside the window.

1	2	3
4	5	6
7	8	9

front plane

10	11	12
13	14	15
16	17	18

central plane

19	20	21
22	23	24
25	26	27

rear plane

Figure 17.4.1: cubic array of size 3x3x3

All the 256 convex polyhedrons are classified under nine groups such as A, B, C, D, E, F, G, H and I. Every polyhedron is coded as an 8 bit binary word, and every group is constructed by cyclically permuting its code generator.

17.5 Pextral Coding Of Gray Images

As outlined in the introduction of this section, segmentation based image coding techniques have been considered promising for the reason that they may mimic *Human Vision System* (HVS) while processing contours and textures of the image for coding purposes. These *contour-texture* based techniques usually segment a given image into homogeneous regions surrounded by contours and employ only these parameters in coding. There are a number of segmentation techniques available in the literature. However, we provide here a novel technique which would closely mimic the HVS.

Segmentation Algorithm

Scan the given gray image by a 3x3 or by a 3x3x3 window depending on the image. On every move find the maximum and the minimum gray values inside the window. Find the gray distance, that is, the difference between the maximum and the minimum values observed. Specify a threshold value T based on the statistics of the given image. Now check whether the gray distance is less than or equal to the threshold T. If it is so, then replace the central pixel value by the value given by adding half the value of the gray distance to the minimum gray value inside the window. On the other hand, if gray distance is more than T, then move on to the next pixel. The overall effect is that the entire image is segmented to be the disjoint union of various regions. Now employ the coding technique discussed earlier.

17.6 Transcription Of Pextral Codes

The compressed code has to be in a form that is compatible for processing in a computer and for subsequent transmission. We provide a novel technique called *transcription* proposed by Markov [20]. Let us take the case of 2D pextral codes. As seen earlier, there are 16 pextral icons in the set. Now each icon is uniquely represented by a word of the type 01^i0 , $i \geq 1$. The first transcription would then be 010 and the last $01^{16}0$. Note that any string consisting of these transcriptions could be uniquely decoded. An efficient transcription of a pextral code depends on the logic of employing transcriptions in the increasing order of their lengths for those icons in the decreasing order of their frequencies in a given image. Transcriptions of pextral codes are the binary strings that are recommended for transmission purposes.

Part V

Abstract

This part of the book consists of five sections and they describe various application areas and certain important outcomes of our own research in symbolic processing of signals and images. Section 18 provides the basic areas of research related to symbolic processing of signals and images. Section 19 explores the possibility of modeling solidification process as a thinning lattice gas automaton. The moving boundaries of isotherms in a solidification process correspond to the boundary removal of a digital image, which is also referred as thinning. In section 20, we explain the technique of modeling fluid flow using cellular automata, which are also known as lattice gas automata. Section 21 describes one application of cellular logic array processing techniques to examine the laser scanned data of metal surfaces. Lastly section 22 describes an important application of modeling of collision processes using cellular logic array processing.

Applications of Cellular Logic Array Processing

Section 18

Research Areas Related To Symbolic Processing Of Signals And Images

The various research activities related to symbolic processing of signals and images could be carried out in three directions: (i) computer vision, (ii) pattern recognition and analysis and (iii) modelling and simulation. In this section, we provide a brief account of some of these activities, and identify a few among them for our study in the last part of this book. The major areas of research are shown in figure 18.1.

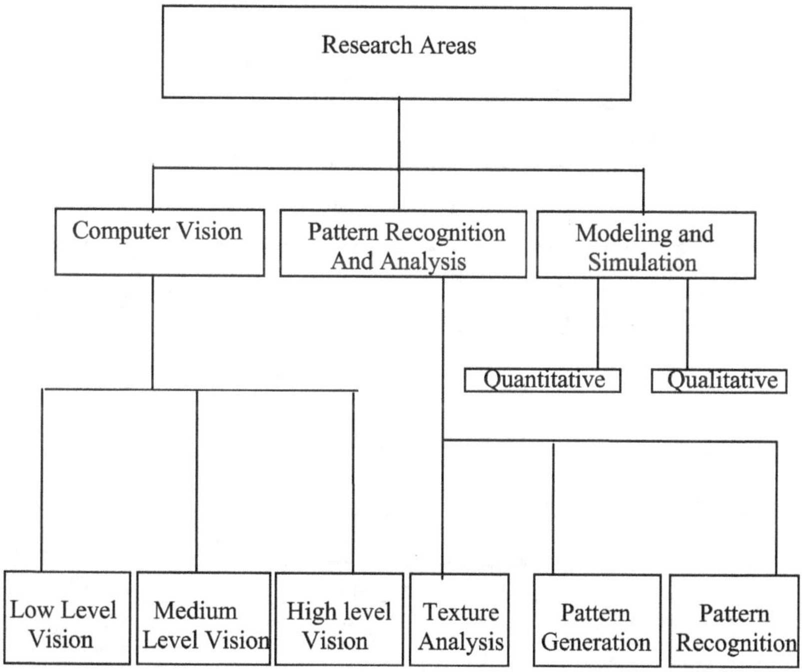

Figure 18.1: Major areas of research in symbolic computation

E. G. Rajan, *Symbolic Computing - Signal and Image Processing*
ISBN 81-7800-047-4

18.1 Computer Vision

The term *Computer Vision* refers to the state-of-the-art of acquiring and processing of images with the help of computers and other devices. The acquisition of images using devices like video cameras with suitable add-on cards, CCD cameras, Infra Red (IR) sensors, optical scanners, ultrasound scanners, Nuclear Magnetic Resonance (NMR) devices and Magnetic Resonance Imaging (MRI) scanners is generally termed as *Low Level Vision*. *Medium Level Vision* is about the processing of digital images using various algorithms and of the development of such algorithms either in a mathematical framework or in a logical framework. *High Level Vision*, on the other hand, deals with the problem of making a system vision sensitive and intelligent. Artificial Intelligence (AI) plays a vital role in this formalism. Figure 18.1.1 shows a typical computer vision system deployed in a research laboratory or an automated industry.

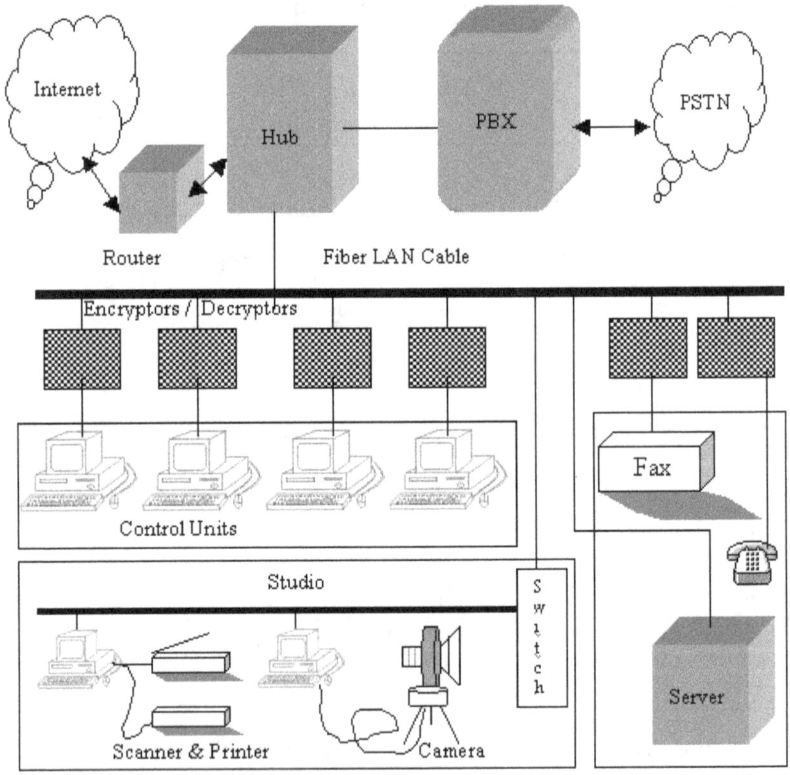

Figure 18.1.1: Computer Vision Systems Laboratory

Figure 18.1.2 shows a tree diagram, which contains many domain specific IT application areas related to computer vision.

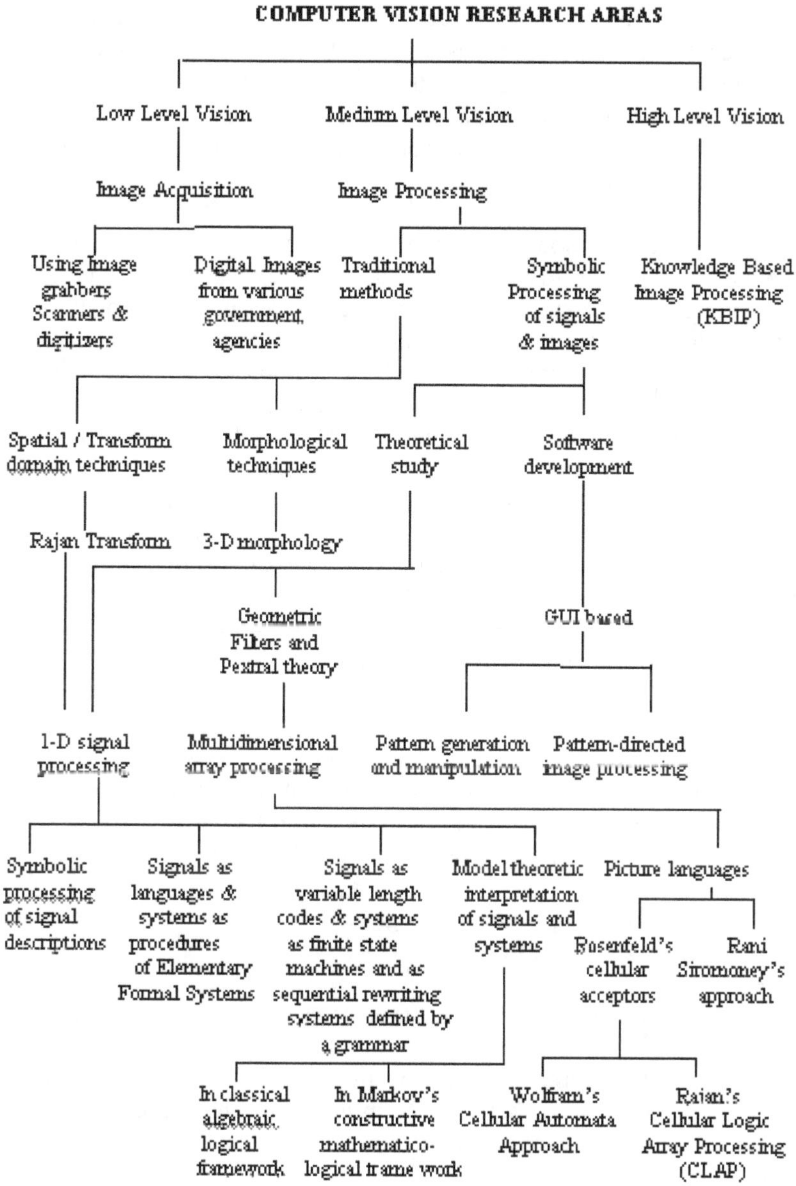

Figure 18.1.2: IT enabled research areas in computer vision

18.2 Pattern Recognition And Analysis

As the title goes, this subsection describes a technique of recognizing an object, say, a target in combat space. The combat space T consists of targets of three types (i) wanted targets W, (ii) rejected targets R and (iii) unknown targets U so that $T = W \cup R \cup U$. An object could be recognized by various techniques among which syntactic pattern recognition technique is generally preferred when high-speed recognition is a matter of concern.

The description of an object is called its pattern. According to the nature of pattern to be recognized, recognition is of two types. It is recognition of concrete items and that of abstract items. Recognition of abstract items is also termed as conceptual recognition, as this involves the recognition of solution to the problem with our eyes and ears closed, where as recognition of concrete patterns is considered as psycho physiological problem which involves a relationship between a person and a physical stimulus. When a person visualizes a scene he perceives a pattern, which he uses to make an inductive inference and associates his perception with some concepts or clues, which he might have derived from his past experience. Thus we view pattern recognition as a classification process of discriminating input data not between individual patterns but between populations via a search for certain *invariant attributes* among members of populations.

The process of pattern recognition can be carried out either on spatial or temporal patterns. Spatial patterns are those, which occupy space, like characters, fingerprints, weather maps, physical objects and pictures. Time based patterns like speech waveforms, ECGs, target signature and timer series are called Temporal Patterns.

The study of pattern recognition problems may be logically divided into two major categories.

(1) Study of pattern recognition capabilities of human beings.

(2) Development of theory and techniques for the design of devices capable of performing a given recognition task for a specific application.

In formal terms, Pattern recognition is the categorization of input data into identifiable classes via extraction of significant features or attributes of the data from the background of irrelevant detail.

A pattern class is a category determined by some given common attributes among the patterns. We need to provide an automatic system by which patterns falling into disjoint classes are categorized into their respective classes. The design concepts for automatic pattern recognition are motivated by the ways in which pattern classes are characterized and defined. Three basic design concepts are discussed in the following.

18.2.1 Design concepts [15]

Membership-roster concept

A pattern class is categorized (characterized) by the roster of its members and thus this technique suggests automatic pattern recognition by template matching. A pattern recognition system stores a set of patterns of a pattern class. When an unknown pattern is shown to the system, it compares it with the existing patterns one by one and classifies this input pattern as a member of a pattern class if it matches with one of the stored patterns. This membership-roster approach works satisfactorily for near perfect noise-free pattern samples.

Common-property concept

Another basic concept used in the design of an automatic pattern recognition system is the characterization of a pattern class by common properties shared by all of its members. In this method the patterns belonging to a class possess certain common properties or attributes, which reflect similarities among these patterns. The common properties are stored in the pattern recognition system. When an unknown pattern is observed by the system, its features are extracted, coded and then are compared with the stored features. If its features match with any of the stored features then the recognition scheme will classify the new pattern as belonging to the pattern class. So, in this approach we determine common properties from a finite set of sample patterns and examine a new pattern for a suitable match.

Clustering concept

When the patterns of a class are vectors whose components are real numbers, a pattern class can be characterized by its clustering properties in the pattern space. Based on the relative geometrical arrangement of the various pattern clusters, the pattern recognition system can be designed. If the clusters are far apart, simple recognition schemes such as the minimum-distance classifiers can be successfully used. On the other hand, when the clusters overlap, more sophisticated techniques are used.

Three categories of methodologies are used in the basic design of automatic pattern recognition systems described above: (i) heuristic, (ii) mathematical, and (iii) linguistic or syntactic. Some times, a combination of these methods is also used in the design of a pattern recognition system. We give a brief account of these three methodologies as follows:

18.2.2 Design Methodologies [15]

Heuristic methods

This approach is based on human intuition and experience, and makes use of the membership-roster and common-property concepts described above. A system designed using this approach would usually consist of ad hoc procedures developed for specialized recognition tasks. Heuristic approach is an important branch of pattern recognition system design. However, since each problem requires application of specifically tailored design rules, generalization of this approach is not easy.

Mathematical methods

This approach is based on classification rules, which are formulated and derived in a mathematical framework, making use of the common-property and clustering concepts. The mathematical approach may be subdivided into two categories: deterministic and statistical. The deterministic approach does not employ the statistical properties of the pattern classes under consideration. The statistical approach uses mathematical classification rules, which are formulated and derived in a statistical framework.

Linguistic (syntactic) methods

In this approach, characterization of patterns is guided by primitive elements (sub patterns) and their relationships making use of the common-property concept. A pattern can be described by a hierarchical structure of sub patterns analogous to the syntactic structure of formal languages. This permits the use of formal languages for tackling pattern recognition problems. A pattern grammar consists of finite sets of elements called variables, primitives, and productions. The production rules determine the type of grammar to be used for pattern recognition. The essence of this approach is the selection of pattern primitives, the assembling of the primitives and their relationships into pattern grammars, and analysis and recognition using the rules of these grammars. This approach is particularly useful in dealing with patterns, which cannot be conveniently described by numerical measurements.

It is important to note here that learning or training takes place only during the design (or updating) phase of a pattern recognition system. Once acceptable results have been obtained, the system is engaged in the task of actually performing recognition on samples drawn from the environment in which it is expected to operate.

Syntactic pattern recognition is a new approach of pattern recognition, which utilizes the concepts of formal language theory. The term syntactic pattern recognition is synonymous to linguistic pattern recognition, grammatical pattern recognition and structural pattern recognition.

The difference between the mathematical approach and syntactic approach is that the former one explicitly utilizes the structure of pattern in recognition process, whereas syntactic approach deals with patterns on a strictly quantitative basis.

As mentioned earlier, syntactic pattern recognition follows the theory of formal languages. Therefore we shall now get acquainted to the basic concepts of formal languages.

The origin of formal language theory may be traced to middle 1950's with the development by Noam Chomsky of mathematical model of a grammar related to his work in natural languages. The concepts that are helpful to comprehend the formal language theory are defined below:

- An Alphabet is any finite set of symbols.
- A word over an alphabet is any string of finite length composed of symbols from the alphabet. For example, valid words of alphabet {0,1}are 0,1,00,01,10,11….
- A word with no symbols is called empty word and denoted by Λ.

- A language is any set of words over an alphabet.

- As every language follows some specific grammar. Similarly the formal language is associated with a grammar which is basically a 4-tuple: $G=\{V_N, V_T, P, S\}$
  where V_N is a set of non-terminals (variables);
  V_T is a set of terminals (constants);
  P is a set of productions or rewriting rules;
  S is a set start or root symbol.

S belongs to the set V_N and V_N and V_T are disjoint sets, whereas V is the union of sets V_N and V_T. V^* denotes the set (free monoid) of words consisting of the empty word Λ whereas V^+ is a set of sentences of $V^* - \Lambda$.

The language generated by G, is denoted by L(G). It is the set of strings that satisfy two conditions:

(i) Each string is composed only of terminals (i.e., each string is a terminal sentence)

(ii) Each string can be derived from S by suitable application of productions from the set P.

The set P of productions consists of expressions of the form $\alpha \rightarrow \beta$. The symbol $\rightarrow$ indicates replacement of string α by the string β, where α is a string in V^+ and β is a string in V^*. Here we use the set of constants denoted by $V_T = \{\alpha,\beta,\gamma,\delta, \bar{\alpha}, \bar{\beta}, \bar{\gamma}, \bar{\delta}\}$ and the root symbols would change depending on the object to be recognized. The set of production formulas are a part of the normal algorithm, which were introduced by A.A. Markov. The normal algorithm recognizes angles from changes in the direction during contour tracking. This is done by what we call *Look Ahead Tracing* (LAT) technique.

Grammars differ only in their productions. Now, various types of grammar are:

- *Unrestricted Grammar*:- It has production formulas of the form $\alpha \rightarrow \beta$, where α is a string and β is another string.

- *Context-Sensitive Grammar*:-It has productions of the form $\alpha_1 A \alpha_2 \rightarrow \alpha_1 \beta \alpha_2$, where α_1 and α_2 are in V^*, β is in V^+ and A is in V_N. This grammar allows replacement of the non-terminal A by the string β only when A appears in the context $\alpha_1 A \alpha_2$ of string α_1 and α_2.

- *Context–free Grammar*:- It has productions of the form $A \rightarrow \beta$, where A is in V_N and β is in V^+. The name context free arises from the fact that the variable A may be replaced by a string β regardless of the context in which A appears.

- *Regular (or Finite-state) Grammar*:- It is one with productions of the form $A \rightarrow aB$ or $A \rightarrow a$, where A and B are variables in V_N and a is a terminal in V_T .

These grammars are sometimes called type 0,1,2 and 3 grammars respectively.

18.2.3 Formulation of the syntactic pattern recognition problem

Suppose that we have two pattern classes W_1 and W_2. Let the patterns of these classes be composed of features from some finite set. We call the set of feature terminals by V_T. Certain primitives are also used instead of terminals in syntactic pattern recognition .The pattern classes W_1 and W_2 are composed of features from some finite set.

If there exists a grammar with the property that the language it generates consists of sentences or words (patterns), which belong exclusively to one of the pattern classes say W_1, this grammar can be used for pattern classification so that a pattern belongs to W_1 if it is a word in $L(G_1)$.

The classification of a given pattern string can be generated by a grammar G. In the case of M-class, there is an M grammar and $L(M_i)$ languages associated with it, where i=1,2,…….M. Refer to section 5 for details of M-grammar. The procedure used to determine whether or not a string represents a word or a sentence, which is grammatically correct with respect to a given language is called *parsing.*

18.2.3.1 Syntactic Pattern Description

The object to be recognized in an image is a two-dimensional pattern. The string grammars of this pattern can be done by simple juxtaposition of a string, to form new strings. Juxtaposition of two strings means placing the objects together, without losing the identity of each object. Concatenation can also be done but it involves spatial rearrangement as well as a loss of identity on the part of the individual objects. Juxtaposition of structures takes place only at two points called a *head* and *tail* of an arrow defined by these two points.

The other useful technique for describing two-dimensional relationship is based on tree structures. A tree is a finite set T of one or more nodes such that:

- There is no especially designated node called the root of the tree

- The remaining nodes (excluding the root) are partitioned into m disjoint sets $T_1, T_2 \ldots\ldots T_m$, $m \geq 0$, where each of these sets is in turn a tree. These trees are called sub trees of the root. A node of degree zero is called a leaf, while a node of higher degree is called a branch node. Finally, the tree representation of a pattern is called a pattern tree and a sample tree diagram is shown in figure 18.2.3.1.1.

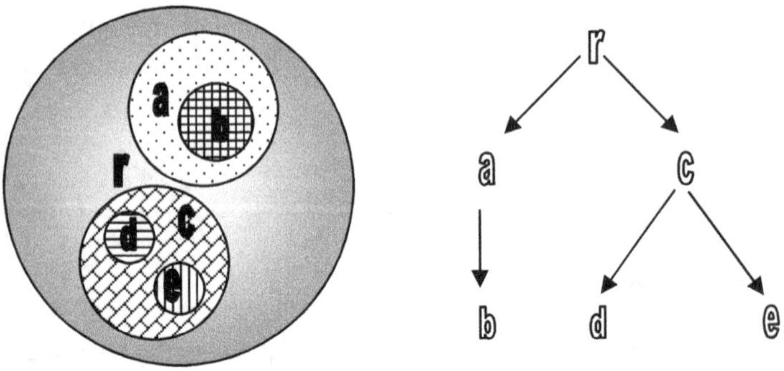

Figure 18.2.3.1.1: Tree representation of patterns

Recognition grammars:

There are three methods of recognizing a pattern. They are (i) *Syntax-directed grammar*, which is a mechanics for determining whether or not a pattern can be generated by a particular grammar, (ii) *Recognition of graph-like pattern*, which deals with the recognition of two-dimensional patterns which can be reduced to an equivalent string representation and (iii) Tree grammars, which are expressed as tree structures, and are used in recognizing patterns.

18.2.3.2 Syntax-Directed Recognition

Once the grammars are known, the basic problem is the development of a procedure for determining whether or not a given pattern represents a valid formula, a word or a sentence. As outlined earlier, the procedure used in formal language theory to accomplish this is called *parsing*. Basically, we consider two types of parsing techniques: (i) *Top Down* and *(ii) Bottom Up*. The top or root of the (inverted) tree is the start symbol S and through repeated application of the productions of the grammar, one can attempt to arrive at the given terminal sentence. The bottom up approach, on the other hand, starts with the given sentence and attempts to arrive at the symbol S by applying the production. In either case, if the parsing fails then the given pattern represents an incorrect sentence and is therefore rejected. The parsing process can be further improved by employing the rules of syntax of the grammar. Syntax is defined as the juxtaposition and concatenation of object. A rule of syntax states some permissible (or prohibited) relation between objects. A *syntax-directed parser* employs the syntax of the grammar in the parsing process.

18.2.3.3 Recognition Of Graph Like Patterns

An interesting application of linguistic concepts of pattern recognition is pthe *Picture Description Language* (PDL). A primitive in PDL is an n-dimensional structure with two distinguished points a *tail* and a *head*. A primitive can be linked to another primitive only at its tail and (or) head. On the basis of this permissible form of juxtaposition and because of the fact that each primitive is abstracted as a directed line segment, it is evident that the structure of PDL are directed graphs and also that these structures can be handled by string grammars. The main rules of juxtaposition of PDL are as follows.

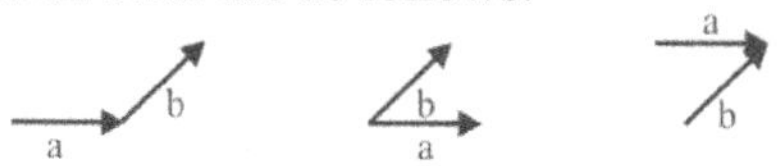

Blank primitives must be used for generating disjoint structures. A null point primitive has identical head and tail. The mechanics of PDL could be used to obtain the contour of a pattern.

To illustrate this mechanism, consider the following PDL grammar

$G = \{V_N, V_T, P, S\}$

where

$V_N = \{S, A_1, A_2, A_3, A_4, A_5, A_6, A_7\}$

$V_T = \{\alpha \rightarrow,\ \beta \setminus,\ \gamma\downarrow,\ \delta /\}$

$$P: \left.\begin{array}{l} S \rightarrow \alpha + A_1 \\ A_1 \rightarrow \beta + A_2 \\ A_2 \rightarrow \gamma + A_3 \\ A_3 \rightarrow \delta + A_4 \\ A_4 \rightarrow \bar{\alpha} + A_5 \\ A_5 \rightarrow \bar{\beta} + A_6 \\ A_6 \rightarrow \bar{\gamma} + A_7 \\ A_7 \rightarrow \bar{\delta} \end{array}\right\} \quad \text{A normal algorithm}$$

where ($\bar{\ }$) indicates the primitive with its direction reversed. The result obtained by applying all the productions is

$$(\alpha+(\beta+(\gamma+(\delta+(\bar{\alpha}+(\bar{\beta}+(\bar{\gamma}+\bar{\delta})))))))$$

The above normal algorithm creates a octagon as shown below in figure

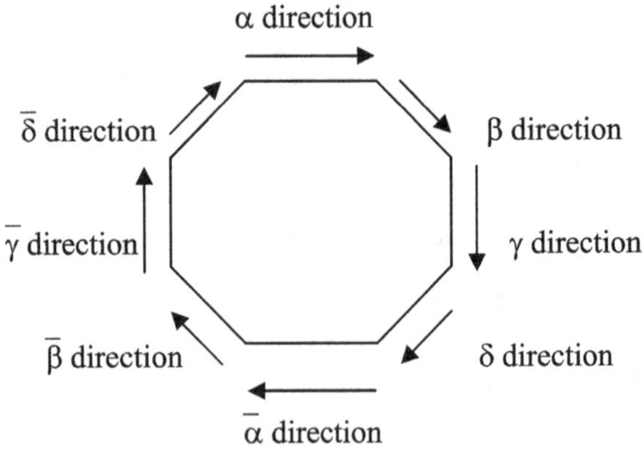

18.2.3.4 Recognition Of Tree Structure:

A tree grammar is defined as a quintuple $G = \{V_N, V_T, P, R, S\}$, where V_N and V_T are sets of non-terminals and terminals respectively. S is the start symbol, P is a set of production of the form $\Omega \rightarrow \psi$, where Ω and ψ are trees; R is a ranking function which denotes the number of direct descendants of a node whose label is a terminal in the grammar.

18.2.3.5 Learning And Grammatical Inference

The term *learning from sample patterns* means learning a grammar from a set of sample sentences. This procedure is commonly referred to as grammatical inference and is a vital subject in the study of syntactic pattern recognition, because of its automatic learning implications.

Inference of String Grammars

Figure 18.2.3.5.1 shows a model of inference of string grammars. The input is a set of sample terminal strings $\{x_i\}$ and the box is an adaptive learning algorithm and the output of the box is a grammar G, which is compatible with the given strings $\{x_i\}$, and which is a subset of L(G).

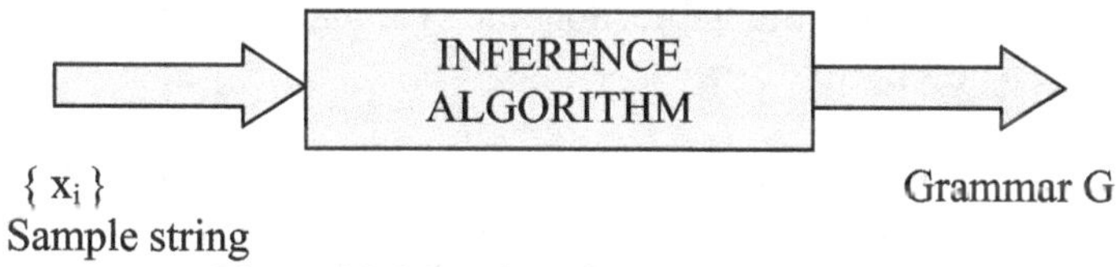

Figure 18.2.3.5.1: Inference engine

The algorithm used to get a string grammar utilizes the Feldmann's method. The algorithm is viewed into three parts based on their functionalities.

- The first part forms the non-recursive grammar
- Second part converts the results to a recursive grammar.
- The last part is concerned with simplifying the grammar.

Inference of Two-Dimensional Grammar

The basic problem of a two-dimensional grammar lies in the specification of juxtaposition rules. Here, we assume that the appropriate two-dimensional positional descriptors are already made available. Then the following procedure holds good,

- Given a set of primitives and positional descriptors, complex structures could be built with the help of them.
- When the process is completed, a grammar is derived using the steps followed in building the structures.

Here, we demonstrate a working model of an inference engine that approximates an object in a digital image to a regular polygon or to a set of regular polygons, determines a syntactic code for it and compares with that of a model code in the knowledge base. If it is matched, then the object is recognized. The pattern vector used here is three valued. This triple valued data is called a vector data of an image. It is a linear chain of triples of numerical values of the spatial coordinates of contour pixels and their gray values.

From this spatial coordinates a normal algorithm is generated. This normal algorithm recognizes the angle changes in the direction during contour tracking using the *Look Ahead Tracing* (LAT) technique. In this technique, a previously recognized direction during a scan is given the first priority status when compared to the other preferential ones. If α is the identified direction, then the other preferential directions are β, γ, δ, $\bar{\alpha}$, $\bar{\beta}$, $\bar{\gamma}$, $\bar{\delta}$.

The vector data consists of both the Direction Code (DC) and the Length Code (LC). The direction data is a string of the elements from the set V_N, that is the set of non-terminals. The string elements are separated by a delimiter, which is denoted by the symbol □. An arbitrary square can be represented by the vector code in the following manner:

$$\alpha \square \gamma \square \bar{\alpha} \square \bar{\gamma} * n \square n \square n \square n$$

In a vector code, the part preceding the symbol * is called direction code and the part following the symbol * is called the length code. The symbol n represents the length of the sides of the square.

Inference engine

The inference engine proposed here consists of different blocks, which are explained below. First the given digital image is segmented and contoured. Then the contours are approximated to regular polygons. These polygons are vectorized in order to extract shape information from them. For example, figure 18.2.3.5.2 shows a human being in a standing posture, which is approximated to a disjoint union of a square, a rectangle below the square, two long rectangles one on each side of the first rectangle, and two more long rectangles just below the first rectangle. The LAT first recognizes the head. During successive scans, the right hand and then the body, left hand, right leg and left leg of the human finger are recognized. The vector code corresponding to the contours of individual blocks is given below.

Head: α □ γ □ $\bar{\alpha}$ □ $\bar{\gamma}$ * H1 □H1 □H1 □H1
Right Hand: α □ γ □ $\bar{\alpha}$ □ $\bar{\gamma}$ * RH1 □RH2 □RH1 □RH2
Body: α □ γ □ $\bar{\alpha}$ □ $\bar{\gamma}$ * B1 □B2 □B1 □B2
Left Hand: α □ γ □ $\bar{\alpha}$ □ $\bar{\gamma}$ * LH1 □LH2 □LH1 □LH2
Right Leg: α □ γ □ $\bar{\alpha}$ □ $\bar{\gamma}$ *RL1 □RL2 □RL1 □RL2
Left Leg: α □ γ □ $\bar{\alpha}$ □ $\bar{\gamma}$ * LL1 □LL2 □LL1 □LL2

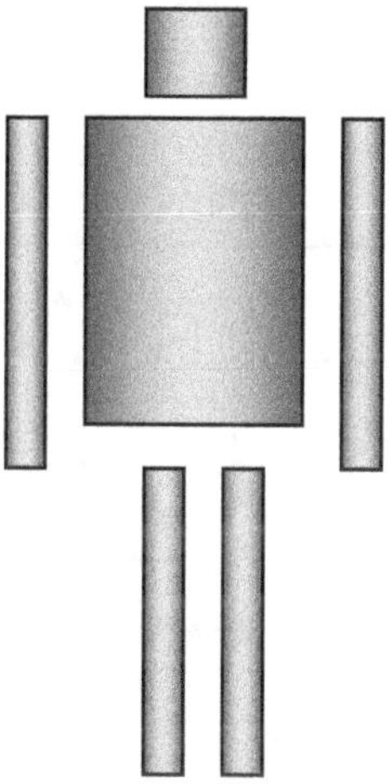

Figure 18.2.3.5.2: Contour map of the geometric model of a human being

The entire compound picture is transformed into a conjoint string of the form:

⌊ α □γ □α □γ*H1 □H1 □H1 □H1⌋
⌊α □ γ □ $\bar{\alpha}$ □ $\bar{\gamma}$ * RH1 □RH2 □RH1 □RH2⌋
⌊ α □ γ □ $\bar{\alpha}$ □ $\bar{\gamma}$ * B1 □B2 □B1 □B2⌋
⌊α □ γ □ $\bar{\alpha}$□ $\bar{\gamma}$ * LH1 □LH2 □LH1 □LH2⌋
⌊α □γ □α □γ*RL1 □RL2 □RL1 □ RL2⌋
⌊α □γ □ $\bar{\alpha}$□ $\bar{\gamma}$*LL1 □LL2 □LL1 □LL2⌋

which is labeled as *Human Being*. The beginning of the scan is denoted by the symbol $\lfloor$ and the end of the scan by $\rfloor$.

The inference engine shown in figure 18.2.3.5.3 is a system of various normal algorithms combined using Markov's combination theorems.

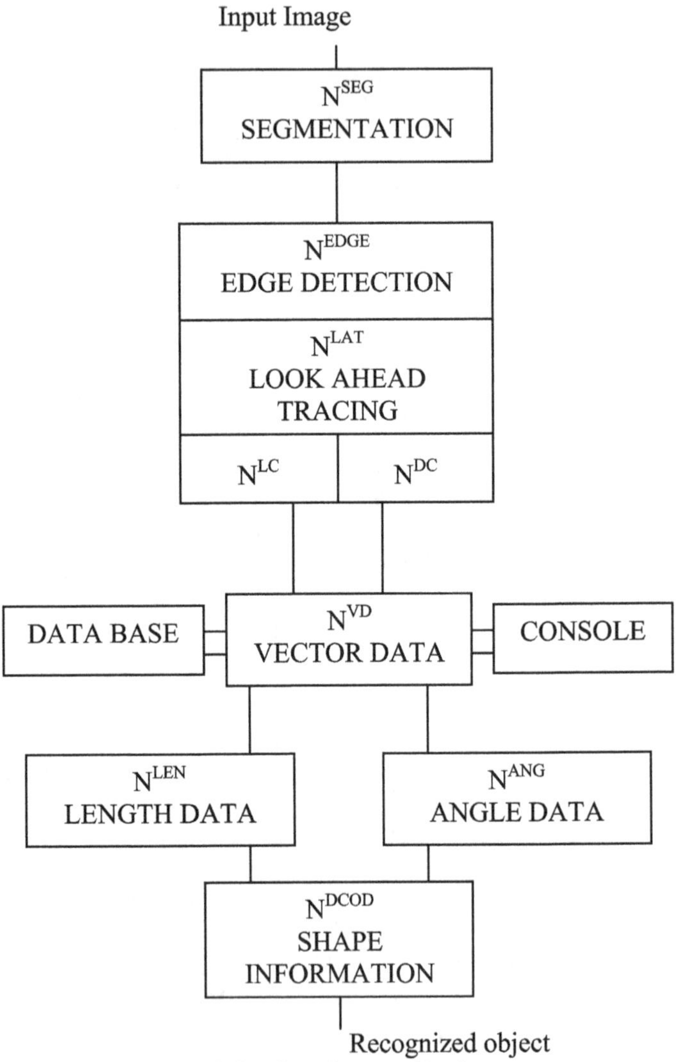

Figure 18.2.3.5.3: Inference Engine

With reference to figure 18.2.3.5.3, the acquired gray digital image is first segmented and then contoured. Then a LAT algorithm is employed to get the angle data and length data from the vector data. These two parts of the vector data are then compared with the ones stored in the database. If they match with the templates, then the shape information is decoded and then object is recognized.

As an example, an image of the contour map of India is shown in figure 18.2.3.5.4 together with the corresponding code. The map of India is not to scale and hence not precise in the form shown in figure 18.2.3.5.4.

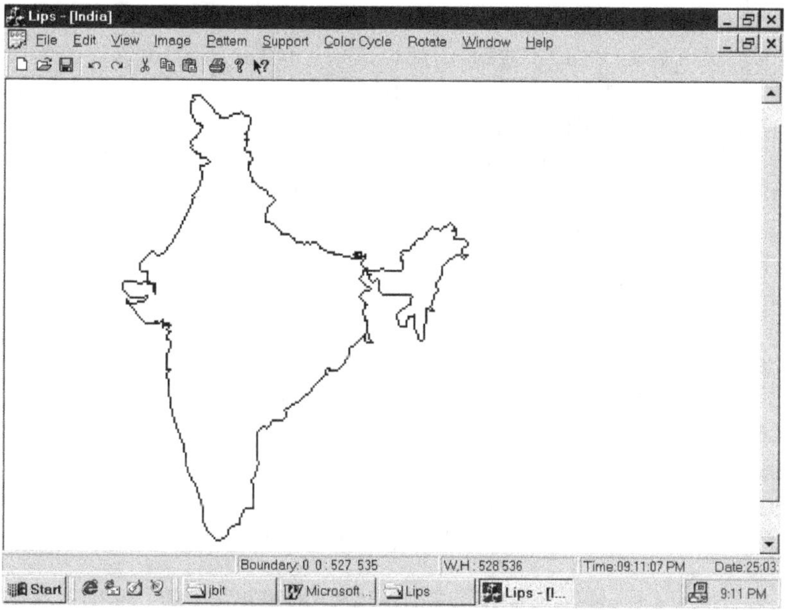

Figure 18.2.3.5.4: Contour map of India

The directional code obtained for INDIA map:

$\beta \square \alpha^3 \square \beta^7 \square \gamma \square \beta \square \alpha \square \beta \square \gamma \square \alpha^4 \square \ \bar{\delta} \square \alpha \square \ \bar{\delta} \square \alpha^3 \square \ \bar{\delta} \square \beta^2 \square \alpha^2 \square \beta \square$
$\gamma^3 \square \delta \square \gamma^2 \square \delta^2 \square \alpha \square \gamma^2 \square \delta \square \alpha^2 \square \delta \square \gamma^2 \square \delta \square \gamma \square \beta \square \alpha^2 \square \gamma^2 \square \beta \square \gamma \square \delta^2 \square$
$\alpha \square \beta^2 \square \alpha \square \gamma \square \delta \square \gamma^2 \square \beta \square \gamma^2 \square \beta \square \gamma^2 \square \alpha \square \beta^3 \square \alpha \square \beta \square \alpha \square \beta \square \gamma \square \beta \square$
$\alpha \square \beta^2 \square \delta^4 \square \gamma^2 \square \delta \square \gamma^4 \square \alpha^2 \square \beta \square \alpha \square \beta^4 \square \gamma \square \alpha^4 \square \beta^2 \square \alpha \square \gamma \square \beta \square \alpha^3 \square \beta$
$\square \ \bar{\delta} \square \alpha \square \beta \square \ \bar{\delta} \square \alpha^2 \square \beta^2 \square \gamma \square \alpha \square \beta \square \alpha \square \beta \square \alpha^3 \square \gamma \square \alpha^4 \square \beta \square \alpha^3 \square \beta \square$

$\alpha^5 \square\ \bar{\delta}^2 \square \gamma^2 \square\ \bar{\beta} \square\ \bar{\gamma}^4 \square\ \bar{\delta} \square \gamma^2 \square\ \bar{\delta} \square \alpha^3 \square \gamma^3 \square \beta \square \delta \square \gamma \square \beta^2 \square \alpha \square \beta \square \alpha^5$
$\square\ \bar{\delta} \square \alpha \square \beta \square \alpha^8 \square\ \bar{\delta} \square\ \bar{\gamma}^3 \square\ \bar{\beta} \square \alpha \square\ \bar{\beta} \square\ \gamma \square\ \bar{\delta} \square \beta \square\ \bar{\delta} \square \alpha^3 \square\ \bar{\delta} \square$
$\bar{\gamma} \square\ \bar{\delta} \square \alpha \square\ \bar{\gamma} \square\ \bar{\delta}^2 \square \alpha^2 \square\ \bar{\delta}^2 \square\ \bar{\gamma} \square\ \bar{\delta}^3 \square \beta \square \alpha^2 \square \beta \square\ \bar{\delta} \square \alpha \square\ \bar{\delta}^2 \square \beta^2$
$\square \gamma \square \delta \square \alpha \square\ \bar{\delta} \square \gamma^3 \square \delta \square \gamma \square \alpha^5 \square \beta^2 \square \gamma \square \delta \square\ \bar{\alpha} \square \delta \square \gamma^2 \square \beta \square \alpha^2 \square \delta^2 \square$
$\bar{\beta}^2 \square\ \bar{\alpha}^2 \square \delta^2 \square\ \bar{\alpha} \square \delta^4 \square \gamma^4 \square \delta \square \gamma \square \delta^2 \square \gamma^2 \square \beta \square \gamma \square \delta^2 \square \gamma^2 \square \delta \square \gamma^2 \square \delta \square$
$\beta^2 \square\ \bar{\alpha}^2 \square\ \bar{\beta} \square\ \bar{\alpha} \square \gamma^7 \square \delta \square \gamma^7 \square \delta \square\ \bar{\alpha} \square\ \bar{\beta} \square\ \bar{\gamma}^2 \square\ \bar{\beta} \square\ \bar{\gamma} \square\ \bar{\beta} \square\ \bar{\gamma}^7 \square$
$\square \delta \square\ \bar{\alpha}^2 \square \gamma \square \delta \square \gamma^3 \square \alpha^3 \square\ \bar{\beta} \square\ \bar{\gamma}^2 \square\ \bar{\beta} \square\ \bar{\gamma}^2 \square\ \bar{\delta}^3 \square \alpha \square\ \bar{\delta}^2 \square \alpha \square\ \bar{\gamma}^3$
$\square\ \bar{\delta} \square\ \bar{\beta} \square\ \bar{\alpha}^{14} \square\ \bar{\beta}^2 \square\ \bar{\gamma}^5 \square\ \bar{\beta} \square \delta^2 \square\ \bar{\beta}^2 \square\ \bar{\gamma} \square\ \bar{\delta} \square\ \bar{\alpha}^2 \square\ \bar{\gamma}^2 \square\ \bar{\alpha}^2 \square$
$\gamma^2 \square \delta^2 \square \beta^4 \square \alpha \square \beta \square \delta \square\ \bar{\alpha}^2 \square \delta^3 \square \beta^4 \square \alpha \square \gamma^2 \square \delta \square \gamma^2 \square \beta \square \gamma^2 \square \alpha \square \gamma^6 \square \beta$
$\square \gamma^2 \square \beta \square \delta \square \alpha^2 \square\ \bar{\beta} \delta \square\ \bar{\alpha} \square\ \bar{\beta} \square\ \bar{\gamma}^3 \square \delta^6 \square\ \bar{\alpha} \square \delta \square \gamma^4 \square \delta^2 \square \gamma \square\ \bar{\alpha}^4 \square$
$\bar{\gamma} \square\ \bar{\alpha} \square \delta \square \gamma \square \beta \square\ \bar{\alpha} \square \delta^7 \square \gamma \square \delta^2 \square\ \bar{\alpha} \square \delta^4 \square\ \bar{\alpha} \square \delta \square\ \bar{\alpha} \square \delta^2 \square\ \bar{\alpha} \square \delta$
$\square \beta \square \gamma^2 \square \delta^2 \square\ \bar{\alpha}^5 \square \delta \square \gamma \square \delta^2 \square\ \bar{\beta} \square\ \bar{\alpha} \square \delta^3 \square \gamma^{14} \beta \square \gamma \square \delta \square \gamma^2 \square \delta \square \gamma^2 \square$
$\delta^2 \square \gamma \square \beta \square \gamma^{12} \square\ \bar{\alpha}^4 \square \delta \square \gamma \square \delta \square \gamma \square \delta \square \gamma^3 \square\ \bar{\alpha}^2 \square \delta \square\ \bar{\alpha} \square \delta^2 \square \gamma^2 \square \delta^2 \square$
$\bar{\alpha} \square \delta \square\ \bar{\alpha}^2 \square\ \bar{\beta}^5 \square\ \bar{\gamma} \square\ \bar{\beta} \square\ \bar{\gamma} \square\ \bar{\beta} \square\ \bar{\gamma}^8 \square\ \bar{\beta} \square\ \bar{\gamma}^2 \square\ \bar{\beta} \square\ \bar{\gamma}^2 \square\ \bar{\beta} \square$
$\bar{\gamma}^2 \square\ \bar{\beta} \square\ \bar{\gamma} \square\ \bar{\beta}^2 \square\ \bar{\gamma} \square\ \bar{\beta} \square\ \bar{\gamma} \square\ \bar{\beta} \square\ \bar{\gamma}^2 \square\ \bar{\beta} \square\ \bar{\gamma}^6 \square\ \bar{\beta} \square\ \bar{\gamma}^4 \square\ \bar{\beta} \square$
$\bar{\gamma} \square\ \bar{\beta} \square\ \bar{\gamma}^2 \square\ \bar{\beta} \square\ \bar{\gamma} \square\ \bar{\beta} \square\ \bar{\gamma}^2 \square\ \bar{\beta} \square\ \bar{\gamma}^2 \square\ \bar{\beta} \square\ \bar{\gamma}^3 \square\ \bar{\beta} \square\ \bar{\gamma}^5 \square\ \bar{\beta} \square$
$\bar{\gamma}^8 \square\ \bar{\beta} \square\ \bar{\gamma}^2 \square\ \bar{\delta}^2 \square\ \bar{\alpha}^2 \square\ \bar{\gamma}^8 \square\ \bar{\delta} \square\ \bar{\gamma} \square\ \bar{\delta} \square\ \bar{\gamma}^3 \square\ \bar{\beta} \square\ \bar{\alpha} \square\ \bar{\gamma}^2 \square\ \bar{\delta}^2$
$\square\ \bar{\alpha} \square\ \bar{\beta} \square\ \bar{\delta}^2 \square\ \bar{\alpha}^2 \square\ \bar{\delta} \square\ \bar{\alpha}^2 \square \gamma \square \delta \square\ \bar{\gamma}^4 \square \delta^2 \square\ \bar{\alpha}^2 \square\ \bar{\delta} \square\ \alpha \square \delta \square$
$\bar{\alpha}^4 \square\ \bar{\beta}^5 \square\ \bar{\gamma} \square\ \bar{\beta}^4 \square\ \bar{\gamma} \square\ \bar{\beta} \square \gamma^2 \square \alpha^5 \square\ \bar{\delta} \square \alpha^3 \square\ \bar{\delta}^2 \square\ \bar{\gamma} \square\ \bar{\alpha} \square \delta \square\ \bar{\alpha}^7$
$\square\ \bar{\beta}^4 \square\ \bar{\gamma}^3 \square\ \bar{\delta}^2 \square\ \bar{\gamma} \square \alpha^6 \square \beta \square \alpha^2 \square\ \bar{\delta} \square \alpha^3 \square \gamma \square \alpha^3 \square \gamma^5 \square\ \bar{\beta} \square\ \bar{\gamma}^4 \square\ \bar{\alpha}^3$
$\square\ \bar{\beta} \square\ \bar{\delta} \square\ \bar{\gamma}^4 \square\ \bar{\alpha}^3 \square\ \bar{\beta} \square\ \bar{\gamma}^3 \square\ \bar{\delta} \square \alpha \square \beta^2 \square \alpha \square\ \bar{\delta} \square \alpha^3 \square\ \bar{\delta}^6 \square \alpha \square\ \bar{\delta}$
$\square \alpha \square\ \bar{\delta} \square\ \bar{\gamma} \square\ \bar{\delta} \square\ \bar{\gamma}^2 \square\ \bar{\delta} \square \alpha^2 \square\ \bar{\delta} \square\ \bar{\gamma}^2 \square\ \bar{\delta}^3 \square \alpha^2 \square\ \bar{\gamma} \square\ \bar{\beta} \square\ \bar{\delta} \square\ \bar{\gamma}$
$\square\ \bar{\beta} \square\ \bar{\gamma}^2 \square \alpha^2 \square\ \bar{\delta} \square \alpha \square\ \bar{\delta} \square\ \bar{\beta}^2 \square\ \bar{\alpha}^3 \square\ \bar{\gamma}^2 \square\ \bar{\alpha}^2 \square\ \bar{\gamma} \square\ \bar{\alpha} \square\ \bar{\beta}^3 \square\ \bar{\gamma}^7$
$\square\ \bar{\beta} \square\ \bar{\delta}^4 \square \alpha \square\ \bar{\delta} \square\ \bar{\gamma} \square\ \bar{\delta} \square\ \bar{\beta} \square\ \bar{\gamma} \square\ \bar{\beta} \square\ \bar{\alpha} \square\ \bar{\beta} \square\ \bar{\gamma} \square\ \bar{\alpha}^3 \square\ \bar{\gamma}^3 \square$
$\alpha \square\ \bar{\delta}^3 \square \alpha^3 \square\ \bar{\beta} \square \alpha^5 \square\ \bar{\delta} \square$

where α, β, γ, δ, $\bar{\alpha}$, $\bar{\beta}$, $\bar{\gamma}$, $\bar{\delta}$ are the basic direction codes.

Now the question of identifying a flying target in a combat space could be viewed as a process of identifying it to be the member of the W-class if a match is found.

The decision of identifying a target not only depends on the output of the inference engine but also on the outputs of other sensors and priority details labeled as $x_1, x_2, \ldots, x_n$. Figure 18.2.3.5.5 shows block diagram of a possible decision process.

After having studied certain basic concepts involved in pattern recognition and analysis, we now proceed to have a cursory look into various related areas of fundamental research and applications research, in the form of a tree diagram.

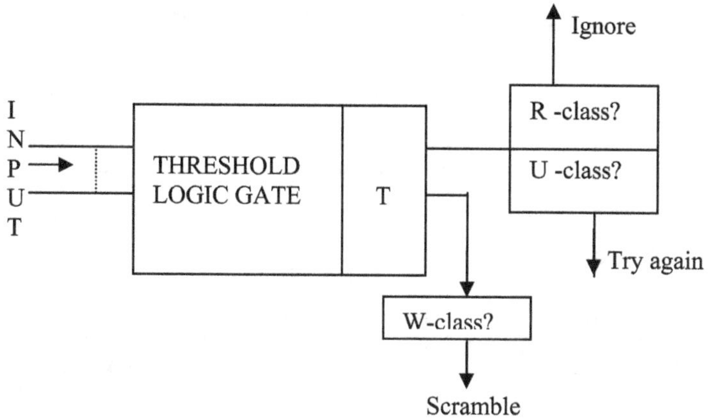

Figure 18.2.3.5.5: Decision process

Thus we have a basic idea of what is meant by pattern recognition and analysis. Most of the research carried out in this area makes use of digital images of different kinds, digitized map, remotely sensed images like satellite imageries and Synthetic Aperture Radar (SAR) imageries, to name a few.

Ground truth evaluation from remotely sensed data, feature extraction from medical imageries, security classification using biometric signals and images, target identification and tracking using optical and Infra Red (IR) imageries and a few other applications require high degree of pattern recognition and analysis capabilities.

Pattern recognition makes use of low, medium and high level computer vision techniques and to a great extent the state-of-the-art techniques of *Artificial Intelligence* (AI). In some mission critical decision making processes, the reliability, precision and speed of the pattern recognition procedures that are used are of paramount importance and special care is taken while designing and developing the relevant algorithms and procedures. Symbolic processing of signals and images seems to provide a rich repertoire of tools in such cases.

Figure 18.2.3.5.6 exhibits some of the research areas related to pattern recognition and analysis.

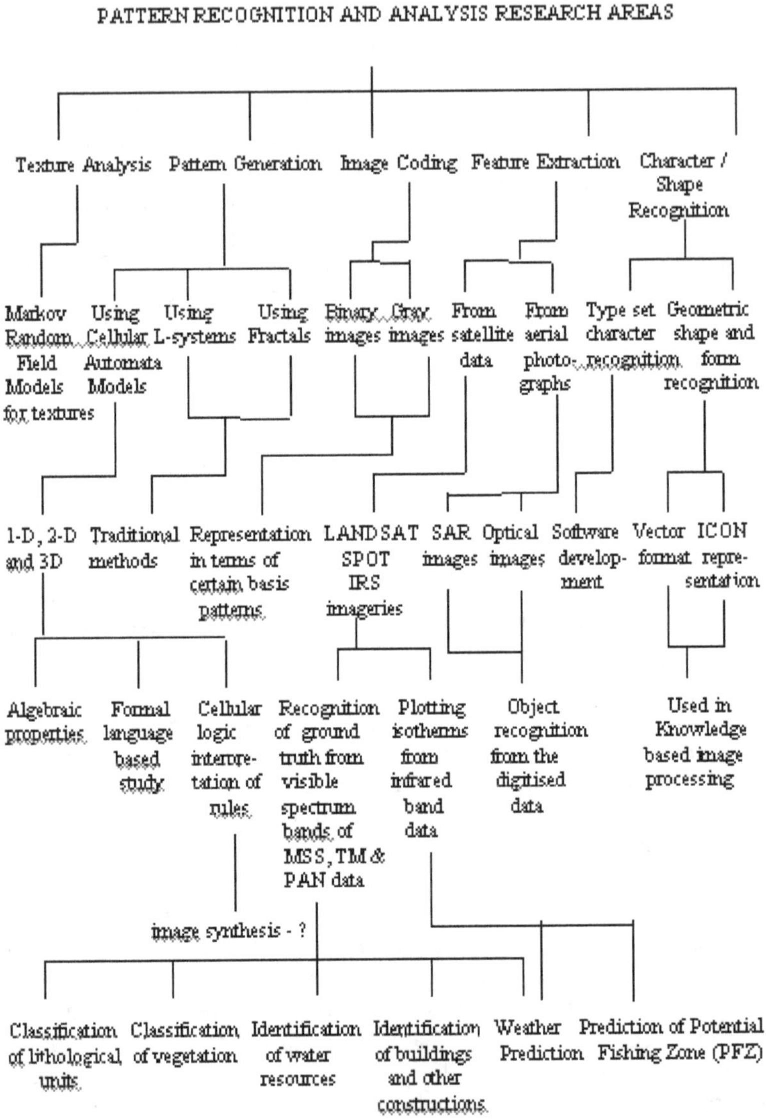

Figure 18.2.3.5.6: Research areas in pattern recognition and analysis

18.3 Modeling And Simulation

Modeling of real systems has been an age-old engineering practice. It is convenient to work on models instead of real systems or physical processes that are not conducive for empirical analysis. For example, subjecting a chemical plant to empirical analysis is not only expensive but also foolish and risky. Alternatively, a model of the plant could be analyzed easily with the help of simulation programs. But the analysis of a model of a system would be meaningful and useful only when the model is a valid model of the system. Consequently, model validation turns out to be an important part of any discipline where computer plays a primary role.

18.3.1 Systems, Models And Validation

A system consists of a number of components each of which functions by virtue of a rule that governs certain other components. On the other hand, a system whose components function independently of other components is called a Hausdorff system. Such systems cannot be modeled in any mathematical or logical framework. We are not concerned here with Hausdorff systems. Figure 18.3.1.1 symbolizes a system with certain measurable parameters $x_1, x_2, \ldots x_i, \ldots x_n$.

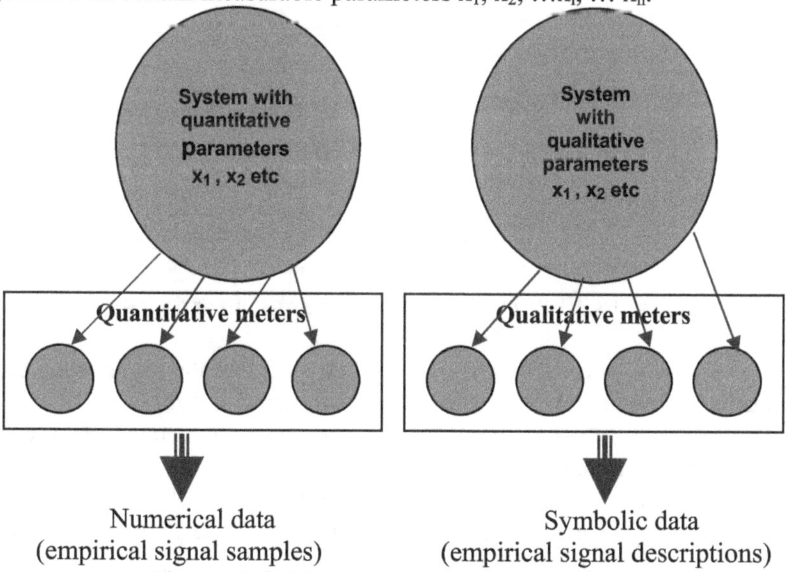

Figure 18.3.1.1: A real system symbolized

If a parameter variable takes on numerical values, then it is termed as a quantitative parameter. If it, on the other hand, takes on non-numerical descriptions or symbolic patterns, then it is called a qualitative parameter. For instance, physical parameters are quantitative whereas human feelings are qualitative parameters.

Model is a construct in an algebraic or a logical framework. It can be either an algebraic or a logical function or a *well formed formula* (wff) in a logical calculus or a formal mathematical structure like a group or a ring or a field or a relational structure like a lattice. Figure 18.3.1.2 shows a functional description of a system and its model.

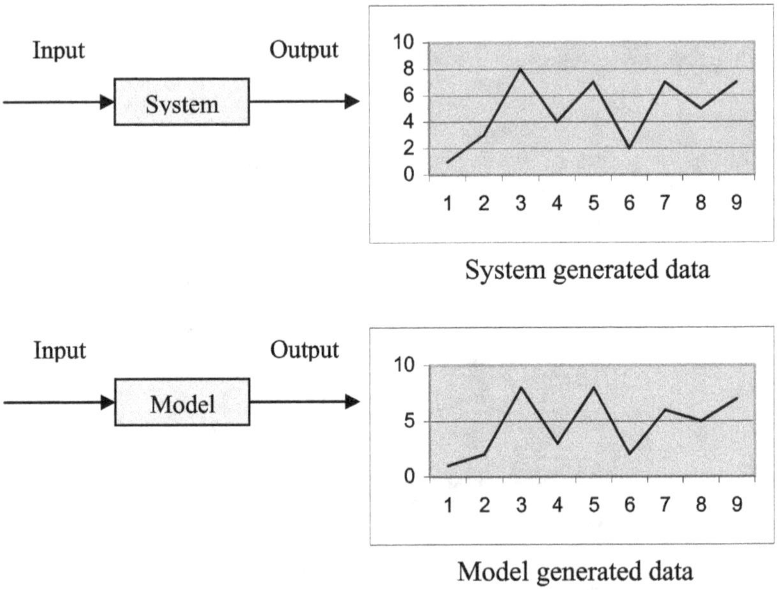

Figure 18.3.1.2: Data generated by a system and its model

It can be observed from figure 18.3.1.2 that the model generated data is approximately equal to the system generated data. So now, the process of checking to what extent the model generated data is in accordance with the system generated data is called validation. The type of validation process depends on the type of model that is used to simulate a system. Simulation is carried out by means of computer programs.

Models are of three types: (i) replicative models, (ii) predictive models and (iii) structural models. Let us have a brief study of these types.

Replicative models

Let us consider a system consisting of a resistor of R ohms. This system is empirically studied by applying varied voltages across the resistor and by measuring the resulting currents. The values are tabulated as system generated data and subsequently viewed in the form of a graph, which exhibits the input-output characteristics of the system.

Figure 18.3.1.3 shows one such empirical setup, data and a graphical representation of the data.

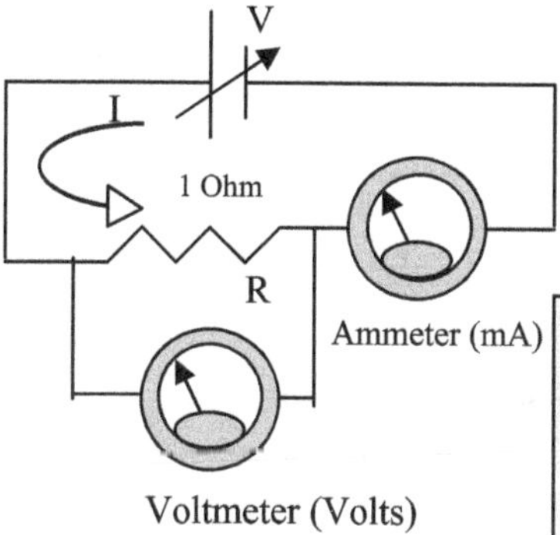

1	2	3	4	5	6	7	8	9	10	11	12
I	2	3	4	5	6	7	8	9	10	11	12

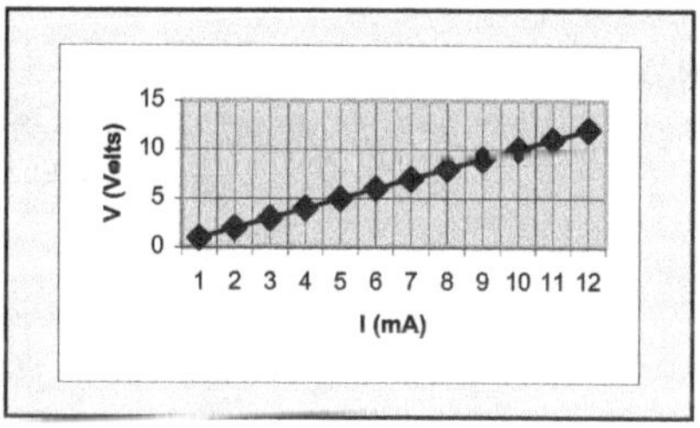

The governing equation is V = RI. So, the best fit is a linear equation y = mx, where m is the slope.

Figure 18.3.1.3: Empirical setup of a system and its model derivation

Such models which are exclusively derived from system generated data are called replicative models.

Predictive models

It is not always possible to derive replicative models for studying complex systems and physical processes. For example, systems like a chemical plant, human brain, tornado, flash flood, war theater are not conducive for replicative modeling. Alternatively, one would prefer to fit a model for a complex system based on probabilistic estimation about the performance of the system and on some stray data available about the system. Such a model is termed as a predictive model. For example, let us consider the case of unidirectional modeling fluid flow. Fluid mechanics is a very complex operation and traditionally the fluid flow is studied using Navier-Stokes equation which in turn is derived from continuity equation. Section 20 provides a detailed study on the predictive modeling of fluid flow using Geometric Filters. Figure 18.3.1.4 shows a predictive model of a unidirectional fluid flow using a one dimensional three neighborhood binary valued cellular automaton.

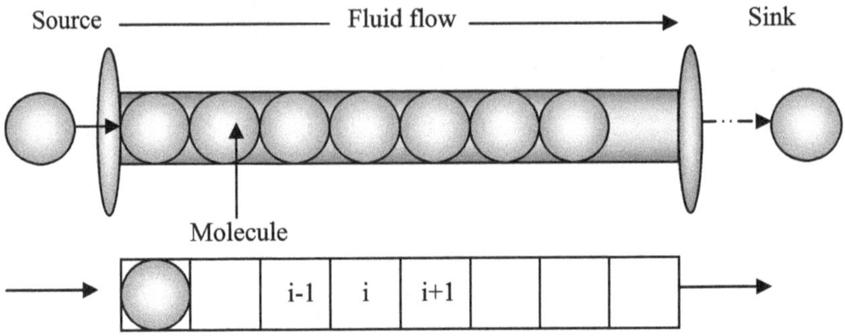

Figure 18.3.1.4: Cellular automata modeling of fluid flow

Assumptions:

- Molecules are perfectly elastic models
- The abstract fluid container is modeled as a linear array of cells
- Each cell will contain just one molecule only
- The first cell (source side) contains a molecule always.
- The last cell (sink side) contains no molecule at any instant.
- A molecule in a cell repels another molecule in adjacent cell.
- Presence of a molecule in a cell is denoted as 1 and its absence as 0.

Based on these assumptions, the unidirectional fluid flow could be modeled as a one dimensional three neighborhood binary valued cellular automaton with the updating rule 10010010. The decimal equivalent of this rule is 146. The rule is shown below in figure 18.3.1.5 both in diagrammatic form and production form. More details about this model are given in section 20.

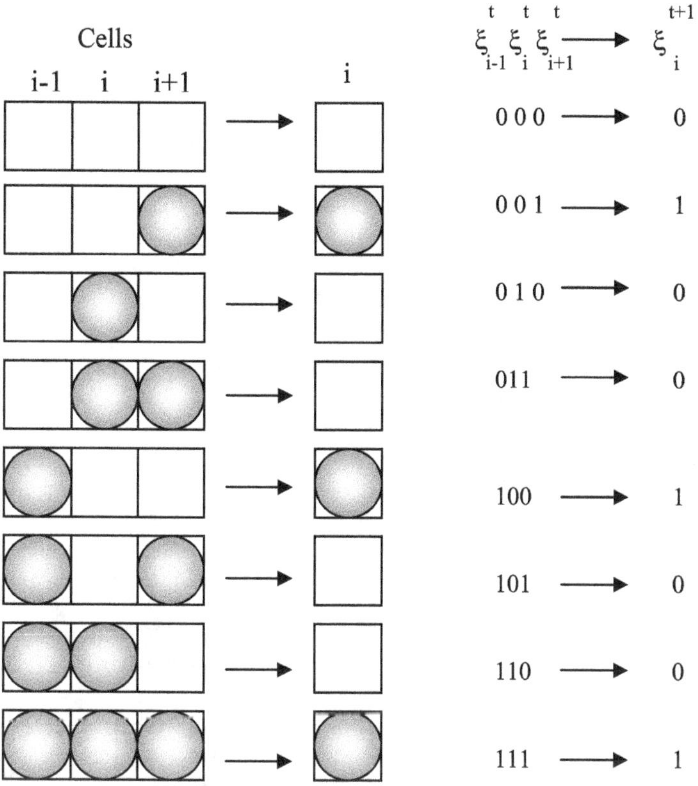

Figure 18.3.1.5: Updating rule for the fluid flow model using cellular automaton

Structural models

Structural models are developed in formal mathematical or relational structures. The basic principle that is mentioned right in the beginning of section 1 is invoked here as the fundamental requirement for developing effective structural models. The principle states that the models of physical sources from which signals originate and the systems that process such signals should belong to the same class or a structure. For example, signals are languages from a free monoid and systems are finite state machines defined by M-grammar.

Figure 18.3.1.6 presents some research areas related to modeling and simulation.

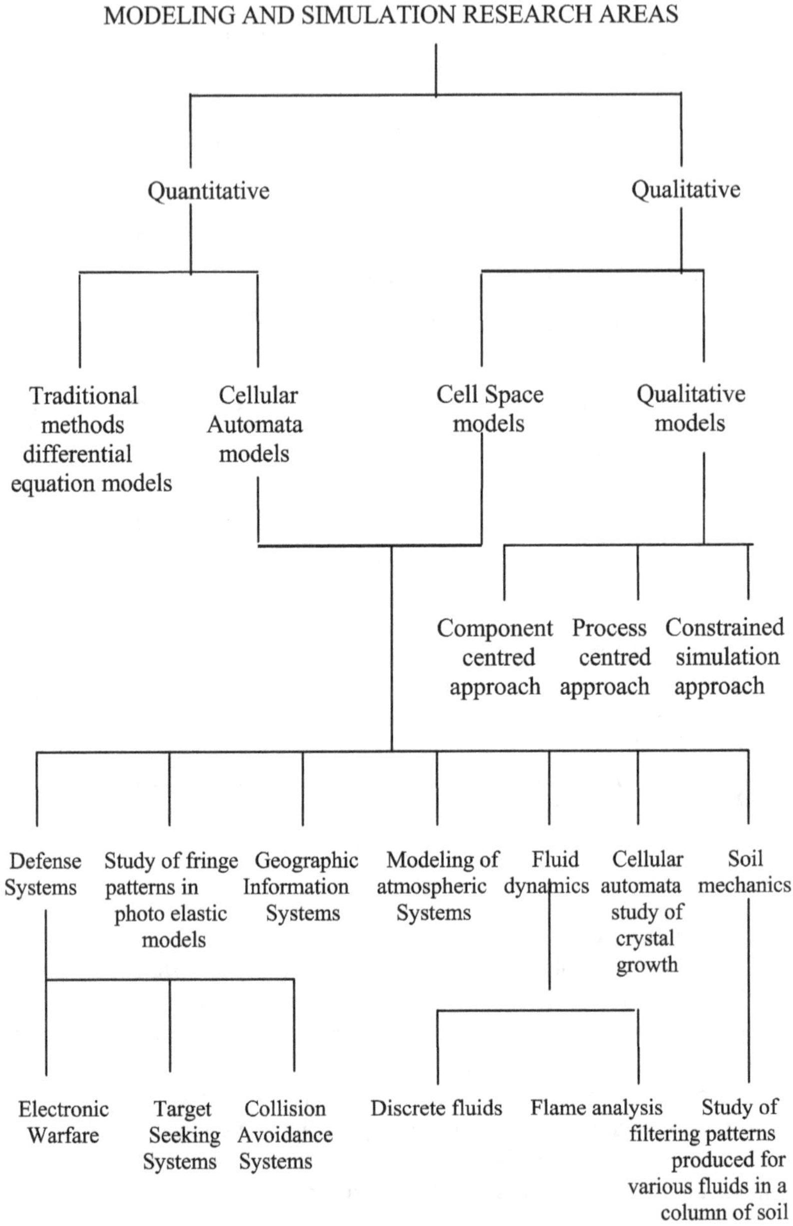

Figure 18.3.1.6: Research areas in modeling and simulation

Section 19

Thinning Lattice Gas Automaton Model For Solidification Process

Abstract

In this section, we discuss the theory of solidification process as the evolution of a thinning lattice gas automaton. This automaton is essentially a cellular automaton which implements the thinning operation of digital images corresponding to objects of different size morphologies. Moving isotherms in a solidification process in an object is considered here as the shrinking boundaries of the object. The shrinking process is modeled as an evolving cellular automaton, which carries out the recursive thinning of the corresponding digital image.

19.1 Introduction

Given a solidifying material, it is assumed here that one can obtain a digital image model of it. The central idea on which the material discussed in this section rests is that the shrinking boundaries of a digital image model correspond to the moving isotherms of the solidifying material. To be more precise, the solidification process of a material is modeled here as a 2-D cellular automaton consisting of a rectangular lattice of sites together with an updating rule given by the following pseudo code:

{The given digital image is scanned by a nine neighborhood empty window; on each move, the sub image covered by the window is examined to see whether the gray distance, say D, that is, the difference between the maximum and the minimum gray values corresponding to that sub image, is less than or equal to a threshold value T; if D is less than or equal to T then the central pixel is retained and the boundary pixels are assigned the value 0; otherwise, the original value of the central pixel is removed; this procedure is continued till the entire image is scanned }

E. G. Rajan, *Symbolic Computing - Signal and Image Processing*
ISBN 81-7800-047-4

The overall effect is that the boundaries of various regions in the given image that appear to be uniform are removed and their interior pixels kept intact, thus giving us the contour removed version of the image. The contour removal should be continued till no further contour is detected. We call this operation as *iterated thinning*, because the updating rule is independent of initial configuration and the number of evolutions. Iterated thinning does not account for losses due to radiation and convection during the solidification process, and so it is not an ideal model. In order to obtain a near ideal model for solidification process, we introduce in this section the concept of a *lattice gas automaton,* which implements *recursive thinning.* The updating rule of this automaton changes evolution by evolution and it depends on the current configuration and the evolution number.

The significance of this technique is that metals in the molten form do not form any lattice arrangement and they form regular lattice structures after solidification, the solidification process being viewed as a neighborhood dependent evolutionary process of forming geometrically viable macro lattices from geometrically not viable micro lattices.

19.2 Solidification Process

The process of solidification mainly includes two heat transfer processes (i) conduction and (ii) radiation. Heat transfer from one molecule to the other inside the liquid metal is carried out by conduction process and that from the surface of the molten metal to external atmosphere by radiation. Numerical methods like Chvorinov's method are generally used to solve such conduction problems. When the heat in the core of the molten metal is conducted out, nuclei will be formed and crystallization will start around them. This growth will continue till the solidification is complete. Nucleation is of two kinds (i) homogeneous and (ii) heterogeneous. The liquid under equilibrium condition would contain a cluster of atoms, some of which would have structures of the corresponding solids. Below a critical size, the clusters of atoms or embryos are not stable. Either the liquid at a particular temperature will nucleate or it will remain in a meta stable equilibrium depending on the relationship between the size of the largest cluster it contains and the critical size. Once a nucleus is formed in super cooled liquid metal, its growth rate will be large and it will be limited by the rate at which the latent heat of solidification is removed from the growing liquid-solid interface. Alternatively, the heterogeneous nucleation is achieved by forming the nucleus of critical size with the help of certain nucleation agents called *nucleants* (solid particles) suspended in the liquid. Crystallographic structures of a nucleant plays an important role in the process of nucleation and subsequent crystal growth. In practice, especially in the case of solidification of metal alloys, a complex type of nucleation of both homogeneous and heterogeneous kinds takes place.

A crystal is a regular assembly of atoms occupying definite positions in the crystal lattice. The actual position of an atom cannot be precisely determined because it undergoes thermal vibrations and imparts kinetic energy to its neighboring ones. So the mean position of an atom could only be approximately evaluated when it vibrates with a minimum energy and is balanced by electrostatic forces exerted by its neighboring atoms. During heating, the thermal vibrations increase, the ordered structure collapses, clusters of ordered structures form for a short duration and they dissociate fast, and then the solid turns out to be liquid. On the contrary, during solidification, the short duration clusters do not act as nuclei for subsequent growth, and so, the tools and concepts that are used for the study of melting processes cannot be used for studying the inverse process of solidification.

A number of solidification models have been proposed so far of which Bernal's model is now considered as the most suitable one. Yet the mathematics of statistical geometry of the heap arrangement in a solidifying metal, as advocated by Bernal's model needs further development and so is incomplete. It is in this situation that one can explore the possible use of the concepts of cellular automata for modeling solidification process.

A cellular automaton, also known as *lattice gas automaton,* evolves in discrete time steps with the values of the variable at a site being affected by the values of the variables at certain sites in its neighborhood. By neighborhood of a site we mean the site itself together with some of its adjacent sites. The sites (cells) may be arranged in the form of a rectangular lattice or of a hexagonal lattice. The site values corresponding to a configuration (array of cell values) at a particular time step, say t, are updated, all at once, based on the values in their neighborhood, according to a definite set of updating rules. The resulting configuration at time step t+1 is the evolved version of the one at time step t.

19.3 Lattice Gas Solidification Models

As outlined earlier, moving isotherms (liquid-solid interface) in a solidifying metal could be modeled as shrinking boundaries of the corresponding digital gray image. As per this iterated thinning model, the shrinking boundaries of isotherms inside the solidifying material will not take into account various losses due to radiation and convection. In reality this is not true. Hence a correction factor is introduced in the thinning algorithm as shown in the following pseudo code.

{The given digital image is scanned by a nine neighborhood empty window; on each move, the sub image covered by the window is examined to see whether the gray distance, say D, that is the difference between the maximum and the minimum gray values corresponding to that sub image, is less than or equal to a threshold value T; if D is less than or equal to T then the central pixel is retained and the boundary pixels are assigned the value 0; else, based on the evolution number, the corner pixel together with an increasing order of its adjacent pixels are removed;} this procedure is continued till the entire image is scanned.

This operation is called *recursive thinning* because the updating rule does depends on the initial configuration and evolution number. Recursive thinning simulates solidification processes where losses due to radiation and convection are taken into account. As an extension to this concept, one can use the 27-neighborhood structure, as shown in figure 19.3.1 for realizing 3-D recursive thinning model for solidification processes.

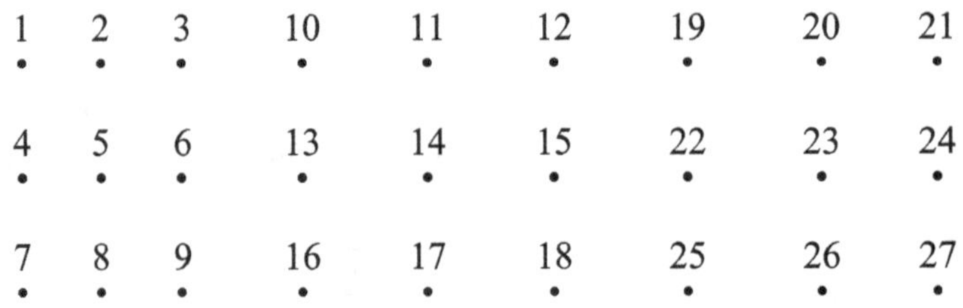

Figure 19.3.1: 21-neighborhood structure P

Hexagonal lattice gas automata are better suited for modeling highly complex nonlinear systems like fluid flow and solidification processes because they exhibit better rotational symmetry when compared to rectangular lattice gas automata. The input configuration would then be a hexagonal array of pixels each being addressed not by a row and a column numbers but by a row and a zigzag. The recursive thinning algorithm could be used to determine the moving boundaries in a given hexagonal digital image but with the help of a 2-D seven-neighborhood structure.

Alternatively, one may prefer to view a solidification process as a 3-D hexagonal prism cellular automaton. With reference to figure 19.3.1, one can easily verify that there are 25 basis prism neighborhood structures, which are listed in table 1. Figure 19.3.1 actually shows the 21-neighborhood structure P with the nodes numbered in a suitable manner and figure 19.3.2 shows a basis prism structures with 90° twist when viewed from the first plane to the third plane.

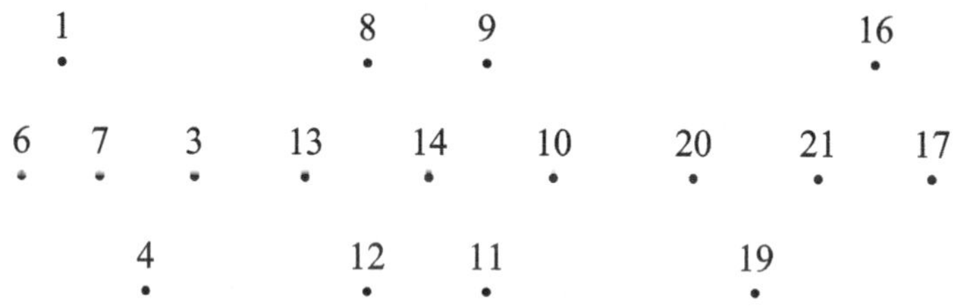

Figure 19.3.2: Basis prism structure with 90° twist

One can use any of the 25 prism structures as a neighborhood structure for the thinning hexagonal 3-D lattice gas automaton to simulate a solidification process. The automata with 0° twist neighborhood structures will simulate regular crystalline structures after solidification, where as, the automata with twisted neighborhood structures will simulate *dendritic* growth and other twisted patterns after solidification. In any case the simulation is simple. A thinning hexagonal 3-D lattice gas automaton will thin the corresponding image exhibiting the isotherms as it evolves.

Table 19.3.1 shows the list of 25 basis patterns that are constructed in the 21-neighborhood hexagonal structure.

Table 19.3.1: Basis prism neighborhood structures

Sl.No.	Prism	Remarks
1	$P_{1,4,15,18}$	
2	$P_{1,4,16,19}$	
3	$P_{1,4,17,20}$	
4	$P_{2,5,15,18}$	4 corners removed
5	$P_{2,5,16,19}$	
6	$P_{2,5,17,20}$	
7	$P_{3,6,15,18}$	
8	$P_{3,6,16,19}$	
9	$P_{3,6,17,20}$	
10	$P_{1,4,15,17,19}$	
11	$P_{1,4,15,18,20}$	
12	$P_{2,5,15,17,19}$	
13	$P_{2,5,16,18,20}$	
14	$P_{3,6,15,17,19}$	
15	$P_{3,6,16,18,20}$	
16	$P_{1,3,5,15,18}$	5 corners removed
17	$P_{1,3,5,16,19}$	
18	$P_{1,3,5,17,20}$	
19	$P_{2,4,6,15,18}$	
20	$P_{2,4,6,16,19}$	
21	$P_{2,4,6,17,20}$	
22	$P_{1,3,5,15,17,19}$	
23	$P_{1,3,5,16,18,20}$	
24	$P_{2,4,6,15,17,19}$	6 corners removed
25	$P_{2,4,6,16,18,20}$	

Molten metals do not form any lattice arrangement and they form regular lattice structures after solidification, the solidification process being viewed as a neighborhood dependent evolutionary process of forming viable macro lattices from geometrically not viable micro lattices. Crystallization like solidification could be ideally modeled using growing binary valued cellular automata.

Highlight

Iterated thinning lattice gas automata are ideal models of solidification processes where losses due to radiation and convection are not considered. On the other hand, recursive thinning lattice gas automata are ideal models of solidification processes where losses due to radiation and convection are considered.

Section 20

Cellular Automata Modeling Of Unidirectional Fluid Flow

Abstract

This section is concerned with the study of discretization of fluids and their flow using lattice gas automata. The basic concepts of Geometric Filters and Cellular Automata play a major role in this study. Fluid dynamics is essentially filled with examples of collective behavior – shocks, instabilities, vortices, vortex streets, vortex sheets, turbulence, to name a few. In this section, an attempt has been made to describe non-equilibrium fluid dynamics by modeling it with simple cellular automata, which contain in them iterative mechanisms for developing collective motion. These cellular automata are idealized models constructed in appropriate geometries and they function as per certain updating rules that describe fluid behavior. This approach to model fluid dynamics is quite drastic and different from conventional techniques like partial differential equation models, and so it is naive in its presentation.

20.1 Introduction

The 3-D fluid flow volume is traditionally modeled as a cube with one face through which fluid enters and the opposite face through which it leaves the unit cube. The traditional generalized continuity equation derived using this model is

$$\frac{\partial \rho}{\partial t} + \frac{\partial (\rho\, u)}{\partial x} + \frac{\partial (\rho\, v)}{\partial v} + \frac{\partial (\rho\, w)}{\partial z} = 0$$

which reduces to

$$\frac{\partial u}{\partial x} + \frac{\partial v}{\partial y} + \frac{\partial w}{\partial z} = 0$$

E. G. Rajan, *Symbolic Computing - Signal and Image Processing*
ISBN 81-7800-047-4

for the steady flow of incompressible fluids. The point which we wish to bring out here is that this continuity equation works as an ideal model for the unidirectional unguided steady flow of fluids. But in practice, we come across cases of guided unsteady flows only. Let us consider a guided flow of fluid inside a tube of very large radius r and length ℓ. The mechanics of fluid flow inside this tube will not be consistent for the entire cross section of the tube. In fact, the velocity profile of the fluid flow at a particular cross section of the tube will be of the form of a paraboloid and not of the planar form. This is due to frictional forces influenced by the boundaries of the tube. Consequently, considering the entire guided fluid as a single flow field model and solving flow problems will not yield correct results.

It is in this situation that a different approach has been tried to model guided flows and certain observations reported in this section. First, the flow volume is geometrically divided into concentric tubes of flow fields. Each flow field is modeled by a specific geometry defined by a geometric filter and continuity equation computed. The set of such continuity equations could then be solved using traditional techniques in order to study the fluid dynamics.

This section proposes the techniques of modeling fluid flow in terms of geometric filter components and of solving related problems with the help of simple combinatorial updating rules of certain cellular automata. 3-D cube lattice gas automata and 3-D hexagonal prism lattice gas automata play important roles in solving such problems.

20.2 123CA Model For Fluid Flow

Rectangular gas automata are basically cellular automata that evolve in digital spatial domains. The spatial domain is not restricted to rectangular lattice alone. For example, hexagonal lattice and the Face-Centred-Hyper-Cube (FCHC) lattice are also admissible spatial domains for the gas automata to evolve. The term 123CA refers to 1-D binary valued three neighborhood cellular automaton. First, let us assume a unidirectional fluid flow from a source to a sink as shown in figure 20.2.1. A tube connecting the source and the sink is assumed to be a hypothetical guide for the fluid motion.

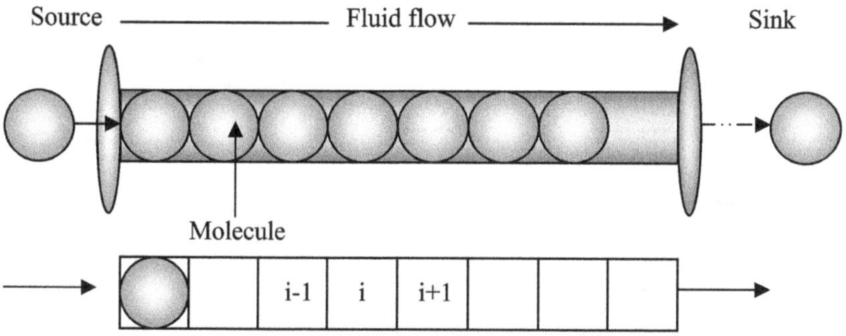

Figure 20.2.1 123CA model for a unidirectional flow

The tube is divided into cells as shown in the above figure. Each cell is assumed to hold one molecule or in other words, one unit volume of an incompressible fluid. Each cell is assigned with a state variable ξ which is binary valued. The presence of a molecule in a cell i is denoted by $\xi_i = 1$ and the absence by a 0. Let us also assume that a molecule in a cell is physically affected by the ones in the cells that are immediate left and right neighbors to it. At a particular instant of time, the configuration of this automaton refers to the positions of molecules or unit volumes in the fluid flow. Their positions would change at successive instants of time and these changes only decides the nature of fluid flow under consideration. Based on these assumptions, the unidirectional fluid flow could be modeled as a one dimensional three neighborhood binary valued cellular automaton with the updating rule 10010010. The decimal equivalent of this rule is 146. The rule is shown below in table 20.2.1 and in figure 20.2.2 both in diagrammatic form and production form.

Table 20.2.1 Fluid flow rule

$\xi^{(t)}_{i-1}$	$\xi^{(t)}_{i}$	$\xi^{(t)}_{i+1}$	$\xi^{(t+1)}_{i}$	Remarks
0	0	0	0	Empty neighborhood
0	0	1	1	Backward motion
0	1	0	0	Unstable position
0	1	1	0	Repelled to left
1	0	0	1	Forward motion
1	0	1	0	Limbo state
1	1	0	0	Repelled to right
1	1	1	1	Compact state

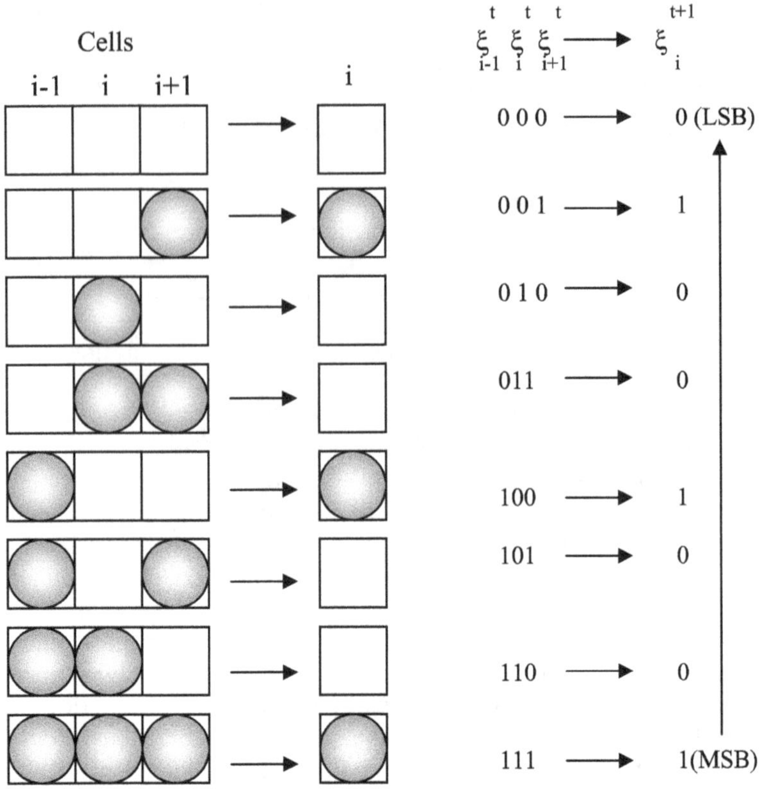

Figure 20.2.2: Updating rule for the fluid flow model using 123CA

The argument follows:

When a molecule is flanked by two other molecules then a compact condition prevails. When a molecule is flanked on both sides by empty cells, then an unstable condition prevails and so there is every possibility that it moves to its right or to its left. Here we rule out the third possibility of the molecule remaining in the same cell due to the assumption that molecules are perfectly elastic bodies and they are in constant motion. When a molecule is flanked by a molecule on one side and by an empty cell on the other side, then it moves to the empty cell. When an empty cell is flanked on both sides by two molecules, then the system is in a limbo state. That is, the empty cell remains to be empty in the next instant of time also. Lastly, when an empty cell is flanked on both sides by empty cells only, then it remains to be empty in the next instant of time. This argument is coded in the form of an updating rule $\xi^{(t)}_{i+1} = \phi(\xi^{(t)}_{i-1}, \xi^{(t)}_{i}, \xi^{(t)}_{i+1})$ which is given as the binary string 10010010 in the second column of the table 20.2.1. This 8-bit word corresponds to the decimal number 146. This rule is expressed as the Linear Boolean Function (LBF):

$$\xi^{(t+1)}_{i} = (\xi^{(t)}_{i-1}\overline{\xi^{(t)}_{i}}\,\overline{\xi^{(t)}_{i+1}}) + (\overline{\xi^{(t)}_{i-1}}\,\overline{\xi^{(t)}_{i}}\,\xi^{(t)}_{i+1}) + (\xi^{(t)}_{i-1}\xi^{(t)}_{i}\xi^{t)}_{i+1})$$

Consequently, 1-D unidirectional fluid flow could be simulated using this simple 123CA model. This model takes into account conservation laws of mass and momentum but not of energy. Next, we proceed with the study of 3-D unidirectional guided fluid flow as *Geometric Filter Models* (GFM) defined over rectangular and hexagonal lattices and their implementation by the respective lattice gas automata.

20.3 Geometric Filters Revisited

Let us consider a 3x3 array of cells over a 2-D rectangular lattice as shown in figure 20.3.1.

1	2	3
4	5	6
7	8	9

Figure 20.3.1: 3x3 rectangular array of cells

There are 16 convex polygons in this array as shown in figure 20.3.2.

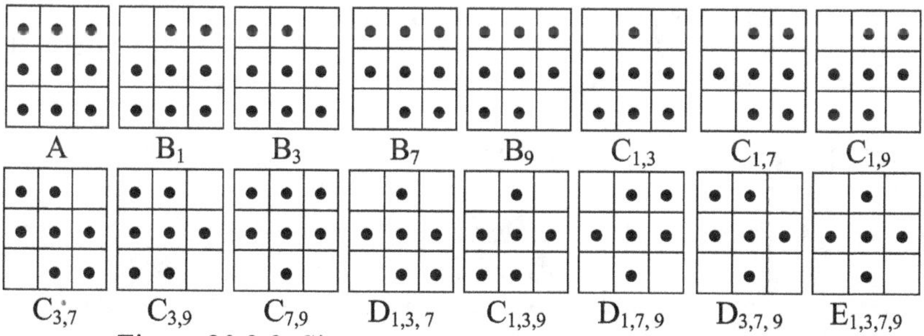

Figure 20.3.2: Sixteen convex patterns in a 3 x 3 matrix

In the same manner, one can construct 256 convex polyhedrons in a 3x3x3 array of cells over a 3-D rectangular lattice. They are classified under nine groups A, B, C, D, E, F, G, H and I. The 3-D polyhedrons A and $I_{1,3,7,9,19,21,25,27.}$ are shown in figure 20.3.3.

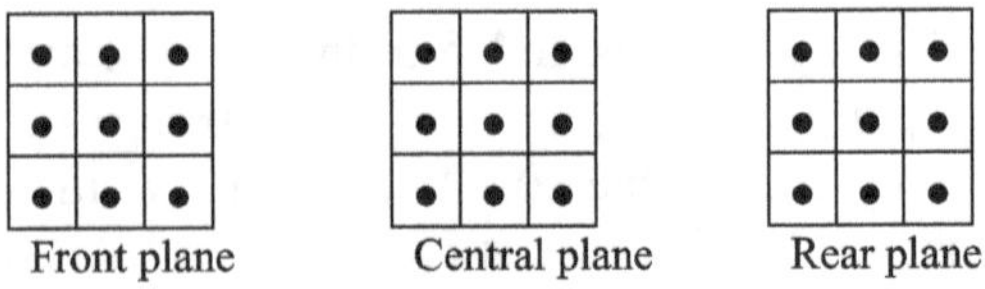

3-D Polyhedron A

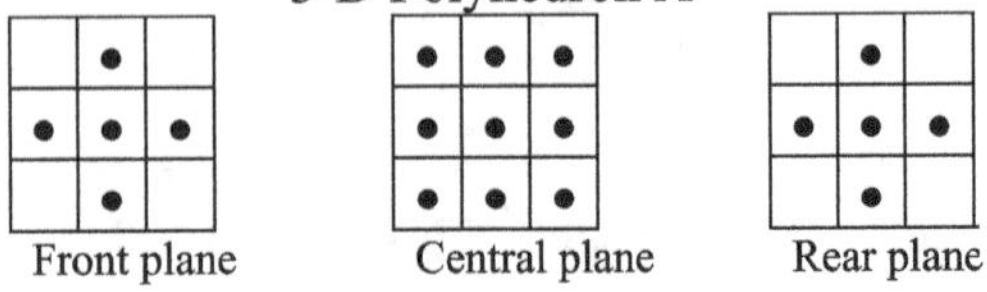

3-D Polyhedron $I_{1, 3, 7, 9, 19, 21, 25, 27}$

Figure 20.3.3: 3-D polyhedron in 3x3x3 cubic array

Let X_2 be the set of all 2-D polygons and X_3 be the set of all 3-D polyhedrons. Then the power set $\mathcal{X}_2$ or X_2 consists of a convex null and $2^{16}-1$ sets of convex polygons. Similarly, the power set $\mathcal{X}_3$ or X_3 consists of a convex null and $2^{256}-1$ sets of polyhedrons. A convex null is an empty set consisting of no polygons or polyhedrons.

Definition 20.3.1

Geometric filter (G-filter) is a subset of the power set $\mathcal{X}_2$ (or $\mathcal{X}_3$) satisfying the following conditions: (i) the filter set should not contain a convex null and (ii) every element in the filter set should ensure the presence of all of its super sets.

For example, the set $F = \{\{A, B_1, B_3, B_7, B_9, C_{1,3}, C_{1,7}, C_{1,9}, C_{3,7}, C_{3,9}, C_{7,9}, D_{1,3,7}, D_{1,3,9}, D_{1,7,9}, D_{3,7,9}, E_{1,3,7,9}\}\}$ is a G-filter defined over the set X_2.

Definition 20.3.2

A geometric filter of evolution type (GE-filter) is a set of polygons (polyhedrons) satisfying the following conditions: (i) the set should not contain a convex null, that is a polygon (polyhedron) consisting of unacceptable geometry or cell values and (ii) every polygon (polyhedron) in the set should ensure the presence of all of its proper envelopes. An envelope of a polygon (polyhedron) is also a polygon (polyhedron) that contains it. Every polygon (polyhedron) is an envelope of itself. If a polygon (polyhedron) has an envelope with more number of corners, then the envelope is said to be proper.

For example the set F = {A, B_1, B_7, $C_{1, 7}$} is a GE-filter defined over the set X_2. Geometric filters are defined over hexagonal lattices also. One can construct 18 polygons over a 7-cell hexagonal arrangement. The above concept could be extended to 3-D hexagonal prismatic lattice also.

20.4 Geometric Filter Model Of 3-D fluid flow

Let us consider a guided flow of fluid inside a tube of radius r and length ℓ. The fluid flow is geometrically divided into 9 concentric tubes of flow as shown in figure 20.4.1.

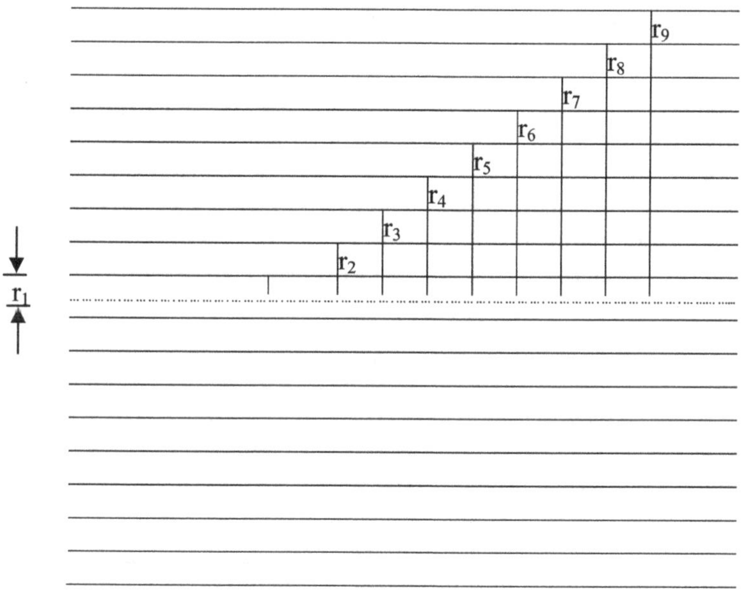

Figure 20.4.1: Flow filed diagram of 3-D rectangular lattice gas automata model

The central flow field has a volume of $2\pi r_1 \ell$. The second flow field has a volume of $2\pi(r_2 - r_1)\ell$ and so on. Now, instead of using a cube model for the entire fluid flow, each flow filed is modeled as a polyhedron from X_2. For example, the central flow field is modeled as A consisting of 27 cells, the second flow field as B_1 consisting of 26 cells, such that the outer most flow field is modeled as a polyhedron with 19 cells, that is $I_{1,3,7,9,19,21,25,27}$. It is obvious from geometrical considerations, that a normal to a cut surface indicates the friction force acting on the central cell. So, $I_{1,3,7,9,19,21,25,27}$ suffers maximum frictional forces and A suffers the least. It is clear from this argument that the proposed modeling technique is suitable for solving problems related to guided fluid flow.

A fluid flow is nothing but a join of nine flow fields, the flow being controlled by a geometric filter of evolution type. There are 40320 types of fluid flow when modeled as 3-D rectangular lattice gas automata. 3-D rectangular lattice gas automata modeling of discrete fluid flow bears a similarity with traditional techniques. In spite of its computational ease and precision, this model does not yield ideal results because of the absence of rotational symmetry in its geometry. On the other hand, a cylindrical modeling of fluid flow would certainly be the best technique for analyzing fluid problems. But this would be non-constructive.

So, we propose 3-D hexagonal prism lattice gas automata models for this purpose. The central idea behind this technique is that the 3-D fluid volume is modeled as a hexagonal prism with one face through which the fluid enters and the opposite face through which it leaves the prism. Now, the guided flow of fluid in a tube is geometrically divided into, say, seven concentric tubes of flow as shown in figure 20.4.2.

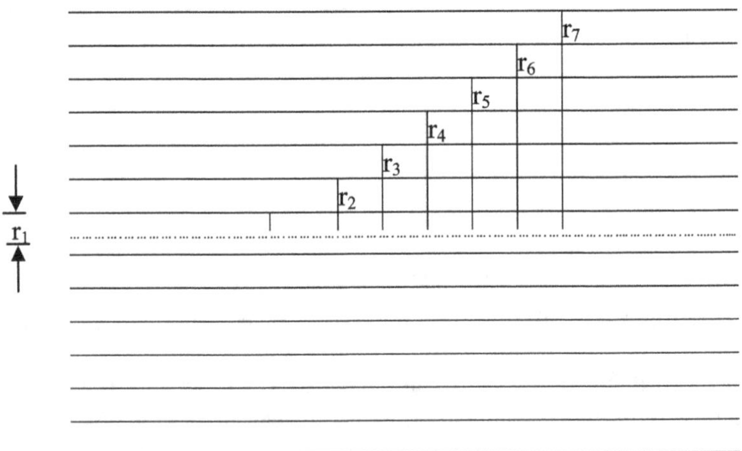

Figure 20.4.2: Flow field diagram of 3-D hexagonal lattice gas automata model

There are 4536 types of fluid flow when modeled as 3-D hexagonal lattice gas automata.

Highlight Of the Section

In this section, an attempt has been made to describe nonequilibrium fluid dynamics by modeling it with simple cellular automata which contain in them iterative mechanisms for developing collective motion. The concept of geometric filters has been used to explain the macro dynamics of fluid flow in a large guide. The fluid motion near the principal axis of the flow suffers minimum resistance, where as, that at the boundary experiences maximum resistance. The changing resistive action in a fluid flow along various layers of the flow could be viewed as the result of a variable grid size sieve placed perpendicular to the flow direction, the magnitude of resistance being inversely proportional to the size of the grid. This filter action has been explained with the help of geometric filters defined over rectangular and hexagonal lattices.

20.5 A Case Study

Traditionally, cube model is used in deriving continuity equation for streamlined fluid flow. Figure 20.5.1 shows the cube model as well as hexagonal prism model, which could be used to derive continuity equation. The convention used in earlier sections is followed here to label the corners of the cube and hexagonal prism.

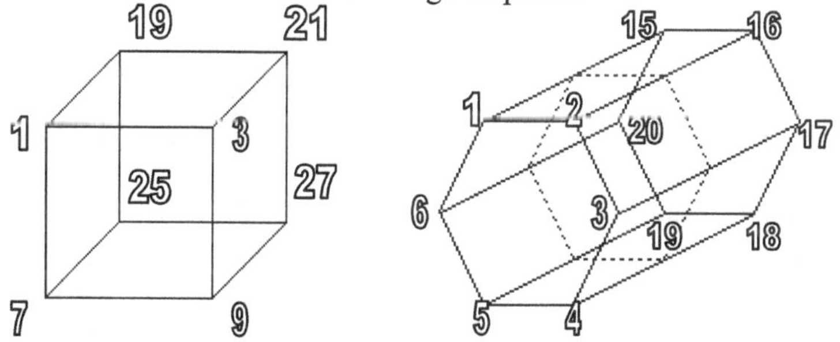

Figure 20.5.1: Cube and Hexagonal prism model for fluid flow

Let us consider a guided flow of fluid inside a pipe of very large radius r and length ℓ. The fluid flow is geometrically divided into say, nine concentric tubes of flow as shown in figure 20.4.1.We shall, for brevity, use a terminology "flow field" to denote a tube of flow inside this pipe. The central flow field has a volume $2\pi r_1 \ell$. The second flow field has a volume of $2\pi(r_2-r_1)\ell$. The third flow field has a volume of $2\pi(r_3-r_2)\ell$ and so on. Now instead of using a cube model for the entire fluid flow, each flow field is modeled as a convex polyhedron in a 3x3x3 lattice. For example, the first (central) flow field is modeled as the polyhedron A consisting of 27 neighbors. One can easily obtain flow equations using this model. Next, the second flow is modeled as the polyhedron B_1 consisting of 26 neighbors and the flow equations computed. The third flow field is modeled as a 25-neighborhood polyhedron and in the same manner, the 9th flow field with the pipe as its boundary is modeled as the 19-neighborhood polyhedron. This discrete modeling technique has some similarities with Finite Element technique but it uses cellular automata tools while computing. The 9th flow field suffers maximum friction due to its boundary and so is modeled as the basis $I_{1,3,7,9,19,21,25,27}$. This basis has eight triangular surfaces and the frictional forces act along the normals of these surfaces thus exhibiting a filtering action. In fact, the resultant of all the eight normal faces would try to arrest the mobility of the central node. However, due to the innate velocity of the fluid, the flow field would experience a slow motion. The $I_{1,3,7,9,19,21,25,27}$ model of the 9th flow field is shown below.

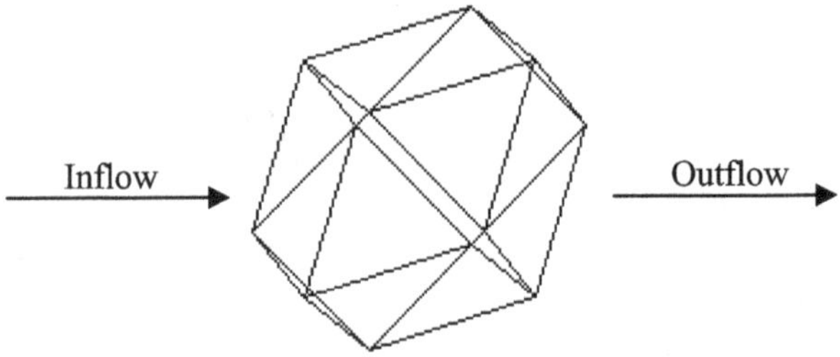

Next, the 8th flow field suffers less friction and thus modeled as a 20-neighborhood polyhedron. There are seven such polyhedrons. Depending on the type of forces acting on the 8th flow field, we shall choose one of these seven. At present we assume the polyhedron $H_{1,3,7,9,19,21,25}$ to be the model of the 8th flow field. This model is shown below.

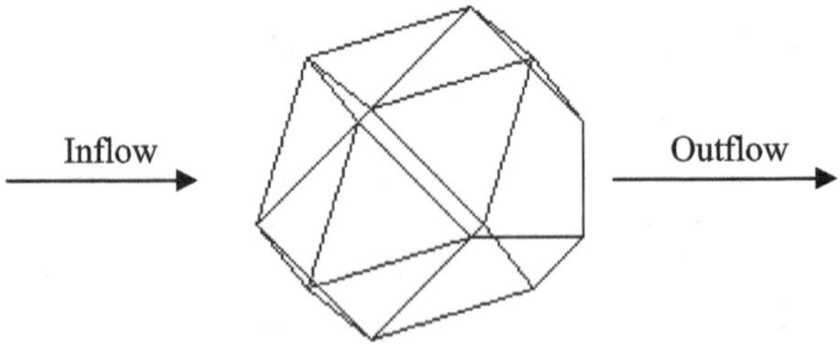

Seven normal forces act on the central node and the resultant force would act towards the 21st node of the lattice. The direction of net velocity of the flow field would be the resultant of the actual field force and the resultant of the polyhedron normal forces.

The polyhedrons $H_{1,3,7,9,19,21,27}$, $H_{1,3,7,9,21,25,27}$, $H_{1,3,7,9,19,25,27}$, $H_{1,3,7,19,21,25,27}$, $H_{1,3,9,19,21,25,27}$, $H_{1,7,9,19,21,25,27}$ and $H_{3,7,9,19,21,25,27}$ can also be used as models of the 8th flow field. All these models yield resultant forces that either counter the actual fluid or retard the velocity of the flow. All these eight possibilities could be used as models depending the type of flow and flow field.

The model of the seventh flow field depends on the model chosen for the 8th flow field. For instance let us assume $H_{1,3,7,9,19,21,25}$ to be the model of the 8th flow field. Then one can choose any of the seven models of G type polyhedrons. They are $G_{3,7,9,19,21,25}$, $G_{1,7,9,19,21,25}$, $G_{1,3,9,19,21,25}$, $G_{1,3,7,19,21,25}$, $G_{1,3,7,9,21,25}$, $G_{1,3,7,9,19,25}$ and $G_{1,3,7,9,19,21}$
Model $G_{1,3,7,9,19,21}$ is shown below.

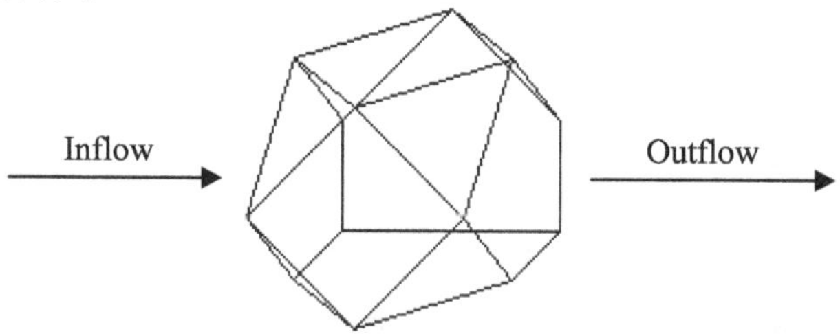

The magnitude of this resistive force would be comparatively less than that of the one in the previous case. Thus the resistive forces go on reducing to a minimum when we model the 1st (central) flow field. A set of nine such polyhedrons is called a GE-filter

Now the highlight of this technique is:

A fluid flow is nothing but a join of nine flow fields, the flow being controlled by a geometric filter of evolution type. There are 40,320 types of fluid flow when modeled as rectangular lattice gas automata.

Figure 20.5.2 shows a collection of Geometric Filter Models in a rectangular grid and figure 20.5.3 shows a collection of Geometric Filter Models in a hexagonal grid.

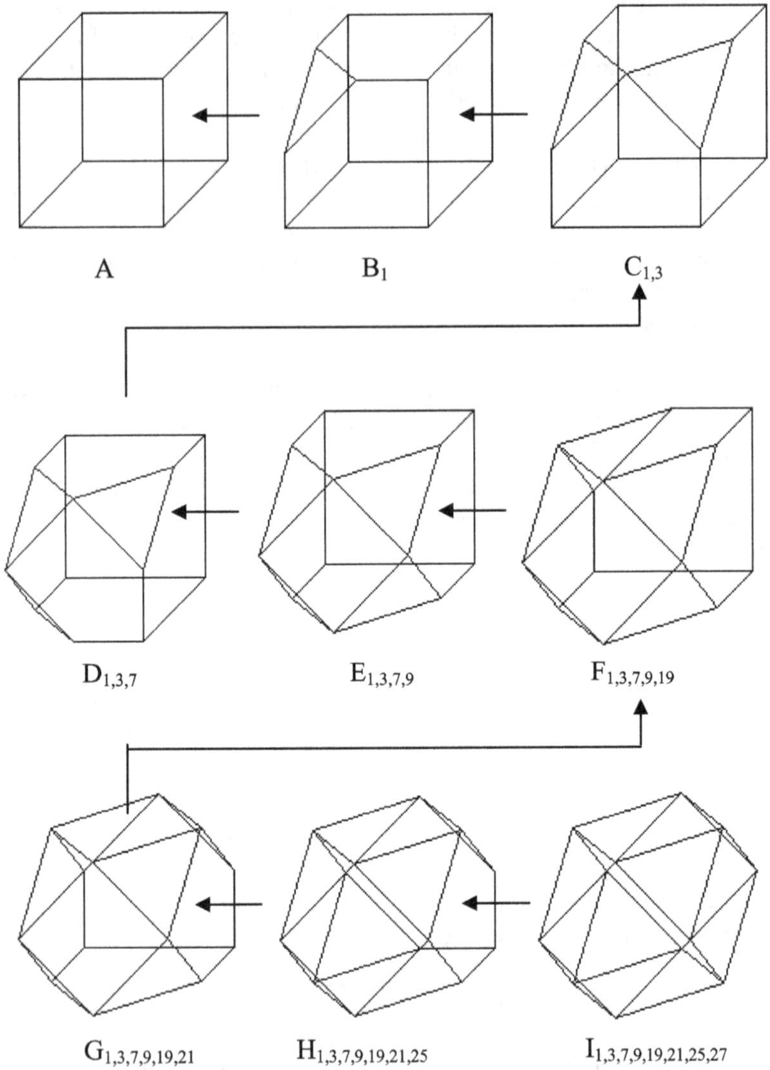

Figure 20.5.2: A 3-D Geometric filter model $\{A,\ B_1, C_{1,3}, D_{1,3,7}, E_{1,3,7,9}, F_{1,3,7,9,19}, G_{1,3,7,9,19,21}, H_{1,3,7,9,19,21,25}, I_{1,3,7,9,19,21,25,27}\}$ of fluid flow in a rectangular grid

Rectangular lattice gas automata modeling of discrete fluid flow bears a similarity with traditional techniques. In spite of its computational ease and precision, this model yields less ideal results because of the absence of ideal rotational symmetry in its geometry. On the other hand, a cylindrical modeling of fluid flow would certainly be an ideal technique for analyzing fluid flow problems. But this would be non-constructive. So, a compromise has to be made by choosing a model which is closer to a cylindrical model and at the same time it is constructive, that is, which, in other words, has better rotational symmetry in its geometry when compared to the rectangular lattice geometry. Hexagonal lattices exhibit better rotational symmetry when compared to rectangular lattices. So, we shall now just mention the possibilities of modeling fluid flow using hexagonal lattice gas automata. The argument related to geometric filters in a hexagonal grid and their utilization as fluid flow models is very much similar to that of the rectangular lattice gas automata models and hence it is not described here. As shown in figure 20.4.2, the flow field is geometrically divided into seven concentric tubes of flow. The overall 21-neighborhood structure is shown in figure 20.5.1. One can construct 4,536 geometric filters of GE type in a hexagonal lattice. One such filter is shown in figure 20.5.3.

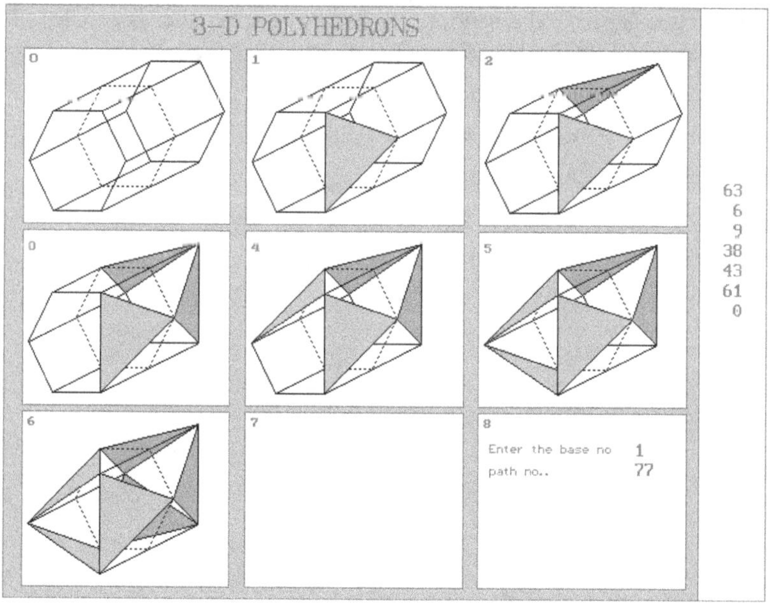

Figure 20.5.3: Geometric filter model of 3-D fluid flow in a hexagonal grid

In simple terms, the changing resistive action in a fluid flow along various layers of the flow could be viewed as the result of a variable grid size sieve placed perpendicular to the flow direction (refer to the diagram given below) which offers variable resistance to the fluid motion, the magnitude of resistance being inversely proportional to the size of the grid.

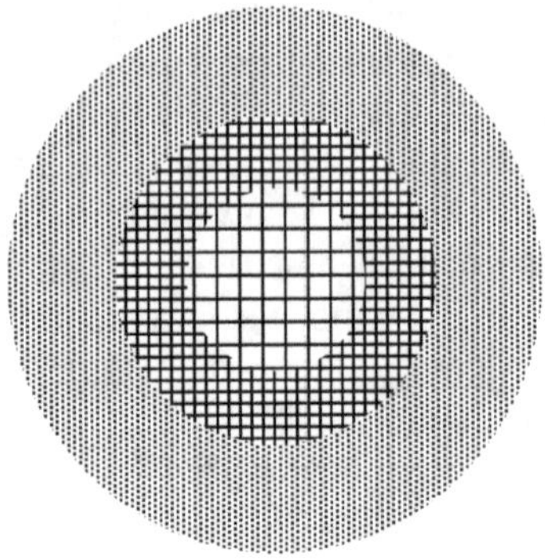

The variable resistance phenomenon is in general heuristically observed, whereas it has been explained in this section with a clear cut mathematico-logical description. In other words, the heuristic filter action has been demonstrated with geometric filter models.

Section 21

Cellular Logic Array Processing Of Laser Scanned Data Of Metal Surfaces

Abstract

In this section, we propose an Interactive Image Processing Language (IIPL) system developed in the framework of Cellular Logic Array Processing (CLAP) for detecting various irregularities and textures on the surface of a metal. Cellular Logic Array Processing is a nonnumerical image processing paradigm developed with the help of certain tools and concepts related to the theory of Markov's Normal Algorithms and the theory of Cellular Automata. Much about this has been treated in detail in earlier sections.

21.1 Introduction

Processing of images of metal surfaces has become an important activity in any machine vision based industry. Usually laser scanned data is obtained from a specimen and analyzed for the presence of bright spots on the surface of the metal under inspection. These spots indicate various kinds of defects on the metal surface and the surface texture could be described in some suitable parametric form. Processing of such laser scanned data plays an important role not only as the best nondestructive testing technique but also as the one with commercial importance. Huge savings could be made if metal is inspected whilst still red-hot, rather than allowing it to cool, inspecting it while it is cold, and then reheating it. The economics achieved in fuel savings are potentially very large indeed.

There are a number of techniques and standards, which could be used to detect textures on metal surfaces and classify them. Traditionally, Electro-Formed comparison standards have been used to classify metal

E. G. Rajan, *Symbolic Computing - Signal and Image Processing*
ISBN 81-7800-047-4

surfaces based on the agreement of their surface roughness with the standard ones. For instance the composite pocket set number 130 introduced by Rubert & Co Ltd., England, contains 30 specimen standards calibrated in μ" Ra (CLA) and in the metric equivalents μm Ra. For many purposes, it is of importance to know also the peak to valley depth of roughness Rt, which varies from 4 to 12 times the Ra values. The classification accuracy, as declared by the company, is within ±10% for Ra and ±30% for Rt from the corresponding actual values. So, visual methods proved to be inaccurate and there was an urge to go in for better methods such as computer aided classification.

Since this problem comes under computer aided texture classification, syntactic and spectral domain pattern recognition techniques play important roles as the classification procedures.

In this section, a novel Interactive Image Processing Language (IIPL) technique is described which is expected to increase the classification accuracy many times when compared to visual comparison standards techniques. This technique advocates the use of a set of fast pattern recognition algorithms, which have been developed in the framework of what is known as Cellular Logic Array Processing.

2.2 Processing Of Laser Scanned Data Using Interactive Image Processing Language

Interactive image processing began in the mid-1970s. Bruce Batchelor and Dr. P.J. Brumfitt were the first people to develop a system called SUSIE (Southampton University System for Image Evaluation) in 1975. Later in 1986, British Robotics Systems Ltd., brought out an IIPL system called Auto view. At present, the IIPL system that is available in the market combines the features of Auto view and SUSIE.

The programs of this IIPL have been developed in Prolog+ which is the standard Prolog enhanced by various image processing predicates. Hence, Prolog+ is viewed as an interactive image processing language as well as a language for representing intelligent procedures.

The latest IIPL system designed by Bruce Batchelor and Frederick Waltz been developed based on seven principles.

(i) If a technique works, use it. If not, find one that does.

(ii) Utility, ease of implementation, speed, cost and adaptability with other algorithmic atoms in the system are of paramount importance.

(iii) There is no single image processing algorithm that stands above all others, in terms of its importance.

(iv) It is vain to do with more what can be done with less, says Occam's Razor. IIPL should adhere to it.

(v) Complexity, if needed, can often be obtained by combining simple operations.

(vi) Machine vision systems need not, in any way, attempt to model natural vision.

In this system, any image processing algorithm design / selection is regarded as the task of putting together sequences of atomic operations to form complete procedures. This IIPL system consists of a collection of interactive logical programs and a piece of computer hardware together with a scanner. Processing of laser scanned data of a metal surface could be carried out using the following IIPL procedures in order to recognize various textures and to classify them. These procedures are not unique and one can try alternative ones for better results.

Laser flying spot scanner is used to acquire digital image of the metal surface under test and the following IIPL procedure (command sequence) is used to process the image.

Program used	Description
DG;	Digitize an image
LOCHM 8, [PT 50]	Preprocess image using a nonlinear filter
OU TEMP;	Save image for further analysis
TEXTUR;	Binary image texture analysis
VO 1,128,128,128;	Copy histogram buffer to right hand column of image
CS;	Copy right hand column to all other column of image
PT 10,1;	10% threshold parameter
PT 25,2;	25% threshold parameter
PT 50,3;	50% threshold parameter
PT 75,4;	75% threshold parameter
PT 90,5	90% threshold parameter
IN TEMP;	Recover semi processed image

YX;	Rotate by 90°
TEXTUR;	Repeat binary image texture analysis
Vo 1,128,128,128;	Copy histogram buffer to right hand column of image
CS;	Copy right hand column to all other column of image
PT 10,6;	10% threshold parameter
PT 25,7;	25% threshold parameter
PT 50,8;	50% threshold parameter
PT 75,9;	75% threshold parameter
PT 90,10;	90% threshold parameter
MR 5;	Match registers 1 – 10 to database

LOCHM is a local area histogram modification macro, and it is an excellent preprocessing filter to convert the textured gray scale images into binary form. In order to learn texture parameters of a surface, one may use the macro 'SR texname, 10;', where texname is the name of a particular texture surface whose parameters one may wish to learn. The macro SR denotes the command 'Store Registers'. In order to detect significant spots on a metal surface, one may use the command sequence:

Program used	Description
DG;	Digitize an image
GO 0,0,0,0,1,0,0,0,0;	Median filter the image
GO 0,0,0,0,1,0,0,0,0;	Median filter the image (Repeated application)
TH 128;	Threshold parameter determined by experiment

The command GO represents a general rank convolution operator which computes a linearly weighted sum of the intensities within the 3x3 window centered at the pixel at (i, j). TH is basically a quantisation operator which quantises a selected range of intensities to a single value. This is generally carried out by trial and error method.

All the macros of the current IIPL system have been developed using numerical algorithms. Alternatively in this section, we purpose a constructive logio-mathematical framework called Cellular Logic Array Processing (CLAP) in which a number of algorithmic atoms related to pattern recognition and image processing could be developed and IIPL procedures constructed.

2.3 CLAP-Interactive Image Processing Language (CLAP-IIPL)

The CLAP-IIPL consists of a number of algorithm atoms developed in this framework and it works exactly as the IIPL due to Batchelor and Waltz. Processing of laser scanned data of a metal surface is carried out as it is done in IIPL, but only with a different version of the TEXTUR algorithm. The CLAP-TEXTUR algorithm extracts the textures in a digital image in the following manner. The given digital image is scanned by the nine-neighborhood structure. On each move, the 3x3 sub image covered by this window is examined and the boundary values are stored in a temporary linear array in a particular order. This ordering plays an important role in extracting the textures.

Figure 21.3.1 shows five different ways of ordering. Now, the values in the array are compared with the central pixel value. If a boundary pixel value is greater than or equal to the central pixel value, then a 1 is assigned to it, otherwise a 0 is assigned. The 8-bit word thus obtained is converted to its decimal equivalent and the central pixel value is replaced by it. This procedure is continued till the entire image is scanned. The overall effect is that the textures of various regions in the given image are extracted thus giving us the texturized version of the original image.

1	2	3
8	X	4
7	6	5

3x3 window with cell numbers

1	2	3	4	5	6	7	8	ORDER 1
7	8	1	2	3	4	5	6	ORDER 2
5	6	7	8	1	2	3	4	ORDER 3
3	4	5	6	7	8	1	2	ORDER 4
8	7	9	5	4	3	2	1	ORDER 5

Linear array with cells differently ordered

Figure 21.3.1: 3x3 window and ordering of linear array

Now, the digital image of the metal surface under test is examined using the following CLAP-IIPL procedure (command sequence).

Program used	Description
DG;	Digitize an image
OU TEMP;	Save image for further analysis
TEXTUR ORDER;	Gray image texture analysis using an order
VO 1,128,128,128;	Copy histogram buffer to right hand column of image
CS;	Copy right hand column to all other columns of image
ORDER 1;	First order of linear array
ORDER 2;	Second order of linear array
ORDER 3;	Third order of linear array
ORDER 4;	Fourth order of linear array
ORDER 5;	Fifth order of linear array
VO 1,128,128,128;	Copy histogram buffer to right hand column of image
CS;	Copy right hand column to all other columns of image
SR 5;	Store registers 1 – 5 to database

One can construct CLAP-IIPL programs for processing any scanned data of metal surfaces of weld joints.

Section 22

Modeling Of Collision Processes

Abstract

This section proposes a logical method of computing various state vectors of a real time control system like a collision avoidance system. The major results of this investigation are:

1. The search space of an intelligent system (robot) has been discretized as (i) blind region, (ii) high risk region, (iii) low risk region as given in the following diagram.

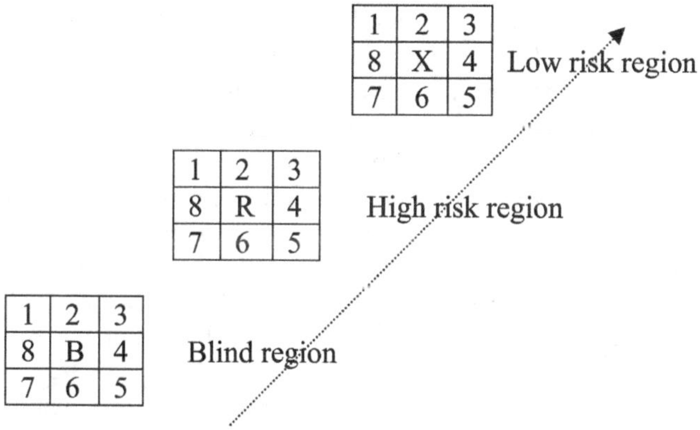

R represents the robot position at the present time instant. It is on the move towards the low risk region. X is the expected position of the robot at the next instant of time. Blind region is the region behind the robot. The position B of the robot was at the previous time instant.

2. Now, the obstacles may be present in the low risk, or in the high risk or in the blind regions with respect to the present position of the robot. Obstacles in the blind region are not of our concern in our study.

E. G. Rajan, *Symbolic Computing - Signal and Image Processing*
ISBN 81-7800-047-4

3. There are 512 possible ways of confrontations that the robot may have at the low risk region.

4. The decision logic for the control of state vector $< D, S >$ is given by a set of nine constructive logical formulas.

5. There are 256 possible ways of confrontations that the robot may have at the high risk region.

6. Now decision logic for the control of state vector $< D, S >$ is given by a set of eight constructive logical formulas.

The formulas have been derived out of a rigorous mathematical treatise on the dynamical behavior of the intelligent robot launched in space with a particular mission direction.

22.1 Introduction

Autonomous Mobile Robots (AMR) are used in different applications like working in a factory, airport, hospital environment or space exploration. In such cases, AMRs have to cope up with static and moving obstacles. The navigation problem in a constraint environment has been treated in many ways, usually the difference lying in the knowledge base. The robot motion is generally decided by taking into account obstacle configuration, robot kinematics and the result of the modification of the local perception. Subject to these basic constraints, several procedures and methodologies have been developed for fixing optimal paths of AMRs in known as well as unknown environment.

Traditionally two basic approaches are being used for path generation of an AMR, fixing of the total path in a known environment, and instantaneous fixing of path directions depending on situations in an unknown environment. The former approach is error free because the nature of the environment is a priori known, where as the latter approach is not. Most of the current research is being focused on to the second approach with an intention of developing a universal technique in order to meet the challenges of obstacle avoidance in any unknown environment by an AMR, the deep space with asteroids and a spaceship, for instance.

We too are concerned here with the problem of identifying a technique for path generation of an AMR in an unknown environment. For the past few years, a number of path fixing techniques have been developed each having its own merits and demerits. Almost all the techniques involve the geometries, velocities, time segments and directions of motion of obstacles and AMR while fixing the path of the AMR instantaneously.

The work carried out in this section centers around a novel path fixing technique in the framework of Cellular Logic Array Processing.

Cellular logic array processing advocates the use of constructive logical formulas constructed in the logico-mathematical, hierarchical and symmetrical system of languages $Я_{\alpha}$ due to A.A. Markov.

The system of languages $Я_{\alpha}$ has been described in detail in section 7.

22.2 Problem Formulation

An autonomous mobile robot is moving in E^3 (Euclidean) space in a particular direction called Mission Direction (MD).

It has the following objectives:

1. To avoid collision by reorienting itself by instantaneously fixing its mission paths in a collision prone environment (Target Avoidance Problem, TAP).

2. To set its aspect straight to a target by instantaneously fixing the attack points in the moving target (Target Seeking Problem, TSP).

Traditional approach :

Traditionally two basic approaches are being used for path generation of an AMR, fixing of the total path in a known environment, and instantaneous fixing of path directions depending on situations in an unknown environment. The former approach is error free because the nature of the environment is a priori known, where as the latter approach is not. Most of the current research is being focused on to the second approach with an intention of developing a universal technique in order to meet the challenges of obstacle avoidance in any unknown environment by an AMR, the deep space with asteroids and a spaceship, for instance.

Our approach :

What is intended in this section is to use a novel approach to instantaneous path fixing for an Autonomous Mobile Robot (AMR) using certain image processing tools and concepts from a paradigm called Cellular Logic Array Processing. These tools are used (i) to find the boundaries of the digital image of an interfering object so that it can be avoided (TAP) and (ii) to find the skeleton of the image of the interfering object (TSP).

Image acquisition is an important activity in such cases. In this regard, we use a technique called "Collision Avoidance Using Conic Projection Image Sensor (COPIS)" for automatic path generation of an AMR in an unknown environment.

Finally, the main aim of this section, that is, control of the Mission Direction (MD) is carried out using constructive logical methods.

22.3 Modeling Of Three Dimensional Space

The three dimensional Euclidean space E^3 is discretized here as a 3-D grid of uniform cells, each cell taking the shape of a cube. The presence of an obstacle in a cell attributes a value 1 to that cell whereas the absence of an obstacle attributes a 0 to it. It is important to note that a cell in the 3-D grid is an abstract model and so it is not limited by morphology and size. Usually these six nodes are called the direct neighbors of the node (i, j, k). This seven node arrangement is extended three dimensionally to form the lattice. Figure 22.3.1.2 shows an extended array of the one shown in figure 22.3.1.1.96

The nodes (i-1, j-1, k), (i-1, j+1, k), (i+1, j-1, k), (i+1, j+1, k), (i-1, j-1, k-1), (i-1, j+1, k-1), (i+1, j-1, k-1), (i+1, j+1, k-1), (i-1, j-1, k+1), (i-1, j+1, k+1), (i+1, j-1, k+1), (i+1, j+1, k+1) are called the indirect neighbors of (i, j, k).

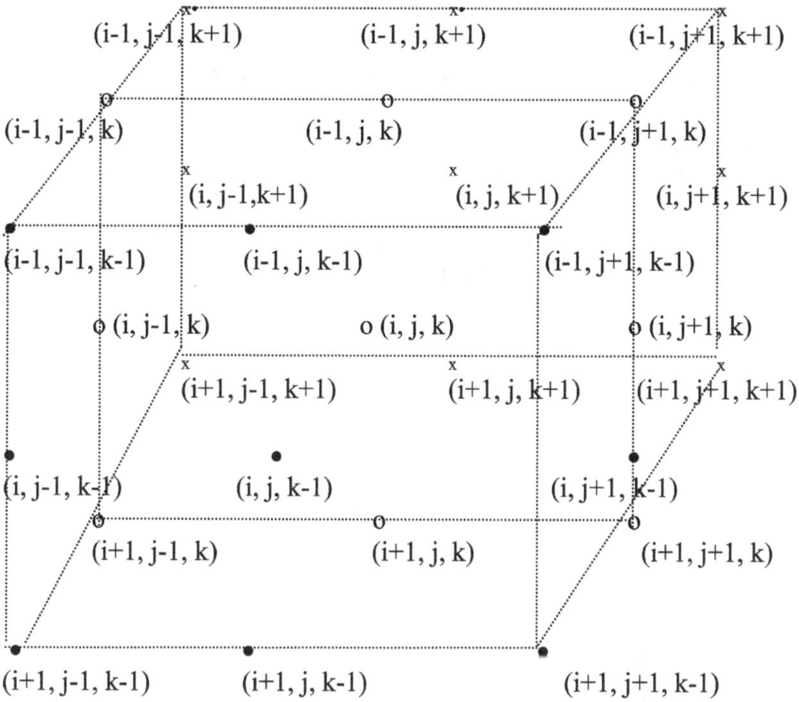

Figure 22.3.1: 27-neighborhood 3-D Lattice arrangement

22.4 Omni Directional Image Acquisition

The collision avoiding omni directional image sensing AMR consists of three components (i) COnical Projection Imaging Subsystem COPIS, (ii) image processing and pattern recognizing subsystem, and (iii) a mobile robot. The digital image acquired by the system is a combination of two images acquired by the digital cameras separately. Digital camera # 1 acquires the image of the environment just in front of it. The digital camera # 2 acquires the image of the omni directional environment projected by the conical mirror. The conical mirror is of 120mm diameter and it is kept along with a digital camera inside a glass tube in such a way that their axes are identical. The image taken by this COPIS is a 2π view around the axis, that is $(4\pi-\omega)$ solid angle view around the optical center of the digital camera # 2, where ω is the solid angle of the blind view hidden behind the camera. Let the vertex angle of the conical mirror be δ and the visual angle of the camera # 2 be γ. The distance between the optical center of the camera and the apex of the conical mirror is ℓ. Now one compute the lower and upper angles of the field of view respectively as $\alpha_1 = \delta$ and $\alpha_2 = (\delta - \gamma/2)$ under optimum setting of ℓ. This is achieved by selecting ℓ such that the circular visual boundary of the camera touches the circular base of the conical mirror.

Figure 22.4.1 shows a typical set up that could be used for acquiring omni directional digital images.

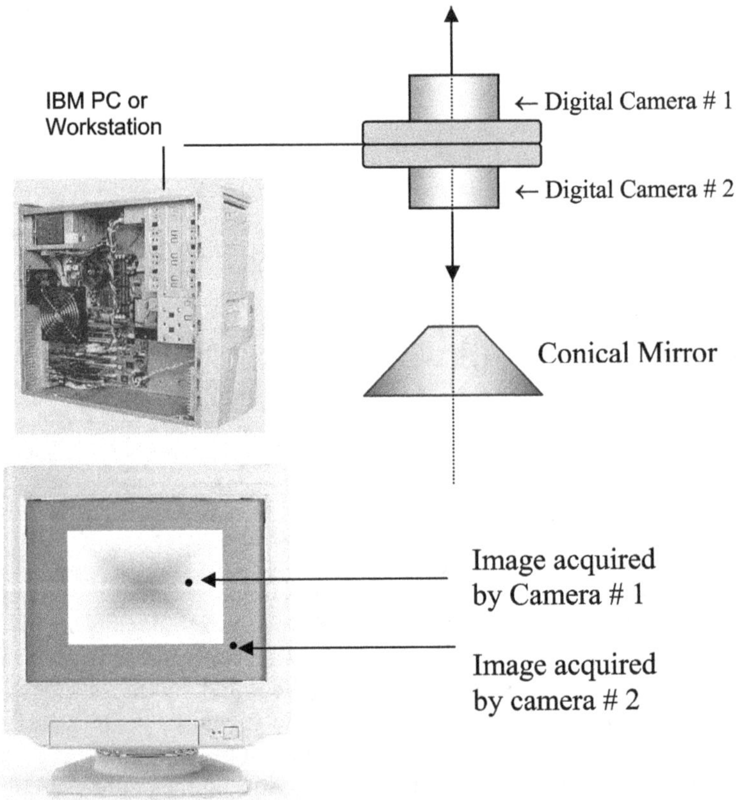

Figure 22.4.1 : Conical Projection Imaging Subsystem

With this kind of a setting, the image acquisition is governed by the following fundamental relations defined in a 3-D co-ordinate system with the camera lens as the origin. Let us consider a point P in the space positioned by the coordinates (X_P, Y_P , Z_P) in the 3-D co-ordinate system XYZ with camera lens center as origin O. The coordinate axes X and Y constitute Euclidean plane, which is vertical to the axis of the mirror and camera. The Z coordinate axis is collinear with the axis of the camera. Let f be the focal length of the camera. This point P when projected by the mirror would form a 2-D picture. Now let θ be the angle subtended by the object to the X axis of the coordinate system. Then,

$$\text{Tan}\ \theta = \frac{Y_P}{X_P} = \frac{y_P}{x_P}$$

where y_P and x_P are the y and x coordinates of the projected point in the image. All points with a same azimuth in space appear on a radial line through the image center. This amounts to saying that objects in the digital image acquired by camera # 2 could be viewed as ones depicted on a polar coordinate system. The elevation, azimuth and range parameters corresponding to an object in space are evaluated in the following manner. The value of θ denotes the elevation and the distance $\mathcal{D}$ from the image center to the object in the image denotes the azimuth. The range could be evaluated by the size $\mathcal{J}$ of the object image. It was obvious then to note that when an object approaches the robot in the head-on direction, the size of the object in the image will increase. Thus the robot will understand the possibilities of a collision. The three parameters θ, $\mathcal{D}$ and $\mathcal{J}$ yield information about the movement of an object. The instantaneous position of an object in space is thus evaluated as a function of θ, $\mathcal{D}$ and $\mathcal{J}$. Based on the present and a few past data sets, the robot will compute the possible direction of the object and decide instantaneous changes in its own direction and speed.

22.5 Instantaneous Path Fixing Using Cellular Logic Principles

An object in space is either captured by camera # 1 or by camera # 2 depending on the position of the object in space. The images acquired by the cameras are superimposed properly to form a composite image. The composite images corresponding to two positions of the object in space are shown below. Figure 22.5.1 shows a model scene captured by camera # 1 of the system COPIS.

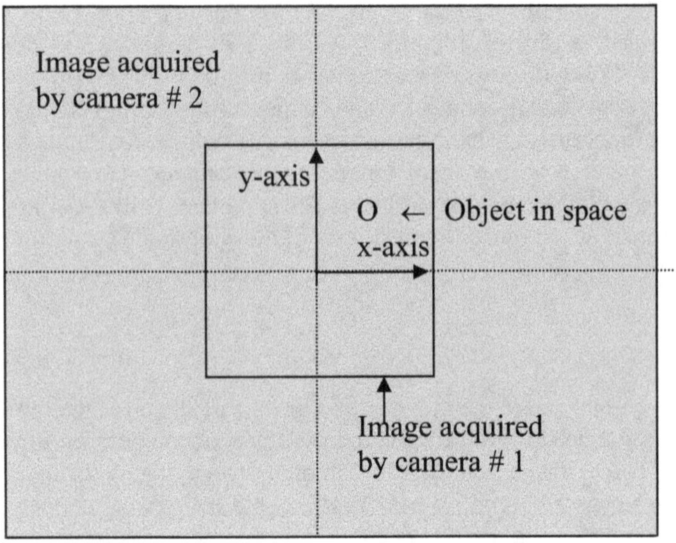

Figure 22.5.1: Image acquired by camera # 1
Object position coordinates: < x, y >

Figure 22.5.2 shows the model scene captured by camera # 2 of the system COPIS.

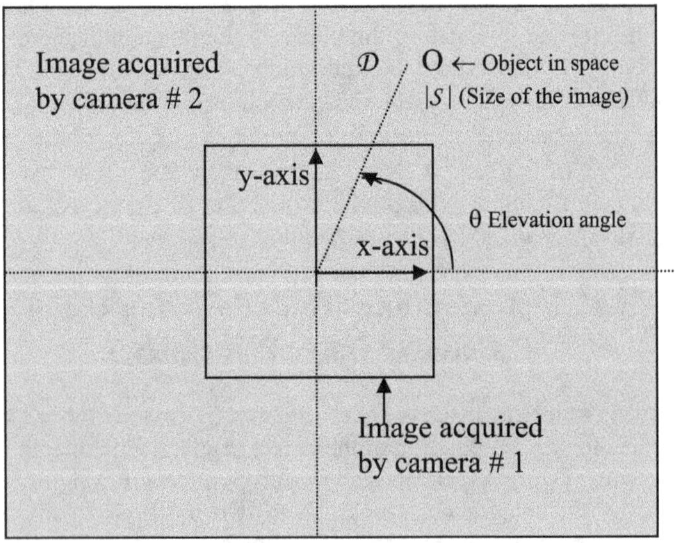

Figure 22.5.2: Image acquired by camera # 2
Object position coordinates: < θ, $\mathcal{D}$, $\mathcal{J}$ >

22.6 Pattern Recognition And Decision Making

The acquired composite image is processed by a PC or a R5000 based Silicon Graphics O2 workstation for the purpose of pattern recognition and decision making. The composite 256 level gray image is of size 512 x 512. The digital image acquired by camera # 1 is also of size 512 x 512 but it is reduced to the size of 128 x 128 in order to be superimposed exactly on the central blind region of the conical mirror. It is to be noted here that the COPIS has two blind regions (i) central blind region and (ii) rear blind region with solid angle ω radians. The central idea on which the decision making is done is that the moving objects in space are recognized either as harmful or as harmless. *Harmful* objects are those which approach towards the robot and *harmless* ones move away from the robot. Less harmful objects are those which are captured by camera # 1, where as, those captured by the other camera are more harmful. The loci of harmful objects are evaluated using cellular logic principles. The logic goes as follows:

Perception space of an AMR is classified as a disjoint union of two subspaces (i) one consisting of recognized entities, (ii) the other consisting of unrecognized entities. In our case, the perception space is treated as a disjoint union of three subspaces (i) one consisting of objectively recognized entities, (ii) the other consisting of objectively unrecognized entities and (iii) the third consisting of subjectively recognized entities. It is clear from this classification that there is an inbuilt fuzziness in characterizing entities belonging to a perception space. It is to be noted here that a perception space of one AMR is not identical to that of another AMR.

We are concerned here with the problem of instantaneous fixing of path of an autonomous mobile robot sent on a mission especially in an unknown space. The formulation of such a kind of technique has been tried theoretically in the framework of cellular logic array processing. The central idea behind this technique is that an AMR decides its direction of movement based on the neighborhood in which it is situated at a particular instant of time. The direction parameter of an AMR for next instant of time is decided by a formula that involves the position and intended direction of the AMR in a neighborhood consisting of obstacles, be them mobile or not, and their positions and estimated directions of motion.

In order to do this it is essential to model the three dimensional Euclidean space E^3 as a digital grid mathematically denoted as Z x Z x Z, where Z denotes the system of integers. In fact there are many ways of discretizing the analog E^3 space: (i) using three dimensional lattice model, (ii) using three dimensional hexagonal prism model and (iii) using three dimensional polyhedron model, to name a few. The first two models are described in this proposal in order to justify the need for discretizing the E^3 space.

22.6.1 Three Dimensional Lattice Model Of E^3 Space

The three dimensional lattice is an array of nodes, each hypothetically connected to six more nodes in mutually orthogonal directions. Figure 22.6.1.1 shows such an arrangement where one node indexed as (i, j, k) is hypothetically connected to six more nodes (i-1,j,k), (i, j+1, k), (i, j-1, k), (i+1, j, k), (i, j, k-1) and (i, j, k+1) .

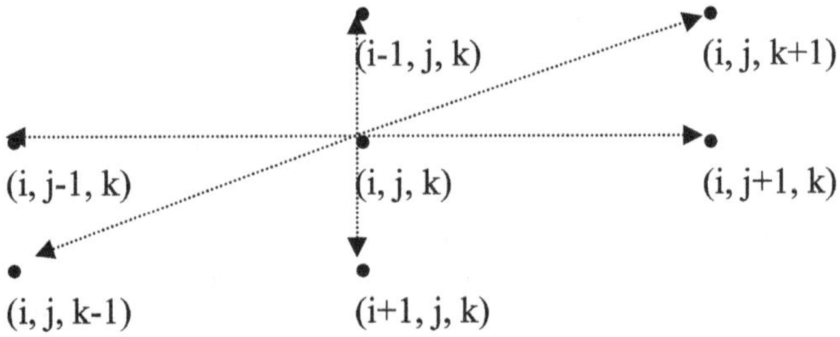

Figure 22.6.1.1: 3-D Lattice arrangement

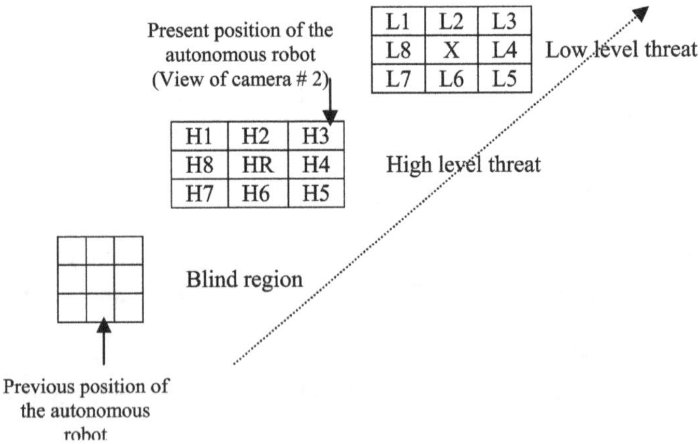

Figure 22.6.1.2: Model of threat positions in E^3 space.

This intended path of the robot is given by R→L0. Normal speed of robot is denoted as S. A path is fixed by the robot depending on the positions and speeds of obstacles. At a time instant the robot dynamics is determined by the ordered pair < S, R →Li > , 1 ≤ i ≤ 8. There are 8 loci corresponding to less harmful objects approaching the robot from 8 directions: Lj→R, 1≤j≤8. So R →Li depends on Lj →R, and S on Hk →R, 1 ≤ k ≤ 8. Now the cellular logic scheme that fixes the instantaneous path is <S, R →Li > = Φ (R →Li , 1 ≤ i ≤ 8, Hk →R, 1 ≤ k ≤ 8).

22.6.1 A THEORETICAL CASE STUDY

Let us assume that R →L0 is the intended direction of an AMR's mission. The first collision possibility is due to a single obstacle approaching the AMR from the direction L0 →R. This low threat position is pictorially represented in figure 22.6.1.1. The presence of a 1 in a cell indicates the presence of an obstacle.

0	0	0
0	1	0
0	0	0

Figure 22.6.1.1: Low threat position indicating head-on collision

For brevity we shall represent this threat position as an array of numbers as shown below.

0 0 0
0 1 0
0 0 0

Now the AMR can change its direction of motion to any one of the following ones: R →L1, R →L2, R →L3, R →L4, R →L5, R →L6, R →L7, R →L8 with the probability of 1/8. The AMR can adjust its speed depending on its relative velocity with respect to that of the obstacle's. Let us assume that the AMR takes on the direction R →L1 with a deviation of $\mathcal{D}°$ and continues in that direction for t_1 time units with the same speed s or with a different speed, say s'. Then it necessarily changes its direction to R →L0 with the deviation of $(2\mathcal{D})°$ exactly for t_1 time units and moves with the same speed. After t_1 time units, the AMR changes its direction once again with the deviation of $\mathcal{D}°$. This strategy ensures regain of original direction of its mission. For brevity, we call this strategy as Restorative Deviation. Next, let us assume that two low threat obstacles approach the AMR from the direction L0→R and L1→R. This low threat position is pictorially represented as:

0 0 0
0 1 0
0 0 0

Now the AMR can change its direction of motion to any one of the following ones: R →L2, R →L3, R →L4, R →L5, R →L6, R →L7, R →L8 with the probability of 1/7. One can construct a total of 8 two obstacle threat positions with an obstacle in the L0 position as shown below in figure 22.6.1.2.

100 010 000	010 010 000	001 010 000	000 011 000
000 010 001	000 010 010	000 010 100	000 110 000

Figure 22.6.1.2: 8 threat positions to an AMR

The following table gives a summary of threat positions for various groups of obstacles.

Table 22.6.1.1: High Low Threat Positions (set # 1)

Sl. No.	No. of obstacles (With obstacle in L0)	Threat positions (No. of obstacles)
1	(L0)	$^8C_0 = 1$
2	(L0, La/1 ≤ a ≤ 8)	$^8C_1 = 8$
3	(L0, La, Lb/1 ≤ a, b ≤ 8)	$^8C_2 = 28$
4	(L0, La, Lb, Lc/1 ≤ a, b, c ≤ 8)	$^8C_3 = 56$
5	(L0, La, Lb, Lc, Ld/1 ≤ a, b, c, d ≤ 8)	$^8C_4 = 70$
6	(L0, La, Lb, Lc, Ld, Le/1 ≤ a, b, c, d, e ≤ 8)	$^8C_5 = 56$
7	(L0, La, Lb, Lc, Ld, Le, Lf/1 ≤ a, b, c, d, e, f ≤ 8)	$^8C_6 = 28$
8	(L0, La, Lb, Lc, Ld, Le, Lf, Lg/1 ≤ a, b, c, d, e, f, g ≤ 8)	$^8C_7 = 8$
9	(L0, La, Lb, Lc, Ld, Le, Lf, Lg Lh/1 ≤ a, b, c, d, e, f, g, h ≤ 8)	$^8C_8 = 1$

The above set consists of a total of 256 high risk threat positions. Similarly, one can construct table 22.6.1.2 summarizing 256 low risk threat positions with out an obstacle in position L0. By low risk threat, we mean that the AMR can continue in its intended direction R → L0 with low risk in spite of the fact there are obstacles present elsewhere in the neighborhood.

Table 22.6.1.2: Low Risk Low Threat Positions (set # 2)

Sl. No	No. of obstacles (With obstacle in L0)	Threat positions (No. of obstacles)
1	( ) (Threat free)	0
2	(La/1 ≤ a ≤ 8)	${}^8C_1 = 8$
3	(La, Lb/1 ≤ a, b ≤ 8)	${}^8C_2 = 28$
4	(La, Lb, Lc/1 ≤ a, b, c ≤ 8)	${}^8C_3 = 56$
5	(La, Lb, Lc, Ld/1 ≤ a, b, c, d ≤ 8)	${}^8C_4 = 70$
6	(La, Lb, Lc, Ld,Le/1 ≤ a, b, c, d, e ≤8)	${}^8C_5 = 56$
7	(La,Lb,Lc,Ld,Le,Lf/1 ≤ a,b,c,d,e,f≤8)	${}^8C_6 = 28$
8	(La, Lb, Lc, Ld, Le, Lf, Lg/1 ≤ a, b, c, d, e, f, g ≤ 8)	${}^8C_7 = 8$
9	(La, Lb, Lc, Ld, Le, Lf, Lg Lh/1 ≤ a, b, c, d, e, f, g, h ≤ 8)	${}^8C_8 = 1$

From the above argument we see that an AMR faces a total of 512 low threats with 256 high risk zones and 256 low risk ones. In addition to the above an AMR faces 256 high threat zones from its sides. The AMR changes its speed depending on the high threat level. Table 22.6.1.3 summaries all the 256 high risk high threat positions.

Table 22.6.1.3 : High Risk High Threat Positions

Sl. No.	No. of obstacles (AMR in H0)	Threat positions (No. of obstacles)
1	(R) (AMR Position, threat free)	${}^8C_0 = 1$
2	(Ha/1 ≤ a ≤ 8)	${}^8C_1 = 8$
3	(Ha, Hb/1 ≤ a, b ≤ 8)	${}^8C_2 = 28$
4	(Ha, Hb, Hc/1 ≤ a, b, c ≤ 8)	${}^8C_3 = 56$
5	(Ha, Hb, Hc, Hd/1 ≤ a, b, c, d ≤ 8)	${}^8C_4 = 70$
6	(Ha, Hb, Hc, Hd, He/1 ≤ a,b,c,d,e≤8)	${}^8C_5 = 56$
7	(Ha, Hb, Hc, Hd, He, Hf/1 ≤ a, b, c, d, e, f ≤ 8)	${}^8C_6 = 28$
8	(Ha, Hb, Hc, Hd, He, Hf, Hg/1 ≤ a, b, c, d, e, f, g ≤ 8)	${}^8C_7 = 8$
9	(Ha, Hb, Hc, Hd, He, Hf, Hg Hh/1 ≤ a, b, c, d, e, f, g, h ≤ 8)	${}^8C_8 = 1$

To summarize, with the three dimensional space being modeled as a discrete grid, an AMR faces a total of 768 threat zones while undertaking a mission in the discrete space, out of which one is totally threat free. The restorative deviation method is adopted by the AMR to avoid different types of collisions. Further, precise modifications could be made if we resort to probabilistic methods in evaluating the relative velocities and assigning suitable priority values to different directions while fixing the path.

With the basic model for a collision avoidance system, our efforts would now be focused on to the possibility of using logical control of the AMR in the framework of Constructive Mathematical framework discussed in detail in the previous chapters. The constructive logical formulas that govern the motion of an AMR are given below:

Case # 1

The MD (Mission Direction) of an AMR is R→L0. It is assumed that there is no obstacle in the L_0 position. It is also assumed that there is no obstacle in the high-risk region. Then the following formulas are valid:

1. $(L_k = 1) \Rightarrow \bigvee_{i=0}^{8, i \neq k} RL_i$

2. $(L_{k_1} \wedge L_{k_2} = 1) \Rightarrow \bigvee_{i=0}^{8, i \neq k_1, k_2} RL_i$

3. $(L_{k_1} \wedge L_{k_2} \wedge L_{k_3} = 1) \Rightarrow \bigvee_{i=0}^{8, i \neq k_1, k_2, k_3} RL_i$

4. $(L_{k_1} \wedge L_{k_2} \wedge L_{k_3} \wedge L_{k_4} = 1) \Rightarrow \bigvee_{i=0}^{8, i \neq k_1, k_2, k_3, k_4} RL_i$

5. $(L_{k_1} \wedge L_{k_2} \wedge L_{k_3} \wedge L_{k_4} \wedge L_{k_5} = 1) \Rightarrow \bigvee_{i=0}^{8, i \neq k_1, k_2, k_3, k_4, k_5} RL_i$

6. $(L_{k_1} \wedge L_{k_2} \wedge L_{k_3} \wedge L_{k_4} \wedge L_{k_5} \wedge L_{k_6} = 1) \Rightarrow \bigvee_{i=0}^{8, i \neq k_1, k_2, k_3, k_4, k_5, k_6} RL_i$

7. $\left(L_{k_1} \wedge L_{k_2} \wedge L_{k_3} \wedge L_{k_4} \wedge L_{k_5} \wedge L_{k_6} \wedge L_{k_7} = 1\right) \Rightarrow \bigvee_{i=0}^{8, i \neq k_1, k_2, k_3, k_4, k_5, k_6, k_7} RL_i$

8. $\left(L_{k_1} \wedge L_{k_2} \wedge L_{k_3} \wedge L_{k_4} \wedge L_{k_5} \wedge L_{k_6} \wedge L_{k_7} \wedge L_{k_8} = 1\right) \Rightarrow \bigvee_{i=0}^{8, i \neq k_1, k_2, k_3, k_4, k_5, k_6, k_7, k_8} RL_i$

9. $\left(L_{k_1} \wedge L_{k_2} \wedge L_{k_3} \wedge L_{k_4} \wedge L_{k_5} \wedge L_{k_6} \wedge L_{k_7} \wedge L_{k_8} \wedge L_{k0} = 1\right) \Rightarrow \bigvee_{i=0}^{8, i \neq k_1, k_2, k_3, k_4, k_5, k_6, k_7, k_8, k_0} RL_i$

Case # 2

Next, the MD (Mission Direction) of an AMR is assumed to be $R \rightarrow L_0$. It is assumed that there are obstacles in the high-risk region. Then the following formulas are valid:

1. $\left(H_{k_1} = 1\right) \Rightarrow \bigvee_{i=0}^{8, i \neq k} RH_i$

2. $\left(H_{k_1} \wedge H_{k_2} = 1\right) \Rightarrow \bigvee_{i=0}^{8, i \neq k_1, k_2} RH_i$

3. $\left(H_{k_1} \wedge H_{k_2} \wedge H_{k_3} = 1\right) \Rightarrow \bigvee_{i=0}^{8, i \neq k_1, k_2, k_3} RH_i$

4. $\left(H_{k_1} \wedge H_{k_2} \wedge H_{k_3} \wedge H_{k_4} = 1\right) \Rightarrow \bigvee_{i=0}^{8, i \neq k_1, k_2, k_3, k_4} RH_i$

5. $\left(H_{k_1} \wedge H_{k_2} \wedge H_{k_3} \wedge H_{k_4} \wedge H_{k_5} = 1\right) \Rightarrow \bigvee_{i=0}^{8, i \neq k_1, k_2, k_3, k_4, k_5} RH_i$

6. $\left(H_{k_1} \wedge H_{k_2} \wedge H_{k_3} \wedge H_{k_4} \wedge H_{k_5} \wedge H_{k_6} = 1\right) \Rightarrow \bigvee_{i=0}^{8, i \neq k_1, k_2, k_3, k_4, k_5, k_6} RH_i$

7. $\left(H_{k_1} \wedge H_{k_2} \wedge H_{k3} \wedge H_{k4} \wedge H_{k_5} \wedge H_{k6} \wedge H_{k_7} = 1\right)$

$$\Rightarrow \mathop{V}_{i=0}^{8, i \neq k_1, k_2, k_3, k_4, k_5, k_6, k_7} RH_i$$

8. $\left(H_{k_1} \wedge H_{k_2} \wedge H_{k_3} \wedge H_{k4} \wedge H_{k_5} \wedge H_{k6} \wedge H_{k_7} \wedge H_{k_8} = 1\right)$

$$\Rightarrow \mathop{V}_{i=0}^{8, i \neq k_1, k_2, k_3, k_4, k_5, k_6, k_7, k_8} RH_i$$

These constructive logical formulas form the control signals that change the state vectors of the AMR moving in space.

References

[01] Aberth, O., Computable Analysis, McGraw Hill, New York, 1980.

[02] Arbib, M.A., Algebraic Theory of Machines, Languages and Semigroups, Academic Press, New York, 1968.

[03] Barwise, Jon, Handbook of Mathematical Logic, North-Holland Publishing company, 1977.

[04] Beeson, M.J., Foundations of Constructive Mathematics, Springer Verlag, Heidelberg, 1985.

[05] Benthem, J.F.A.K.V., The Logic of Time, D. Reidel, London, 1983.

[06] Bishop, Errett, Foundations of Constructive Analysis, McGraw Hill, 1967.

[07] Bobrow, D.G., Symbol Manipulation Languages and Techniques, Proceedings of the IFIP Working Conference on Symbol Manipulation Languages, North-Holland Publishing Company, Amsterdam, 1968.

[08] Bridges, D.S., Constructive Functional Analysis, Pitman, London, 1979.

[09] Clifford and Preston, The Algebraic Theory of Semigroups, American Mathematical Society, Providence, 1961.

[10] Copi, I.M., Symbolic Logic, MacMillan Publishing Company, 1979.

[11] Dalen, D.V., Logic and Structure, Springer Verlag, Heidelberg, 1980.

[12] Ershov, Yu.L., and Palyutin, E.A., Mathematical Logic, Mir Publishers, Moscow, 1984.

[13] Giardina, C.R., and Dougherty, E.R., Morphological Methods in Image and Signal Processing, Prentice Hall Inc., 1988.

[14] Gleason, A.M., Fundamentals of Abstract Analysis, Addison Wesley. 1966.

[15] Griswold, R.E., Poage, J.F., and Polonsky, I.P., The SNOBOL4 Programing Language, Pretice Hall, 1971.

[16] Grzegorczyk, A., An Outline of Mathematical Logic, D. Reidel Pub. Co., 1974.

[17] Kushner, B.K., Lectures on Constructive Mathematical Analysis, AMS, providence, Phode Island, Vol 60, 1984.

[18] Lallement, Gerard, Semigroups and Combinatorial Applications, John Wiley and Sons, 1979.

[19] Lothaire, M., Combinatorics on Words, Addison Wesley Pub. Co., 1983.

[20] Markov, A.A., Theory of Algorithms, The Isreal Program for Scientific Translations, 1961.

[21] Mittelstadt, Peter, Quantum Logic, D. Reidel Publishing Company.

[22] Pin, J.E., Varieties of Formal Languages, Plenum Press, New York, 1986.

[23] Shanin, N.A., On Constructive Real Numbers and Constructive Function Spaces, AMS, providence, Rhode Island, 1968.

[24] Shanin, N.A., On the Constructive Interpretation of Mathematical Judgements, AMS, Translations 23, 1963.

[25] Toffoli, Tommaso, and Margolus, Norman, Cellular Automata Machines, The MIT Press, Cambridge, Massachusettes, 1987.

[26] Wolfram, Stephen, Theory and Applications of Cellular Automata, World Scientific Publishing Company, 1986.

[27] Birkhoff, G., and Von Neumann, The Logic of Quantum Machanics, Annals of Mathematics, Vol 37, No.4, 1936.

[28] Finch, P.D., On the Structural of Quantum Logic, Jr. of Symbolic Logic Vol. 34, No.2, 1969.

[29] Gunson, J., On the Algebraic Structure of Quantum Mechanics, Commun. Math. Phys. 6, 1967.

[30] Jauch, J.M., and Piron, C., On the structure of Quantal Proposition systems, Helvestia Physica Acta, Vol 42, 1969.

[31] Markov, A.A., Normal Algorithms which Compute Boolean Functions, Soviet Math. Dokl., 5, 1964.

[32] Rajan, E.G., Study of Signals and Systems in the Framework of Markov's Constructive Mathematical Logic, Ph.D thesis, Indian Institute of Technology, Kanpur, January, 1990.

[33] Rajan, E.G., and Sinha, V.P., Image Processing using Normal Algorithmic Cellular Automata, Technical Report, TR/IP-4-91, Department of Electrical Engineering, Indian Institute of Technology, Kanpur, January, 1991.

[34] Rajan, E.G., and Ramprasad, V.V., Pattern-Directed Array Processing, Technical Report, TR/IP-5-91, Department of Electrical Engineering, Indian Institute of Technology, Kanpur, January, 1991.

[35] Rajan, E.G., Cellular Logic Array Processing, Techniques for high throughput Image Processing Systems, SADHANA, Special Issue on Computer Vision, Volume 18, Part 2, June 1993, pp. 279-300, Indian Academy of Sciences.

[36] Rajan E.G., High-Throughput Cellular Logic Array Processing of Remote Sensed Imageries, International Conference on Remote Sensing and GIS, ICORG-92, Jawaharlal Nehru Technological University, Hyderabad, 1992, Proceedings, Tata McGraw Hill Publishing Company Pvt. Ltd., pp-347-440.

[37] Rajan, E.G., High-Throughput Cellular Logic Array Processing of Satellite Data for Geophysical Surveying, Paper No A.1-S.1.08. The World Space Congress, Washington, D.C., U.S.A., 28 August to 5 September 1992.

[38] Rajan E.G., Fast Algorithm for Detecting Volumetric and Superficial Features in 3D Images, Proceedings of the International Conference on Recent Advances in Biomedical Engineering Osmania University, January 6-8, 1994.

[39] Rajan, E.G., Object Recognition and Tracking in a Multiple Target Environment, 1994 IEEE International Conference on Systems, Man and Cybernetics, San Antonio, Texas, U.S.A., October 2-5, 1994, pp-2390-2395.

[40] Rajan, E.G., Fast Algorithm for Skeletonising 3-D Digital Images, 8th International Conference on Biomedical Engineering, December 7-10, 1994, Singapore, pp. 151-153.

[41] Rajan, E.G., A Genetic Algorithmic Fixing of Attack Points in a Moving Target, 1995 IEEE International Conference on Systems, Man and Cybernetics, Vancouver, B.C., Canada, October 22-25, 1995, pp. 217-222.

[42] Rajan, E.G., Genetic Algorithms in the Framework of Markov's Constructive Mathematical Logic, 1995 IEEE International Conference on Systems, Man and Cybernetics, Vancouver, B.C., Canada, October 22-25, 1995, 223-228.

[43] Rajan, E.G., Neural Automata Based Object Recognition, 1995 IEEE International Conference on Systems, Man and Cybernetics, Vancouver, B.C., Canada, October 22-25, 1995, 1882-1887.

[44] Rajan, E.G., The Notion of Geometric Filters and their use in Computer Vision, 1995, IEEE International Conference on Systems, Man and Cybernetics, Vancouver, B.C., Canada, October 22-25, 1995, 4250-4255.

[45] Rajan, E.G., Cellular Logic Array Processing, Invited paper, World Congress for Nonlinear Analysts, organized by the international Federation of Nonlinear Analysts, Florida,\ Institute of Technology, July 10-17, 1996, Athens, Greece.

[46] Rajan, E.G., On the Notion of a Geometric Filter and its relevance in the neighborhood processing of digital images in hexagonal grids, Fourth International Conference on Control, Automation, Robotics and Vision, Westin Stamford, Singapore, December 3-6. 1996, organized by the Nanyand Technological University, Singapore.

[47] Rajan, E.G., Medical Imaging in the framework of cellular Logic Array Processing, 15th International Conference of Biomedical Society of India,INCONBME'96, Coimbatore Institute of Technology, December 12-14, 1996.

[48] Rajan, E.G., Markov's Normal Algorithms and their generalizations, World Conference on Systemics, Cybernetics and Informatics, Caracas, Venezuela, July 1997.

[49] Rajan, E.G., Symbol Manipulating techniques using Markov's normal algorithms, World Conference on Systemics, Cybernetics and Informatics, Caracas, Venezuela, 1997.

[50] Rajan, E.G., Nonnumerical signal processing using Markov's normal algorithms, World Multiconference on Systemics, Cybernetics and Informatics, Caracas, Venezuela, 1997.

[51] Rajan, E.G., An Elementary Formal System for representing constructive systems, World Multiconference on Systemics, Cybernetics and Informatics, Caracas, Venezuela, 1997.

[52] Rajan, E.G., Special Automata for Normal Algorithms and their Transcriptions, World Multiconference on Systemics, Cybernetics and Informatics, Caracas, Venezuela, July 1997.

[53] Rajan, E.G., MEDIMAGE - A PC Based Medical Image Understanding System, invited paper, National Conference, Model College of Engineering, Cochin, organized by All India Council of Technical Education, Government of India, 1997.

[54] Rajan, E.G., Fast Algorithm for collision avoidance by autonomous mobile systems in the framework of cellular logic array processing, 13th international conference on CAD/CAM Robotics & Factories of the Future, Universidad Technologica de Pereira, Columbia, South America, December 15-17, 1997.

[55] Scott, D., Suppes, P., Foundational Aspects of the Theory of Measurement, Jr. Symbolic Logic, Vol. 23, No.2, January 1958.

[56] Sinha, V.P., Certain Logical Considerations in Finite Discrete System Theory, First International Workshop on Fault Detection and Spectral Techniques, Oct. 12-14, 1983, Boston University.

[57] Steiglitz, K., The equivalence of Digital and Analog Signal Processing, Information and Control 8, 1965.

Index

R

S

T

U

W

www.ingramcontent.com/pod-product-compliance
Lightning Source LLC
Chambersburg PA
CBHW062057160726
48282CB00003B/32